TRANSPORT AND DISTRIBUTION Made Simple

The Made Simple series
has been created
primarily for self-education
but can equally well
be used as
an aid to group study.
However complex the subject,
the reader is taken
step by step,
clearly and methodically,
through the course. Each volume
has been prepared by experts,
using throughout the
Made Simple technique of teaching.
Consequently the gaining
of knowledge now becomes
an experience to be enjoyed.

Accounting	English
Acting and Stagecraft	French
Additional Mathematics	Geology
Advertising	German
Anthropology	Human Anatomy
Applied Economics	Italian
Applied Mathematics	Journalism
Applied Mechanics	Latin
Art Appreciation	Law
Art of Speaking	Management
Art of Writing	Marketing
Biology	Mathematics
Book-keeping	New Mathematics
British Constitution	Office Practice
Chemistry	Organic Chemistry
Childcare	Philosophy
Commerce	Photography
Commercial Law	Physics
Company Administration	Pottery
Computer Programming	Psychology
Cookery	Rapid Reading
Cost and Management	Russian
Accounting	Salesmanship
Dressmaking	Soft Furnishing
Economic History	Spanish
Economics	Statistics
Electricity	Transport and
Electronic Computers	Distribution
Electronics	Typing

TRANSPORT AND DISTRIBUTION Made Simple

Don Benson, M.C.I.T., M.Inst.T.A., and
Geoffrey Whitehead, B.Sc. (Econ.)

Made Simple Books
W. H. ALLEN London
A division of Howard & Wyndham Ltd

Printed and bound in Great Britain
by Richard Clay (The Chaucer Press) Ltd, Bungay, Suffolk
for the publishers W. H. Allen & Company Ltd,
44 Hill Street London W1X 8LB

ISBN 0 491 01674 3 casebound
ISBN 0 491 01684 0 paperbound

Foreword

This book introduces the reader to the whole field of transport and physical distribution, as practised in the 1970s. It is an exciting study, for we have just experienced the greatest leap forward in distribution since the railway-building age. Transport has become a world-wide intermodal activity. Enormous capital expenditure has made it possible to move cargoes directly, or with a minimum of transshipment, from continent to continent and door to door.

This book will prepare the reader for a wide range of examination syllabuses at an intermediate and higher level. It covers the introductory syllabuses of the Chartered Institute of Transport and the Institute of Traffic Administration. It is ideal for adoption by H.N.C. and H.N.D. students selecting a transport option, or seeking background knowledge for this aspect of Applied Economics. It will be excellent reading for a CNAA degree with a transport option, and for Sociology students considering the impact of transport on the environment.

In describing the latest responses of engineers and administrators to the basic problems of transport we have assumed little prior knowledge on the part of the reader. In places we may be accused of stating the obvious, but we have found over many years of experience that students, especially those new to the industry, fail to see what seems obvious to experienced practitioners. Many other readers, particularly in developing countries, are unfamiliar with the rich transport background of developed countries like the United Kingdom, and appreciate the detailed descriptions included in the text.

In other places we may stray from what is strictly relevant to the chapter heading in order to comment upon problems, causes and effects which could not be inserted conveniently elsewhere. We have devoted considerable space to discussing terminals, as we feel that in some previous publications these have not received the attention they deserve. In this area, we feel, lies the greatest scope for future increased efficiency.

In preparing this book we have received help from many firms and institutions, who have courteously supplied illustrations, photographs and detailed descriptions of their equipment, organisation, procedures, aims and objects. We have had inevitably to leave out a good deal of the material supplied, but have included a very considerable amount. The courtesy of these firms is gratefully acknowledged, as is the co-operation of the institutions listed in Chapter Twenty-One. While acknowledging this help we must emphasise that the statements made in this book in no way represent the firms, organisations or institutions concerned but are essentially our own points of view on controversial matters.

We are grateful to Mr. F. R. Pywell for his appraisal of the script and the many useful suggestions he made.

DON BENSON
GEOFFREY WHITEHEAD

Acknowledgements

Australian High Commission, Office of
Bacat Line
Boltless Systems, Link 51 Ltd.
British Airports Authority
British Aircraft Corporation Ltd.
British Railways Board
British Rail Hovercraft Ltd.
British Road Services
British Waterways Board
Carmichael and Sons (Worcester) Ltd.
George Cohen 600 Group Ltd.
Crane Fruehauf Ltd.
Croner Publications Ltd.
Dover Harbour Board
J. Evershed & Co (Bow) Ltd., St. Albans
Felixstowe Dock and Railway Co. Ltd.
FIATA Airfreight Institute
Finspa Engineering Co. Ltd.
Freightliners Ltd.
Gibbons Brothers Ltd.
Goodyear Tyre and Rubber Co. (Great Britain) Ltd.
Gush and Dent Ltd.

Her Majesty's Customs
Her Majesty's Stationery Office
Jaloda Transport Equipment Ltd.
Lancer Boss Ltd.
Lansing Bagnall Ltd.
London Transport
Lufthansa German Airlines
Mathews Conveyor Company (Canada) Ltd.
National Data Processing Service
National Freight Corporation
Overseas Containers Ltd.
Peninsular and Orient Steam Navigation Co. Ltd.
Port of London Authority
Ready Mixed Concrete Group Services Ltd.
Shell International Petroleum Co. Ltd.
St. John's Ambulance Headquarters
Tibbett and Britten Ltd.
Townsend Thoresen Car Ferries Ltd.
Transmeridian Air Cargo Ltd.

Table of Contents

CHAPTER ONE

TRANSPORT AND THE MODERN WORLD

Transport in the Framework of Production

Production occurs as a result of economic activity of one kind or another. The natural resources and the human resources of the earth are combined for the purpose of creating some marketable product wanted by mankind. Usually in this process i t is helpful to take advantage of tools, equipment and techniques made available in previous periods. These 'producer goods' or 'capital goods' speed up production and raise output. Economic activity is therefore a combination of three 'factors of production': land, labour and capital. Land, to an economist, means all the non-human natural resources of the earth; 'labour' means all the human resources; and 'capital' means all the accumulated wealth of tools, equipment, techniques of production, etc., inherited from the previous production period. Economic activity aims to satisfy man's wants by creating 'utilities'—the name given by economists to any good or service which yields satisfaction. Food has utility, for it satisfies hunger; clothes have utility, for they keep us warm; dentistry has utility; so have theatrical performances, holidays on the Côte d'Azur and power from atomic reactors. Few of the satisfactions available to men in sophisticated societies are possible without transport, which must either move the goods to where we can enjoy them, or move us to where the goods and services are located.

Transport is that part of economic activity which is concerned with increasing human satisfaction by changing the geographical position of goods or people. It may bring raw materials to places where they can be manufactured more easily, or finished goods to places where consumers can make best use of them. Alternatively it may bring the consumer to places where he can enjoy services which are being made available; patients to hospital; the weary to centres of recreation; the young to institutions of education and learning; the bored to places of entertainment.

Many areas of the world, even today, are largely uninhabited and their resources unexploited. We may not experience quite the same thrill that Balboa felt when he climbed a tree on the Isthmus of Panama and saw the Pacific Ocean stretched limitlessly before his eyes; but the television screen daily depicts for us out-of-the-way places where simple men still lead simple lives ignorant of the wealth that lies in their sun-drenched hills or frozen tundra. Transport can release these resources. It has been said that 'Transport creates the utility of space'. It is a liberating force, setting free natural, man-made and human resources from situations where they are yielding little satisfaction, and transferring them to places where their full utility can be realised. But equally it may, by giving access, release utilities which have been unable previously to realise their true potential *in situ*. The canals built in Britain in the eighteenth century transformed the districts through which they

1

were cut. The countryside was opened up, populated and developed. Wild heathland became farmland; ores, stone, coal and other natural products could be exploited; villages and towns grew up. It is a process that is taking place even today. It is no accident that the African republics have only now begun to exert an influence on world affairs, for the jet aeroplane has at last liberated their utilities. In a single generation the camel has been replaced by the V.C.10. The beaches of Tanzania have always been beautiful, with coral strands scented with cloves and spices, but until the long-haul jet made them accessible to European tourists they were of little value.

Transport releases resources from their geographical bondage. It makes available formerly inaccessible utilities. The breakfast cereal made in North London reaches the housewife in Birmingham, Aberdeen or Penzance. The power supply of Kittimat in British Columbia is released as aluminium saucepans for the kitchens of West Germany, the United States or Argentina. *We may therefore define transport as a means for increasing human satisfaction by the movement of goods and passengers, so that inaccessible goods may be moved to those points where consumers require them or consumers may be moved to those points where otherwise inaccessible service facilities may be enjoyed.*

The Nature of the Modern World

The earth today is commonly described as a 'shrinking' world; one in which transport has reached such a level of performance that very rapid movements of goods and people can be made, from one part of the globe to another. Goods manufactured in Finland or Sweden on Monday arrive in San Francisco by 8 a.m. the next morning. It is possible to leave Seoul in Korea on Thursday afternoon, spend a day in Alaska and, with a little help from the international date line, reach London on Friday morning. The distances we have to cover are as great as ever, but the time required to traverse them has shrunk drastically.

The chief features of this shrinking world affecting transport may be listed as follows:

(*a*) a complex pattern of trading nations;
(*b*) a growing population;
(*c*) an increasing affluence of nations;
(*d*) a decline in strategical interferences with transport;
(*e*) a ceaseless quest for economies of scale in transport operations;
(*f*) increasingly serious environmental problems.

While these are dealt with more fully later in this book, a preliminary glance at the outstanding features is desirable at this point.

The Pattern of Trading Nations

The modern world still consists of a collection of nation states, each exerting its own dominion over its territory or territories, and imposing its own legal and administrative controls over its citizens and the economy which provides for them. While the ultimate destiny for mankind must be world citizenship, we are not likely to see this ideal attained for many years yet. Instead we see a tendency for all but the very largest states to associate together in trading groups. These groups at least as far as the free-enterprise nations are concerned are not based on the domination of a single powerful member, as in former times. Instead nations tend to link up with nations similar in size and wealth to themselves. Their mutual interests draw them together, and their similar bargaining strengths incline them to arrive at agreements acceptable to all. Besides the two major powers—themselves really federations of states—America and Russia, we have the European Economic Community as a really affluent grouping of nations. There is also a residual E.F.T.A., or European Free Trade Area. At less affluent levels we have organisations like CARIFTA, the Caribbean Free Trade Area, E.A.C., the East African Community, C.A.C.M., the Central American Common Market, and L.A.F.T.A., the Latin American Free Trade Area. There is also an Eastern European block, COMECON, which forms a Communist Economic Community in association with Russia. These bodies and others like O.P.E.C. (the Organisation of Petroleum Exporting Countries) represent member nations at international conferences on trade and transport matters, and bargain for the best possible terms in international negotiations.

Despite these groupings, the essential feature of the modern world economic scene is the mutual interdependence of all nations. The essence of trade, and the transport associated with it, is that it must be mutually beneficial. Where it is not, the nation that is at a disadvantage will eventually cease to trade. While it is to some extent true that the strong can still extort what they want, and the weak still yield what they must, the general tendency is towards greater egalitarianism. The balance of power is more evenly divided between nations today, and economic power is more susceptible to international opinion than perhaps at any time in history. In transport this has led to a series of international conventions in the last fifty years which have regulated most aspects of international transport. The resulting agreements have done much to ensure fair play between nations and between carriers and customers. They have also done much to eliminate the more wasteful features of free competition.

The Growth of Population

One feature of the modern world that affects transport is the enormous increase in population. Tables 1.1 and 1.2 show the same facts in two different ways. In Table 1.1 the growth in world population to the year A.D. 2000 is shown, as estimated by the demographers.

Table 1.1. Estimated World Population, 1650–2000

Year	Estimated world population (millions)
1650	450
1900	2,000
1960	3,000
1970	3,600
1980	4,000
2000	6,250

A convenient unit for considering the change in population is the megabirth. A megabirth is 1,000 million people. The term 'megabirth nightmare' has been used to describe the incredible growth in world population envisaged in the last two decades of this century. In Table 1.2 we have these figures presented in a different way, by showing the speeds with which a megabirth increase has taken place.

Table 1.2. World Population Trends

Population (thousand millions)	Reached by A.D.	Number of years needed to produce an increase of one thousand million inhabitants
1	1830	From the dawn of life, say 100,000 years
2	1930	100
3	1960	30
4	1980	20
5	1990	10
6	2000	10

The staggering increase predicted for 1980–2000 (twice as large an increase in 20 years as was produced in the period from the dawn of history to 1830) gives some idea of the transport problems to be faced. Not only will this enormous population need to be fed, clothed and housed, it will increasingly demand to see the world. In 1972, after serious crop failures in Russia and China the movements of grain from the United States and Australia sent freight rates soaring to record levels. The shipping capacity just was not available. The greatest increases in population are likely to come in precisely those areas where famines most easily occur. If the population of the developing world is to double by the year 2000 it may well prove impossible to fulfil the demand for shipping in times of emergency. Population growth requires increases in transport: transport of raw materials, vegetables and other crops, meat, milk, cheese and other proteins, of manufactured goods and of the people themselves.

The Increasing Affluence of Nations

The volume of traffic reflects not only the numbers of people requiring to be fed, clothed and sheltered, but also their affluence. Not only are more nations affluent today than ever before, but the spread of that affluence down into the masses of their populations is greater than at any time in history. Egalitarianism is inevitable in modern societies, for it is easy enough for the dispossessed to disrupt the pleasures of the well-to-do. A rich nation whose wealth is enjoyed by the few generates little trade, and that chiefly in luxury goods. An affluent nation which has an egalitarian structure generates enormous volumes of trade, for there are millions of people demanding broad ranges of goods and services. Home trade, community trade within a free trade area, and international trade must inevitably grow, and generate increased demand for and use of transport facilities of every type.

It is not only the volume of goods transported which increases in an egalitarian society, the people themselves are on the move. Nations pass successively through a bicycle era and a motorcycle era to a private motorcar era. A good test of an affluent nation is the extent to which the mass of the people have personal transport. A second guideline at present is the volume of air passenger traffic, which only becomes possible for the vast mass of the people once they have achieved a certain affluence. The enormous growth of packaged holidays by air has been one of the most significant developments in European transport since 1960, reflecting as it undoubtedly does the increased affluence of the ordinary European.

The Decline of Strategical Interferences with Transport

Transport is vitally affected by geography, particularly the topographical features, mountain chains, plains, valleys and coastlines. These features represent major problems to the various modes of transport. Political and strategic interferences with access are also obviously a great inconvenience, particularly where the natural, or shortest route to a given destination lies across territory which may not be traversed for these reasons. The most notable example of such restrictions was the almost total closure of the Soviet Union in the first half-century of Soviet rule. This particularly handicapped the development of logical air routes to the Far East and the Antipodes. The aircraft is the one form of transport which is little affected by geographical topography, but this advantage could not be fully used while the trans-Soviet routes were closed.

In the last few years some relaxation of these strategic restrictions has been made, because of the development of satellite observation techniques. When satellites can observe every 90 minutes the developments of even the most inaccessible installations there is little point in preventing air traffic flying along normal corridors. The short air routes across the Soviet Union, first to Malaya and Singapore, later to Vladivostok and Japan, have been opened up, while the Trans-Siberian railway route for containerised traffic is becoming increasingly important. The latter route achieves a saving of two to three weeks on the shipping time to the Far East.

The Search for Increasing Efficiency in Transport

At one time the concept of efficiency in production was largely associated with the manufacturing processes. Henry Ford's definition of mass production as 'the focusing upon a manufacturing project of the principles of power, accuracy, economy, system, continuity, speed and repetition' enabled him to achieve enormous economies of scale in the manufacture of motor vehicles. His ideas were quickly copied, not only by rival motorcar manufacturers but throughout the whole manufacturing field. By the 1950s firms were forced to look elsewhere for economies which would keep them ahead of their rivals. Naturally transport and distribution activities came under scrutiny, if only because an increased scale of manufacturing operations inevitably requires longer distribution chains to market the increased output. The result has been the focusing of attention upon the total distribution process, and a continuing search for economies in transport operations. This search for a system offering the 'smallest total distribution cost' has revolutionised transport since 1960. (For a full description of this concept see page 106.) The most notable changes to achieve economies in physical distribution are the following:

(*a*) An increase in bulk carriage, especially by sea, with the development of specialised bulk carriers for oil, ore, refrigerated gas, wheat, cellulose and other commodities.

(*b*) An increase in unit loads, chiefly by containerisation, but also by palletisation, pre-slinging, roll-on roll-off systems and by the packaging of timber.

(*c*) An increase in air transport, no longer reserved for valuable lightweight cargo, but extended into a range of other traffics, like the 'Fad today and Fade tomorrow' commodities so appealing to teenagers, and those products where 'total distribution costs' can be minimised by using air freight if it effects savings in other directions such as 'idle plant' costs, warehousing costs, etc.

(*d*) The streamlining of documentation by 'aligned systems', in which a variety of documents is produced from a single spirit or offset-litho master.

(*e*) Groupage—a process whereby specialist firms assemble the goods of several small shippers into a unit load, for which they assume responsibility for the major part of a transit, dispersing them to their individual destinations on arrival at the foreign port.

Transport and the Environment

The enormous developments in transport during the last quarter of a century have not been without their social costs, and transport is at present under heavy criticism for the adverse effects it is having upon the environment. Much of this criticism is unjust, since transport only reflects the ordinary aspirations of mankind for an increased standard of living. The conservationist who protests loudly about aircraft noise will be found booking his packaged tour with the rest of us. The village dweller protesting about juggernaut lorries still buys his groceries in the supermarket of his local town where the juggernaut unloaded.

Notwithstanding this inconsistent behaviour of transport's critics, the environmental issue is one that gives most transport men cause for concern. No one should plan transport operations without giving at least some thought to ways of minimising the nuisance likely to be caused by any new system that is proposed. The public image of any firm is a matter of concern to its management, and that image is increasingly endangered by transport activities which appear to effect the environment adversely.

The Study of Transport

We have defined transport as a means of increasing human satisfaction by the movement of goods and passengers. The problems of moving goods and passengers are great, and in their solutions to these problems transport engineers and others have shown great ingenuity. The infinite variety of vehicles and units of propulsion means that no comprehensive study of the subject can be short. Transport has its own interesting history, and the pace of development is such that obsolescence overtakes many transport components before their anticipated working life is ended. While this book will do its best to give a world-wide picture, it cannot hope to deal fully with all the branches of transport and of the associated fields which affect and are affected by it. The major headings we shall attempt to cover are as follows:

(a) The functions of transport, in particular its part in bridging the gaps between producers and consumers.

(b) The physical components of transport; the 'ways' over which vehicles move, the units of carriage and of propulsion, and the terminals where interchanges occur between one transport system and another.

(c) The nature of traffic, both goods and passengers. The special characteristics of each type of traffic and the responses made by engineers and others to accommodate the traffic and meet the peculiar nature of each.

(d) The modes of transport, road, rail, sea and air, and the typical operations of each type.

(e) The structure of the industry, and its forms of ownership.

(f) The associated fields of human activity bearing upon transport, particularly communications, finance, import and export trade, law—in particular international law—industrial relations, the social implications of transport and its effects upon the environment and the biosphere.

At the end of each chapter there is a bibliography of further reading on the topics discussed.

Suggested Further Reading

Faulks, R. W., *Principles of Transport*, Ian Allen Ltd., 1973.
Schumer, L. A., *The Elements of Transport* (3rd edition), Butterworths, 1968.

CHAPTER TWO

THE FUNCTION OF TRANSPORT

Transport and Economics

Economics has been defined as 'the study of mankind in the everyday business of life'. The everyday business of mankind is concerned with the production of goods and services which satisfy man's wants. There are many solutions to man's economic problems, and economies differ according to the pattern of solutions adopted. In the modern world there are three chief types of economy. There are the free enterprise economies, such as the economy of the United States of America; centralised economies, such as the economies of the Soviet bloc countries; and mixed economies, of which the British economy is perhaps the best example. These alternative solutions to the problems of mankind in providing goods and services to satisfy wants are alike in one respect at least: that transport is an essential element in each system. Only the most primitive economies can operate without transport. The village cobbler of a simple community, having made a pair of shoes for the elder of some family, walks with them to his customer's house and a simple cash transaction, or even a barter transaction, takes place. The advanced manufacturing systems of the modern world require more sophisticated arrangements. In economic terms the 'scale' of operations is greater. Large-scale production of footwear requires supplies of skins, hides and synthetic materials to be transported into the production unit. Design staff, production workers, marketing and distribution teams and management have to be attracted to the area and moved in. The finished product has to be packaged, transported to regional depots, warehoused, displayed, sold and finally distributed to the localities where consumers are waiting for supplies.

To the economist transport is an essential part of the production process. A 'good' has not been fully 'produced' in the economic sense until it has actually reached the final consumer who will enjoy it. Therefore the transport worker who brings it from the point of production to the point of consumption is fulfilling a useful and productive service. Similarly a service made available at any given point is not productive until someone is present to take advantage of it. The airline pilot who transports holidaymakers to the Costa Brava is productive because he enables his passengers to achieve the satisfactions experienced on vacations.

Transport is therefore an element of Economics, and the demand for transport derives from the economic needs of mankind.

The Demand for Transport

To some extent all economies are free enterprise economies, for it is in the nature of mankind to find personal solutions to the problems of demand and supply. When we feel a need for some particular good, or service, we seek out someone who can supply it, and offer him an inducement to do so. Economists have therefore divided elementary economic studies into the studies of demand and supply. When a person wants something sufficiently to be prepared to pay for it—that is to say, he will offer an inducement to any supplier prepared to supply it—he is said to 'demand' the good. Payment is most often arranged in 'cash': some officially sponsored form of 'legal tender' such as pounds or dollars. The demand for a good, or service, is therefore that quantity of the good or service which people are prepared to pay for at a certain price.

Many goods are demanded 'directly', that is to say they are wanted for the satisfaction they yield. The demand for fish and chips arises directly from the hunger of consumers for that particular combination of foods. The demand for houses arises directly from the need for shelter.

There is another kind of demand which is indirect rather than direct. Here the object demanded is not demanded for itself alone, but only as a means to provide other desirable goods and services. The demand for sewing machines is great, and continuing, but no one actually 'wants' sewing machines. You cannot eat them, drink them or wear them. We want them because they are producer goods; they help us produce clothing and furnishings which are directly beneficial in our everyday life, bringing warmth, comfort and privacy. The demand for sewing machines is a 'derived demand', derived from our need for clothing, curtains, etc.

The demand for transport is this type of demand, an indirect demand. It stems from mankind's need for goods and services of every type. We demand the transport of Japanese transistor radios because we demand the entertainment they provide. Our demand for a taxi to the dentist derives from the demand for his services. Transport facilities are 'producer goods'; goods which have a part to play in the production process. Their particular function is to bridge the geographical gaps between producers and consumers.

Bridging the Producer–Consumer Gaps

Economists recognise two producer–consumer gaps, the 'time gap' and the 'geographical gap'. The time gap arises because goods produced today may not be required until tomorrow, or next month, or next year. This gap is bridged by the warehousing process, with its techniques for preserving goods against deterioration.

The geographical gap arises because producers and consumers are rarely in the same place. Zambian copper is demanded all over the world, but chiefly in Western Europe, the United States of America and in Japan. Ghana's cocoa finds its readiest markets in London and in the United States; Volvo cars are sold in Sweden, but also throughout Europe and indeed, the world. The Spanish hotel industry offers entertainment and recreation to all visitors prepared to pay its very reasonable charges, but the 'consumers' of these services live in Britain, France, Germany, Scandinavia and North America. *It is the function of transport to bridge the geographical gap between producers and consumers, so that goods and services may be exchanged to their mutual benefit.*

Strangely, transport itself is a major factor in producing larger and larger gaps between producers and consumers. It seems paradoxical that a device designed to overcome the gaps between producers and consumers should frequently result in their enlargement, but since time immemorial this has been so. The explanation is to be found in another economic concept, the concept of 'economies of scale'. Generally speaking, it is true to say that larger production units are more efficient than smaller production units. This is because the larger organisation can usually make use of more productive equipment, specialised tools and machinery of every sort. For example, the jobbing printer does not require a computer, but the large-scale printing firm can take advantage of computerisation to set books more cheaply. The power tools of a modern motor vehicle plant, unscrewing two dozen nuts simultaneously, effect economies of operation which lower the price of motor vehicles. However, this growth in the scale of operations which results in a better, yet cheaper product, cannot take place if the goods cannot reach the market. In the eighteenth century in Britain the production of bricks was largely carried on locally, in small brickworks all over the country. Bricks are heavy, and difficult to transport. The expense of moving bricks by carts and pack mules was great, and the number that could be carried was small. When the canals were dug, a great improvement in transport occurred. Canal traffic is particularly suitable for the transport of heavy, non-emergency traffic like bricks. The result was that the number of local brickworks declined; fewer, larger brick kilns could supply the market, now that the new form of transport was available. Transport, bridging the gaps more effectively, made possible the economies of scale achieved in the bigger plants. Later the railway train, and today the lorry, bridge the geographical gaps so effectively that one or two brickworks supply the whole of the United Kingdom.

The Concept of 'Safe Arrival'

Transport provides the means of bridging the geographical gaps between producers and consumers, but its function will not have been carried out properly unless the goods or passengers arrive safely at their destination. Transport is peculiarly susceptible to interference from outside agencies, for by its very nature it requires carriers to go 'over the hills and far away'. Who can say what fate lies in store for those who travel, or what dark deeds may be done by those entrusted with other people's goods. As we shall see later, English law from time immemorial has regarded the carrier as being in a special category of bailee. He has, from early times, been regarded as a 'common carrier' and the peculiar characteristic of the common carrier is that he is liable for every loss that occurs, whether it was his fault or not. He has always been required to put safe arrival before speed—delay is no justification for excessive speed which causes injury to passengers or damage to goods. It is true that later a few exceptions were permitted to this harsh rule of absolute liability: not even a common carrier can be blamed if he is struck by lightning, or if the Queen's enemies fall upon him, but if he is robbed by anyone else he will be held liable. The concept of safe arrival as an essential element in the carriage of goods and passengers has therefore been recognised from very early times as an essential element in transport.

Transport—An Economic Catalyst

Transport is demanded to bridge the consumer–producer gaps, and is supplied by those willing, or empowered, to provide facilities. In free enterprise economies transport tends to be provided by enterprising individuals who see prospects of profitability for themselves, yet it confers great benefits on others in the process. When the Duke of Bridgewater built the Worsley–Manchester canal Parliament required him to sell his coal in the streets of Manchester at a maximum price of 4d per cwt. for 40 years. This was about half the price of coal in Manchester before the canal was dug. Not only did the Duke make excellent profits from his canal, but he was able to sell coal at a lower price than 4*d* per cwt. to the general satisfaction of the community. In controlled economies there is some central, nationalised body to provide transport. State railways are extremely common throughout the world, state airlines are to be found in many countries, and even road-haulage—an extremely difficult form of transport to nationalise—is operated by nationalised corporations in many countries.

A catalyst—as those who learned chemistry will remember—is a component which enables some other process to be carried on more quickly and efficiently. Transport in many ways acts as a catalyst, raising the level of activity in an economy. It has already been said that it releases utilities trapped in under-developed areas of a country, or of the world. It enables the scale of industry to be increased, bridging the producer–consumer gaps on both sides of the production process. Thus the crude oil of the primary producing nations of the Middle East, Indonesia, Nigeria and South America reaches the refineries of the advanced nations, and the sophisticated petrochemicals produced by those refineries make an enormous range of fuels, solvents, plastics, drugs and paints available to customers throughout the world. The commercial activities of businessmen depend enormously on the contacts they are able to make with one another. While these contacts are promoted and assisted by increasingly sophisticated communications networks, travel for business reasons is still essential. Problems are most easily solved when businessmen meet face to face, and assess the difficulties at first hand. The expert flies in to extinguish the blazing oil gusher; mini-submarines are rushed to effect spectacular sea-bed rescues; at more routine levels marketing men catch their Inter-City express trains to inaugurate a sales drive, while the goods to be featured in the campaign are containerised to catch the Freightliner next morning.

The catalytic effects of transport on an economy are not confined to business activities, for economic welfare is not achieved by bread alone. We need transport to attain levels of domestic satisfaction not possible in former times. We live in pleasant suburbs and commute to work in busy cities. At least one London businessman lives near Edinburgh and flies to and fro daily. We visit aged parents more regularly; choose schools for our children at a distance from our homes; travel in to area technical colleges for our education; arrange appointments with consultants at specialist hospitals; fly around the world to the university of our choice; visit theatres, exhibitions, eisteddfods and festivals, and generally enrich our lives by travel.

For the transport operator these catalytic effects of transport on the economy are a challenge and an opportunity. Densely populated urban areas generate traffic: commercial traffic, business passenger traffic, domestic convenience traffic, recreational traffic, vocational traffic and vacational traffic. To the extent that these traffics are catered for by the customers themselves, using personalised transport, the operator is prevented from playing his full part. To the extent that he can provide more efficient, more economic transport services than the customer can provide with his 'own account' fleet of vehicles or his personal transport, the operator is able to contain personal transport, perhaps with environmental advantages to society in general. Let us briefly consider the provision of transport.

The Provision of Transport

Transport is only provided if it meets some need, which is brought to the attention of those willing, or empowered, to provide facilities. The facilities made available at any time may be regarded as the response of transport engineers and entrepreneurs to the needs of society at that particular time, in view of the technology currently available. These responses have called forth enormous ingenuity from transport engineers, and the variety of prime movers, units of carriage, types of way and types of terminal is truly astonishing. Stand on any overpass above a motorway and ponder the traffic passing below, if you wish to review the ingenuity of transport engineers. Besides a wide variety of cars and light vans each with its own specialist features the enormous range of heavy vehicles is a tribute to their designers' skill. Specialised tankers for fuel oils, chemicals and powders are a main feature of our modern traffic. Articulated vehicles consisting of a motive unit, or tractor, and trailers of enormous variety are a second feature. Ready-mixed cement and similar traffics are a third type of specialised vehicle. The wide range of vehicles fitted with their own lifting devices is a fourth tribute to the ingenuity of the industry. Compared with the traffic of, say, the 1930s, there has been a great leap forward. The increased efficiency, economy, adaptability and capacity of road traffic is matched by other transport systems; the railways, the airlines, shipping and even pipelines display an endless variety and a restless activity. This activity has not only responded to the needs of mankind, it has generated much of the affluence it serves. While some conservationists put their heads in their hands, and their hands over their ears, the transport engineers and operators are seeking new systems which will control the social costs without killing the goose that lays the golden eggs. As he fits a television set to give the driver a view of his reversing vehicle the transport engineer ponders how to make the transport he is providing a safe, reliable servant of the community.

Free enterprise firms will only provide transport if they can do so profitably, for profit is the reward for enterprise. Every investment made by a sole operator, a partnership or limited company must in the end yield a return on the capital invested. If it does not, the investment will not be renewed when the existing asset depreciates or becomes obsolete. If left to the free play of the market, transport undertakings would nearly always yield profit. In times gone by the monopolistic nature of transport made transport undertakings exceedingly profitable. This monopolistic nature may not be apparent to every reader. Clearly it would be pointless to run two separate railway lines from A to B, with a few trains a day on each line. The capital costs of railways are so enormous that even in the days before taxation, when a man's profit was available for his own use entirely, no one could be found to finance such investments unless reasonable guarantees of a monopoly were given by the State. In Great Britain a running battle between the railways and successive governments lasted for most of the nineteenth century, from 1825 until 1888. The railway monopolists sought to preserve their power and the profits which represented the return on capital invested. The Government sought to reduce profit margins to a 'reasonable' level. From 1888 onwards, when reasonably firm control of fares and charges was established, the railways began to decline. Investment was less attractive, and, despite the extension of amalgamations to the point where there were only four main companies, with all the economies thus achieved, the railways in the face of competition from new forms of transport ran down steadily into an antiquated and outdated transport service, which only nationalisation could restore.

A nationalised industry provides transport facilities with different reference points from those of the private operator. Often there is a recognition that the services provided cannot be provided profitably. The service itself is the vital thing. Society needs an adequate service, and the industry must provide it. Criteria of efficiency will be laid down, which attempt to predict the nation's needs and the degree of 'loss' that can be suffered. Political decisions replace the test of profitability which is applied by private enterprise, and within the criteria laid down by the legislature the operators provide the services required. The transport facilities are effectively subsidised to the benefit of firms and private citizens who pay through taxation for the balance of the costs.

In a mixed economy, where some facilities are provided by private enterprise and some by corporations run as public enterprises, the pattern of transport facilities will be complex. From time to time attempts will be made to improve the arrangements being made, so that the public are better served. Calls for co-ordination of services will be heard, so that trains meet buses and feeder services meet ships or aircraft. Integration of services under a single unified control may be proposed so that these arrangements can be more perfectly made. The transport student, and the reader of this book, must consider all these proposals if he is to understand the policies that have been tried, or are being tried, in the transport field.

Suggested Further Reading

Bonavia, M. R., *Economics of Transport*, Nisbet, 1954.
Faulkes, R. W., *Principles of Transport*, Ian Allen, 1973.
Schumer, L. A., *The Elements of Transport* (3rd edition), Butterworths, 1969.
Sharp, C. H., *Transport Economics*, Macmillan, 1973.
Thomas, R., *Economics of Traffic Congestion*, Open University, 1972.
Thompson, J. M., *Modern Transport Economics*, Penguin, 1974.
Whitehead, G. M., *Economics Made Simple* (4th edition), W. H. Allen, 1974.

CHAPTER THREE

THE PHYSICAL COMPONENTS OF TRANSPORT: PRELIMINARY CONSIDERATIONS

Introduction

At first sight there appears to be little in common between an elephant and a jumbo jet, except that the largest of the land mammals has given its name to the largest type of aircraft. They are, of course, both forms of transport. Though widely different in their nature, when we compare them in their transport rôles we can find many points of similarity. In fact, if we take any mode of transport and compare it with the others, we find a number of factors common to all. In any attempt to study the various forms of transport we need to examine these common factors to discover the extent to which they affect each particular mode. Having studied the similarities, we can then look at the differences. In this way we can acquire an understanding of the problems which are common to all modes of transport and learn the needs and difficulties of particular modes. We can then assess a particular mode of transport and its suitability for the specific tasks we wish to perform.

In the next few chapters we will be concerned principally with the physical components of transport (sometimes called the essentials of transport), but before studying them we need to examine a requirement that is vital to successful transport operation: the need to keep transport moving.

The Need to Keep All Forms of Transport Moving

Any form of transport earns revenue only when it is doing the job for which it was designed, viz. carrying people or goods. At all other times it is generating costs.

The need to keep transport moving is so important that it could be called the first principle of successful transport operation. The professional operator who loses sight of this principle could be heading for financial failure. Consider the cases of two small road haulage operators.

Smith has a lorry engaged on contract work which keeps his vehicle and driver fully occupied for 10 hours per day, 5 days per week. Routine inspection is given to the vehicle at the end of each day and periodic maintenance is carried out at weekends.

Brown has a similar lorry, but has been fortunate in securing a contract under which the vehicle, with two drivers, is used for two shifts each of 10 hours per day for 5 days per week. Inspection and maintenance schedules are similar to those adopted by Smith.

At the end of any given period, Brown's lorry will have carried twice as many ton/miles as Smith's. But what of the costs? Brown's labour, petrol and oil will be double those of Smith, maintenance will be somewhat higher, but the capital cost of his vehicle, premises, tax and insurance will be the same. Brown's total costs per ton/mile will be lower than Smith's, because he has achieved a higher utilisation.

If we take an entirely different mode of transport, shipping, we find the ship operator is particularly conscious of the need to obtain maximum utilisation of his vessels. During the anticipated life of his vessels, he must recover the very high capital costs involved, the interest incurred on that capital, his operating costs, and at the end of the day earn sufficient profit to make the whole operation worthwhile. This money can only be earned by the carriage of passengers or freight. Every additional journey he can make is an extra opportunity to earn revenue. He is concerned therefore to see that as little time as possible is spent in port. Not only does a short turn-round time increase the time available for additional voyages, it reduces the very heavy costs incurred while a vessel is in port. Similar illustrations can be found in all modes of transport, and the higher the cost of the transport facility, the more important it becomes to ensure that the maximum possible utilisation is obtained.

Continuous operation such as is achieved in some industries is rarely attained in the transport industry. Nevertheless transport operators should be striving to achieve maximum performance within the constraints imposed upon them. These constraints may result from the availability of traffic, national and international legislation, and the physical components of the particular mode of transport.

The Components of a Transport System

Every mode of transport uses four major components, or essential elements of transport. These are the *way*, the *terminal*, the *unit of carriage* and the *unit of propulsion*. The 'way' is the route along which the traffic moves. Natural ways are cheap and free, and have no maintenance costs unless we try to improve them artificially. The sea, the air, the rivers, and footpaths and bridleways are all natural ways. Being natural they are subject to the whims of Nature, and this often requires that they be improved artificially. Rivers are subject to controls to prevent flooding in wet periods and insufficient flow in dry periods. They are dredged to maintain a channel and locks are built to improve navigation in the upper reaches. Bridlepaths are made up and turned into roads. Highways and motorways, canals, railways, tramways, tunnels and monorails are similarly constructed. Clearly these are not 'free' like the sea or the atmosphere, but for historical reasons some of the costs may be borne socially rather than privately. If the costs are borne by the ratepayer and tax-payer we may have what is an apparently free way because no actual charge is made to the user. If the way is privately built the owner usually has sole use of it. He then charges for its use by other persons, to recoup his capital expense.

The terminal is the interface where one transport network ends and another begins. Nearly every journey involves junctions where we can transfer from one form of transport to another. A port is usually regarded as a terminal for ships, but in fact it is also a terminal for trains, roads, pipelines and aircraft. In planning efficient transport systems, commercial firms and transport authorities must view the interchange of facilities as being part of a unified whole. Congestion in terminals in the past has spelt the death of a transport system, as it did when the congestion on the canals led to the growth of railways.

The unit of carriage is that part of the transport system where passengers or goods are accommodated. The efficiency of the mode of transport depends to some extent on the flexibility and adaptability of the unit of carriage used.

Road vehicles are more adaptable than railway rolling stock. Because they are less rigidly bound to the way they can overtake preceding vehicles and switch to alternative routes with much greater ease than can their railway counterparts. Aircraft and ships are even less tightly bound by the 'way' on which they travel.

The propulsion unit drives the vehicle or craft in use. Every vehicle must be driven, and the choice of a propulsion unit depends upon the strength of the vehicle, the speed required, the available fuel and other factors. Today the steam engine, the first great prime mover, has been largely replaced by the petrol engine, the jet engine, the diesel engine and the electric motor.

In any particular mode we may find two or even three of these components combined. For example, the pipeline is at the same time a way and a unit of carriage, while the pump house, which is the unit of propulsion, is itself an integral part of the way, the product in transit passing through the pump. Similarly the family car is both a unit of carriage and a unit of propulsion, travelling over a roadway but not using any particular terminal except the family garage.

These four components require detailed study, so that the variations between the components in different modes of transport can be studied. To assist this study each component has been given a separate chapter.

Suggested Further Reading

Faulkes, R. W., *Elements of Transport* (2nd edition), Ian Allen, 1969.
Faulkes, R. W., *Principles of Transport*, Ian Allen, 1973.

CHAPTER FOUR

THE PHYSICAL COMPONENTS OF TRANSPORT: THE WAY

Definition

The 'way' is defined as the medium on or through which the transport unit travels in performing its function.

There are three classifications of ways: natural ways, artificially improved natural ways and artificial ways.

Natural Ways

The air and the open sea are the examples which spring most readily to mind in the first category, but they are not the only ones. Navigable rivers were the main highways of many countries for centuries before the development of road transport and the advent of the railways, and many continue to fulfil that rôle today. Large areas of inland water are almost always utilised as commercial highways, e.g. Lake Geneva and the Great Lakes of North America. The importance of these inland lakes and waterways to the development of civilisation can be seen at a glance from maps showing the location of towns and cities two to three centuries ago. The only inland communities of any size had developed on the shores or along the banks of inland lakes and waterways, because these were the only places with supply routes capable of maintaining concentrations of population.

Throughout the world there are vast tracts of land over which suitably designed vehicles can operate with comparative ease. Deserts and prairie lands are good examples of this type of terrain, where for centuries the unimproved surface of the land has provided the natural ways used by the scattered population. The exploitation of the natural resources of those areas, bringing increased populations and the establishment of towns and cities, has resulted in the provision of artificial ways, better able to serve the needs of the areas. In some parts of the world large areas of swamp and marsh lands have lain relatively undeveloped until the past few decades. The development of specialised vehicles such as marsh buggies and more recently hover-vehicles is enabling these areas to develop economically, in a world where land of any sort is a scarce commodity. In the past, the cost of creating artificial ways has been so disproportionate to the economic benefits obtainable, that it has been necessary to develop vehicles suited to the natural way rather than provide artificial ways suitable for existing vehicles. Examples are the 'snowcats' used in Arctic tundra conditions, with wide caterpillars which spread the weight of the vehicle over the snow surface. As the demand for land grows, the less difficult areas are being drained and artificial ways created to aid the exploitation of the land.

As the level of economic activity increases, so does the demand for efficient transport. This means, so far as the user is concerned, low cost, speedy and reliable transport. In the examples given above, natural ways soon become inadequate to meet the demand for efficient transport, and it becomes necessary either to improve the existing natural ways or to provide entirely artificial ways.

Natural Ways Artificially Improved

Man soon learned that however useful natural waterways and lakes were to him, their usefulness could usually be increased by artificial improvements. At first such improvements consisted of such things as removing loose rocks and obstructions, strengthening banks where collapses impeded navigation, and such dredging as could be accomplished with manual labour and crude dredging devices. Then as man's engineering ability increased, the scale of possible improvements was enormously extended. Where solid rock had formerly frustrated attempts to increase the depth of water, now this could be blasted away to achieve the desired result. Permanent artificial banks could be created, containing the river within fixed limits, so increasing the depth and flow of water, and utilising its 'self-scouring' power. Finally, difficult bends could be removed and where necessary massive engineering projects could be mounted for the purpose even of diverting the river from its natural course.

What medieval men called roads, we would call tracks, i.e. unimproved natural ways across land which offered fairly easy passage. As the need for more efficient land transport grew with the growth of economic activity, it became necessary to improve these natural ways. Considerable improvement could be secured simply by removing obstructions such as rocks and fallen trees, by filling in holes and by draining marshy sections. Further improvement could be achieved by pounding broken rock into the surface, and by digging ditches on either side to assist drainage. This was the pattern of road improvement, other than in town and cities, in the developed countries, until recent times, and remains the principal form of road improvement in many parts of the world today. But the weight, volume and speed of modern road transport, demand roads of a much higher standard, and these can only be created artificially.

Artificial Ways

Modern roads are often relegated to a minor position in discussions of artificial ways, because roads have been with us for so long that there is a tendency to think of the majority of them as being natural ways, artificially improved. The opposite is the case, the majority of roads being the deliberate creations of engineers and planners. Road transport has reached its position as the most important form of inland transport in many countries because of the universality of its 'ways', i.e. there are few places that are inaccessible by road.

The distinction between natural ways, costing nothing to provide and maintain, and artificial or artificially improved ways which may require enormous capital expenditure in their construction and continuous expenditure on maintenance, is significant. Because the former cost nothing to provide and maintain, they can be made free to all—there is no economic justification for restricting their use, although it may be politically desirable or expedient to do so. With artificial or artificially improved ways, the question of 'free' use does not arise. Whether the costs of providing and maintaining the way are borne by the transport undertaking, as in the case of railways and canals, or by the community as a whole, as is the case with most roads, those costs must eventually be recouped. Broadly speaking, railway and canal undertakings recover their costs directly from the users by means of tolls and charges. Where the level of income is insufficient to meet the costs, Government subsidies, financed from taxes, may be considered necessary. Roads on the other hand, excepting certain toll-ways, are financed partly from specific taxes on road users and partly from general taxes on the whole community.

The amount which the community, as a whole, contributes towards the provision and upkeep of the way must be carefully balanced against the benefit which the community gains from the mode of transport using that way. If the benefit derived from providing ways for one mode of transport is less than that derived from another, then more of the community's resources should be directed towards that mode which proves most beneficial. Unless this is done, adherents of one mode of transport will claim that the elected representatives of the community (e.g. the Government) are unfairly favouring one mode of transport to the detriment of others and to the community. Determining the rights and wrongs of such claims is no simple matter, even trying to quantify benefit is a most complex process. In this context 'benefit' is used to denote a concept far wider than simply monetary return against capital outlay, and may even go so far as to embrace the quality of life itself.

The Ownership of Ways

We have seen that the provision of ways, other than natural ways, is a costly business, and the money expended must be recovered in one way or another—the user does not get the way for nothing. Some ways may be provided by an individual or an undertaking solely for his or its personal use. Roads or railways, wholly within the boundaries of an industrial estate, are examples of such *private ways* which have been provided solely for the benefit of the undertaking. Members of the public in their dealings with the under-taking may make use of those ways, but they do not have the freedom to use them for purposes of their own (except with the express or implied permission of the owners). The cost of such ways must be borne by the individual or undertaking for whose benefit they were constructed, without the benefit of contributions from other sections of the community.

Other ways, to which the public have access, *for their own private purposes* can be called *public ways*. These may be *publicly owned* ways or *privately owned* ways.

Publicly Owned Public Ways

In this category we find most roads. These are financed from money received from rates and taxes, and their provision is regarded as a service essential to the community. For this reason, some users—e.g. pedestrians and cyclists—make no contribution towards their provision and upkeep, other than through general rates and taxes. Other users, who are considered to obtain a greater benefit from the roads and who, by their heavier use of the roads, create higher maintenance costs, pay an additional charge by way of special taxes, e.g. vehicle taxation coupled with fuel tax.

Privately Owned Public Ways

Some artificial or artificially improved natural ways are provided by private undertakings, for public use. In many cases the provision of the way is intended primarily to benefit the undertaking by providing easier access and more efficient transport, and, by allowing the public to use it, it becomes more attractive financially. This may be because:

(*a*) The financial burden of providing and maintaining the way would be too great for the undertaking to bear, or

(*b*) Payment for the use of the way by other members of the public is a source of additional profit.

Many of Britain's early canals, like the Bridgewater Canal completed in 1767, which was constructed to carry coal from the Duke of Bridgewater's estate at Worsley to Manchester and Liverpool, were built primarily to benefit specific undertakings. But because canals were regarded as common highways, they were open for use to all who were prepared to pay the tolls and obey the bye-laws of the canal companies. The recovery of capital and maintenance costs, plus a percentage profit, can be achieved by the providers of these privately owned public ways, by two methods:

(1) The payment of charges based upon the degree of use, e.g. a charge per ton or per passenger carried, or

(2) The payment of tolls, i.e. a charge based on the carrying unit, irrespective of the degree of use, e.g. a per vehicle charge, based on the carrying capacity of the vehicle, not on the load carried.

Where the undertaking providing the way is also the carrier, then the first method is likely to be adopted. Where, as is often the case, the provider of the way does not engage in the actual transport of passengers and goods, then the second method is more likely to be used. If, however, the provider of the way acts as a carrier, alongside other carriers, then a combination of the two methods will probably be adopted.

The Control of Ways

Some ways, particularly non-congested ways, are not strictly controlled except by a framework of rules or laws laid down for the mutual benefit of all travellers. They are 'sight' ways, where travellers move so long as they can see their way to be clear. Other ways are rigorously controlled, sometimes with automatic signalling which excludes another unit of carriage from any section of the way that is already in use. Such are the train signals on the London underground railway. Other ways have radar-assisted control points like the air traffic control of modern airports and the estuarial control in busy rivers. These systems and devices are expensive to operate and must be considered when comparing ways.

Where for some reason control breaks down, severe interruptions to traffic may occur. This is particularly so where the system is inflexible, as with tramways. A single tram breakdown may hold up all the trams behind. A flexible way, by contrast, allows units of carriage to by-pass stoppages. This flexibility is an important aspect of ways.

The Characteristics of Different Ways

Roadways

Roadways are usually public ways. Until the end of the eighteenth century most roads were improved natural ways of ancient origin. The tracks made by our ancestors became pathways, footways, bridleways and eventually highways, deliberately raised above the level of the surrounding countryside to give an advantage against footpads and other outlaws. Some were based upon Roman roads laid down during the Roman occupation from A.D. 43 to A.D. 410. Others were laid down during the great roadbuilding period from 1760 to 1836, when road transport was greatly improved in Britain. Because of this ancient origin roads have tended to be 'free'—that is, no charges are made to road users for the use of ordinary roads. Certain road tunnels, bridges and in some countries motorways, are financed by tolls, and the imposition of charges for the use of congested city centres is continually under discussion, but the freedom of ordinary roads is a chief characteristic of the present-day situation.

A second characteristic is the universality of the road network, which makes all places accessible and forms the link between all other modes of transport. Other specialised ways come to an end at some terminal, and the road is used to link that terminal with the next stage of the transit, or the final destination of the passengers or goods. Of course there are some places which are not accessible by road, and the helicopter, aeroplane or hovercraft may take over, but these are relatively rare destinations for goods and passengers. The universality of the road network is the great advantage of this type of way—it gives door-to-door service for the vast majority of business firms and private citizens in advanced nations. This door-to-door service is also under the personal control of managements using 'own-account' vehicles. They are able to control the utilisation of their vehicles and the movement of their goods, and with electronic aids like the cab radio can maintain complete control of a vehicle throughout the working day.

Road 'ways' are flexible. By this we mean that each vehicle operates independently of other vehicles. The breakdown of one does not affect the others, which quickly drive round the stoppage or are diverted into alternative routes. Computerised route planning can be employed to select optimum routes for particular vehicles; obstructions, floods or subsidences can be by-passed. It is also flexible in that the way may be used by many types of vehicles. The transport engineer designs vehicles and units of carriage to suit a great variety of traffics. Many of these vehicles are specific to particular products, like milk, cement, petroleum products, etc., but if the demand is constant and continuing this is no disadvantage.

The road is durable, and even permanent provided reasonable maintenance is carried out. It is today of solid construction, usually in concrete, but often of tar macadam, featuring a 'camber' to assist the run-off of water. It is usually controlled and repaired by local authorities charged with the duty of caring for the roadway, but the payment for repairs, lighting, etc., may not be a local matter, but financed from national funds.

Lastly, congestion is a characteristic of the roadway today. With many users, each pursuing his own route and not subject to control, a conflict arises between the demand for road space and its provision, particularly at peak hours. It is impossible to provide enough 'way' at peak periods, and devices such as 'one-way' systems, parking restrictions, clearways, flyovers, traffic lights and roundabouts are introduced as means of increasing the volume of traffic a particular road can support.

Roads do not have any system of traffic control apart from ordinary police activities to detect the bad driver who is breaking the rules. Each driver is legally responsible for the movements his vehicle makes and operates within a framework of laws much of which is embodied in a highway code. A highway code usually includes many recommendations which, though not having the force of law, will tend to enhance or prejudice a case coming before a court of law according to whether or not they have been observed. Traffic lights exercise some degree of control at busy points, but there is no electronic all-powerful control panel to make decisions about traffic flows. It seems inevitable that such control systems will be developed and an experimental system in Southampton displays traffic density on a main panel to permit an operator to take appropriate action.

Railways

Railways consist of two parallel metal strips which give a smooth hard surface. Today rails are made of steel, but in the early days they were made of wood, and later of iron. The surface thus provided offers little resistance to rolling, especially on level ground, and very heavy weights can be moved with relatively small motive power. Railways present major engineering problems during their construction, for it is essential that gradients are kept to a minimum and the problems of overcoming terrain are severe. Bridges, viaducts and tunnels are needed to overcome land barriers and the consequent costs of construction are great. Other solutions to the problems of severe gradients are: (i) *racked railways*, which have steel cogs (the rack) laid between the lines, and pinions on the engines, which engage in the cogs of this rack; and (ii) *cable ways*, which engage with the unit of carriage between the rails and haul it up very steep sections of track. Besides the actual way, stations, signalling and other apparatus must be provided and maintained, so that the capital cost is high.

Most railways began as private ventures and the track, when built, constituted a private way for the sole use of the proprietor. In Britain, Parliament introduced into early Railway Acts requirements that the line should be available to other users who had the right to run trains on it. For safety reasons this practice was discontinued, and the operations were performed by the railway company concerned. For a variety of reasons railways are now usually operated as a nationalised industry in many countries. In any case rail movements are outside the control of the owner of goods being moved, who is forced to rely on the efficiency of the railway organisation to ensure that his goods proceed with proper dispatch. This loss of control over one's own goods is a major disadvantage of rail transport. It is offset in continental countries by the increased speed which is possible on long-haul journeys. Over 200 miles the advantages of rail transport—high speed and low labour cost—exceed the disadvantages of terminal delays experienced when the terminal is outside the personal control of the consignor. Below 200 miles the advantages can only be achieved if terminals are very efficiently handled, as with the Freightliner system. Medium and long distance transport of heavy density is therefore best catered for by railways, with their ability to move large numbers of people and large quantities of goods very easily. For this reason concentration of rail transport on a small number of main lines with heavy through traffic makes good sense.

Very high concentration of commuter traffic over relatively short distances can best be handled by rail, from an operational viewpoint, because of the greater carrying capacity of trains. Unfortunately, this may be inefficient economically because of the under-utilisation of staff and facilities during off-peak hours.

Railways are inflexible in that any interruption along the specialised way holds up all traffic behind. With a dense network of lines it may be possible to re-route trains around an obstruction, but any major accident on a trunk line is going to cause delay to both goods and passengers. Railways today do not provide door-to-door service except to the very largest industrial firms. Private sidings built in earlier times are less useful today since industry has re-located itself in other areas, and only major firms in the motor vehicle, petrochemical and similar industries find it economic today to install private sidings.

Another feature of railway systems today is the reduction of depots and stations. The 'slow train' is generally uneconomic, and in the interests of economic operation the convenience to customers and passengers of the local depot has been sacrificed. By concentrating reception and delivery of goods at a few larger depots the railways achieve economies of large-scale operations and greater total utilisation of the way.

Waterways

Waterways are usually improved natural ways or artificial ways. They have the advantage that a floating unit of carriage is weightless and can be moved by a small motive power unit. This makes for economical transport, but speeds are relatively slow. While the water itself needs no repairing, the way may include artificial banks, locks and other devices which require to be preserved, maintained and possibly manned. In busy waterways radar controls, river police and pilots may be necessary. Barges may be as large as 3,000 tons on major river and canal networks, carrying bulk ores, coal, iron and steel products, chemicals, timber and wheat. These traffics are generally non-urgent, so that slow speed is no disadvantage. In recent years the development of 'lash' ships (lighters aboard ships) makes a very effective use of inland waterway networks (see page 88). A feature of water traffic today is the environmental advantages to be achieved by the use of waterways. Where waterways link the interior of a country to the sea, the port area near the estuary will generally be a major city with a complex road structure. Barges slipping up river from a mother ship in the estuary avoid this congestion, taking goods inland to depots on the far side of the conurbation, where they may be transshipped to rail and road transport for the hinterland above the navigable part of the river. A really huge interconnected river and canal network exists in Europe which enables goods to move by water from the Mediterranean to the Rhine and North Sea. Further improvements and extensions, planned or under construction, will eventually make possible journeys right across Europe and Asia.

Seaways

The sea is of course the best waterway of all; a huge linking waterway between continental land masses, with continuous access to the interior of many countries along major estuaries. Its size enables higher speeds to be achieved than are possible on inland waterways, the wash created by the high speeds dissipating itself in the vastness of the waters. Vessels can be very large, and modern bulk haulage (see page 92) takes full advantage of this. For passengers the size of ships ensures comfortable accommodation and recreational facilities, but the slow speed has meant a loss of business and other passengers to air transport. This has not been the case with cruise travel, where the ship can offer the passenger who is not in a hurry a vacation which combines the advantages of foreign travel with those of a holiday at home. The ship may be of his own nationality, the crew speaking his own language, serving traditional food and yet calling at exotic places with strange sounding names.

Airways

Like the sea, the atmosphere is a way which requires no artificial preparation, has no repair bills and no private costs. It is more universal than the oceans, since all parts of the world are equally accessible. It is no accident that the great continental powers, the U.S.A., the U.S.S.R. and China, have had to wait for the air age before reaching full stature in the world. Apart from taking off and landing air transport is quite free of terrain, the topography of most countries lying far below the flight paths. Only one or two major land masses, the Rockies and Andes in America and the Himalayas in Asia, present obstacles to some flights, and even these may be taken advantage of by 'pressure-path' navigation in which the pilot seeks to fly in 'jet-streams' created by the mountain patterns.

The chief characteristic of air transport is speed. The aircraft is fast, and follows the 'least time track'. This may not be as straight as the crow flies, but takes advantage of pressure patterns which vary from day to day. The short journey time offsets the high cost of aircraft, the expensive labour necessary and the costs of surveillance to ensure safe arrival. These can be considerable, but frequent journeys and the maximum utilisation of the airframe keep fares low.

In evaluating air transport the 'least total cost' concept has been developed. This holds that the ticket cost or freight charges—which are usually higher than other forms of transport—must be reduced by the benefits gained. Examples are the more efficient use of executive time where top management flies instead of going by sea, and the production benefits enjoyed when machinery, flown to its destination, is installed and working when it would previously have still been on its way by sea. Although air transport charges are nearly always more expensive there are some goods which would be carried 'ad valorem' by sea but at ordinary freight by air. This is not the case with passenger journeys which may take several days or weeks by sea—the cost of feeding, service, entertainment, etc., over a much longer period, raises the cost of sea fares. Air transport is flexible, since each flight is unique and cannot affect other flights. Finally, the majority of flights are international in character and require international co-operation and agreement if they are to proceed without interruption.

Pipelines

The pipeline is a unique method of transport. Of the four elements of transport—the way, the unit of carriage, the propulsion unit and the terminus —three are combined. The way, i.e. the pipeline, is also the unit of carriage and embodies at intervals along the way propulsion units (pumping stations), which are themselves part of the pipeline system. Only the terminus—for example, a tank farm—is separate.

The 'way' in transportation by pipeline is essentially an artificial way, constructed usually by a private user for his own particular purposes. The commonest examples today are crude oil and natural gas pipelines owned and operated by oil and gas companies. The capital costs are high, requiring the negotiation of way-leaves (permission to cross land belonging to others); the digging of a trench about one metre deep; the installation of the pipeline in the trench; and the construction of booster stations at regular intervals according to the requirements of the installations. Particular problems have to be faced when the landscape is interrupted by ravines or other natural features, and in mining areas where subsidence is possible. Once established this route is inflexible in two ways: (*a*) as to direction, and (*b*) as to use. We cannot easily turn a pipeline off in another direction should the product no longer be required at its present delivery point, so that before we construct a pipeline we must be confident that the demand will be a continuing one. As to the use of the pipeline, it is inflexible in that the product to be carried can only be varied within certain limits. It does no harm to vary the product from motor spirit to aviation spirit or paraffin oil, but we cannot vary it to beer or milk. Where a pipeline is constructed by the user for his own particular purposes these are not serious disadvantages.

Once constructed, continuous flow transport replaces batch transport by ship, train or road vehicle, with twenty-four-hour operation at high speeds. Pipeline transport is very competitive with other forms of transport over short distances, especially if full utilisation of the pipeline is possible at all times, but it cannot compete with long distance batch transport by sea in very large bulk containers. On overland routes, where environmental factors such as reduction of traffic congestion enter into the calculations, or where climatic conditions are unfavourable to other surface routes, the pipeline is competitive.

The pipeline is a very efficient method of ensuring safe arrival under normal circumstances, but a pipeline which traverses several countries is vulnerable to interruption for political reasons, and to sabotage by dissident elements. Most pipelines are also subject to leakages. There are many joints and welds in a pipeline and external and internal pressures quickly discover weak points.

Corrosion is a great problem and the presence of anaerobic bacteria can play a major part in a particular type of corrosion. For this reason glass fibre and asbestos wrappings have replaced jute and cotton, which provide a source of food for these bacteria. Electric currents passing between pipelines also cause serious corrosion, but only at the positive unit in any coupling. Nearly all pipelines therefore are today protected by cathode voltages, i.e. negative potential of about one volt is applied at intervals along the pipe. Being at negative potential, corrosion due to electric currents cannot take place. An added advantage of cathodic protection is that the escape of these voltages into the earth, which can be detected, indicates that the insulation on the pipe has broken down—perhaps stones have penetrated the insulation or subsidence has caused abnormal pressure at some point. Such breakdowns are the chief causes of water rusting the pipes, at the point where the coal-tar wrapping has broken down. By carrying out a repair job on the pipe before it has had a chance to rust the 'way' is preserved, and continued safe arrival is ensured.

Suggested Further Reading

Allen, G. F., *British Rail Atlas*, Ian Allen Ltd., 1967.
British Railways Board, *The Reshaping of British Railways*, 1963.
Faulks, R. W., *Principles of Transport*, Ian Allen Ltd., 1973.
Rolt, L. T. C., *Navigable Waterways*, Longman, 1969
Sealy, K R., *The Geography of Air Transport*, University Library, 1966.
U.K. Ministry of Transport, *Roads for the Future*, Cmnd 4369, 1970.
U.K. Ministry of Transport, *Traffic in Towns*, S.O. Code No. 55–402, 1963.

CHAPTER FIVE

THE PHYSICAL COMPONENTS OF TRANSPORT: THE TERMINAL

Introduction

Traffic (i.e. goods and passengers) needing to use the way must be provided with places of access to vehicles operating on that way, and places where interchange between different vehicles of the same mode of transport or between different modes of transport can take place. These points of access and interchange are called terminals.

Confusion sometimes arises between the two words 'terminal' and 'terminus'. A terminus has been defined as the point where something (e.g. the way) comes to an end. A terminal formerly meant the same thing, and in many contexts still does, but in transport usage it has the much wider meaning given above. So the word terminus can be used to describe a terminal situated at the end of a way, but not one situated in an intermediate position.

Functions of the Terminal

A terminal has three main functions:

(a) To allow access to vehicles operating on a specialised way;
(b) To permit easy interchange between vehicles operating on that way, and between different modes of transport;
(c) To facilitate consolidation of traffic.

People and goods to be transported are referred to collectively as traffic. A specific lot of goods sent forward at one time, by one consignor, for one consignee, to one destination, is called a *consignment*. It is not usual to refer to one passenger or group of passengers as a consignment, but for convenience when discussing traffic, consignment can be used in that way.

The arrival of a consignment will frequently not coincide with the availability of the unit of carriage. Even when it does, it is not usually efficient to transport that consignment on its own. Except where the consignment in itself constitutes a full load, it is necessary to combine it with other consignments until a vehicle load has been assembled. This process is called *consolidation*, and the length of time needed to achieve it depends upon the volume and characteristics of the traffic.

Terminals range in size from a simple roadside bus stop to the huge complex of a major port. The latter can be regarded as a single very large terminal, or alternatively as a series of separate terminals grouped together for convenience, efficiency and economy—each individual berth being considered as a terminal in its own right. Variation in the size and equipment of terminals is found between those provided for different forms of transport, and between passenger and goods transport. As with the time taken to consolidate traffic, the variation in the size and equipment of terminals is governed by the volume and characteristics of the traffic to be moved. Therefore before looking at terminals in detail, we should now examine the characteristics of passengers

27

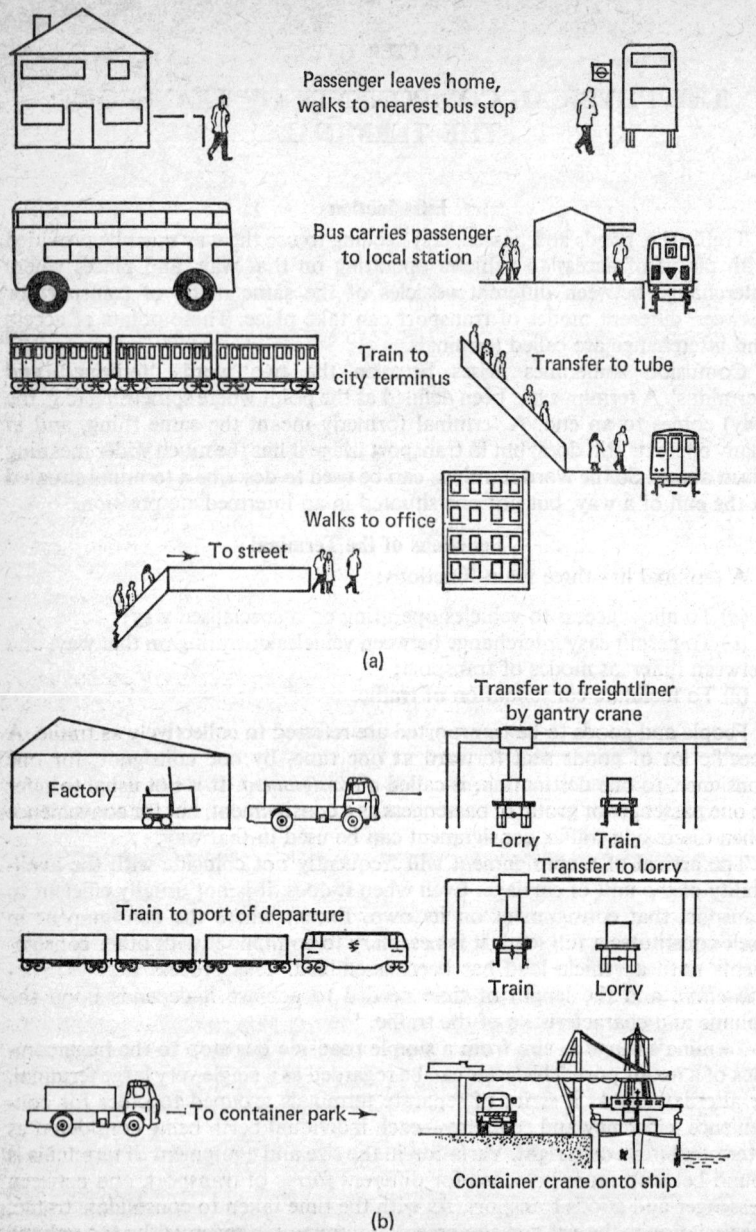

Fig. 5.1. The need for terminals: (a) for passengers; (b) for goods.

and goods, so far as those characteristics affect the type of terminal and the range of services which must be provided (see Fig. 5.1).

The Effect of Traffic Characteristics on Terminals

Generally speaking, passengers are self-loading and self-discharging and capable of moving themselves from one mode of transport to another. Unless the passengers are infirm or disabled, the transport operator needs to provide little assistance in loading and discharging; only where long distances, or changes of level are involved between the terminal entrance and the conveyance, or in interchanges between vehicles, does he need to provide ancillary transport. Moreover, passengers are capable of reading timetables and following instructions, and so can be in a sense self-consolidating. Whereas goods can be accumulated over a period of time and stored until a vehicle load is available, passengers 'store' themselves. If given a time and place and, where necessary, instructions detailing how to get there, passengers will present themselves, ready for transport. This relieves the operator from the task of collecting together the individuals that are to make up a vehicle load. Nevertheless, the extent to which passengers are self-consolidating has its limitations. The length of time a passenger is willing to remain in 'store', i.e. between vehicle departures, is shorter than the time that can be allowed to elapse between the dispatch of loads of goods on journeys of comparable distances. The longer the journey, the longer the interval between vehicle departures which will be tolerated by the passengers.

Few passengers arrive at the terminal at the precise time fixed for the departure of the conveyance. This may be due to personal preference, the time-tabling of other forms of transport bringing them to the terminal, or because it is essential for operational, administrative and governmental purposes for them to arrive some considerable time before the vehicle is due to depart. Where interchange between vehicles and modes of transport is concerned, some time-lag is necessarily involved. Firstly, there must be sufficient time allowed to enable the changeover to be accomplished, and secondly additional time may be allowed to offset any delays to connecting conveyances. In addition to these deliberately built-in time-lags, some waiting time at interchanges may arise simply because it is impossible to timetable neat connections between all services.

During these waiting periods, the transport operator (or the terminal operator, if a different body) must provide certain services and facilities for the passenger. These services will vary according to the volume of traffic, the size of the carrying units, the length of journeys, the degree of comfort expected by the passengers, any special considerations peculiar to the mode of transport, and whether the journey is internal to one country or international. They will usually include seating, toilet accommodation and refreshment facilities.

Goods, being inanimate, do not require the range of services necessary for the comfort and convenience of passengers, but present a different set of problems. Because goods are immobile it is essential to provide suitable mechanical handling appliances to facilitate the loading and unloading of vehicles, for sorting and for stacking and unstacking goods in the storage areas, and for transporting them around the terminal. Many of the goods to be transported will have been accumulated beforehand, and others having completed the major leg of their journey will need to be temporarily accommodated, pending collection, payment of dues and charges, Customs clearance, etc. Adequate temporary storage space must be provided to permit these goods to be stored without creating congestion and avoiding the overstowing of some consignments by others. At some terminals, goods will arrive in mixed loads, to be sorted, before individual consignments are consolidated with others bound for common destinations. Great care must be exercised in the design, layout and equipment of terminals where this type of operation is performed, to ensure that it is carried out expeditiously and efficiently.

It must be apparent from the foregoing that ample space and considerable forethought in the planning of terminals are essential prerequisites to efficient operations. Possible future expansion must be taken into account in the planning stage, for an efficient terminal can soon be crippled if the success of its operation generates additional traffic with which it cannot cope.

The Location of Terminals
Road and Rail

The planning and equipment of a terminal, important factors though they are, will be of little avail if the terminal is not in the right place. Terminals should be sited so far as it is possible in places convenient and readily accessible to those wishing to travel or to forward goods. This means close to concentrations of population or where large quantities of goods originate or are consumed. Towns and cities are by definition the places where we expect to find concentrations of people, and until the latter half of this century the greatest density of population would be found in the centre. Over the past few decades there has been a movement of people out of the centres of towns and cities, for residential purposes, but many of those who have homes outside the centre, still work there. Moreover, in those places we will also find the greatest concentration of shops supplying goods for domestic use, as well as places of entertainment, and other essential community services, e.g. doctors, dentists, solicitors, estate agents.

Industrial activity presents a different picture. Extractive industries and those concerned with the production of basic raw materials, though attracting some build-up of population, rarely create a sufficient concentration of population to cause the industry to become completely surrounded, and eventually become the core of a large town or city. The opposite is often the case with manufacturing industry. Old established industries are often found in the heart of towns and cities, surrounded by workers' houses. In this sort of situation the town has been born because the industry located there, and in an earlier era of poor transport people had to live within easy walking distance of their work. This necessity no longer applies, so that we find newer industries locating on the outskirts of towns and cities, where land is cheaper, but the sites are easily accessible to their workers, and close to the market for their products.

From this we can deduce that the centres of towns and cities could be important locations for terminals for some modes of transport, though not for all. However, these central sites may be unavailable to or unsuitable for the terminal operator, for various reasons:

(*a*) Most land in or near the centre of a town or city is likely already to be occupied, and any vacant land will be very expensive.

(*b*) Where there are no vacant sites, occupied sites might be acquired and re-developed, but this would involve even greater expenditure than the acquisition of vacant sites.

(*c*) The additional congestion created by road vehicles using the terminal may be unacceptable to the local authority and planning permission might be refused.

(*d*) The environmental effects of noise, fumes, vibration and visual intrusion may be unacceptable to the community.

Points (*a*) and (*b*) above are likely to make city centre sites economically unsuitable for goods transport, unless the site was obtained at an early stage in the city's development, when land was still relatively cheap. This is often the case with railway goods depots, and we find extremely valuable sites being used for activities which today would not justify their being acquired on either economic or environmental grounds. The high cost of land in the city centre and the non-availability of sites have given rise to a tendency for new industrial undertakings to locate on the periphery of the city, and road goods terminal operators tend to do likewise. By so doing, they get the benefit of cheaper land, proximity to younger developing industrial undertakings, yet remain near enough to be able to serve the industries and consumers located in the centre.

The choice of location for road passenger terminals (bus and coach stations) is usually more straightforward because in most cases the town or city centre is the focal point for numerous road passenger services.

A model showing the pattern of road passenger services in a typical area would reveal the following:

(*a*) Networks of local services within the city and within the large towns of the area.

(*b*) Radial services connecting the city and the large towns.

(*c*) Services connecting the large towns with their neighbours.

(*d*) Radial and circular services linking the large towns with the smaller towns and villages.

In almost all cases, the focal points of the services will be the town and city centres, which act like magnets in attracting the surrounding population. Passengers demand to be set down within easy walking distance of their destinations, or if changing vehicles, that the interchange be made as convenient as possible. If these conditions are not satisfied, the result will be that many passengers will transfer to personal transport. Planners of new towns are well aware of this situation and endeavour to fulfil the conditions from the start, but in older, established towns this has not always been possible. However, it is now becoming necessary to re-develop the centres of many old towns, and where this is happening it often becomes possible to incorporate a bus station in or near the town centre, when the re-development of the area is planned.

Two towns in adjoining areas of Essex provide interesting illustrations of the two situations described, i.e. the provision of bus stations in new and old towns.

Basildon is a new town built since the Second World War, primarily to accommodate the overspill from London. Unlike many old towns which have main routes running through their centres, Basildon is located between two almost parallel arterial roads. The older London–Southend road, the A13, runs to the south, while the newer A127 passes to the north of the town. Wide roads link up the industrial area, residential areas and the main shopping and recreational area. The bus station is located close to the main shopping area giving good access for shoppers, and convenient for passengers to and from Chelmsford to the north, Southend to the east, and the Grays area and London to the west. The railway station at Basildon was not built until twenty years after the town was started, since the new town was built between two existing stations and good, convenient bus services to the nearest stations were therefore adequate. With the increased town size and the large number of people who commute to London to work, or travel there for other purposes, this became inconvenient and a town centre railway station was built.

Grays, an old town which has grown up over several hundred years, though chiefly in the nineteenth and twentieth centuries, presents an entirely different picture. The nucleus of the town was located on the north bank of the Thames where a chalk outcrop gave access, unhindered by marshes, to the river, and firm building land. Industrial development has spread along reclaimed marshland to the west and east and residential development to the north, so that the town has grown in a fan-shape from the nucleus. Until the First World War the town could be said to be bounded to the north by the A13 but subsequent growth has caused the town to spread well beyond that boundary. Other residential developments on the outskirts of the fan have placed the residents some considerable distance from the main shopping centre and other services. The High Street is bisected by the London–Tilbury–Southend railway line, with a station and goods yard in the 'town centre'.

A large part of the working population, particularly white-collar workers, commutes to London and many other workers travel daily to the factories and docks of industrial Thameside. Those travelling to London depend to a large extent upon bus services to carry them to and from the railway station and the surrounding towns and villages. Where shorter journeys to work are involved, buses and cars are the preferred modes of travel. For the bus users, this frequently means changing from one service to another in the centre of Grays. The lack of a bus station makes it necessary for boarding and alighting points to be scattered some distance from each other, and the railway station, in various streets in the centre of the town. Passengers changing from one bus service to another, or from bus to train, have to proceed on foot for two or three hundred yards, and sometimes further. This can be unpleasant in inclement weather, and frustrating when delays to one mode of transport result in missed connections with another, despite a frantic rush between two terminals. Now the town centre is being re-developed and a bus station will be provided alongside the railway station. This should result in much greater convenience to users of public transport, will perhaps lessen the use of personal transport, and will improve traffic flows once main boarding and alighting bus stops have been removed from the principal streets.

In this country, the railway system has been long established and therefore consideration of where to locate new terminals rarely arises. In recent years the pattern has been to close many of the smaller goods depots and to concentrate facilities on larger central depots. The problem has therefore been not where to locate new terminals, but which terminals to retain and develop, and which to close down.

Before leaving the consideration of the location of road and rail terminals it is interesting to note that whereas it has become customary to locate road terminals in or close to centres of population, railway terminals have often in the past been responsible for creating centres of population and industry.

Although many early railways were built initially to link specific towns or to serve specific industries, a common effect was for some small communities situated along the line of the railway to develop into important towns, while other communities in the same area, but not similarly served by the railway, remained small and unimportant, perhaps even disappearing altogether. Industrialists seeking new locations for their factories appreciated the value of good transport facilities. In consequence they established their undertakings alongside the railways, close to the developing towns, and towns and industries prospered together.

Airports

The process of choosing a site for a new airport would seem at first to be comparatively easy—find a piece of flat land close to a large centre of population, and build it there. This may have been near the truth in the early days of flying, but the process has now become extremely complicated. Three sets of considerations must now be taken into account: (1) customer requirements, (2) operational requirements, (3) community requirements; and these three sets of considerations are unlikely to be compatible.

Let us examine the requirements of each of these conflicting forces to see how and why the conflict arises.

Customer Requirements

As already mentioned, the airport will need to be located close to a large centre of population, probably a city. Much of the traffic using the airport will originate from the city itself; other traffic, especially passengers, will be drawn from surrounding areas to road and rail terminals in the city centre. The customers will almost certainly have selected air transport because of its speed. They will therefore wish the terminal to be as near to the city as possible to reduce the journey time from the city to the airport, and to keep the overall transit time as low as possible. Passengers will demand good transport services between the city centre and the airport, while for freight traffic there must be good access for surface transport.

Operational Requirements

The terminal operator will look for a site having the following attributes:

(*a*) A large area of flat well-drained land. As aircraft have become larger and faster, so the need for longer and more heavily constructed runways has increased. In addition more space is required for aircraft parking and manoeuvring, and very large areas to accommodate the ancillary services.

(*b*) It must be away from mountains or large hills, which would make approach and take-off difficult and could create dangerous air currents.

(*c*) The site should, as far as possible, be free from fog.

(*d*) It should not be surrounded by concentrated development. Since cities continue to grow, future development must be taken into account, otherwise there is a real danger that in a relatively short space of time the airport will be hemmed in, with no further land for expansion and hampered by restrictions imposed on operations in built-up areas.

Community Requirements

Airports require very large areas of land, as we have seen, and these need to be located near to large centres of population. In countries not so densely populated as the United Kingdom, such sites may be readily available, but in this country suitable sites are few and have alternative uses. Those open spaces sufficiently large to be considered as airport sites that are to be found in the vicinity of our major cities, are either valuable agricultural land or areas set aside for recreational purposes. Even when not densely populated there are certain to be some scattered houses in the area, and probably one or more villages. We find therefore that any proposal to locate an airport in one of these areas must be measured against the value to the community of its alternative uses. Can we as a nation afford to sacrifice valuable farming land? If we give up open park-land, where are town and city dwellers to go for recreation? What is to happen to the people who have homes and jobs in the selected area? It may be possible to find them new jobs—indeed many new jobs may be created by the airport—but there is no guarantee that these jobs will fit in with the chosen way of life of those displaced. Similarly, it may be possible to rehouse people who have been forced to leave their old homes, but will this compensate for the loss of homes that have been cherished and which may have been family homes for generations? These questions have no easy answers; each case must be judged on its merits and whatever decision is reached, it is likely to be a compromise solution, not wholly satisfactory to any of the three conflicting forces.

It must be emphasised that these problems are particularly severe in this country, which is so densely populated and where open space is at a premium. Other countries with much greater land areas do not have the same problems except where large conurbations have developed. Moreover, because of the much greater length of many inland journeys, air travel is much more commonplace. Here, only a small percentage of the population uses air transport and for most of them, one trip a year is their limit, although it is also true to say that the percentage is rising every year. The present situation does, however, raise another question. Are we justified in appropriating a large open space for an airport, and subjecting the surrounding population to almost perpetual aircraft noise, and heavily increased road traffic, simply to benefit a small section of the population?

If the airport is designed primarily to meet the needs of the local population justification may not prove too difficult and the facility may meet with general approval from the local inhabitants. If, however, the airport is to be primarily concerned with international traffic, resistance to the proposed siting may become very strong indeed. A country can only support a limited number of major international airports. Although some local people may use it, the majority of passengers and freight will have originated from or be destined for other parts of the country, or be merely passing through, in transit. It becomes very difficult in these circumstances to convince local inhabitants that their area should be used in preference to another. While most people will agree that an international airport is desirable, few will be happy to have it located in their own vicinity.

The Roskill Commission's report on the site for the proposed Third London Airport demonstrates the complexities involved in reaching an acceptable solution.

Ports

Because they represent the earliest form of transport terminal, a study of the location and growth of ports can be a fascinating exercise. Some ports established over a thousand years ago have continued to grow and to thrive; some, once flourishing, have faded into obscurity; while others have remained, little changed in size, for the past few hundred years. The enterprise of their owners or controllers may have had much to do with their success or failure, but often the result was due to their natural attributes, to changing patterns of trade or to technological developments. Before examining the factors which lead to the location and growth of ports, we need to establish clearly in our minds exactly what we mean by a port.

The word 'haven' is used in some countries to describe what we call a port, and 'harbour' is often used in a similar manner (some Government reports refer to 'trade harbours'). In common with many other words used in the port industry, it is often difficult to distinguish between them with any degree of precision because the usage varies from place to place and according to the context in which they are found. Both haven and harbour indicate a place of refuge, somewhere that a ship may lie safely at anchor, protected from wind, wave and current. Generally it is true to say that whereas a haven can be a place of refuge fashioned by nature, a harbour usually indicates some degree of artificial improvement, though this is not always so. A port is something more than simply a place of refuge. Its Latin root *portus* means a gateway, and that meaning roughly describes its function. It is the place through which passengers and goods pass from land transport to water transport and vice versa. There are of course river ports and canal ports, but we usually employ the word port to mean seaport, and it is on that meaning that we shall concentrate. If we subscribe to the 'chain of transport' concept, then a seaport can be defined as 'that link in the chain of transport where sea transport is exchanged for inland transport'. The essential difference then between a haven or harbour and a port is that the latter is essentially concerned with the handling of passengers or cargo or both.

Let us now examine the factors which lead to the location and growth of a seaport, and seek to discover why some prosper while others stagnate.

Shelter

A ship at anchor is more at the mercy of the elements than one at sea, unless it is anchored in a sheltered spot. Faced with a violent storm at sea, and depending of course on the size of his vessel relative to the severity of the storm, a master can run before it or head into it. What he would not choose to do would be to sail broadside on to the direction of the storm. If he did so, this would present the greatest surface area to the force of the wind and waves, with the biggest risk of damage and disaster. Should a storm strike suddenly when a ship is at anchor, there might be no time to alter its position so as to minimise the force of wind and waves. This could result in the vessel being pounded against the quay wall if tied up alongside, or if in an open anchorage possibly in the vessel capsizing. For this reason, as well as for ease in handling cargo or in embarking and disembarking passengers, it is essential that a port should give good protection from the elements.

This shelter is naturally found in land-locked bays, where the surrounding land affords protection, or in the estuaries of rivers, where it is supplied by the sides of the river valleys. Sometimes a site which in other respects may be admirable, is unable to give the required protection. In this case, it may be possible to create the necessary shelter artificially, for example by erecting breakwaters. These must not only be able to break the force of the waves, but be sufficiently high to give shelter from the wind. Dover harbour is a good illustration of a harbour with artificial breakwaters. Breakwaters are expensive and their construction is unlikely to be undertaken unless there is no better site in the area, or the port is long established but the existing protection is no longer adequate for the much larger modern vessels.

Deep Water

Although some small vessels are constructed with specially strengthened bottoms to enable them to 'sit on the mud' at low tide, most modern vessels do not have this facility and must 'remain always afloat'. Should a large modern vessel settle on the bottom it would almost certainly suffer severe structural damage unless by some freak chance it settled in a natural cradle so that all parts of the hull were equally supported. This is because the immense weight of a modern vessel bearing down on an unsupported section of the ship's bottom would cause distortion or fracturing of the structural steelwork. It follows that not only must there be a sufficient depth of water to enable a ship to enter port, but that there must be a sufficient depth of water to support it at all times.

We have already noted that the estuaries of rivers provide excellent shelter, and in Chapter Four we saw that rivers were the principal means by which goods were conveyed before the advent of canals and railways. Rivers, on their way to the sea, cut themselves channels, deeper in the centre than at the sides, so that even at low water there may be sufficient depth in the centre of the channel for a vessel to remain afloat. The nearer the river gets to the sea, the greater the depth of water available. It is not surprising therefore that given shelter and deep water, many early ports were established in the estuaries of rivers.

Rivers were great highways, but they were also barriers. The nearer one got to the mouth of a river, the wider it became and consequently more difficult to cross. It was likely too, that as the river neared the sea, the speed of flow dropped and marshes formed on either bank, making crossing even more precarious. It would be necessary to travel some distance upstream before a point could be found where it was possible to ford the river. At this point early settlements usually developed, and as this was the farthest upstream that large vessels could safely penetrate, it was here that ports were established. Port and settlement developed together; as one flourished so did the other, each dependent upon the other. Most of the major ports of the world began like this, centuries ago. London is a prime example, a settlement and later a port growing up where a gravel outcrop made it possible to ford the river.

In some estuarial ports, vessels moored in midstream and transferred their cargoes to and from shore in smaller craft—lighters, barges, etc. Sometimes quays and jetties were built along the banks, and by dredging the area around them vessels were able to lie alongside to load or discharge their cargoes. For many centuries the size and draught of vessels changed only very slowly and such growth as there was in the size of ships could be accommodated by the majority of ports, especially if assisted by dredging. But gradually the growth in size of vessels and the demands of shipowners that their vessels should always remain afloat brought about the introduction of enclosed, impounded docks in many places.

Whether or not enclosed docks are necessary or desirable depends upon the following factors: (1) the depth of water available at all states of the tide; (2) the depth of the approach channel at low water; (3) the size of the ships using the port; (4) the tidal range, i.e. the difference between the depth of water at high tide and low tide.

The principal advantage of enclosed docks is that a constant depth of water can be maintained so that vessels remain always afloat. A further advantage is that the additional shelter provided makes cargo-handling easier than in rough, open water.

The principal disadvantage is that where there is an insufficient depth of water in the approach channel, except around high tide, large vessels are restricted to a relatively short period before and after high tide during which they can pass into and out of the docks. Missing a tide can result in a delay of almost twelve hours and this can prove very costly where today's highly expensive ships are concerned. Even in the case of smaller vessels which have a longer period within which to negotiate the locks, the time wasted in waiting to lock in and out, and in passing through the locks, can be inconvenient and expensive especially if the vessels are engaged in short-sea, ferry-type services.

A further important problem connected with lock entrances concerns their size. Dock installations in general involve very heavy capital expenditure and are built with an intended long life. In planning dock entrances, future possible increases in the size of vessels must be taken into account. If this is not done, entrances will be unable to cope with the new larger vessels which will be excluded from the docks with consequent loss of revenue if the trade is transferred to other ports. On the other hand, if an over-estimate is made of the future increase in size of vessels and the lock entrance is made unnecessarily large, the extra capital expenditure incurred may prove a heavy financial burden to the port. Port planners in the past could not possibly have foreseen the tremendous growth in size of vessels which has taken place in the past two or three decades. The result has been that many ports have found themselves saddled with enclosed docks with insufficient depth of water and lock entrances too small to accept the new larger vessels, and have seen their trade lost to other ports with more suitable facilities.

Access

It is not sufficient that vessels should be able to lie at anchor sheltered from the elements; they must be able to reach the anchorage easily and safely. A harbour whose entrance is guarded by dangerous rocks or sandbanks is unlikely to prove popular with seafarers. But these obstacles are not insurmountable. Rock can, if necessary, be blasted away and safe channels can be dredged through the sandbanks, but it is important that any impediments are clearly marked by lighthouses, lightships, beacons, etc., and the safe channels clearly marked by navigational buoys.

On its way to the sea a river carries with it quantities of silt and debris, the amount varying according to the nature of the land through which the river passes, and whether or not it is subject to violent flooding. As it nears the sea, especially if it passes through an extensive coastal plain, its speed drops, and the material carried in suspension may be deposited in the estuary or the immediate surrounding sea areas. In this way sandbanks are created which may reduce the use of an otherwise admirable harbour. If the speed of flow of water is sufficient natural channels will be formed through the river-made barrier which may be adequate for navigation. Where the river is sluggish, a delta may form with numerous channels the width and depth of which may make navigation impossible. The once important port of Chester on the River Dee is now completely defunct as a result of the silting up of the Dee estuary, whereas the swiftness of its current saved the neighbouring estuary of the River Mersey from a similar fate. As a result, and helped by considerable engineering ingenuity, Liverpool developed into one of Britain's largest ports. (For an account of Liverpool's problems and how they were overcome see *The Major Seaports of the United Kingdom*, by James Bird.)

Just as the growth in the size of vessels affected the depth of water that had to be provided to enable vessels to lie safely afloat, so it affected the depth and width of the approach channels that were necessary. Some dredging has always had to be provided in almost all major ports to prevent docks, anchorages and channels from silting up (maintenance dredging), but as vessels grew in size it often became necessary to dredge deeper and wider approach channels, or to cut entirely new ones (capital dredging). The cost of dredging has been a major item of expenditure for many ports and is reflected in the charges they make for the use of the port. Dredging cost can therefore be an important item in determining the competitiveness of two rival ports. For some ports blessed with deep water approaches, very little dredging is necessary, sometimes none at all. For others, the amount of dredging required could be so great that the financial returns from being able to accommodate larger vessels would be insufficient to cover the heavy cost involved. These ports, unless heavily subsidised, have had to resign themselves to their inability to accommodate vessels beyond a certain size. The most successful ports in this category are those that recognised their limitations early, and have concentrated on securing those traffics best suited to smaller vessels.

We have looked at the problem of access from the sea, and some of the ways in which difficult access can be improved. Equally important is access to the port on the landward side. A fine natural harbour, with deep water and good easy access from the sea is unlikely to have developed into a major seaport if, on the landward side, cliffs rise almost vertically from the sea, or it is surrounded by extensive marshes. With today's technology, it would not be impossible to develop such sites, although the capital cost would be high, but in the past an alternative site would have been sought and developed. In all probability the chosen site would not have been so desirable from a seaward aspect, but the deficiencies could have been more easily overcome. This again illustrates the point made earlier that when selecting a terminal location, only on rare occasions does an ideal site emerge. Usually the chosen site represents a compromise between what is desirable and what is easily attainable.

A serious problem of access often arises in the case of long-established ports. The natural sequence is for a town or city to develop as the port develops, the growth of one feeding the growth of the other until the prosperity of each is dependent upon the other. Where this development has occurred over several centuries, as with many of the world's major ports, the port becomes enclosed in a built-up area that may extend to a depth of many miles. Some of this urban development will have taken place prior to the age of motor transport, and much of the remainder during a time when the present volume of motor transport seemed inconceivable. If this has resulted in the landward approaches to the port consisting of mile after mile of narrow congested streets totally inadequate for today's high-capacity road vehicles, port developers are faced with a problem over which they frequently have no control. Unless the port authority is also the municipal authority, the provision of a road system adequate to meet the needs of the port will be the responsibility of other bodies whose priorities may not coincide with those of the port authority. When this happens a situation may arise where the efforts of the port developers in providing up-to-date facilities in keeping with the demands of modern ocean transport and the 'through transport' concept are in part frustrated by inadequate road approaches. But whoever is the responsible road authority, clearing the way for wide new approach roads will be a very costly undertaking.

Large Flat Land Areas

Earlier port developers probably did not consciously select sites which had large areas of flat land available for industrial development. They would, however, seek sites where land was available to build warehouses and houses for the community which would follow the port's establishment. In many cases the land available would be far in excess of their immediate needs or would have been viewed as favourable for agricultural development. The most successful ports would have attracted industries to them, and the availability of land would have assisted the industrial development.

Today, when economies of scale are well understood both in transport and industrial activity, port developers must search for large areas of land, capable of industrial development, and having access to deep water as sites for their new ports. These sites have been named M.I.D.A.'s (Maritime Industrial Development Areas). Some may be associated with existing major ports, e.g. Rotterdam's Europort; others associated with what were relatively small ports, e.g. Dunkerque. Often it may be necessary to create the land area required, as with Rotterdam and the development proposed for the Port of London on the Maplin sands at the extreme limit of the port authority's jurisdiction. In the developed countries M.I.D.A.'s will almost certainly be associated with existing ports, for although there may be many sites having all the attributes previously mentioned as necessary for the establishment and development of major ports, they may lack the final necessary attribute, a flourishing hinterland.

Hinterland

One well-known dictionary defines hinterland as 'the district behind that lying along the coast (or along the shore of a river); the back country', and it is in this sense that most people use the word. It has, however, developed an additional special meaning when used in connection with ports, i.e. the area from which a port draws its trade. This means the area from which it receives its exports and to which it sends its imports.

In order to be successful a port usually needs to develop a two-way trade. For this it needs people and industries to create a demand for imported goods, and to produce raw materials or manufactured goods for export. (The word 'industry' here is used in its widest sense, i.e. including agriculture, extractive industries, etc., and not merely manufacturing.) The exception to this rule is the port which predominantly imports or exports one or more bulk commodities in such quantities that it is a viable economic entity on the basis of that traffic alone.

Ports then exist to serve people and industries; these are its hinterland, and without that hinterland a port cannot develop, no matter how ideal the site is in terms of its natural advantages. A good example of this situation is found in Scapa Flow. Scapa Flow is a 12-mile wide anchorage encircled by the South Isles of the Orkney Islands off the north coast of Scotland. It has good approaches and deep water and is sheltered by the islands that surround it. It was used as a naval anchorage in both the First and Second World Wars, and it has been said that the entire Allied fleets could have anchored there at the same time. Yet it has never become a major port, simply because the population of the islands is inadequate to support one—there is no hinterland.

Whiddy Island, Bantry Bay, in the south-west corner of Ireland seems to contradict the proposal that a port cannot flourish without a hinterland, for here is a recently established port in a sparsely populated part of Ireland. But this port was not established to serve south-west Ireland, it was located there because the 312,000-ton tankers which use it require 30·4 metres (100 ft.) of water and are unable to enter the North Sea to deliver their cargoes of oil to Western European ports. The oil must be transshipped in smaller tankers (80,000–100,000), but the economies of scale obtained on the long haul from Kuwait justify the transshipment costs. What seems to be a port without a hinterland is really a port separated from its hinterland by the barrier of inadequate depth.

The world's major ports tend to fulfil several rôles simultaneously. They are at the same time bulk ports, often with industries processing imported raw materials in close proximity; transit ports concerned with the rapid exchange of goods between land and sea transport, to and from inland destinations; transshipment ports where cargoes are transferred in large quantities from large vessels to smaller vessels or to other modes of transport for onward transport to destinations not served by the major ocean carriers; and entrepôt ports involved in the warehousing and marketing of imported goods. Because of this multi-rôle character of major ports they can be said to have not one hinterland but many, according to the particular aspect of the port's operations or the specific traffic that is being examined. For example, it may be found that the hinterland of the port in relation to its bulk cargo operations extends only as far as those industries located in the immediate vicinity of the port. Where its transit and transshipment traffic is concerned, however, it may extend hundreds of miles in several directions.

In earlier centuries, when inland transport was poor, ports tended to serve the needs of local communities. Much of the traffic was coastal, this being the easiest way of moving goods from one part of the country to another. Many ports would be involved in some degree of short-sea trade with not-too-far-distant countries while a few would establish reputations as starting points for voyages of discovery and trade with distant parts of the world. Where a country had a long, indented coast-line, as in Great Britain, innumerable small ports would be established. As world trade developed, the better endowed ports attracted most of the trade and transshipped to other areas in coastal vessels and along inland waterways. The Industrial Revolution brought changes in the pattern of population and industrial activity. Instead of the population being thinly spread throughout the country with relatively small concentrations of population in the towns and cities, much larger conurbations began to develop. These favoured the growth of those ports best situated to serve the new conurbations.

When shipping companies began to establish liner services they naturally based their regular calls on those ports able to offer the largest quantities of traffic on a regular basis, with less frequent calls at some smaller ports, and omitted others from their schedules which consequently had to be served by transshipment. At the same time improvements in inland transport enabled importers and exporters to by-pass the smaller ports in favour of those with more frequent sailings to and from a wider range of overseas ports. In this way the major ports extended their hinterlands at the expense of smaller ports located nearer to the origin or destination of the goods. This feature is particularly noticeable in connection with particular types of goods distributed on a world-wide basis, e.g. London would hardly seem to embrace Scotland with its hinterland, yet because it has more sailings to more parts of the world than any other port in Great Britain, it is the favoured port for the shipment of large quantities of Scotch whisky. An apparent paradoxical situation has arisen in recent years; some smaller ports have been attracting traffic away from major ports, while at the same time some major ports have been capturing trade from their rival major ports. This situation has been made possible firstly by the tremendous improvement in inland transport in the post-war years, resulting from the provision of motorways and the railway Freightliner services, and secondly by the growth of containerisation.

Failure on the part of major ports in this country to use effective techniques to establish the cost of handling specific commodities but instead relying on the principle of charging 'what the traffic would bear', placed them in a vulnerable position. It meant that some commodities handled in large quantities but requiring little in the way of specialised services, were subsidising the handling of other commodities whose handling costs were very much higher but which were not reflected in higher port charges. Other commodities carrying high port charges were being handled in obsolete, labour-intensive facilities in an economically inefficient manner. A number of small ports, on examining the charges schedules of the major ports, realised that they could offer much more attractive terms which would outweigh the additional transport costs now that the improved inland transport services no longer placed them at a geographical disadvantage in terms of transit time. They were able to offer much lower charges because they were dealing with selected commodities rather than trying to supply a full range of services. This meant that their capital costs and overhead charges were much lower. Often their labour charges were lower and they did not suffer losses resulting from bad industrial relations. Finally, where necessary, they could provide modern facilities which could handle selected cargoes at a much cheaper rate than could ports with obsolete facilities. Typical of this type of resurgence were ports such as Shoreham and Sheerness.

The development of roll-on roll-off vessels and containerisation gave other small ports the opportunity they required. Provided they had good road and rail links, these new developments enabled many smaller ports to capitalise on their geographical positions relative to the mainland of Europe. The shorter sea distances between East Coast ports and the ports of West and North-West Europe enable vessels to complete a greater number of voyages within a given period of time. Felixstowe, an outstanding example of small-port growth in the post-war period, is so situated that to achieve the same frequency of service to Rotterdam, two vessels would be required to operate from London, compared with one from Felixstowe. This progressive little port has been so successful in attracting traffic from outside its former hinterland that it is not uncommon to see container lorries passing through London en route for Felixstowe and by-passing the country's premier port. These containers are not necessarily bound only for European destinations, for by being first in the field in providing facilities for specialised container vessels, Felixstowe succeeded in securing a considerable volume of deep-sea container traffic. It is possible, however, that as container ships become larger some of this traffic may be lost because of draught limitations in the port's approaches.

The decisions of various container shipping consortia, notably those in the Australian and Far East trades, to limit their ports of call to one port per country and to arrange inland transport to and from that port from all parts of the country with no difference in freight charges has led to some major ports losing large quantities of traffic to others. The decision to base Australian sailings on Tilbury has meant that London has gained at the expense of other ports. At the same time, London has lost some traffic due to the decision to base Far East trade on Southampton.

From the foregoing it can be seen that radical changes have taken place with regard to what were fairly well-defined hinterlands, due to changes in transport systems and organisation, and improvements in inland transport. Established ports have had to try to learn to adjust to these changes, and by offering modern facilities and efficient working to attract a reasonable share of trade. Some have succeeded better than others. In this country, with far too many ports for its size, port authorities now realise that the time has passed when they could rest comfortably knowing that traffic would come to them because of their geographical location. There is no longer any guarantee that in future the largest vessels will make direct calls to this country. Unless conditions are favourable, they could call at European ports, and transship the British portion of their cargo.

Given the existence of competition between ports in different countries for the same traffic, the survival or growth of individual ports no longer rests on the natural attributes that we have discussed or on the foresight and energy of port authorities, but is affected by political decisions. Political consideration may decide which ports in a country are to be given government support and the extent and manner in which the support is to be given. The decisions may be based on a need to protect the national economy, to safeguard national security or perhaps simply to preserve national pride.

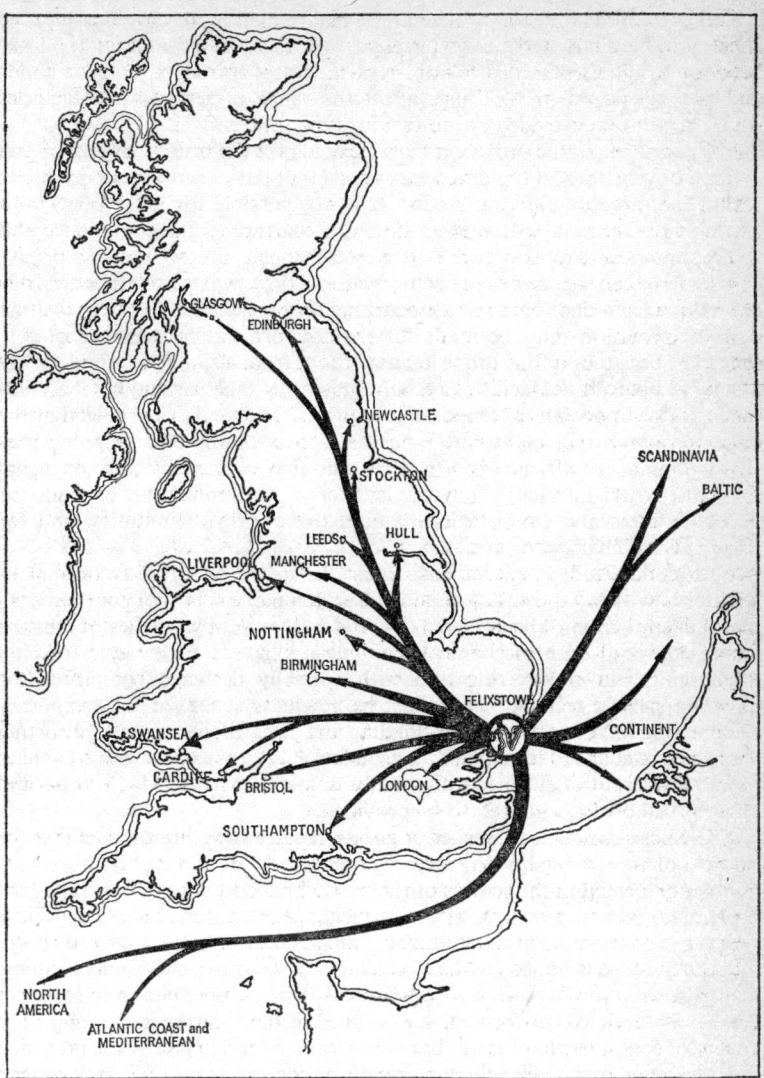

Fig. 5.2. Felixstowe's situation relative to seaways and hinterland.

(courtesy of Felixstowe Dock and Railway Co. Ltd.)

Services and Facilities Required at Terminals

Earlier in this chapter we looked at the main functions of terminals and the effect of traffic characteristics on terminals. We also noted the variation in size between terminals provided for different modes of transport, and for goods and passengers. All these things affect the range of services and facilities which need to be provided at the various types of terminal.

For passenger traffic provision must be made for the orderly discharge and loading of vehicles and rapid and easy transfer of passengers between vehicles within the same or differing modes. It is not possible for all passengers to arrive at the terminal at the exact time of departure of the conveyance and some waiting time must occur. Where interchange is involved, unless precise connections can be arranged, some waiting time will result between disembarking from one vehicle and embarking on another. During these waiting periods, provision must be made for the comfort and convenience of passengers. The extent of this provision may range from a simple seat and shelter at a bus stop, to toilet facilities, restaurants, shops, cinemas and hotel accommodation at important international terminals. The facilities provided at the larger terminals will be available not only to incoming and outgoing passengers, but also to friends and relatives who may be meeting them or seeing them off. Where international traffic is involved, provision must be made for H.M. Customs and Immigration officials to perform their duties, and for passengers to change currencies.

With goods traffic, the emphasis must be on the speed of turnround of vehicles and of rapid transfer of goods between modes. This of course means that the terminal must be designed to avoid congestion by vehicles. It must be amply equipped with mechanical handling appliances for general loading, discharging and transferring and with specially designed equipment for handling specific traffics. There must be adequate space for the temporary accommodation of goods prior to loading and after discharge, and for sorting goods where consolidation and deconsolidation take place. As with passenger traffic, if international transits are involved, facilities for H.M. Customs and Health Authorities will need to be provided.

All vehicles, whether passenger or goods, require servicing and facilities for this are often provided at the larger terminals. Road and rail terminals are frequently located in the centres of towns, on high cost sites where space is at a premium. Because of this, major servicing is often done at less expensive sites some distance from the terminal, though care is usually taken to ensure that the distance is not so great as to create heavy costs due to empty running. Nevertheless, even at town centre terminals it is not uncommon to see some degree of servicing performed, e.g. re-fuelling and carriage cleaning. The advent of containers has meant that in addition to servicing vehicles, provision must be made for the cleaning and repair of containers and this is becoming an important service to be provided at those terminals handling a large volume of container traffic.

Road Transport

Passengers

The simplest form of road passenger terminal is the roadside bus stop. In some country districts where buses stop when hailed, the stop may not even be marked with a sign, but may be a spot where by custom the local population elect to wait to be picked up. Usually, though, it will be indicated by some form of permanent sign affixed to a post or a building. The next step up is the provision of a shelter, with or without seats, for the protection and comfort of waiting passengers. The final stage is the provision of bus and coach stations of varying size in town and city centres. Depending upon size, the following facilities are likely to be found: toilet accommodation, an enquiry/booking office, and waiting rooms, with perhaps a bookstall or shop and some provision for light refreshments. At the larger terminals, especially those associated with long-distance coach journeys, greater provision for refreshment and shopping may be provided, depending upon the distance to similar facilities in the town or city centre.

Goods

As with other modes of transport, the type of operation and the variety of traffic has a considerable bearing on the range of services and facilities which must be provided. But nevertheless certain basic facilities will be required at most road haulage terminals. Congestion is the enemy of efficient working, and therefore a large circulating area is necessary. Office accommodation will be needed from which to administer the business. The office block may well embrace other staff facilities such as rest rooms, locker rooms, a canteen, etc. Vehicles will need to be parked, garaged and maintained, and for these operations adequate space is needed. The emphasis of the Transport Act 1968 on quality licensing means that great importance must be attached to the provision of proper maintenance facilities, an aspect which did not always receive proper priority before the Act. Finally, goods will need to be handled and this means providing a variety of mechanical aids.

Long-Distance Haulage (*Full Loads*)

This type of operation often consists of two parts: (*a*) the trunk haul and (*b*) local collection and delivery, in which the separate parts are performed by different drivers using articulated vehicles. The loaded trailer is brought into the terminal by the local or shunt driver and is parked ready for pick-up by the trunk or long-haul driver, and vice versa. The operation calls for plenty of parking space for vehicles awaiting pick-up. Although it is not intended that loads should be transferred from one vehicle to another, vehicle breakdowns may sometimes make this unavoidable. With some loads the transfer could be done manually, but this is often impossible. Heavy individual packages and the increasing use of pallets and containers make the provision of mechanical appliances such as fork-lift trucks, mobile cranes and overhead gantry cranes a virtual necessity.

Local and Medium-Distance Haulage (*Full Loads*)

This operation usually calls for the same vehicle and driver to pick up and deliver the load in the same day, without the goods passing through the terminal. On occasion, however, it is convenient for the load to be picked up, held at the terminal overnight and delivered the following day. Similar facilities as in the previous category are required.

Consolidated Loads

Goods may be brought into the terminal by either local or long-haul vehicles and consist of a number of consignments, none of which is large enough by itself to constitute a full vehicle load or to warrant a vehicle to itself because of value or urgency. The loads are broken down, sorted according to destination and consolidated with other part loads for either trunk haul or local delivery. For this kind of operation to be performed efficiently, a loading bank is essential.

The Loading Bank

This consists of a platform at tailboard height, against which vehicles can be backed for easy loading and unloading. The bank will usually be backed by a large shed or warehouse, with a canopy extending over the platform and vehicle to give protection from the weather. Sometimes, instead of an external bank, the raised floor of the shed acts as a platform, and vehicles are backed up to shuttered openings in the walls of the shed. A canopy is still necessary, but it need not be as large, since it needs only to cover the vehicle. A further variation consists of a large, raised, covered area, with open sides. This involves lower capital expenditure, but is less secure, gives less protection from the weather, and is unsuitable for some kinds of goods, when the structure is also required to serve as a warehouse.

Whichever system is used, it is essential that adequate room is provided for sorting, and that the area is well lit to enable work to continue expeditiously and safely during the hours of darkness. Because of the increased amount of handling required, particularly of smaller packages, compared with the previous type of operation, a greater variety of handling equipment will be needed. In addition to that already mentioned, this is likely to include: hand trucks, pallet trucks, platform trucks and belt conveyors. (For detailed descriptions of various mechanical handling appliances and conveyor systems see Chapter Ten.)

Parcels Traffic

This will require facilities similar to those described in the previous category, with much greater emphasis on the space required for the sorting and temporary accommodation of goods awaiting consolidation. If the volume of traffic is sufficiently large, it may justify the installation of complete conveyor systems. These are designed to speed up the sorting process by minimising the number of individual movements and to lower costs by reducing the labour content of the operation. A parcels office will be required to facilitate the delivery to and collection from the terminal of those parcels for which local collection and delivery services have not been requested.

The various categories of road haulage operation which require terminal facilities have been dealt with separately, but in practice more than one and often all categories are dealt with at the same terminal. This enables considerable economies to be made in the use of vehicles, equipment and manpower. At the same time it calls for great care in planning the layout of the terminal and in selecting the most appropriate items of equipment or heavy losses due to congestion and unsuitable equipment can soon occur.

Rail Transport

Passengers

Terminals range in size from small country halts to those main-line stations which handle local, national and international traffic. At a country halt, a simple shelter, lavatories and perhaps a ticket office are the only facilities likely to be provided. As stations get progressively larger, other facilities are added—viz. waiting rooms, book-stalls and refreshment rooms—until at the largest main line stations more extensive toilet facilities, restaurants, shops, banking and foreign exchange facilities, and provision for Customs and Immigration procedures are necessary. Passengers are mobile and capable of carrying small amounts of luggage themselves. The terminal operator must therefore concentrate on providing those facilities which minister to the passengers' comfort and convenience, rather than in physically moving them as is necessary with goods traffic. Nevertheless, he must not lose sight of the need to move passengers swiftly and without confusion through the terminal, especially where a large volume of commuter traffic is concerned, and to ensure that boarding and alighting from vehicles is carried out with the minimum of delay to vehicles.

Passengers undertaking long rail journeys are much more likely to have baggage with them than short-distance travellers. Where their stay is likely to be prolonged, the amount of baggage accompanying them may be more than can be easily carried, so that porters and baggage trolleys must be provided. During waiting periods, while taking refreshments, etc., or when breaking their journey, passengers need somewhere to deposit their baggage in safety, to permit them to move around freely. This generates a need for baggage lockers and baggage rooms.

The rail terminal is not generally within easy walking distance of the origin or destination of the majority of passengers, so that good access to and from other modes of transport must be provided. At the large city terminal with heavy commuter traffic a large proportion of the passengers will be transferring to and from buses and underground railway systems. Other passengers will be arriving and departing by taxis and private cars. For passengers transferring between surface rail and underground systems escalators must be provided. To simplify transfer between rail and road, access for road vehicles should be as near to the rail platforms as possible.

The larger the station, the greater the opportunity for confusion. To overcome this, clear and reliable information and instructions must be given to the public. Traffic indicator boards, colour-coded direction signs, multi-lingual notices, and regular announcements over public address systems are all ways in which this essential exercise in communication is carried out.

The increasing use of the private car has meant that greater numbers of passengers arrive at the station by this mode of transport. This is especially so with commuter traffic. The commuter uses his car for the short journey between home and the railway station, travels by rail over the long distance, and completes his journey by underground railway, bus or taxi. This means that car parking facilities have to be provided in or near the station premises. Failure to provide parking space results in lost passengers to the railway. This happens when former rail travellers decide to complete the whole journey by private car. Frequently the car owner persuades other rail travellers to join him as passengers to share expenses, or where several car owners are concerned a rota system is established using a different car each week. If further restrictions are imposed on the use of cars in cities, greater provision of car parks will have to be made at railway stations (and bus stations) on the outskirts of cities, to enable car users to park and continue their journeys into the city by public transport.

Goods

As with road goods traffic, rail traffic can be divided into several categories: (*a*) train load, (*b*) truck load, (*c*) less than truck load, (*d*) 'smalls' (*e*) freightliner traffic. It is important always to remember that apart from private siding traffic, rail traffic will begin and end its journeys on road vehicles. Rail terminals must therefore be designed not just with the needs of railway operation in mind, but to facilitate the transfer of goods between road and rail.

Almost all full train load traffic will originate from private sidings. If we apply our original definition of a terminal, viz. places of access to vehicles operating on the way, it will be seen that private sidings fall within this definition. Most train load traffic will be of a bulk nature, e.g. coal, ores, cement, oil, etc., although unit trains (i.e. operated for one consignor) of manufactured goods such as motor vehicles and parts, are becoming more common. Homogeneous traffic lends itself to handling by specialised equipment, and this we would expect to find at the private siding from which the goods originated, with corresponding facilities at the receiving end where this is a regular destination for a specific traffic. Typical equipment for bulk goods would be loading hoppers and conveyors, with truck-tipping mechanisms at the receiving end or elevated tracks for gravity discharge of trucks fitted with bottom doors. For motor vehicles conveyed by rail, end-loading and discharging ramps would probably be used.

Some truck-load traffic originates from private sidings, where separate trucks bound for different destinations may form part of a complete train load destined for the nearest marshalling yard. Or it may be picked up as individual truck loads, a truck here, two or three trucks there, by a local train collecting from small stations and private sidings on its way to the marshalling yard. Unlike road transport consignments of a similar size and weight, a truck load on the railway cannot under present conditions travel by itself from origin to destination, but experiments are being conducted with this end in view. At present such loads must be linked up with other truck loads to make up a train load of trucks bound for a common destination or area. It is this process of consolidation, or marshalling into train loads, that makes the marshalling yard so essential to a large proportion of railway goods traffic operation.

The Marshalling Yard

A marshalling yard consists essentially of a number of incoming or reception sidings from which fan out a large number of train assembly sidings. Incoming trains of mixed destination trucks are pushed towards the sorting point, where they are disconnected and dispatched to the opposite siding where they will be joined up with other trucks to form a train for a common destination. This operation is either carried out using shunting engines, or by utilising gravity in connection with a hump (see Fig. 5.3). A 'hump' is an

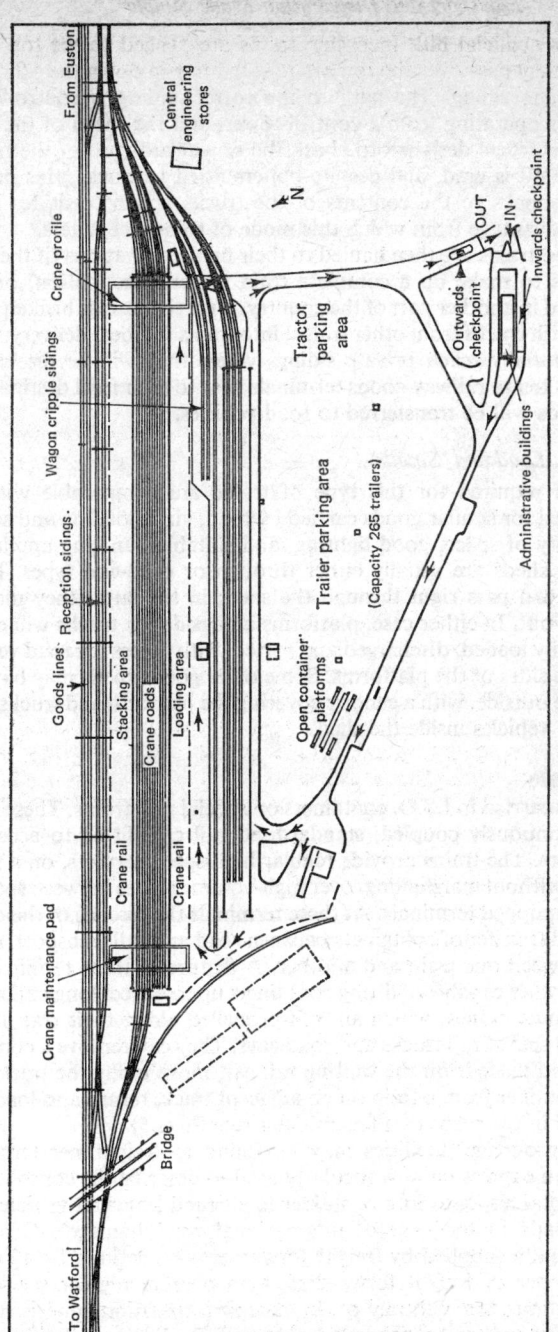

Fig. 5.4. Willesden Freightliner Terminal.

(courtesy of Freightliners Ltd.)

embankment or artificial hill. Incoming trains are pushed to the top of an incline, and as they pass over the top are released to run down the other side to the appropriate siding. The path to the correct siding is controlled by switching points operating from a control tower, and the speed of the truck controlled by retarders designed to check the downward rush of the trucks. Whichever method is used, and despite buffers fitted to trucks, this process causes violent shocks to the contents of the trucks and necessitates heavy packing, a disadvantage from which this mode of transport suffers.

The assembled trains are then hauled to their final destinations (if there are sufficient trucks to make up a complete train for one destination) or to a marshalling yard in another part of the country. Here the train is broken down and re-sorted with trucks from other trains, into trains for local delivery. Some trucks will eventually reach private sidings where they will be discharged, others will be taken to railway goods terminals near to their final destinations, where their loads will be transferred to road vehicles.

Less than Truck Load and 'Smalls'

The facilities required for this type of traffic are comparable with the facilities required for similar goods carried by road, viz. a loading and sorting bank with plenty of space, good lighting, and suitable handling appliances. Railway goods sheds are usually either through or dead-end types. In the former, trucks can pass right through the shed; in the latter they must be shunted in and out. In either case, platforms alongside the trucks will enable goods to be easily loaded, discharged and sorted, with access for road vehicles on the opposite sides of the platforms. Some older goods sheds may have the platform on the outside, with a canopy covering the platform and trucks, with access for road vehicles inside the shed.

Freightliner Traffic

This is traffic carried in I.S.O. containers on special unit trains. These trains consist of continuously coupled, standardised rail cars fitted to accept all I.S.O. containers. The trains provide regular high-speed services, on a point-to-point basis, without marshalling, over high-volume routes between specially designed and equipped terminals. At these terminals the essence of the operation is the rapid transfer of containers between road and rail transport, and in some cases between one train and another. A feature of these terminals are the container cranes capable of lifting containers up to 40 feet long and weighing 30 tons. These cranes, which are self-propelled along their own tracks, straddle several sets of rail tracks and roadways. They can remove a container from a lorry and place it on the waiting rail car, move along the track, pick up another container from a train on an adjacent track, return and load it on to the lorry, all in the space of a few minutes (see Plate 5).

Sometimes 'groupage' facilities may be found at freightliner terminals. 'Groupage' is an expression now regularly used to describe the consolidation of less than container loads into container loads (and less than vehicle loads into vehicle loads in the case of international road haulage). Groupage services are usually supplied by freight forwarders—sometimes by a consortium of a number of freight forwarders, who operate regular services to specific destinations. As with any other transport operation concerned with less than vehicle load traffic, a covered area with loading banks, mechanical

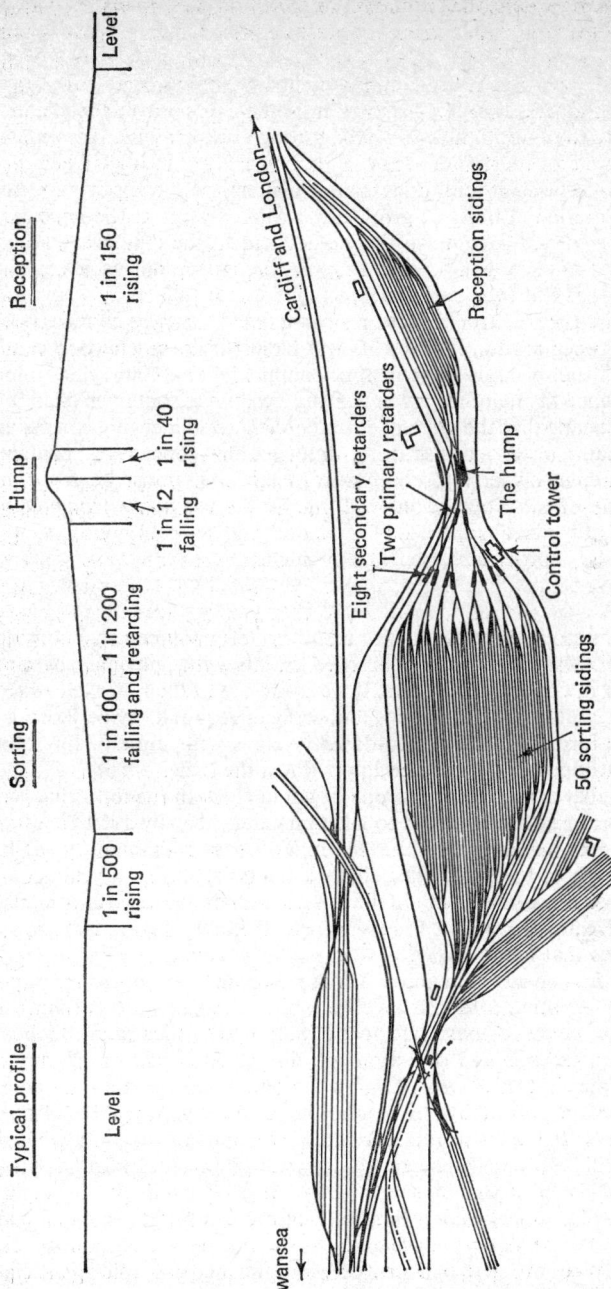

Fig. 5.3. Margam marshalling yard, showing profile and configuration.

(courtesy of British Railways Board)

handling appliances, etc., is required. In addition, because international traffic is likely to be involved, facilities must be provided for Customs clearance.

It will be obvious that as freightliner terminals are involved in the rapid transfer of containers, the greatest care must be exercised in the planning stage, to ensure the smooth flow of traffic through the terminal. Ample space must be allocated for the manoeuvring of road vehicles. Although freightliner terminals have been dealt with under rail transport, road transport to, from and within the terminal must be given equal consideration if the terminal is to operate efficiently. Space must also be devoted to the temporary accommodation of containers awaiting loading on to road or rail vehicles, when direct transfer has not been possible (see Fig. 5.4).

However fast the rail transit, and no matter how quickly containers are transferred between modes, the benefits will be lost if documentation cannot keep pace with the speed of movement of containers, or if a lorry has a long wait for clearance at the office, or is delayed because a container cannot be located. This means that the systems for recording container movements and container locations, for transmitting information concerning container numbers, contents, ownership, etc., between terminals must be rapid and accurate. Many of these operations will involve the use of electronic equipment, which in turn means the need for well-trained staff, all housed in well-planned offices, if bottlenecks are to be avoided.

Air Transport

As with other modes of transport, air transport terminals can vary considerably in size from small airports concerned mainly with light passenger aircraft, to major international airports. If we study one of the latter, Heathrow, we can see the full range of facilities and services required, while bearing in mind that the former will be scaled-down versions with some of the refinements being dropped as we proceed lower down the scale.

The first regular air service to Europe began in 1919. In the following years air passenger transport has grown to such an extent that by 1969 Heathrow airport alone was handling over thirteen million passengers and by the late seventies is expected to be handling thirty million passengers a year. Goods traffic developed more slowly, but in the last decade has increased enormously. Again citing Heathrow, freight has risen from 115,000 tons in 1962 to more than four times that figure today.

This enormous expansion in air traffic has posed many problems for airport authorities. As existing airports have become inadequate to deal with the growing traffic, new sites have had to be found. Ideal locations which will satisfy the requirements and objections of all interested parties are rare, as mentioned earlier in this chapter. Even when an apparently suitable site has been selected, the airport authority cannot be certain that it will be adequate for future needs. No one can forecast with any degree of certainty what the future growth of air traffic will be, or what new developments in aircraft design and size are likely to emerge in, say, 15–20 years. Meanwhile the airport will have created a fairly large conurbation (Heathrow supports approximately 250,000 people) and what was once an open site may now be a built-up area with no further room for expansion, or where further expansion is socially unacceptable. As aircraft grew larger and faster, longer runways were needed, and the introduction of much larger, heavier jets has meant that stronger runways have had to be built. These larger aircraft also need much more room for manoeuvring on the ground and occupy more space on the traffic apron. They require greater space separation between aircraft because of the increased blast from their more powerful jet engines.

The greater passenger capacity of new aircraft which are now coming into service in increasing numbers, and the even larger capacity aircraft being developed, may absorb some of the projected traffic increase, but there is still likely to be a trend towards increased aircraft movements at most major airports. This could lead to the airspace in the vicinity of existing airports becoming dangerously overcrowded, or air traffic control being stretched to breaking point. Even where sufficient space is available on the ground, new airports may have to be established to reduce the load on existing ones. At Heathrow in 1968, a peak of 71 aircraft movements in an hour was recorded, and a total of 901 movements in a day. These figures illustrate the magnitude of the problem, and show why airport planners must look well to the future in anticipating demand. A miscalculation in the level of future demand could lead to a potentially dangerous situation, or a curtailment in the growth of services in a particular area.

Because an aircraft cannot be brought to rest on its specialised way, unlike land and sea transport, the standards of safety and maintenance required must be more exacting than those required for other modes. These of course necessitate very frequent and meticulous maintenance schedules, and strict safety checks. Many of these require to be done between landing and take-off and so require facilities to be provided at the terminal.

Modern aircraft consume enormous quantities of fuel; for example, a B.A.C. One Eleven flying between Gatwick and Palma will consume, depending upon weather and traffic conditions, between 5,160 and 5,860 kilograms of fuel. This must be loaded quickly to avoid unnecessary delay, yet, because of the potential hazard, with maximum regard to safety. At older airports, fuel is taken to the aircraft by road tankers, but at more modern airports permanent underground pipelines are laid from the storage areas to hydrants at the aircraft refuelling points, where it can be pumped aboard under pressure at high speed under strict safety control.

Passenger Facilities

As would be expected from previous discussion on the facilities required by passengers at the major terminals of other modes, aircraft passengers would expect to find shops, restaurants and banking facilities. Because many long-distance flights involve overnight stops, and because aircraft are subject to delays due to weather, etc., hotel accommodation must be provided adjacent to or at the terminal. Heads of State, politicians, major figures in the commercial and industrial worlds, film stars, 'pop' stars and other celebrities are usually accorded special facilities. The abbreviation V.I.P., standing for Very Important Person, was probably coined by airlines to describe these categories of passenger, and it is customary to find V.I.P. reception rooms set aside at major airports where important travellers can be received, interviewed or may wait in privacy. When strict security must be observed, special landing areas are sometimes set aside.

Apart from light hand baggage, passengers do not accompany their baggage to the aircraft. It must be checked, weighed, transported to the aircraft and carefully stowed so as to maintain the trim of the aircraft. At the end of the flight the procedure is reversed, with an additional Customs examination where necessary. With some aircraft now taking hundreds of passengers on a single flight, and remembering the number of flights per hour that may be involved, this must be done speedily and efficiently if delays to aircraft and passengers are to be avoided. This requires the provision of extensive baggage handling systems (see Plate 12).

Cargo Facilities

An aircraft is designed to fly in a particular attitude; that is to say, with the tail in a particular position in relation to the nose when in normal flight at a given speed. If the plane is nose-heavy or tail-heavy it could result in the aircraft failing to take off properly or stalling when in flight. Therefore the trim of the aircraft must always be correct before it is permitted to leave the ground. To ensure that the aircraft's trim is correct, great care must be taken to ensure that the weight carried is properly distributed. Many variables other than weight of cargo must be taken into account: the weight of the aircraft itself, weight of fuel which varies according to distance, weight of mail, the weight of aircrew and baggage, and, since a large proportion of cargo is carried on passenger aircraft, the weight of passengers and their baggage. All these factors, and others, including any special stowage requirements of the cargo itself, must be considered to guarantee a proper trim.

The detailed attention that must be paid to the stowage of an aircraft means that it is often necessary for cargo to be delivered to the airport transit shed four to five hours before take-off, even though the actual flight may only take the same length of time. During this pre-flight time, the cargo must be check-weighed, documented and labelled. Then a stowage plan, load sheet and trim sheet must be prepared, and the cargo loaded.

Since a large proportion of the cargo sent by air consists of small packages, much of it will be palletised in the airport transit sheds, particularly if it is to be carried in all-freight aircraft. To handle large quantities of small packages, sophisticated handling and conveyor systems are required, and these are a feature of the cargo-handling facilities at modern airports. The loading doors of large aircraft are often a considerable height from the ground, and could present problems in loading. Sometimes direct access can be obtained by means of a ramp. In other cases, specialised pieces of mechanised handling equipment, such as scissor-lifts, have been developed to overcome the difficulty.

The total tonnage handled by airports is small by comparison with that handled by major seaports. Nevertheless if a comparison is made in terms of value of cargo, the picture is very different, and the high value of a large percentage of air cargo is clearly demonstrated. On this basis, Heathrow ranks second only to the Port of London in the handling of Britain's international goods traffic. Because of this high proportion of valuable goods, particular attention must be paid to security arrangements, and since much of the cargo is subject to Customs or Excise duty extensive facilities must be provided for the temporary accommodation of dutiable goods.

The principal benefit derived from the use of air transport is speed of transit, but this benefit could soon be dissipated by delays on the ground due to non-arrival of documents, and slow Customs clearance. The various

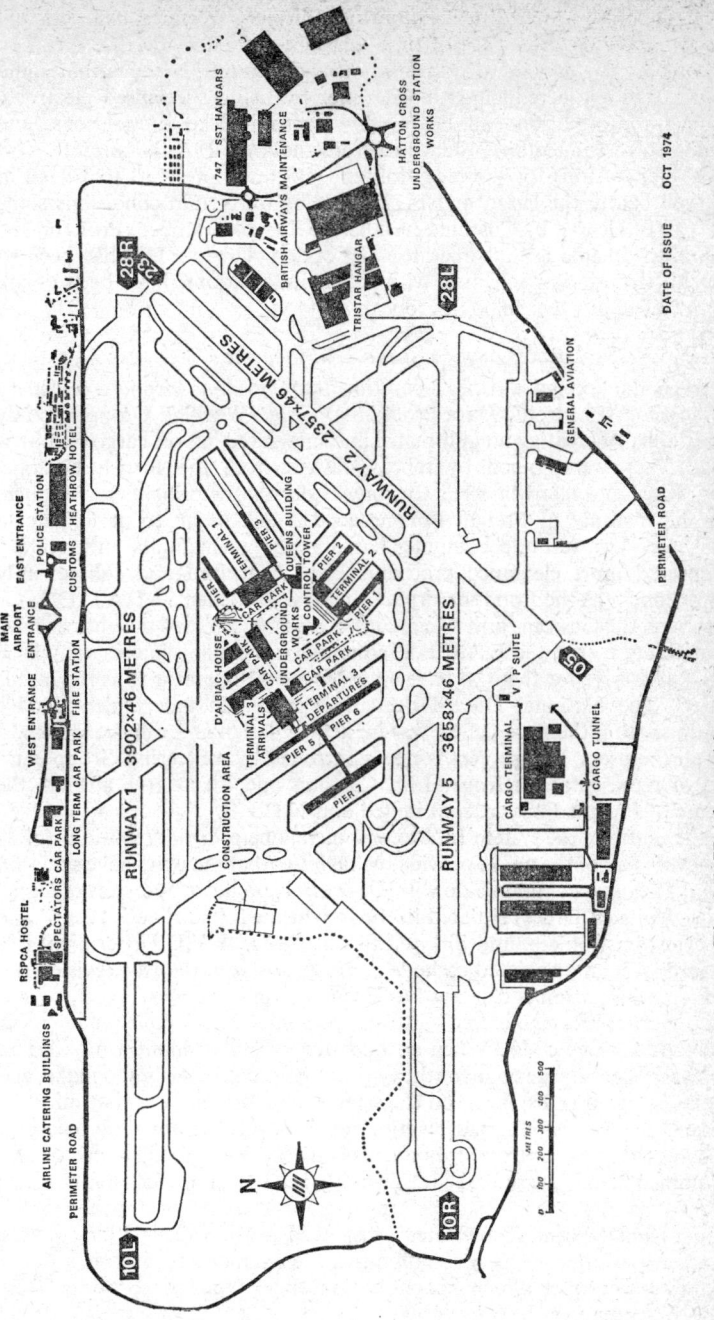

Fig. 5.5. Heathrow Airport, London: general configuration.
(courtesy of British Airports Authority)

agencies involved—viz. airport authorities, airlines, freight forwarders and Customs—have devoted a lot of time, thought and effort over the years to the problem of producing documentation and clearance systems that could keep pace with the reducing transit time. By using specialised electronic equipment, information can be rapidly transmitted to destinations, and facsimiles of documents reproduced before the arrival of the aircraft. This enables preparations for the reception and clearance of cargo to be put in hand well before the cargo arrives. Depending on certain conditions some goods can be cleared by Customs even before they have landed. Probably the best known scheme is that operated at London Airport. This has been so successful that similar schemes, with local modifications, have been or are being installed at other major European airports.

L.A.C.E.S.—*The London Airport Cargo EDP Scheme*

In 1966 the foreign airlines operating into London Airport decided to form an EDP (Electronic Data Processing) Cargo Working Group to study the feasibility of creating an automated and integrated import cargo clearance system. They were joined by representatives from the British National Corporation, and Her Majesty's Customs endorsed the principles laid down. Later the Institute of Freight Forwarders Limited began to participate in the scheme. As a result, a computer-based system to maintain an inventory and speed import clearance procedures was conceived and subsequently became known as the London Airport Cargo EDP Scheme—L.A.C.E.S.

Although the Customs and Excise authorities and most of the airlines have the capability to run the L.A.C.E.S. computers, the many interests involved made it attractive for them to have an independent operator to perform this function. The National Data Processing Service, an independent service operating within the Post Office, was invited to design and run the system to serve all the users. The project is now controlled by a Steering Group composed of representatives from H.M. Customs and Excise, the airlines, the Institute of Freight Forwarders Limited and N.D.P.S.

At the centre of the system I.C.L. computers, operating in 'real-time' for 24 hours every day of the week, provide the facilities that the users have said they require. The users communicate with the central computer by means of Visual Display Units (V.D.U.s) situated in the freight area, in airlines', agents' and H.M. Customs' offices, and airlines' transit sheds. A V.D.U. terminal is a keyboard with an associated cathode ray display screen (like a television set) on which information is displayed as it is keyed in.

Each type of message is known to the computer by a two-letter reference called the 'message code'. When an operator wishes to input a message he first keys in the message code for the type of input that he wishes to make, and the relevant form is displayed on the screen. The form shows what information can be input and at what position on the screen it should be recorded. This helps the operator to record information accurately. A full screen of data is assembled before the message is transmitted to the computer, thus enabling errors to be easily corrected before transmission. After transmission a response from the central computer is displayed on the screen within seconds. The other main item of user's equipment, the character printer, is a device similar to a teleprinter, which is capable of receiving typed outputs direct from the central computer.

Lack of space prevents a detailed description of all that can be done within the system, but a brief description of how a consignment is processed through the system illustrates just one facet of its operation.

Progressing a Consignment Through the System

The aim of the system is to record the state of a consignment as each external event occurs. As the various inputs for recording these events are made, the computer checks the stage reached. Before a consignment, or part of a consignment, can be released for delivery the record must have passed three significant stages, which may be achieved in any order.

Status of a Consignment

The computer sets a STATUS indicator as each significant stage is reached. When set they record:

(1) That the number of packages expected (NPX) from the air waybill (AWB) input equals the number of packages received (NPR), from the package check-in input—Status 1.

(2) That the airline is satisfied as to the creditworthiness of the consignee and/or that any other conditions placed upon a consignment have been satisfied—Status 2.

(3) That the Customs authority placing the goods out-of-charge has been given and that they may be released—Status 3.

A check for Status 1 is made as package input is made or at the time of AWB input if package input has already been made. If the full number of packages is not input within a given time, a discrepancy report is produced. On the other hand, if an over-shipment is recorded a discrepancy report is produced immediately.

If the airline and H.M. Customs are satisfied that a consignment can be released (Status 2 and 3) but only part of the consignment has been checked into the shed (Status 1 not set), the record can be split into subsidiary records. In this way one of the sub-records can achieve Status 1 and the part-consignment released. Status 2 and Status 3 may be set at the time of the AWB input, where in the case of the former, the airline and consignee have agreed conditions for release, and in the case of the latter, when the computer is told that the consignment is domestic or is in transit to another final destination airport.

After an Entry input is made, Customs allow clearance of the goods either automatically by computer programme after a pre-determined delay or by the input of a Customs clearance message. Customs clearance (Status 3) is recorded on the computer record. (Further information on L.A.C.E.S. can be obtained from a booklet available from National Data Processing.)

Sea Transport

The terminals for sea transport range in size from small, riverside wharfs capable of accommodating vessels of a few hundred tons in size, and perhaps built with strengthened bottoms to enable them to sit on the bottom at low tide, to huge complexes covering an area of many square miles. In fact what we often refer to as ports at the present time, are not so much terminals for sea transport as industrial areas with port connections, in which the actual area devoted to purely port work is only a small part of the total complex.

It is not possible to deal with the various facilities and services to be found at ports of various sizes according to some ascending or descending ladder of size, for the number of steps on such a ladder would be almost as large as the number of ports themselves. Instead, as we did with airports, we will look at the provisions made by major ports and remember that these will be scaled down or dispensed with as the ports decrease in size and complexity.

We have already seen, earlier in this chapter, the necessity for providing shelter, deep water and safe access from the sea. Immense capital expenditure will have been necessary to provide the fixed installations, viz. enclosed docks, lock entrances, quay walls, etc., where these are necessary; to provide extra protection in the form of breakwaters where extra protection is needed; or to dredge deeper channels to keep pace with the ever-increasing draught of modern vessels. After these provisions much more needs to be done. Maintenance dredging must be carried out on a continuous basis to preserve the depth of water, and a multitude of other services and facilities must be provided for the safe reception and handling of the vessel, its passengers and cargo.

First, the vessel must be brought safely to its berth. This may involve a tricky navigation from the outer limits of the port to a berth in an enclosed dock some miles upstream. Unlike aircraft, which for the most part operate in strictly controlled air lanes and are virtually handed on from one air control point to another, ships while on the high seas are free from regulation, and it is not until they reach the approaches to a port that they come under the jurisdiction of the port authority. Even then, the degree of control exercised by the port or harbour authority is much less than that which applies to aircraft. It has been said that a ship's master is 'Master under God'; that is, that in all matters relating to the safety of his ship, passengers, crew and cargo, he is the sole arbiter, and while port authorities may have statutory powers to 'regulate' the passage of his vessel, they do not 'control' it.

Some time before its actual arrival, perhaps a few days, perhaps weeks, sometimes even months before, the shipping company will have advised the port authority of the ship's intended visit. The longer the voyage, and the larger the number of ports of call, the more difficult it will be to give a precise arrival and this may be adjusted several times as a more accurate picture of the vessel's progress emerges. When the vessel is a tramp rather than a cargo liner, its expected arrival date is likely to be more imprecise, because the loading of extra cargo will always take priority over the need to sail on a planned date. Unless the ship is destined for an allocated berth, i.e. one leased or rented for the exclusive use of a specific shipping company (or a specific stevedoring company in the case of many European ports), a provisional allocation to a common user berth will be made. This allocation may have to be amended several times before the ship actually arrives, depending upon how the discharging and loading of preceding vessels has progressed—for example, whether the programme has been upset by late arrival of preceding vessels, bad weather, breakdowns, labour disputes. Once en route to the port, the shipping company or its agents will give an E.T.A. (estimated time of arrival) to the port authority. This will later be confirmed by the ship's VHF radio to the port navigation service, as the vessel draws nearer.

It will, it is hoped, assist the reader who has no knowledge of the workings of a large modern port to understand the parts played by the many services and organisations if we follow the progress of a vessel from the time it arrives at the outer approaches to a port, until it reaches the safety of its berth. The description which follows of organisations and procedures is based loosely on those applicable to the Port of London, but they are not always identical and considerable variations will occur from port to port.

Long before the vessel reaches the outer limits of the port authority's jurisdiction it will require assistance in avoiding natural hazards such as rocks and sandbanks. Coastal lightships, lighthouses, buoys and beacons placed in position by the lighthouse authority will serve to guide the vessel safely on its way.

Lighthouse Authority

The general lighthouse authority for England and Wales, the Channel Islands, the adjacent seas and islands and Gibraltar, is the Corporation of Trinity House of Deptford Strand, London. In association with the Commissioners of Northern Lighthouses and the Commissioners of Irish Lights, the Corporation controls and maintains the lighthouses and lightships on and around our coasts. To finance the construction, maintenance and administration of these and other seamarks, money is raised by means of special dues levied on shipping using the ports of the British Isles. These dues, called 'light dues', are collected on behalf of the Corporation by H.M. Customs, and the accounts are submitted annually to Parliament. A number of other bodies having a limited local jurisdiction perform a similar service. In other countries this function may be performed by government services or departments, e.g. a 'Ministry of Marine' or a 'Coastguard Service'.

Having reached the outer limits of the port, especially an estuarial port such as London, the vessel may now face the problem of navigating a considerable distance before entering the actual estuary, and then many more miles of estuary and finally the river itself, before arriving at the lock entrance of the enclosed dock. From its surface the water gives little clue as to what lies beneath. To an experienced mariner 'broken water', i.e. where the surface appears very disturbed, may indicate rocks or shoals, but there can be little to indicate a difference in depth between 30 ft. and 40 ft. and this may be critical to the safe progress of the vessel. The master needs to know where the safe channels lie. These will be marked by positioning navigation buoys (as opposed to mooring buoys) along the length of the deep-water channels. Each of these will be of a different shape or system of marking, will be named individually and recorded on the charts. Navigation information for the port will give a detailed description of each one so that they can be easily identified and the ship's position accurately located even in conditions of poor visibility when shore marks may be hidden. The provision of these navigation buoys may be undertaken by the Port Authority or the Lighthouse Authority. In London, they are provided and maintained by the Corporation of Trinity House.

Pilotage

Buoys alone are not sufficient to ensure that the vessel can safely navigate in confined waters. Difficult currents, tricky crosswinds, speed of tide and ferry crossings are just a few of the difficulties that create the need for the assistance of someone with extensive local knowledge. It is here that the pilotage service plays its part. Pilots operate under licences granted either by the Port Authority (which may be designated as the Pilotage Authority) or an independent Pilotage Authority. In London the Pilotage Authority is another department of the Corporation of Trinity House. Licences are granted to satisfactory applicants only after they have passed tests and gained experience in the work they will have to do, e.g. by a period of training under other experienced pilots. In some ports possession of a Master's Certificate for Foreign Going Ships is a prerequisite for acceptance as a trainee, at others this is not required and the pilot progresses under experienced pilots, through several stages of competency to handle vessels of increasing size. In some ports pilotage is compulsory, in others it is optional. Even in non-compulsory ports few masters will dispense with the services of a pilot, except where they are in command of a small vessel operating a very frequent service so that they have acquired an extensive local knowledge. In compulsory pilotage ports, the masters of small vessels that are frequent visitors will sometimes qualify as pilots so as to avoid the necessity of having to employ one each time they enter and leave the port. It is important to note that even where pilotage is compulsory, control of the vessel and responsibility for its safety and conduct remains with the master; the pilot acts in an advisory capacity only.

Towage

It is difficult for large vessels to navigate and manoeuvre in confined, congested waters without assistance. Even when barely moving, considerable power is required to halt the forward momentum of a large vessel, and the damage it can cause by a slight collision with a fixed structure such as a pier can be enormous. Imagine an elephant leaning gently against a garden shed and you can probably visualise the effect of a 100,000 ton tanker still moving, though very slowly, bearing down on the steel structure of an oil jetty. Furthermore, a vessel which is hundreds of feet long finds it impossible to change direction quickly. A considerable time must elapse after the rudder has been moved before the vessel's head comes round. To counter these two difficulties, tugs must be used. These small, but immensely powerful vessels can pull, push and check the movement of giant vessels and enable manoeuvres to be performed with much more success than could be achieved by the ship's engines and rudder alone. Although Port Authorities themselves frequently maintain fleets of tugs for work in enclosed docks, towage on the river, in the estuary, and some dock work is usually performed by tugs belonging to firms of tug owners established in the port.

Port Navigation Service

Although by no means a universal feature, most major ports now have some form of navigation service. This, as its name implies, is a service designed to assist vessels in safely navigating the confined waters of a port area. Mention has already been made of VHF radio which permits easy communication between ship and shore. This enables the latest information regarding availability of berths, anchorages, weather conditions, temporary hazards such as dredgers working, etc., to be passed to incoming vessels. As vessels have grown larger over the years it has become necessary for Port Authorities to take powers to regulate and control water traffic in the areas under their jurisdiction. For example, at ports where the tidal range has necessitated the provision of enclosed docks and lock entrances, it may be vital to regulate the order in which vessels proceed upstream. This is to ensure that those vessels with the deepest draughts have the benefit of the deepest water when entering dock, i.e. their arrival will need to coincide with high water at the lock entrance. In this situation they may be required to remain at an appropriate anchorage in the estuary, and to proceed upstream, in sequence, on instructions from the navigation service. Other smaller vessels will be limited to entering the locks before and after the deeper draughted vessels, and their progress will be regulated so that they do not impede the larger vessels.

The reverse procedure will operate for vessels leaving the docks, and where the arrival of a number of large vessels coincides with the departure of others, strict adherence to a plan is necessary to ensure that vessels do not miss a tide. When very large tankers are turning in midstream to go alongside or leave riverside oil terminals, such manoeuvres would be very hazardous if other vessels were moving upstream or downstream at the same time. In this situation the navigation service would have to regulate the movements of other vessels, in the interests of safety.

Most readers will be aware that tide tables are published giving the predicted times and heights of high and low water for principal ports around our coasts. These predictions are usually based on official tide tables provided by the Liverpool Observatory and Tidal Institute, and are as accurate as science can make them. But it must be emphasised that they are only predictions and must be used with care. Meteorological conditions nearly always affect both times and heights of tides. For small and medium-size vessels differences of a few feet and some fluctuation in the actual time of high or low water are unlikely to be serious, especially if even at low tide there is likely to be ample depth for them to navigate in safety. With larger vessels, and especially in the case of giant tankers, such discrepancies could be disastrous if undetected. For this reason a very careful watch must be kept on the height and timing of the tides when very large vessels are due to enter or leave the port. In London, for example, not only are there tidal gauges in the estuary and its approaches, but others are located on the coast many miles to the north and south of the mouth of the Thames. The readings from these automatic gauges are transmitted to visual displays in the Thames Navigation Service Centre at Gravesend. A higher or lower, or earlier or later, reading than that predicted will show up on these coastal gauges an hour or more before a similar reading would appear at the mouth of the Thames. This early warning of any deviation from the prediction will enable a very accurate estimate of the time and height of the tide in the Thames to be made. Such information is invaluable when dealing with vessels exceeding 100,000 tons deadweight, which may have only a few feet of water under their bottoms when proceeding upriver on a rising tide.

Lastly, the navigation service will almost certainly have shore-based radar coverage of the estuarial waters. The Thames Navigation Service is able to provide coverage from the Sunk and Tongue light buoys on the seaward limit of the Port to the entrance to the King George V Dock, a distance of 50 miles. A common question asked in connection with shore-based radar is: 'Why is it necessary when nearly all vessels have their own radar?' The answer is that radar cannot see round corners and a vessel proceeding upstream or downstream cannot tell what is around the next bend because the image will be hidden by the high banks of the river and any buildings or trees upon the banks. Additionally, the multiplicity of other ships, cranes and other shore equipment and buildings would present a confused picture. Shore radar has the advantage of being mounted on high buildings and towers; the equipment is probably more powerful than can be mounted on most vessels; and the operators have the advantage of local knowledge when interpreting the image. In foggy weather, shore-based radar can be of tremendous assistance to vessels enabling them to be guided into and out of the port and thus avoiding the delays which would occur if vessels were forced to drop anchor.

Berthing

If a vessel is passing through an entrance lock on her way to a berth she will need assistance in negotiating the lock. The operation of lock gates and raising the level of the water will almost certainly be performed by staff of the Port Authority's Dockmaster's Department (or some equivalent name). The handling of the ship's ropes when passing through the lock, and when she is finally secured at her berth, may be carried out by Port Authority's staff, or by other men licensed to do this work. At river berths this will probably be performed by licensed boatmen and watermen.

H.M. Customs

At some point on the inward journey to her berth the vessel will be boarded by H.M. Customs officials who will search the vessel for hidden contraband. While this search is in progress, the master will be interviewed by a Customs officer and will receive two very important documents, viz.

Pratique. This is the ship's health certificate, and is issued only if there is no infectious disease on board. Neither passengers nor crew may land pending issue of Pratique. Should there be infectious disease on board, or if it is suspected, then the Port Health Authority will be called in.

Certificate of clearance inward. The master supplies the Customs officers with a list of dutiable goods declared to be in possession of each member of the crew. Duty is charged on these after a small allowance for personal use has been made. The master is given a certificate of clearance inwards after the bonded ship's stores remaining on board have been checked against the Report and sealed up by the Customs. (After the ship has discharged, the bonded stores will again be checked and re-sealed and the master will be given a jerque note, in duplicate, one copy of which must be handed in at the Customs House before the ship can be given an outward clearance.)

Reporting Inwards

Most people are aware that an entry must be made to H.M. Customs for all goods imported into the country, irrespective of whether or not they are subject to duty. But many are unaware that it is also necessary for all vessels from abroad to be 'entered inwards'.

As soon as possible after the arrival of the vessel, the master or his agent must report the vessel's arrival to H.M. Customs' Long Room. (Even if it is a square room or a round one, it is still called a Long Room, after the original one in London.) When reporting, the master must produce the REPORT, which contains details of the ship, its cargo, the name of the master, port of origin, present berth, dutiable stores, cargo intended for other ports, number and nationality of passengers, name of the ship's agent, and a declaration that the ship has not 'broken bulk', i.e. landed any cargo, since leaving the port of origin. Where a large variety of cargo is carried, this will probably be described on the Report as General Cargo, and a copy of the Manifest will be attached to the Report. He must also produce the certificate of Pratique, and where applicable, a Pilotage slip, showing details of any pilotage done, a Deck Cargo certificate, a Grain Cargo certificate, and a Tonnage dues slip showing the dues to be paid. Finally the master will make a declaration of any unusual sightings, icebergs, wrecks, etc.

Before sailing, the reverse procedure is adopted. Before outward clearance is given, the following documents must be presented at the Customs House:

(1) Clearance Outwards and Victualling Bill, giving details of bonded and drawback stores on board.
(2) Load Line Certificate
(3) Ship's Certificate of Registry.
(4) Wireless Certificate.
(5) Light Dues Certificate.
(6) Safety Equipment Certificate.
(7) Passenger Number Certificate.
(8) Inward Clearing Bill (Jerque Note).

On completion of these formalities the ship may leave port, but it is important to note that within six days of the clearance of the ship, the ship's agent must submit to the Customs House a copy of the ship's manifest and a list of the names of passengers carried.

Dredging

While not strictly part of a ship's progress into port, the activities of port authorities in the dredging and conservation of the river channel are vital to the movement of ships. Engineers make painstaking studies of the ebb and flow of tidal waters, in some cases using research models of entire estuaries. These models, which are very accurate representations of the topography of the estuary, its banks, bed and approaches, faithfully reproduce the effect of tidal variations and changes in the force and direction of the flow of water. Through the study of this model, and by constant monitoring of the actual channel, silting up and erosion can be detected and remedial measures taken. Sometimes the careful study of a tidal model will reveal that a realignment of a dredged channel will harness the self-scouring effect of the tides, to reduce or eliminate the need for dredging in the future.

It is not only the river which is affected by silting. Every time a ship passes through the enclosed locks, water carrying fine particles of soil in suspension is admitted. In the calm waters of the dock, this silt settles out and gradually builds up a layer of fine sand on the bottom of the dock. In London, this deposited spoil amounts to a million tons per year, which must be dredged out and pumped ashore to reclaim low-lying marshy land.

Many estuaries yield high-quality gravel and sand which can be sold after being dredged up or used in port developments as the basis of concrete for piles and jetties. Our ship, oblivious of this valuable work, proceeds to its berth through channels kept clear by the Marine Services Department.

Conservation

Estuaries must also be conserved in other ways. The problem of pollution is one that requires constant vigilance. Even to fall into some rivers is dangerous, not because you might drown but because you might swallow some of the water. Where River Conservators are appointed, as in the Port of London, to monitor oxygen levels and detect pollution as soon as it occurs, steps can be taken to prevent repetitions of pollution by offending factories, municipalities or agricultural enterprises. Similarly, river banks can be regularly inspected, flood prevention organised in low-lying areas, animal pests controlled, fisheries promoted, etc. Driftwood collection prevents damage to small vessels, and floating debris which would make banks and sea shores unsightly can be collected and destroyed.

Security

The security of any port area is vital. In the port we have a concentration of desirable commodities, ready to be pilfered, re-routed or stolen. Every conceivable kind of theft and malpractice has been tried at one time or another, from petty theft to major robberies. A port police authority, or river police authority, working in conjunction with other land-based police forces in the hinterland, preserves and safeguards this valuable collection of property. Unauthorised entry to dock areas is forbidden, and patrols must enforce this prohibition. Cargoes and vehicles must be checked at gateways, and only authorised movements permitted. Customs officers will be alert for unauthorised movements of goods seeking to avoid customs duty; will maintain records and checks on movements of vehicles through port areas where roll-on roll-off facilities make smuggling easier; and will watch for illegal entry of drugs and other prohibited articles. Immigration officials will check the movements of foreign nationals, exclude prohibited immigrants and detain for investigation those visitors whose documents are defective.

Health

The Port Medical Officer will supervise the admission of people from areas where outbreaks of infectious diseases have been notified. Veterinary officers will quarantine animals which may be carriers of diseases, such as rabies, foot and mouth disease or swine vesicular disease. Similarly, infested cargoes which could spread pests like the colorado beetle may need to be fumigated or excluded.

Ship's Services

A ship at sea is a self-contained unit, generating its own power, often distilling drinking water, baking its own bread, disposing of its own waste products, etc. In port the engines are still and the ship relies temporarily on shore-based services. It will almost certainly link up to shore power supplies to keep essential services going while in port. The ship will take on board, and pay for, a fresh water supply sufficient to meet most needs of the coming voyage. She will be re-victualled, and re-supplied with countless items such as table linen, bed linen, cleaning materials, lubricants, paint, cutlery, etc. She will discharge accumulated waste products, and dispose of rubbish ashore. She will link up to the public telephone network so that external calls can be made.

The services of shore-based craftsmen will be engaged to effect repairs of a major nature, and at times the facilities of the dry dock will be used. A dry dock is a basin which has an entrance mouth which can be closed by a floating plug called a 'caisson'. First the dock must be made ready to receive the ship which is to be dry-docked, by preparing within it a cradle which will exactly match the configuration of the keel. Then the dock is flooded, the ship brought in, the plug is repositioned and sunk in the entrance by filling it with water. This seals off the basin from the main harbour. Now the dry dock can be pumped clear, the ship settling on to the cradle and being supported as the dock is emptied by suitable methods so that it does not fall over. The entire hull of the ship can now be cleaned and painted, and the cathodic protection renewed. Dry-docking is an annual event for passenger ships, and slightly less frequent for other vessels, but may also take place at other times for the inspection of damage. It does not take too long, and other re-fit work can be carried out at a wet berth to free the dry dock for other vessels.

Bunkering Services

Today bunkering is largely a matter of taking on oil. This is easily supplied by pipeline from shore-based pumps or from small tanker craft specially built for the purpose and can often be taken aboard while the cargo is being turned round. A chain of bunkering facilities around the world has made the task of re-fuelling a simple process, compared with the time-consuming, dirty business of refuelling with coal at special berths, which often entailed loading by basket.

Cargo Handling Facilities and Services

Although a tremendous change has occurred in the transport of cargo by sea during the past few decades with the advent of unitisation and the development of bulk carriers and other specialised vessels, a very large proportion of cargo is still carried in conventional vessels, i.e. those carrying heterogeneous cargo, manually stowed in the holds, and this situation is likely to persist for very many years yet, though in diminishing quantity. It is convenient therefore to describe the services and facilities required at a general cargo berth and then to describe a selection of specialised berths.

It cannot be emphasised too much that time lost and excessive labour costs incurred at the interface can prove very expensive to all concerned. Where the interface is a port, these are the shipowner, the Port Authority, the importer or exporter, the consumer, and ultimately the nation itself. Thus all are concerned, but too often all are not concerned enough. Inefficiency and inadequate facilities are felt in the following ways:

By the shipowner. Slow turn-round means that a ship, which represents a very considerable capital investment, is spending time in port which could otherwise be profitably employed in earning freight. At the same time, dock dues are being incurred. These are based on the net registered tonnage of the vessel, and *the time it spends in port*. The initial dues payment allows for the ship remaining at a berth for a set period; if that period is exceeded additional dues will have to be paid. While it remains in port its crew will have to be paid and fed, and payment will have to be made for certain services supplied from shore, e.g. an electricity supply. Finally, labour charges for loading and unloading cargo will have to be paid. Where all or any of these charges are excessive, i.e. due to inefficiency, the shipowner is faced with several alternatives. He may attempt to recover the extra costs by passing them on to his customers by means of extra freight charges. This may not be possible in view of fixed Conference rates or intensive competition from other shipping companies. He may decide to trim his margin of profit, i.e. to absorb the extra costs himself. This may be impracticable if his profit margins are already low. Finally, he may decide to transfer his operations to a competing port with lower charges and faster turn-round times.

By the Port Authority. Slow turn-round will mean that the Port Authority will be able to accommodate fewer vessls at any berth in a given period of time. Although extra dues may be incurred when a vessel exceeds the period of stay allowed for in the initial dues payment, the extra dues received will not produce the same revenue as could be earned by accommodating extra vessels. The Port Authority also earns revenue from cargo passing through its facilities—more vessels, more cargo, more revenue, or conversely fewer vessels, less cargo, lower revenue. Where the Port Authority is involved in cargo handling, if its operations are labour intensive and if through inefficiency these labour costs are higher than need be, the Port Authority can incur labour costs at an alarmingly high level. If the port is to remain operative, these costs together with fixed costs arising from the provision of capital assets must be recovered from its customers, viz. shipowners, importers and exporters. Where higher charges result in shipping companies transferring to other ports, or merchants transferring their business to other ports (which could eventually lead to shipping companies following), a snowball effect can occur. The Port Authority, which must still cover its fixed costs, may now have an underemployed labour force which it may be unable to reduce because of labour agreements, yet which must still be paid. The consequence is likely to be that the remaining shipping companies, and cargo passing through the port, will have to face still higher charges. This action in turn may force more of them to transfer their allegiance to other ports.

By Importers and Exporters. In addition to the extra charges mentioned above, merchants will face higher costs due to capital being tied up in goods in transit for longer periods than necessary, higher insurance premiums will have to be paid because goods will be at risk for longer periods, and there is a danger of orders being lost through delays or the inability to meet required supply times.

By the Consumer. Increased costs are inevitably reflected in the selling prices of commodities, and as transport and distribution costs may represent anything between 15 and 30 per cent of the final cost of a manufactured item, any increased costs incurred at the interface will have a marked impact on the final price.

By the Nation as a Whole. Great Britain lives by exporting. A large part of our exports is made from imported raw materials. Therefore any increased cost of imported goods due to inefficient ports, will not only be reflected in the cost of imports for our own consumption but also in the cost of exports made from them. Those exports, already inflated in price by higher import prices, will then incur further unnecessary costs if they pass through inefficient ports on their way to overseas markets, and result in lower sales. Loss of exports and increased cost of imports would have an adverse effect on our Balance of Payments and could eventually lead to a lowering of the standard of living of most people living in this country.

The last statement in the above paragraph may seem rather exaggerated, and of course any deterioration in the standard of living (or its failure to improve) through this cause may be small in comparison with the effect of increased oil prices on the economies of the developed countries. Nevertheless, the authors feel that the effect of our ports on the economy is underestimated or misunderstood by many of the people who are best placed to effect changes, viz. workers and managers in the port industry, and perhaps most importantly by politicians and governments whose business it is to create the economic environment in which ports operate.

Although it has taken us some time to reach this point, we can now see that in providing facilities and services for handling cargoes through ports, the emphasis must be on ensuring that vessels are turned round in the shortest space of time, i.e. must be discharged and loaded expeditiously, and at least cost. In addition, arrangements should ensure that cargoes pass through the port as rapidly as possible, and at least cost. To achieve these aims, the provision of certain conditions would seem to be essential.

(1) Shift-working to ensure that the operations of discharging and loading can proceed on a continuous basis and so release the ship in the shortest space of time. This would also give the advantage of reducing the transit time of goods, and making maximum use of very expensive mechanical handling equipment which would otherwise stand idle.

(2) Good management, for example, by planning to ensure that operations are not hampered by lack of equipment, by failure of vehicles and cargo to arrive on time or by shortage of labour.

(3) Good industrial relations. The most modern equipment is no use if the labour force is on strike, or refuses to use it.

These things cannot be achieved by port managements alone; many other interests must play their parts. The following examples will serve as illustrations of this need:

(*a*) Appropriate equipment can only be designed and installed if port managements are kept advised of shipping companies' plans, particularly as they relate to new developments, and can be given some guarantee that if installed the equipment will be used sufficiently to warrant the heavy capital expenditure involved.

(*b*) Liaison and co-operation between manufacturers, inland transport operators, shipping companies and port authorities are essential. Too often in the past, the loading and discharge of vessels was hampered by lack of information concerning the cargo expected, making pre-planning difficult; by 75 per cent of cargo arriving for shipment on the last few days of the receiving period (usually longer than the actual loading period) when much of it could have been sent forward earlier; by space in transit sheds for the receipt of cargoes from import vessels being reduced due to the failure of importers and their carriers to clear cargo from previous vessels, thus slowing down the discharge of the current vessel. Although improvements have taken place in these areas in recent years, there is often room for further improvement, and merchants and carriers who complain of high charges and delays to vehicles might well consider to what extent they are responsible for them.

(c) Good industrial relations cannot be created by one side alone, but only where there is a genuine desire by both sides of industry to work together for the common good. Given the past history of industrial relations in the port industry, this is much easier to say than to achieve. Nevertheless, the type of industrial relations climate desired can be obtained, but only if:

(i) The employers can earn the trust and respect of their employees by themselves trusting and respecting those employees; by providing fair wages and conditions of work; by keeping workers fully informed of future developments and through consultation seeking to minimise any possible adverse effects of such developments;

(ii) The employees can give employers the opportunity to make good the mistakes of the past, by not regarding every new proposal as an employer's trick to extract more work without adequate compensation; by co-operation in the use of new methods and equipment; by giving a fair day's work and by agreeing to greater flexibility in working arrangements.

If all these things can be achieved, and great progress has already been made, much more efficient ports will emerge.

General or Conventional Cargo Berths

By general cargo we mean cargo of a non-specialised nature, i.e. a heterogeneous collection of bags, bales, boxes, crates, cartons, drums, etc., stowed in the holds of a vessel as individual pieces or packages. Despite the revolution which has taken place in the transporting of goods in specialised ships, much of the world's maritime trade is still conducted in conventional cargo vessels, and general cargo plays an important part in producing revenue for port authorities. Indeed, general cargo produces more revenue, ton for ton, than container traffic and bulk cargoes. It is, however, the form of cargo whose handling requires the greatest input of labour and incurs high costs per ton handled. So that although a generator of high revenues, if inefficiently handled it can rapidly become a high loss maker. It is therefore important not to neglect the pursuit of efficiency in general cargo handling while pursuing the development of traffic at the more 'glamorous' berths handling cargo by the new methods. Unfortunately, in many ports general cargo is still being handled at facilities built well before the Second World War and in some cases before the First World War. Well-designed and well-equipped modern general cargo berths are capable of throughputs that would be inconceivable at those outdated facilities.

The following are the essential requirements of a modern general cargo berth:

(1) A plentiful supply of quay cranes. Although most general cargo vessels are equipped with their own cargo derricks, these are generally much slower working than quay cranes, so the latter will usually be preferred in the interest of faster working. The quay cranes will probably be of 5-ton lifting capacity. A decade or so ago, a 3-ton capacity was the more general rule, but the average weight of lifts has increased making the higher capacity necessary.

(2) A wide quay apron (i.e. the space between the quay edge and the transit shed). The increasing use of mobile mechanical handling equipment has made this necessary to allow plenty of room for manoeuvring and to avoid vehicles obstructing one another. It was customary a few years ago to have rail tracks running along the quay apron and at the rear of the transit shed. In recent years, however, the proportion of rail cargo to and from ports (apart from Freightliner and certain bulk traffics) has decreased. For this reason these are usually omitted in this country so as to provide a smooth surface on the quay apron and unhindered access for road vehicles at the rear. Where traffic originates from or is destined for rail transport, it is transported between the berth and the nearest rail terminal by road vehicles. In some European ports, where railways carry a much bigger proportion of port traffic, rail served berths are still important. Where quayside tracks must be provided, it is important to have at least two sets of tracks, with frequent crossovers, to avoid disrupting work along the length of the quay while shunting is in progress.

(3) A modern transit shed. This should incorporate the following features:

(a) A roof of cantilever construction so that space inside the shed is unobstructed by supporting pillars.

(b) The roof should be extended at the rear and ends of the shed to give weather protection to vehicles loading and unloading. The canopy should be high enough to permit mobile cranes to operate beneath it.

(c) A strong floor, capable of supporting heavy loads when cargo is piled high.

(d) Loading platforms at lorry tailboard height at the rear and ends of the shed.

(e) Good natural lighting through transparent roof panels, and good artificial lighting both inside and outside the shed to permit safe and speedy working during the hours of darkness.

(f) Good ventilation so that fumes from mobile equipment and other vehicles working in the shed are quickly dispersed.

(g) Wide, high doors to permit easy access by mobile equipment.

(h) Lock-up facilities for bonded, valuable and pilferable cargoes.

(4) An adequate supply of mobile equipment, e.g. forklift trucks and mobile cranes for handling palletised cargo and packages too heavy for manual handling. Wherever possible, non-palletised cargo should be made into pallet loads during the 'striking' operation, i.e. unloading goods from road vehicles. If this is done the palletised cargo can be taken into the shed by forklift trucks, stacked several pallet loads high to conserve space, and removed from the shed and lifted on board as complete units. This will minimise the number of individual handling movements, reduce the amount of labour required, and speed up the whole process. Pallets used in this way will of course have to be returned from the ship to the shore, as stowage in the hold progresses. To ensure the success of this method of working, a plentiful supply of stevedore's pallets must be available.

(5) Where a shipping company operates a pallet scheme, i.e. supplying pallets so that cargo can be loaded in palletised form, banding machines must be available for making up pallet loads of cargo received in non-palletised form.

Unless a large number of heavy lifts (i.e. exceeding the capacity of the normal quay cranes) is regularly received at a particular berth, it is neither economical nor desirable from a space and congestion point of view to supply a heavy lift crane at a general cargo berth. Instead it is better for these to be received at a specially designated heavy lift berth. One such berth will satisfy the needs of a large number of conventional berths.

Heavy Lift Berth

This will be equipped with a heavy lift crane, possibly the Scotch Derrick type, of sufficient capacity to cope with the generality of heavy lifts. Loading and unloading heavy lifts on to and off conventional vessels is usually accomplished by means of the ship's 'Jumbo' or heavy lift derrick. This takes several hours to rig, and while it is in use other cargo cannot be worked.This means that to avoid continually interrupting the general working of the vessel, all heavy lifts on one vessel must be dealt with during the same period, or at worst in several batches. To make this possible, vehicles carrying heavy lifts must be timed to arrive at specific times during the loading or discharging periods and can be involved in long periods of waiting. Where a heavy lift berth is used this problem is avoided. Heavy lifts for loading can be brought to the berth at a convenient time, removed from the vehicle and subsequently transferred to the loading berth in barges or on dock trailers at the appropriate time. The reverse process takes place with imported heavy lifts. An alternative to the use of ships' derricks is the use of floating derricks provided by the Port Authority. These will invariably be used when very heavy lifts are encountered, the larger among them being capable of lifting weights of several hundred tons.

An interesting innovation in recent years has been the introduction of special heavy lift vessels such as those used by the Central Electricity Generating Board for the coast-wise transport of very heavy pieces of power station equipment. 'Heavy lift vessel' is rather a misnomer, as these are a specialised form of roll-on roll-off vessel designed to accommodate road low-loaders complete with loads. Where these are used heavy-duty ramps must be provided.

Many conventional vessels carry a small number of containers, usually stowed on deck or in the square of the hatch. It is usual for them to be handled by ships' derricks directly to or from road vehicles or trailers. Where direct handling is not possible, they may be received and delivered through lift berths as described above, or at container reception depots, e.g. Freightliner terminals, and moved between berth and terminal by tractor-drawn trailers.

Container Berths

Vessels using purpose-built container berths will vary in size from those operating short-sea feeder services and carrying 30–40 containers, to large ocean-going cellular container ships capable of carrying 1,200–1,800 containers, including a large number of refrigerated containers. Where a berth is reserved solely for short-sea container services it is likely to be a multi-user berth, i.e. used by several shipping companies, operating high frequency services. In consequence there may well be around 2,000 containers on the berth at any one time, either awaiting shipment or having been discharged, awaiting clearance and delivery. At deep-sea berths accommodation for

2,000–3,000 containers may be necessary. The following facilities are essential to the successful operation of a purpose-built container berth:

(1) *Space*. A large area must be available to accommodate the large numbers of containers that will be present on the berth at any one time. A minimum of 15 acres was frequently quoted, but many port operators feel that with increasing numbers of larger vessels coming into service, 20 acres would be a more realistic figure.

(2) *The stacking area* must be capable of supporting heavy vehicles, and containers stacked three high. In certain locations, where space is at a premium, it may be necessary to provide special facilities for five-high stacking, and there have been suggestions that seven-high stacking will eventually be necessary, although this would present many problems to container selection and could cause a slowing down of handling operations.

(3) *Container cranes*. Although in the initial stages of trans-ocean container traffic many existing berths succeeded in handling container vessels through adaptation, utilising heavy lift cranes, as the volume of traffic increased this temporary measure proved inadequate and purpose-built berths and container cranes became essential. These special cranes must have gantries which can be raised to avoid collision with the ship's superstructure on arrival and departure. They must be self-propelled along their own tracks to permit correct positioning in relation to the cells or 'slots' on board ship. Single-lift cranes must have a lifting capacity of 30 tons (the maximum loaded weight of a 40-ft. container) and must have a fast working rate capable of sustaining a discharging/loading cycle of approximately 3 minutes. Twin-lift cranes will have a correspondingly higher lifting capacity.

(4) *Handling equipment*. If a discharging/loading cycle of 3 minutes is to be maintained, it means that as a container is landed on shore, another must be in position to be picked up and loaded on board. Before the next container is landed the previous one must be taken away for stacking, and another for loading placed in position. This sequence of operations requires several shore-based vehicles to serve each container crane. These container handling vehicles may be straddle carriers, heavy-duty forklift trucks or other vehicles specially designed for rapid container handling.

(5) *Refrigeration equipment*. Where refrigerated containers are handled, facilities must be provided to maintain the refrigeration process on shore. These facilities may consist of points where containers can be plugged in to an electrical supply, or when cold air is used for refrigeration the containers must be connected to a shore-based system similar to that used on board ship.

(6) *Office accommodation* should be located at the rear of the berth to permit a clear working area as large as possible. Facilities for vehicle maintenance and container repair, if these are provided at the berth, should also be located at the rear. Consolidation depots, for the 'stuffing and unstuffing' of containers should not be located on the berth at all, but some distance away to remove possible congestion. Where this is not possible, these facilities should be kept at the rear of the berth.

Timber Berths

Most people will have heard or seen something of the revolution in transport which has been brought about by containerisation because of the wide publicity it has received and from the large numbers of containers moving on the roads. They are perhaps not so likely to be as aware of the revolution which has taken place in the transport of timber, although it is no less important to those involved. The packaging of timber, another form of unitisation, is what this revolution is all about.

Packaged timber consists of timber made up into sets or 'bundles', each containing pieces of the same length, breadth and thickness, weighing 2–4 tons, held together by wires or steel bands and remaining in that form throughout the journey.

To appreciate what difference this simple concept has made, we should first look at a berth for handling timber in the conventional or traditional form.

Traditional Timber Berth

When timber is shipped in the traditional manner, i.e. non-packaged, its discharge is a slow, time-consuming, labour-intensive process. This is because the stowage in the ship consists of layer after layer of random lengths in the holds, and often a considerable amount carried as deck cargo. Many of the vessels engaged in this trade are quite small, carrying only a few hundred tons. To discharge their cargo each piece must be picked up separately until the 'deal porter' has sufficient to carry ashore over plank runways. As discharge proceeds and the level of the timber gets lower in the holds, runways are no longer possible and the pieces must be bundled into sets and discharged by crane. Once ashore the timber must be sorted and carefully stacked in large open-sided sheds. Where timber is to remain in the storage sheds for any length of time, the stack must be 'sticked', i.e. thin pieces of timber inserted between each layer, at right-angles to the length of the boards, to ensure proper ventilation. It may take over a week to discharge just a few hundred tons in this manner, whereas at a packaged timber berth rates of discharge between 3,000 and 4,000 tons per day are not unusual.

Packaged Timber Berth

Packaged timber vessels tend to be much larger than traditional timber ships, often exceeding 40,000 N.R.T. in size, and both vessels and cargo require different facilities from those required by their smaller counterparts.

(1) Because of their size the vessels can only be handled at berths with deep water and if these are in enclosed docks, large entrance locks are necessary.

(2) To accommodate very large cargoes, extensive stacking grounds must be provided.

(3) To maintain a fast rate of discharge, and therefore a quick turn-round, this must not be linked too closely with the shore operations of sorting and stacking. It is customary to provide a very large quay apron which acts as a 'surge' area. This enables the vessel to maintain a fast rate of discharge, even when there is a temporary slowing down of shore operations, e.g. when handling vehicles are diverted to load road vehicles.

(4) An ample supply of mechanical handling equipment must be available, e.g. forklifts, side-loaders and straddle carriers, to ensure that removal to the stacking ground can keep pace with the ship's discharge and, when necessary, load road vehicles simultaneously. Because of the extent of the parking area,

and high stacks making vehicle location and control difficult, vehicles are frequently fitted with VHF radio to make communication easier.

(5) Cranes. The method of discharge varies: sometimes quay cranes are used but most bulk timber ships are fitted with their own discharging equipment. Where forestry products other than timber are also carried the cranes are frequently gantry type with interchangeable lifting gear for handling packaged timber, bales of pulp and reels of paper. Where vessels commonly using the berth are equipped with self-discharging gear, quay cranes are often dispensed with so as to leave the quay apron as clear as possible.

(6) Where other forestry products, such as liner board, pulp, newsprint, plywood, are regularly carried temporary storage accommodation must be provided to protect them from the weather. Special handling equipment should be provided: for example, large pallets designed for use with straddle carriers enabling several bales or reels to be carried at one time, and squeeze clamps for fitting to forklifts for easier handling of reels and bales when stacking or loading.

Grain Berths (*usually called Grain Terminals*)

Since the Second World War the pattern of grain imports to this country has undergone a rapid change. Where before the bulk of grain shipments arrived in parcels of 1,000 tons or so in general cargo vessels, with occasional shipments by relatively small bulk grain carriers, the pattern has reversed and the bulk grain carriers have increased in size. This increase in size, though small compared with the growth in size of oil tankers because of the much smaller total demand for grain, is nevertheless very considerable in its own particular sphere. The average size of bulk grain carriers is now 25,000 tons with the larger vessels around 60,000 tons. Facilities which a few years ago were adequate to deal with the generality of ships and their cargoes are no longer able to cope with the large modern vessels. Floating grain elevators, capable of discharging at a rate of a few hundred tons per hour, will not suffice when discharge rates approaching 20,000 tons a day are required, and grain silos capable of holding 20,000–30,000 tons are of little use when one ship after another follows in quick succession, each carrying cargoes in excess of 20,000 tons. As a result we have seen those ports which are able to accommodate the much larger, deeper draughted vessels and are willing to provide larger and faster working shore facilities, capture the major part of the grain trade. The remaining ports are left with the smaller vessels and cargoes transshipped to them.

The most modern terminals incorporate the following features:

(1) *The Berth:* capable of accommodating vessels of 60,000 tons, with provision made for even larger vessels in the years to come.

(2) *Elevators:* multiple bucket elevators, each capable of discharging rates of 750–1,000 tons per hour, with supplementary pneumatic elevators for clearing the holds when there is insufficient grain remaining to feed the bucket elevators.

(3) *Storage Silos:* capable of holding 100,000 tons or more, with automatic equipment for weighing and delivery to bulk rail and road vehicles.

(4) *Associated Mills:* to reduce transport costs, millers are keen to locate new facilities alongside grain terminals, so that their mills can be fed directly

by conveyors. Sufficient space must be available for a number of such mills.

(5) *Transshipment:* all grain received will not pass directly to associated mills or to rail and road vehicles for inland carriage. Most mills throughout the country are located on waterways, some on major rivers, but many smaller mills on quite small rivers where they were once fed by sailing vessels and now receive their supplies from small coasters and short-sea traders. A major grain terminal must therefore provide facilities for transshipment to these smaller mills. This can best be secured by arranging for the large bulk carrier and other smaller vessels to berth on opposite sides of a deep-water jetty (see Plates 8 and 9).

There are many more examples of specialised berths which may be found at major ports and brief descriptions follow of a few of the more common ones. For more detailed descriptions, the student is advised to consult books and publications dealing solely with ports and port operations.

Oil Terminals

Oil terminals frequently have long jetties extending into deep water to accommodate deep-draughted vessels with the minimum of dredging. At loading terminals pumping equipment at the tank farm must be capable of a very rapid rate of loading to ensure a fast turn-round for the vessel. Whether or not a receiving terminal is directly associated with a refinery, an extensive tank storage farm will be necessary to act as a holding facility until the very large cargo can be absorbed by the refinery or inland receivers.

Roll-on Roll-off Berths

These are equipped with loading and discharging ramps and require extensive vehicle parking areas for lorries and trailers awaiting shipment or awaiting collection after unloading. If vessels also carry containers and pallets, the berth will require heavy-duty platform trucks and forklift trucks for loading and discharge, and for handling loads in the stacking area.

Side-loading Berths

Side-loading vessels have ports or doors let into their sides instead of the more conventional hatch openings in the deck. Quay cranes are unsuitable for working this type of vessel and should be dispensed with, the quay apron being kept as uncluttered as possible. This will allow freedom of operation for the forklift trucks, which are used to pass cargo to and from the ship through the side ports. Electric trucks are most suitable for operation on board ship as they do not give off fumes, which would be undesirable in the closed space of a ship's hold. Recharging stations must be provided for the forklift trucks, whose batteries must be recharged after every shift.

Fruit and Meat Berths

A feature of both meat and fruit traffic is the necessity to remove large quantities of cargo from the berth in a relatively short space of time. In most cases this will involve large numbers of road vehicles awaiting their turn to load. Provision must be made for several vehicles to be loaded simultaneously. To avoid congestion in the working area, lorry parks should be provided from which vehicles can be called forward in batches as required. Various forms of automatic discharging equipment may be installed to speed up the process of discharge and to simplify sorting. Where meat is concerned, cold store facilities must be available in the vicinity of the berth, or at not too great a distance from the port.

Bulk Wine Berths

Wine was traditionally shipped in barrels or already bottled. The increased demand in recent years, particularly for the lower-priced dinner wines, has led to the introduction of bulk shipment in tanks. The wine is pumped ashore for storage in glass-lined or fibre-glass tanks. It is not necessary for the tanks to be situated on the berth itself but they can be housed in buildings to the rear of the berth, provided that suitable piped connections are installed. This frees the berth itself for the handling of other cargoes.

Pipeline Transport

Terminals for pipelines take the form of pumping stations and tank farms. Each tank farm acts as a buffer zone, where cargoes arriving out of phase with the demand can be stored until required. Ships do not observe strict schedules—delays occur for a variety of reasons. Sometimes no ships will come in, and another day several may arrive together. Refineries miles away may be working at a steady pace. Supplies must be available at times when ships do not arrive and when several ships arrive together there must be tank capacity to unload the ships and turn them round. This is the function of the tank farm.

The pipelines themselves vary in size. From ship-to-shore tank units we have large diameter pipes to unload ships rapidly. On the exit side of the tank farm smaller capacity pipes will distribute the oil in a steady stream to the refinery.

Each pumping station has two or three pumps in series. They are often in the open air, with control instruments housed in buildings near by. A typical unit is shown in Plate 16.

An interesting example of a pipeline system incorporating both termini and terminals is the pipeline from the Thames Refinery Complex to the Ellesmere Port Refinery Complex. Not only is there a terminus at each end, with 'both-ways' pumping facilities, but there are a number of spur pipelines off the main line which lead to terminals where distribution facilities and storage tanks permit the marketing of refined products.

Suggested Further Reading

Faulks, R. W., *Principles of Transport*, Ian Allen, 1973.

Hurren, B. J., *Airports of the World*, Wolfe Publishing Ltd., 1970.

Jackson, A. A., *London's Termini*, David and Charles, 1969.

Thompson, B. A. (Bridges, R. K., Ed.), *Croner's Road Transport Operation* (Current Edition as revised), Croner Publications.

CHAPTER SIX

THE PHYSICAL COMPONENTS OF TRANSPORT: THE UNIT OF CARRIAGE

Introduction

Every mode of transport must have a unit of carriage in which the goods or passengers actually move. This unit of carriage will be designed to suit the particular mode. Thus a supersonic aircraft will be designed to different specifications from an underground railway train, since it must encounter different stresses and strains. While there will be many points of similarity there will be countless points of difference between any two units of carriage reflecting the modified requirements imposed by the way, the motive power, the class of traffic to be carried and even the termini to be used. *The unit of carriage represents the response of transport engineers to the requirements of a particular class of traffic, moving on a particular way, powered by a particular method of propulsion across a particular pattern of interfaces*. Each particular solution to these problems will be a compromise, in which the engineer seeks to achieve the best of all possible worlds but in fact inevitably falls somewhat short of this ideal.

Principles in the Design of Units of Carriage

The chief principles the engineer will bear in mind in designing a unit of carriage are:

(a) the need to embrace the widest possible market;
(b) the requirements of the particular way;
(c) the requirements of the traffic concerned;
(d) ergonomic aspects;
(e) cheapness.

A word or two about each of these aspects is desirable.

The Need to Embrace the Widest Possible Market

Any unit of carriage has heavy design costs, which must be recouped out of sales. It will therefore most easily recoup the costs if it is able to sell in a wide range of markets to a variety of users. Thus we find the basic design for motor vehicles being used in a variety of models to appeal to different tastes and needs. It will have its basic and cheapest design for general use, its hotted-up version for the enthusiast, its estate version for the salesman or the family man who needs plenty of space. The container manufacturer will provide a range of containers covering a wide variety of markets, general cargo containers, top-loading containers, open-sided containers, tank unit containers, etc., all using standard parts to a considerable extent but appealing to different customers in particular details. The principles of simplification and standardisation are applied to the design of units of carriage so as to achieve the maximum number of alternative uses for a particular unit, which thus sells in a wide variety of markets.

The Requirements of the Particular Way

The character of the way has a very great impact on the unit of carriage. A few examples will illustrate this point. Aircraft operate in a way, the atmosphere, which is unable to support them except when they are in motion. The aircraft cannot pull up and stop along the way, except for very specialised machines, e.g. helicopters and jump-jets, which can hover. Even then the pilot cannot step out to service the machine. Aircraft must therefore be perfectly manufactured, almost flawless in the excellence of their craftsmanship and meticulously maintained. The way imposes strict limitations on the size, shape and speed of these units of carriage.

Air

Aircraft designers are forced by the contraints of the way into concentrating either on carrying capacity or speed. They cannot seek big improvements in both, simultaneously, without major increases in the size of power units. To do so would necessitate disproportionate increases in fuel consumption and render the aircraft uneconomic to operate. (This constraint does not necessarily apply to military aircraft, for which economic operation is not a prime consideration.)

To increase the carrying capacity of an aircraft not only must the size of the body be increased, but the surface area of the wings must be increased to create additional lifting capacity in proportion to the extra weight to be carried. To utilise the extra lifting capacity of the wings, more powerful engines are required to generate the forward speed necessary to create lift-off and sustain that speed as the aircraft climbs to operational height. More powerful engines will consume more fuel. The extra fuel will have to be carried and this means added weight. The extra weight will mean that greater lifting capacity will be needed, which will mean . . ., etc. Somewhere the designer must strike a balance. If the aircraft is to operate over relatively short distances it will require less fuel to reach its destination, and the saving in weight of fuel will permit more passengers or cargo to be carried. If the same aircraft is to operate over much longer distances, then passenger and cargo weight must be sacrificed to allow a greater weight of fuel to be carried on board.

To achieve faster forward speeds, the aircraft designer must produce a shape that offers the least resistance to forward movement, i.e. to minimise drag, and to incorporate more powerful motive units to thrust the aircraft along. The most suitable shape is a pointed, pencil-like fuselage, with minimal wings, for although large wings may be needed to enable it to leave the ground, once it has reached operational flight it no longer requires the same wing area to sustain it in forward flight. The so-called variable-geometry machines, by changing the shape of the aircraft, seek to improve the engineer's command over lift-drag problems which affect its operation.

Sea

The problem of space versus speed also faces marine designers, though perhaps not to the same extent as it affects aircraft designers. Although the vessel relies on the water for support, and compared with land-carriage is relatively free from friction, as speeds increase so bow-waves build up and resistance to forwarded progress is impeded. To overcome this problem a slim knife-like shape would appear to be most suitable, enabling the vessel to slice through the water. Unfortunately if this slim profile is carried too far, problems of stability are created and of course cargo-carrying capacity would be limited. By constructing more and more powerful engines speeds could be considerably increased, but the cost of the extra fuel consumption involved in overcoming the increased water resistance encountered at higher speeds would far outweigh the benefits to be obtained from faster transit times.

Thanks to the buoyancy of water, no problems like those associated with 'lift' in aircraft arise, and enormous vessels can be constructed. However, the designer is still limited as far as size is concerned by the constraints of the way. Because the oceans, seas and rivers of the world are not of uniform depth he must take into account the depths available in those areas in which the vessel will operate, and the availability of terminals able to accommodate it.

Paradoxically, the problem of friction which must be overcome if economic speeds are to be achieved works in reverse as far as large vessels are concerned. The absence of friction which enables very large weights to be moved by water, with relatively small units of propulsion, creates problems when very large vessels seek to come to a halt. Sudden stops are impossible and the vessel must be slowed down gradually, and finally halted with the assistance of tugs.

Road

Roads are narrow ways, often carrying heavy flows of traffic which are not separated according to grade or speed of vehicles, and are often flowing in conflicting directions. They are also used by animals and pedestrians, except for motorway-type roads, and particularly in urban areas hemmed in by buildings, many of which were constructed decades or even centuries before road traffic developed to its present weight and intensity. Roads frequently pass under or over bridges which impose limitations as to the height and weight of vehicles. All these factors, some concerning the character of the way itself, others derived from the method of use, have resulted on limitations being placed on the size and speed of the units of carriage. These limitations, though arising initially from the character of the way, have been given the force of law through Parliamentary and Ministerial enactments. The designer must therefore operate within strict size and weight limits and very detailed regulations concerning construction, while the operator must observe speed limits and restrictions on use.

Rail

Railways are artificially constructed private ways, usually under the sole control of the undertaking. Despite this, they impose limitations on the vehicle designer. Like roads, they frequently pass over or under bridges, which impose limitations on the height and weight of vehicles. Most railways were constructed in the latter part of the nineteenth century or the early part of the twentieth century, and the dimensions established at that time largely determine the dimensions of present-day rolling stock. Vehicles cannot be made wider because of vehicles on adjoining tracks, and their length is governed by the severity of the curves which they must negotiate. Similarly, their speeds are governed by the extent to which curves are present in any particular section of track and whether or not it has been designed and maintained for high-speed running.

The Requirements of the Traffic

While for marketing reasons the unit of carriage seeks to be as versatile as possible, it will often fail to capture a particular traffic unless it caters specifically for it. Specificity within a versatile general framework is what is aimed at. Thus a road tanker manufacturer might—from a standard design—offer specific vehicles for milk, petroleum products, corrosive liquids and bulk powders. The linings of tanks, internal construction and pumping mechanisms might vary, but a standard unit of carriage underlies all the types offered. Nowhere is the specific nature of vehicles more evident than in the problem of the 'empty leg' journey. For example, milk moves in tankers from the agricultural areas to big cities all over the advanced world. Yet what use is the vehicle on the return journey to the countryside? Clearly its specific nature renders the return journey an 'empty leg'. It cannot be filled with fertiliser for the farms, or with furniture for rural households. At least one big firm has found a useful solution to the problem of the empty leg in the container-sized plastic bag. A huge plastic bag the same shape as a container is filled with fruit concentrate and transported in a container. On arrival it is pumped clear, cleaned and sterilised, and returned rolled up for re-use. The non-specific container sets off on its next, unrelated journey; the plastic bag returns at a very economic rate.

Other firms which have tried this solution have found that the cleansing and return of the plastic container is inconvenient and unsatisfactory for their purposes and have discarded the idea in favour of stainless steel lined tanks. Using various solvents, detergents and high-pressure steam they can be thoroughly cleaned in a very short space of time. If the method is to be employed successfully, cleaning facilities must be available at a very large number of centres to avoid excessive empty mileage to and from cleaning stations. By arranging for reciprocal use of each other's facilities, a number of road haulage undertakings have established a chain of these centres throughout the country. It is now possible for a load such as lubricating oil to be carried on the outward journey and, after cleansing, for the vehicle to return loaded with bulk wine.

Such happy solutions to the 'empty leg' problem are rare and only possible if a suitable return load is available. Generally speaking, you must have a specific vehicle for a particular class of traffic and if you do not, you will not capture the market. 'Facilities create traffic' is an old rule in transport, and the unit of carriage catering specifically for a particular traffic will not only capture the existing market but divert traffic away from other less efficient units to increase its share of the market to the general benefit of the economy.

Ergonomic Aspects

Many units of carriage require someone to work in the unit of carriage, or in and out of the unit of carriage. Thus an air hostess must perform her duties in the aircraft, moving up and down the gangway or gangways, with trays of food, liquid refreshments, etc. A baker's roundsman not only drives the unit of carriage but climbs in and out of it two hundred times a day.

A study of the work done by these servants of the transport and distribution industry will enable many useful features to be incorporated in the design of the unit of carriage. Access points can be varied to reduce strain. The delivery van which has direct access from the driver's cab to the unit of carriage enables the driver who has stopped the vehicle to leave his seat and enter the unit of carriage to collect the order for delivery. Previously he had to get out, go round the back and get in again.

Inevitably, with units of carriage ergonomic aspects include two related studies. The maintenance of units of carriage in good order and condition is an enduring requirement. The accessibility of vital points to the maintenance engineer will be an important preoccupation for design teams. They will need to know how the mechanic works to ensure that his activities are performed as quickly and effortlessly as possible. The other aspect is that the total operation of the unit of carriage must be socially and environmentally acceptable. The operation of units of carriage is an extension perhaps of ordinary work study, yet it may impose upon the design staff requirements which modify the unit's size, speed and efficiency, in the interests of ensuring a wide sale unrestricted by official or public disapproval.

Ergonomics is the study of work and the way it is performed. It gives cost saving benefits in the design, layout, maintenance and operation of units of carriage.

Cheapness

Henry Ford once defended his system of mass production with the following definition: 'Mass production is not buying cheap and selling dear. It is the focusing upon a manufacturing project of the principles of power, accuracy, economy, system, continuity, speed and repetition.' It is an enduring definition. Units of carriage lend themselves particularly to mass production for they are required in large numbers, by people who are not rich and therefore need a cheap unit. Even the most advanced technological units, like the airframes and engines of supersonic aircraft, are best produced in this way, for perfect components can only be made by people who repeat a small range of activities and thus acquire skill by repetition. Perhaps where aircraft are concerned it could best be called 'repeat production', since the techniques of the mass production line are not quite applicable.

Had Ford been asked to give a full definition of the entire physical distribution process he would have included in his analysis two further sections. Before mass production can begin design teams must prepare plans for the unit of carriage which embody the principles outlined in this chapter. The design of units of carriage requires us to focus attention upon the needs of society, so that units are produced which are fit for the purpose of many potential customers; appropriate to the way on which they must travel and for the traffic they must bear; convenient to work with; easy to maintain and cheap to buy. After mass production has taken place according to the principles given in Ford's definition, the units of carriage must be cheap to operate, to service and to renew as and when required. They must conform with the law, and be socially and environmentally acceptable. If the result of all these activities is in the end the cheapest possible product to perform that particular class of carriage, the capital employed in its production will not have been wasted but will yield a satisfactory return based upon repeated orders from contented customers.

The Unit of Carriage and the Unit of Propulsion

Sometimes the unit of carriage embodies the unit of propulsion and with other systems they are separate. In so far as they form a single unit the flexibility of the system is reduced. The engine of the family motorcar propels that unit of carriage only, and is of no use unless that unit of carriage is required. A tractor unit of an articulated vehicle is free from this inflexibility. When a trailer has to wait for some reason, such as Customs inspection or the availability of space on a ship, the tractor unit can be uncoupled and proceed to other trailers.

A second point is that the tare of a unit of carriage (its unladen weight) relative to the payload is a vital point in the economy of operations. If the unit of propulsion is embodied in the unit of carriage it must be designed to reduce the fraction of tare weight to total weight, if operation is to be economic. A heavy tractor unit will represent a less serious problem, since its weight will pull many units of carriage and be proportionately less important in the tare weight to total weight fraction.

Units of Carriage by Road

Passenger Units

Today the tram and trolleybus have largely disappeared from our roads, and the typical unit of carriage is the private motor vehicle. The 1973 figures for licences current show that in that year there were 13,497,000 motorcars on the roads of Great Britain against 106,500 buses, coaches and taxicabs. Small wonder that those who use them complain that buses are few and far between. We have become a property-owning democracy, and the outward symbol of property is the motorcar. It is in many ways an inefficient means of transport, with the propulsion unit embodied in the unit of carriage and unutilised when the unit of carriage is not required. It is an expensive user of space—both road space and parking space—but all such costs count as little compared with the convenience of personalised transport.

The bus is the general workhorse of public passenger transport, in the short-haul field. They may be single-decker or double-decker units of carriage, and of impressive length and size. They may offer seating to the majority of passengers, or seating to those travelling some distance, while the short-distance traveller crowds into a standing area (see Plate 1). They may be operated by a driver and conductor, or be one-man operated. Many of the latter have mechanical slot machines for payment on entry. In country areas where two-man operation is prohibitively expensive, buses are either one-man operated single deckers or mini-buses. The latter have between twelve and sixteen seats, and operate on routes where traffic is light. The development of Post buses by the Post Office Corporation is an interesting use of its new powers, and of the grants available for this type of service. Briefly the service implies the use of a postal vehicle to carry passengers on a once-daily trip to the local town and back. Usually a mid-morning bulk delivery of mail to outlying villages drops off mail on its outward run and on the return journey picks up passengers wishing to spend a day in town. The return journey for the passenger is in late afternoon, and is followed by the use of the bus to collect bulk mail from the outlying villages for sorting and onward transmission in the evening.

Coach services tend to be limited-stop services which operate on long-haul routes. The vehicles provide a greater degree of comfort and frequently require pre-booking of seats. Their wide use for tours in areas of scenic beauty has led to the provision of luxury coaches with wide-view windows, storage for hand luggage and capacious luggage compartments. Their ability to use motorways on the long-haul routes has made them an express form of transport competitive in price with railway travel, and very short journey times are possible with adequate facilities available for passenger comfort at motorway service centres. The unit of carriage embodies comfortable seating, ventilation facilities, adjustable shades and personal lighting points for night travel.

Goods Units

The responses of design engineers to the needs of road hauliers are legion, and no short paragraph can adequately describe the infinite variety of size, shape and facility made available. Certain broad classes, however, must be referred to here. The two basic groups are the *rigids* and the *articulated vehicles*. A rigid embodies the propulsion unit and the unit of carriage in a single vehicle, and is therefore less versatile than the articulated vehicle which has a separate motor unit (the tractor) which can be linked in a few minutes to the trailer or semi-trailer. This means of course that the trailer may be left at the loading bank or Customs depot pending loading or inspection, while the tractor is used elsewhere. A very important economy which can be achieved is the saving in driver's time, which becomes increasingly important as the 'permitted driving time' is reduced. The extension of the swap-body arrangement has increased the use of these vehicles, which can be used successively to load three or four bodies at a central dispatch point, take them to a regional transit point, demount them and pick up yesterday's empty bodies to return to the dispatch centre. The individual bodies are now picked up by local tractor units and taken off to do the deliveries. The local depot is eliminated, goods being supplied from the central dispatch point. The regional transit point only needs to be a piece of hard standing (concrete or tarmac parking space) large enough to carry out the switch. By arrangement with a suitable firm this exchange could simply take place at a nominal daily charge at the depot of some existing carrier; or reciprocal arrangements could be made.

The articulated vehicle is also very manoeuvrable, able to turn in a relatively small circle for a long vehicle. Rigids can only be made manoeuvrable if the body is short, with consequent increases in height for a given weight. This poses stability problems.

Within these general classes there are many sub-classes, of which the following are important:

(*a*) *Covered vans*. These range from light vans and delivery vehicles up to pantechnicons for removals and bulk deliveries of furniture and equipment.

(*b*) *Open trucks*. These have sides and tailboards, but are not covered in. They may be used for goods which do not spoil in wet weather.

(*c*) *Tippers*. These are usually very large open trucks, used for carrying bulk deliveries of non-spoiling commodities such as aggregates, ores, etc., which can be easily discharged by tipping.

(*d*) *Platform vehicles or 'Flats'*. These have no sides or tailboard, and are used for containers or packaged timber, or crates and boxes stacked on the platform and restrained by ropes, chains and/or tarpaulins.

(*e*) *Tankers*. These are usually of large size, with capacities up to about 5,000–6,000 gallons, for the carriage of petroleum products, corrosive and other liquids, bulk powders like sugar and flour, or pellets and grains.

(*f*) *Hopper vehicles*. These are used for carrying bulk grains, cement and similar products.

There are many more, and a particular feature of many of them these days is their independence of facilities at either end of the transit, since they are equipped with cranes, tail lifts, cylinder lifts and similar devices to assist loading and unloading (see Plate 3).

Units of Carriage by Rail

Passenger Units

Railway journeys are of three types: long-distance, suburban and 'in-town' services. Railway carriages reflect the differing needs of these three types of journey. Long-distance journeys require comfortable carriages, insulated from outside atmospheric conditions at the limited number of stopping places. The number of access doors can be few, usually at the ends of the carriage and in the centre, so that passengers who are alighting or embarking do so with the minimum of discomfort to through passengers. Access to toilets and to restaurants cars requires a corridor train, and flexible connections between carriages from one end of the train to the other. In Pullman carriages tables are provided for the convenience of passengers, and luggage stowage is possible between seats or above the backs of seats. Couchette type seating is sometimes provided on long-distance trains, while sleeping cars for overnight journeys are also used.

Suburban services require more frequent stopping places and consequently a greater need to disgorge passengers rapidly. This requires a door to every bank of seats, rather than at the ends of coaches only. Since toilet accommodation is less necessary the corridor can be dispensed with, and a multi-compartment carriage each with its own access doors be used instead. The standing room available is less convenient than in a corridor train, but rapid access and egress and the extra seating available compensate for this.

Many railway lines, particularly underground railways, have frequent stops very short distances apart. The time spent in stations must be reduced as much as possible, and so a large number of wide doors must be provided. To avoid harm to passengers in very crowded circumstances doors do not open inwards or outwards but slide into the hollow walls of the carriages. Operated electrically, they give rapid ingress and egress, and as a safety measure may be over-ridden in an emergency.

Today computer-controlled train systems of short units of carriage operating at very frequent intervals are beginning to be used. The most famous recent addition to this is the BART system in San Francisco. The name stands for Bay Area Rapid Transit, and it is reducing very considerably the road commuter problems in that area. The computers send the fleet of carriage units round the circuit at intervals of 90 seconds. They anticipate peak loads, and adjust speeds to compensate for any delay caused at stations and to bring the carriages back on schedule. The multiple-journey tickets issued at electronic booths permit travel to the value of the money paid, the ticket being reduced in value on each trip. The journey across the Bay has been cut to 9 minutes compared with the 40 minutes it takes by road, due to congestion at the road bridges.

Goods Units

A full description of rail units of carriage for bulk transport is given in Chapter Twelve. The vast majority of goods rail traffic is now bulk haulage, which is most logically and effectively carried in company trains or on the Freightliner networks. General cargo frequently travels on passenger trains, or in special wagons attached to passenger trains. This was not possible to any great extent before the goods wagons were modernised and fitted with pneumatic brakes similar to those on passenger carriages. The result has been very considerable improvements in the services offered to customers. Speeds were formerly very low, and damage to the goods carried in loose-coupled trains was considerable. Although the coupling of pneumatic brakes is a considerable disadvantage in marshalling yards, the advantages of high speed —coupling where appropriate to passenger trains—and reduced damage probably outweigh the capital cost involved and the more awkward marshalling activities.

Units of Carriage by Sea

Ships are large, costly units of carriage, much less susceptible to standardisation than road and rail units. They tend to be built to a particular specification, and although there are economies to be achieved by producing sister ships of largely similar layout, few firms are large enough to order an entire fleet at one time, and the need to sell similar models to different owners results in their modification in major or minor ways to suit a particular need. Even apparently similar sister ships in the same fleet tend to differ in minor ways.

Ocean-going ships, as their names implies, sail the major ocean routes. They carry a wide variety of products on the long-haul routes. The short-sea trade routes by contrast are concerned with inter-European movements across the North Sea, the English Channel and Irish Channels and the North African and Near East traffics across the Mediterranean. Many of the units used on these short sea routes are roll-on roll-off vessels, though the roll-on roll-off type of operation has now also been proved to be economic with trans-Atlantic vessels.

Every ship, like any other unit of carriage, represents a response on the part of the ship-building industry to the needs of world trade. The last quarter of a century has been a very fertile period, with an immense variety of solutions to particular problems resulting in a very large broad range of vessels being produced. These include a large variety of conventional-hull ships, hydrofoils and hovercraft. Some of these are referred to elsewhere in this book, and reference here is for the purpose of establishing a list giving brief descriptions of the more common types. The list includes:

(a) General cargo ships
(b) Cellular container ships
(c) Roll-on roll-off ships

(*d*) Barge-carrying vessels
(*e*) Very large crude carriers (V.L.C.C.s)
(*f*) L.N.G. carriers
(*g*) L.P.G. and clean product carriers
(*h*) Hydrofoils
(*i*) Hovercraft

A few details about these different units of carriage are appropriate at this point.

General Cargo Ships

The general cargo ship is still the chief type of vessel carrying goods around the world, though the container ship and the barge-carrying vessel are making inroads into its traffic. Fig. 6.1 shows the latest SD14 class of general cargo ship built by Austin and Pickersgill, in this case for the P. & O. Line. The SD14 is largely a mass-produced ship, and was originally conceived as a replacement for the utility Liberty ships built during the Second World War. It has now become a ship type in its own right, and more powerful versions are being developed to meet the evolving needs of shipowners.

The five spacious holds have fluorescent strip lighting and MacGregor single-pull mechanical weather-deck hatch covers to aid cargo working in port. All cargo spaces have smoke detectors and CO_2 firefighting equipment.

Among the other modern features of the ships can be included Marconi true-motion Radiolocator 16 radars with Seachart C echosounders and associated Seascape visual depth metres. The Radiolocator sets combine the latest in conventional radar technology with an almost total use of solid-state devices and advanced circuitry techniques, giving all normal marine radar facilities with picture auto-alignment, electronic bearing indicator and interference suppression devices.

Air-conditioned single-cabin accommodation is provided for the ship's complement of thirty-two officers and men.

Cellular Container Ships

The specialised container ship will largely replace the conventional cargo liner on the major cargo routes of the world in the next few years. The latest ships have holds designed to accommodate I.S.O. 10-ft., 20-ft., 30-ft. or 40-ft. containers, which can also be stored on deck. A typical ship of about 60,000 tons holds upwards of $2,000 \times 20$ ft. units, of which about three hundred would be carried as deck cargo. About 250 containers of a typical cargo would be refrigerated. The ships may be provided with gantry cranes if they are likely to use ports inadequately equipped with heavy lift gear. They usually reach speeds of 25–28 knots, and spend only a quarter of their total time in port, compared with about half for conventional ships. Because of their high volume, high speed and fast turn-round each ship of this type can carry about seven times the cargo in a year that a conventional cargo liner would carry.

In an age when fewer and fewer passengers go by sea the specialised cargo ship is clearly more economic. However, frequency of service is also vital, and the operators of large container ships, by operating in a consortium of ships from several countries, can offer customers regular fast services leaving every

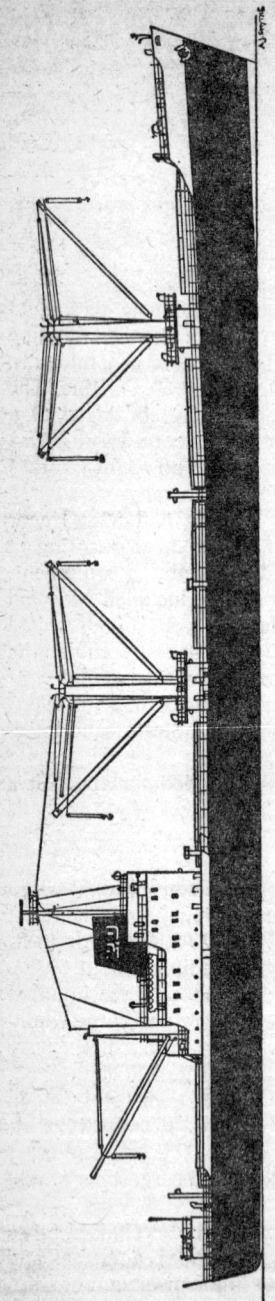
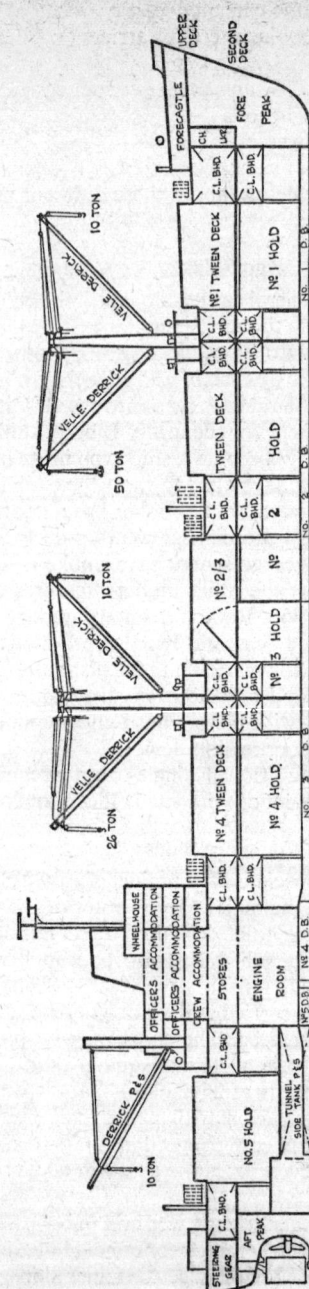

Fig. 6.1. Water-line profile and view of cargo holds and cargo-handling equipment of a modern general cargo vessel.

(courtesy of Peninsular and Orient Steam Navigation Co. Ltd.)

a

b

Plate 1. One-man operated bus, with pay booth on the lower deck.

(courtesy of London Transport Executive)

Plate 2. An Inter-City passenger train (**a**) and the Advanced
Passenger Train (**b**).

(courtesy of the British Railways Board)

Plate 3. The HIAB lorry loader in operation.

(courtesy of George Cohen 600 Group Ltd)

Plate 4. (a) Bulk sugar tipper. **(b)** Ready-mixed concrete vehicle.

(courtesy of Carmichael & Sons (Worcester) Ltd. (a), and Ready Mixed Concrete Co. Ltd. (b))

a

b

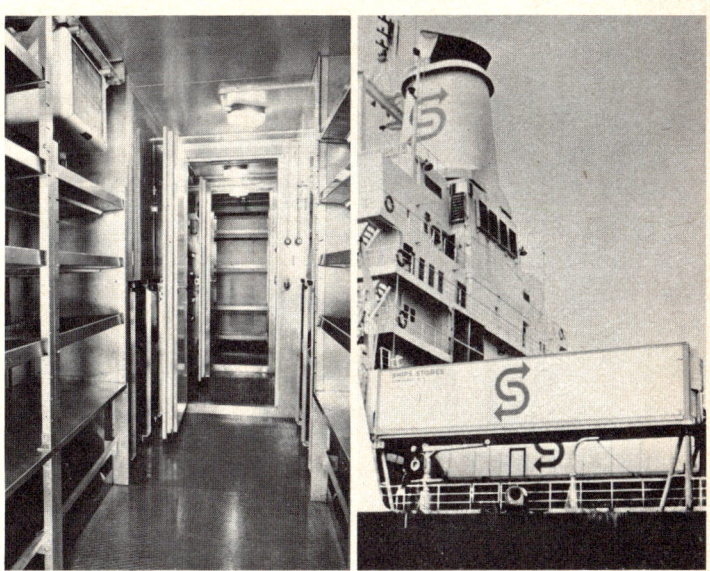

Plate 5. (a) Freightliner terminal with gantry crane in operation.
(b) Containers as ship's stores – a Crane Fruehauf special.

(courtesy of Freightliners Ltd. (a), and Crane Fruehauf Ltd. (b))

Plate 6. (a) A 'Cartic' company train carrying cars for export.
(b) Quarried stone in 37-ton hopper wagons.

Plate 7. A straddle carrier, a skeletal chassis articulated vehicle and a Paceco-Vickers container crane.

(courtesy of the Port of London Authority)

Plate 8. Aerial view of Tilbury Docks, showing container park and lock entrance.

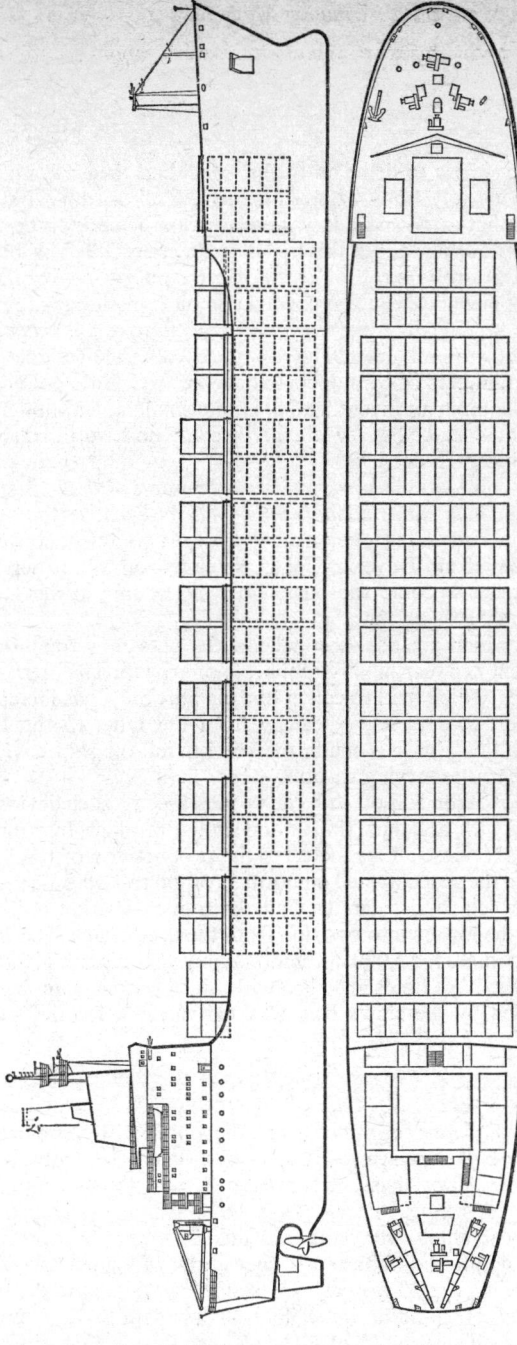

Fig. 6.2. A cellular container ship showing the stacking arrangements.

(courtesy of Overseas Containers Ltd.)

day or two for major trading areas of the world. Plate 10 and Fig. 6.2 show container ships.

Roll-on Roll-off Ships

These ships enable vehicles to drive on to the vessel and then drive off at destination. They are usually bow- or stern-loaders. Roll-on roll-off ships have the disadvantage that cargo space is wasted between the deck of the ship and the lorry or trailer floorboard, but this loss is made up by the ships' many advantages. In many ways roll-on roll-off ships offer the purest form of inter-modal transit, in that the vehicle is not unloaded and no transshipment really takes place. They are very flexible in the type of load they carry, accepting everything from flat beds to tank units. The roll-on roll-off operator does not have to invest in vast numbers of containers (which are frequently not where they are wanted). His equipment inventories are quite small, and although he may carry containers on deck he has fewer expensive and under-utilised shore based gantry cranes or scotch derricks.

Cargo is carried in considerable safety, with a minimum of damage from weather or spray, while the greatest advantage of all is the speed of the ship's turn-round. This is most advantageous on very short sea routes, such as the English Channel crossing from Dover to Calais. Since roll-on roll-off services began in 1953 Dover has become the busiest passenger port in the U.K., handling 5 million passengers a year.

Cargo movements, which are not seasonal like the passenger trade, have increased by 50 per cent per year, a very rapid rate of growth. The operation of large container ships, which tend to call at one big port only, has increased the traffic on the short sea routes, especially from the U.K. to the Low Countries and the Baltic. This has made the roll-on roll-off ship a viable proposition on all the routes serving this busy area.

The versatility of the roll-on roll-off ship can be increased by such devices as roll-on roll-off loading with packaged timber and similar products by straddle carriers belonging to the vessel. This increases the productivity of the long-haul routes by utilising the space wasted on normal roll-on roll-off operations. One group of ships which carries cars to Canada in one direction only has four car decks which she lowers into position from the deck-heads. The ships become vast floating garages for 2,000 automobiles, but on unloading, the car decks are raised and the huge holds are filled with forest products, newsprint and wood-pulp, loaded by the ship's own straddle carriers, for the return journey to Europe.

Barge-carrying Vessels

While some transport operators have been pressing ahead with containerisa-tion, and others with bulk haulage, a further solution to the problems of securing efficient sea transport has been developed by a third group. The solution is a system consisting basically of a large vessel, carrying many smaller vessels which can enter river estuaries while the main vessel proceeds on her way after having lifted on board a further group of loaded barges for transit in the reverse direction. Two basically similar systems have evolved: the Lash system (L.A.S.H. standing for 'lighter aboard ship'), first operated by the Norwegian firm T. Mosvold of Kristiansand, and the Seabee (sea-

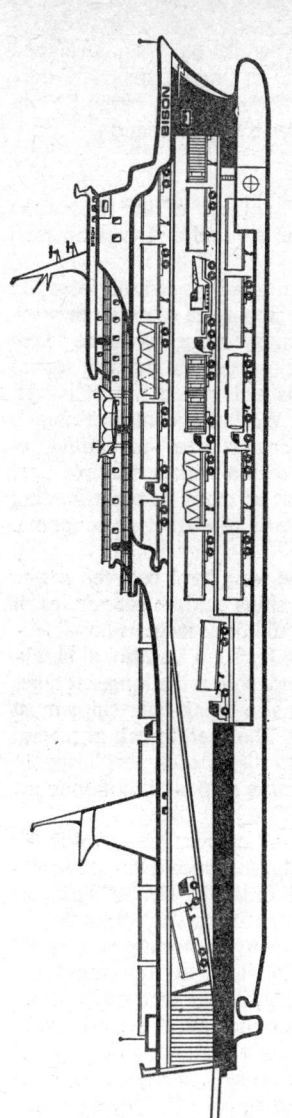

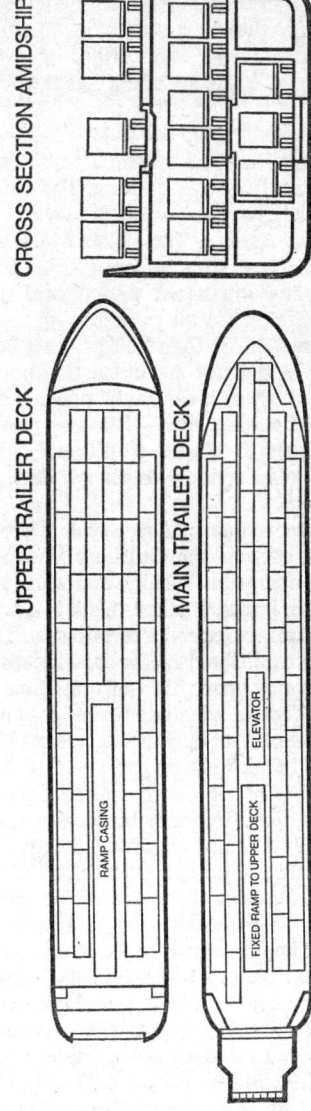

CROSS SECTION AMIDSHIPS

UPPER TRAILER DECK

RAMP CASING

MAIN TRAILER DECK

FIXED RAMP TO UPPER DECK

ELEVATOR

Fig. 6.3. A roll-on roll-off ship.

(courtesy of Peninsular and Orient Steam Navigation Co. Ltd.)

barge) system operated by Lykes Lines. The material in this chapter is drawn from literature made available by this firm.

The Lash and Seabee systems are both intended for trans-ocean traffic. A third variant of the Barge-on-Board (B.O.B.) as these have also been called, is the B.A.C.A.T. system (Barge aboard catamaran) which has been developed primarily for the short sea trades (see Fig. 6.4). At present there are over thirty barge-carrying ships either operating or being built, a barge leasing company is in existence and a barge pool is under active discussion.

Why Use a Barge-carrying Vessel?

The barge-carrying system combines the advantages of all the recent developments in cargo handling. The points borne in mind by Lykes Lines in devising their system were as follows:

Multi-port Pattern. The Lykes Lines have traditionally operated from the Gulf ports. These stretch from Florida to Texas, a complex of nineteen ports all generating important agricultural and manufacturing produce. These Southern States are all experiencing rapid development as industry moves into the area. More than half of these new plants have access to waterways, and many of the rest are in existing port areas. While the container ship is best utilised where it can make one call at a major port area—unloading, re-loading and sailing away—it is less useful in a region with a multiple port pattern. In the Gulf area traditional ships call at as many as eight loading ports, and offer services to several destination ports to attract an economic mix of cargo.

The Diseconomies of Large-scale Ships. On the long haul between major port areas, such as the Gulf and Europe, large ships achieve economies of large-scale operation. Ideally, therefore, ships should be as large as possible— up to certain limits. Against this it is a regrettable fact that traditional break-bulk ships cannot exceed a certain size. The bigger a ship is the longer it takes to load by traditional methods. Therefore large size break-bulk ships must spend a greater proportion of total time in port. The need to call at several ports to collect an adequate mix of cargoes, and to stay at each port longer to load and unload its huge holds, means that the large ship is uneconomic for traditional break-bulk cargoes.

The Nature of the Cargoes to be Carried. Not all cargoes are suitable for containerisation. This may be because the firms that produce them are small-scale firms and do not generate full container loads of traffic. The utilisation of containers then requires the development of groupage firms, who will assemble, and break, loads at either end of the transit. Many agricultural products are uneconomic to containerise, but time-consuming to load by traditional methods. The problem is to load these goods by traditional methods without wasting the time of a large ship. If this can be done the final delivered cost of the product can be kept low, and competitive on world markets.

The Need for Flexibility. The container ship, which achieves economies of large scale, rapid cargo handling and rapid turn-round, does so at the expense of flexibility. It only calls at one port, leaving multi-port areas to be served by a short-sea distribution network. Often this port is a big port, with the shore facilities to unload and stack a large collection of containers in a very short period. The ship and the port are thus very specialised, while the cargoes handled are limited to those which are easily containerised. The problem was to build a ship which was large enough to achieve the economies of large-scale operation but which did not have to spend very long in port; which could be loaded by traditional break-bulk methods where these were cheaper and more convenient, while at the same time carrying containers where movements of pilferage-proof unit loads were advantageous.

The Mother Ship

The barge-carrying ship offers all the advantages of the container ship, the roll-on roll-off ship, the lift-on lift-off ship, the traditional break-bulk ship and the small tanker. It can be employed with almost any type of cargo. It is not so much a ship as a 'system' of transport. The Lykes Line 'Seabee' system has mother ships—barge-carrying hives of the Seabee system. Each mother ship is 875 ft. long and 106 ft. wide, with stabilizer systems which give 'passenger trade' size, stability and speed to the cargo trade. It is equipped with a 2,000-ton submersible elevator which can raise or lower two fully loaded 'Seabee' barges from deck to sea level. The three decks will accommodate 38 'Seabee' barges (out of a total fleet of 246 such units) stowed fore and aft. They can be taken aboard at a speed equivalent to 2,500 tons per hour, each barge holding 832 tons of freight.

The mother ship never enters dock, or pulls in to a pier. She loads and unloads barges away from any port installation. It is the barge units which enter ports, or estuaries, where they act as flexible extensions of the mother ship. They are of shallow draft and can reach wharves and jetties inaccessible to conventional break-bulk ships, let alone container ships. The 'Seabee' system thus restores the inland waterway network to importance, opening up connections to areas inaccessible for decades, and sometimes a century.

The Barge Units

Each barge unit is a cargo-carrying vessel of shallow draft, with double-hulled construction, watertight compartments, and watertight hatch covers which when removed reveal the entire cargo compartment. The cargo can thus be placed directly into its point of rest for the entire journey. This loading takes place in traditional docks, at riverside wharves and jetties far from the mother ship, which has proceeded on her way to other roadsteads where she will hive off yet more 'bees' and collect returning ones which have been filled at the leisure of the shipper. The barges are designed to accommodate pallets, containers and 'intermediate decks' for large units of pre-stowed cargo. The arrangements are entirely at the direction of the cargo shipper, who supervises the stowage in the barge unit which has been delivered to his own location, possibly under cover, since its size is small. Finally, containers may be carried on special support beams above the closed hatch covers.

It is difficult to imagine a more versatile, flexible and economical system (see Plate 15).

The Bacat system, although developed later than the Lash and Seabee systems, is intended for intensive use on the short sea routes, and has been successfully operated. Fig. 6.4 and 6.5 show how the barges are propelled by pusher tugs, and how they are taken on board.

Fig. 6.4. The BACAT (Barges Aboard Catamaran) system.

(courtesy of Bacat Line)

Very Large Crude Carriers

V.L.C.C.s have been referred to elsewhere (see Chapter Twelve) but one or two interesting features of these particular units of carriage are worth mentioning here. First, the draught of the tankers may be as great as 81 ft. and this poses difficult navigational problems in the relatively shallow North European waters.

Many North European ports are at present unable to accept the very largest V.L.C.C.s afloat and can only accept those slightly less small, with great difficulty. As even larger vessels become operational the position will become even more critical, except for a few ports blessed with deep water inshore and with deep-water approaches. For the present, a number of devices have been used to overcome this natural obstacle of inadequate depth.

Dredging is an obvious solution, and where there is deep water at a relatively short distance from the port, the approaches and berths can be progressively deepened to keep pace with the ever-increasing draught. However, as time passes and draughts become larger and larger, it may become necessary to extend the dredged channel further and further seawards until the cost of dredging is no longer economically viable and the port must forego the revenue and prestige which would accrue from handling the largest ships.

An alternative is to utilise the very high 'perigee' spring tides, when the depth of water available will be at its greatest, to bring the vessel to its terminal. A peculiarity of the super-tanker is that it bobs up out of the water quickly as the load is reduced. Since most super-tankers can discharge at

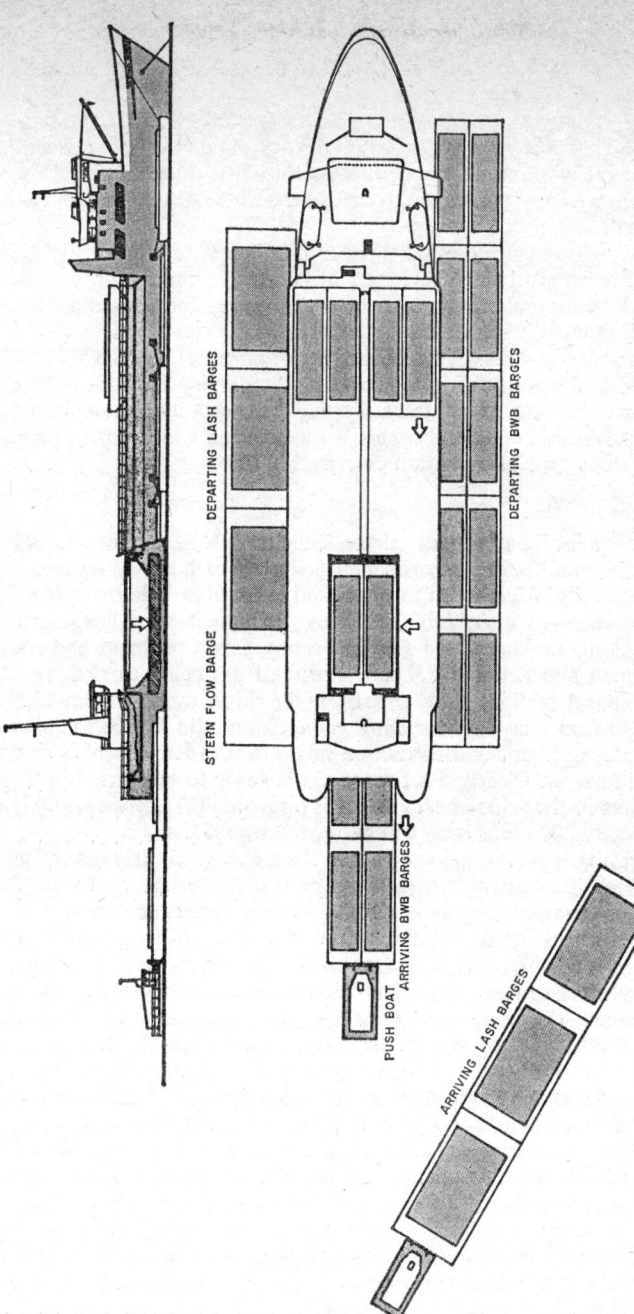

Fig. 6.5. The BACAT barge transporter system.

(courtesy of Bacat Line)

about 13,000 tons per hour, enough cargo can be discharged as the tide ebbs to leave them still afloat at low tide.

A second alternative is to dredge a hole at the terminal and in its vicinity deep enough to ensure that a loaded vessel, brought in on the 'top of the tide' could remain safely afloat at low tide, even without lightening her. This of course is much cheaper than trying to dredge the whole of the channel to the depth required.

In practice, a combination of all three of these possible solutions is used: channels and terminals being deepened until costs become prohibitive, very fast discharge being undertaken to lighten the vessel, and advantage being taken of high tides to bring vessels to their berths.

A fourth solution ignores the established major ports as far as the V.L.C.C.s are concerned and concentrates on providing discharging facilities in places where natural deep water exists, transshipping the cargoes to the major ports with their established hinterlands. This is the solution which has given rise to the Bantry Bay type of operation described in Chapter Five.

L.N.G. Carriers

L.N.G. stands for liquefied natural gas. The first L.N.G. carrier was called *Methane Pioneer* and began experimental deliveries of liquefied natural gas from the gas fields of Algeria to Canvey Island in Essex early in the 1960s. By 1974 there were seven main L.N.G. schemes in operation: Algeria to the United Kingdom, Le Havre and Fos in France, Libya to Spain and Italy, Alaska to Japan and Brunei to Japan. The total gas being carried was 21 milliard (thousand million) cubic metres, in 17 ships, ranging from 27,500 tons to 87,600 tons (the *Norman Lady* plying from Abu Dhabi to Japan). Another 44 ships are under construction or on firm order, of which 36 are 120,000 tons or over. Clearly a lot more gas is going to be carried in these L.N.G. carriers in the years ahead, and it is estimated that between 100 and 150 carriers of 125,000 tons each will be needed by 1985.

Over the years experience has shown that the best way to carry natural gas, which liquefies either under refrigeration or under pressure, is to use the refrigeration process and carry at $-165\,°C$. At this extremely cold temperature insulation between the tank and the hull of the ship is of vital importance. The insulation is of polystyrene. The tanks may be large spherical tanks of 9 per cent nickel steel, or aluminium construction. Alternatively, the tanks may be double-walled, the inner one being a flexible corrugated stainless-steel membrane. A third type, the M.V.T. (multi-vessel tank), has a large number of relatively small vertically positioned cylindrical units. These are safer from the point of view of damage to the ship—only those tanks actually damaged will leak—and the insulation problems are also easier. There are four to eight tanks in each vessel. Wherever possible the tanks are rectangular, to ease the problems of calibrating the tanks for content, but at the fore and aft parts of the ship tanks are shaped to suit the vessel. Difficult problems arise at 'custody transfer' points, such as shore-to-ship on the start of a voyage and ship-to-shore on delivery at the end of the voyage. The mere pumping of the liquid causes heat-inleakage and consequent vaporisation of the more volatile products. The resulting gas reduces the volume delivered and must be refrigerated again, or even burned off in a flare.

Clean Product Carriers and L.P.G. Carriers

Clean products, as distinct from crude oil, are carried usually at normal temperatures, being liquefied by pressure if they are not liquids at ordinary temperatures. They are not usually carried in such enormous quantities as L.N.G., and ships can be quite small. They are often called mini-bulk carriers as a result. They may carry several different products, for different customers.

L.P.G. stands for liquefied petroleum gas, usually propane and butane. Methanol, or methyl alcohol, can be prepared from natural gas and shipped at normal temperatures instead of in L.N.G. carriers. Clean product carriers are rarely bigger than 26,000 tons and the vast majority are in the 1,000–5,000 ton class, but the world's largest, the *Esso Fuji*, is 62,300 dwt., and carries gas from the Arabian Gulf States to Japan.

Hydrofoils

A hydrofoil is a ship fitted with foils, which operate very much like the aerofoil of an aircraft, i.e. pressure from below creates lift. (Aerofoils on racing cars operate in reverse, the shape of the aerofoil being designed to ensure that downward pressure is exerted so that contact is maintained with the road surface.) Perhaps a better illustration would be to liken them to water-skis. A water-skier starts off with his skis submerged in the water. As the tow-boat increases speed, the skis are angled and the pressure created by the water rushing underneath causes them to skim over the water, supporting the weight of the skier. When a hydrofoil is at rest, or moving slowly, it floats with its hull partly submerged, like any conventional vessel. As forward motion increases, pressure on the angled foils causes them to skim the surface, raising the hull clear of the water. This reduces drag and permits increased speeds. The wash of a hydrofoil is much less than an ordinary ship's wash. This is helpful in rivers and other enclosed waterways, where banks and other property can suffer damage from wave action created by fast-moving vessels.

Hovercraft

The Hovercraft principle was originally developed by Christopher Cockerell around 1954, out of two coffee tins, with a space between them. Air was blown through this space with a small industrial drier and the lift he had predicted occurred. Since that date, after many trials and tribulations and with considerable help eventually from the National Research Development Corporation, a whole range of hovercraft types has developed, and wide industrial uses, particularly load removals, have been developed.

While the ordinary Hovercraft has conquered the world, crossing Africa coast to coast and sweeping over South American jungle waterways, its most testing performance has undoubtedly been the Seaspeed Hovercraft cross-Channel service from Dover to Calais. This service operates 364 days a year, with from three to fifteen flights daily, and represents an engineering maintenance achievement of no mean quality.

The Hovercraft operates on a cushion of air built up inside the skirt by a powerful engine. Each Proteus gas turbine, for example, produces 4,250 h.p. at 12,000 r.p.m. The Hovercraft is thus an aircraft and not a sea craft, although its basic design is that of a buoyancy raft and if the skirt fails it can in fact proceed at about 6 knots. In flight its normal speed is about 70 knots and it operates over land or water equally well, so that where appropriate it can take short cuts across mud flats and sand bars. The SRN4 which operates the Dover service can take wave variations of up to 10 ft., and carries nearly 300 passengers and more than 30 vehicles. An American firm is currently developing a 2,000 ton 'Surface Effects Ship', the skirts of which are to be made by the British Hovercraft Company. She will be ten times as big as the Dover ferries.

Units of Carriage by Air

The aeroplane is the typical unit of carriage, but helicopters and airships are alternatives. The aeroplane is fast, safe and reliable, and in 67 years—from 1908—has moved from the Deutsch Archdeacon prize for the first officially observed flight of a single aviator around a circular course, to the carriage of millions of passengers over billions of flight miles. In 1973 Heathrow Airport, London, alone carried 21 million passengers with 293,968 aircraft movements. On the busiest day 972 aircraft movements took place, with 80,000 passengers passing through.

The aircraft is a heavier-than-air machine, which is raised from the ground by the flow of air over the aerofoils or wings. This lifts the aircraft, partly by a build-up of pressure under the wing, but even more by the suction effect created above the wing due to the design. This increases the speed of the air above the wing and hence reduces its pressure. The unit of carriage and the engines are embodied in the same frame, but the engines have been placed in almost every conceivable position. The wings, nose, mid-fuselage, rear fuselage and tail plane have all borne engines in recent years, and the comfort of passengers is certainly increased with modern high-speed aircraft if the engines are to the rear, as with the V.C.10.

All modern aircraft are pressurised, to avoid the use of oxygen when flying at altitudes. A non-pressurised aircraft can only be operated at about 10,000 ft. without oxygen. At the sort of heights at which modern aircraft operate huge supplies of oxygen would be necessary. Pressurised cabins are the only practicable solution. They do mean that greater stresses are put upon the skin metal and careful examination for metal fatigue is necessary.

A Typical Unit of Passenger Carriage—the Boeing 747

It is impossible to describe fully all the many types of aircraft which are in operation around the world. The Boeing 747 is a typical aircraft in the sense that it is flying the major long-haul inter-continental air routes for many airlines today. It is an economic aircraft even in these days of high fuel costs, giving about 60 miles per gallon per passenger, against the family car's 40 miles per gallon per passenger on average. It is an American aeroplane, with four Pratt & Whitney JT9D-3D engines, slung on underwing pods. These develop a thrust of 80,000 kg. The aircraft when fully loaded with its economy class load of 496 passengers and 6,190 cu. ft. of cargo weighs 340 short tons (680,000 lb.). Its wing span is 195 ft. 8 in., its length 231 ft. 4 in., its height 63 ft. 5 in. and it carries 41,900 gallons of fuel. It cruises at 565–600 miles per hour, at altitudes of 30,000–45,000 ft.

The British Airways 747s have five cabins, one first class and four economy class. The walls are straight, the ceilings flat and high, seats are arranged in rows of nine in the economy class cabins, with two wide aisles intersecting the seating into groups of three. The first class cabin has seats in rows of four separated into two-abreast seating by a wide aisle. There is also an exclusive lounge bar, furnished with comfortable chairs and settees, where passengers can enjoy drinks and snacks. There are six galley areas, with automated ovens able to serve hot meals to all passengers, with a personal choice individual service for first class passengers. Full-length feature films are shown, and there is a selection of audio entertainment.

Concorde—the Supersonic Unit of Air Carriage

Concorde is not yet operational, though it is in the final stages of its flight tests and arouses enormous interest wherever it goes.

The aircraft is supersonic, flying at a speed of 1,450 m.p.h., which is greater than Mach 2. It operates at altitudes of 50,000–65,000 ft., and has a range of 3,910 miles, carrying 136 economy class passengers. The great advantage Concorde offers is the speed at which travel is possible. It will reach Australia in $10\frac{1}{2}$ hours, and although the Jumbo jets offer it severe competition where maximum time-saving is not all-important, there are many who believe that passengers who must travel fast will be glad to pay a premium fare for the savings thus obtained.

The Air Freighter

From the earliest times in aviation the cheap way to carry freight has been on the passenger aircraft. It has been a happy coincidence that while most passengers travel at weekends most goods travel on weekdays. It has thus been possible to fill up the mid-week passenger planes with extra cargo in the freight holds. In recent years, however, the air freighter has begun to appear—a response to the increased appreciation of air transport by the freight forwarding industry. Specialised 'igloo' containers, special loading channels and scissors lift devices have been developed to assist in the loading of air freighters, and extremely rapid transit times—two days from the United Kingdom to New Zealand is typical—have been achieved.

Pipelines and Tubes

The pipeline is a unit of carriage which is fully described in other sections of this book. It is both a way and a unit of carriage and requires no further description here. However, the use of pneumatic pipeline systems for the transport of freight, a king-size development of the pneumatic systems used in some department stores for centralised cash desk operations, is a distinct possibility. The Soviet Union claims to be developing a pneumatic freight pipeline which will move 10 million tons of freight a year over 50-km distances. Units of 25 tons are to be moved at 45 m.p.h., in freight cars which fit tightly into the pipe.

Suggested Further Reading

Cannell, J., *Design of Urban Transit Vehicles*, Open University, 1972.
Finlay, P. (Ed.), *Jane's Freight Containers*, S. Low, 1971–2.
Williams, J. E. D., *The Operation of Airliners*, Hutchinson, 1964.

CHAPTER SEVEN

THE PHYSICAL COMPONENTS OF TRANSPORT: MOTIVE POWER

Introduction

The modern transport scene is dominated by enormously powerful motive power units. Aircraft weighing 300 tons roar off into the sky, supertankers weighing half a million tons glide up estuaries to dock at oil terminals, streams of traffic start up within seconds of traffic lights changing colour and the Saturn rocket reaches an escape velocity of over 20,000 miles an hour in less than a minute. Clearly we have moved a long way from the days of natural power, when becalmed mariners whistled for a wind, and a team of horses was needed to drag a single oak tree down the many 'timber-log-lanes' that led to the naval dockyards. We still row our university boat races, we pedal our bicycles, we race our sailing dinghies in innumerable inlets and the prize is still on offer for the first man-powered flight, but in the developed countries the world of transport has forgotten about natural power, and is preoccupied with mechanised units of propulsion.

Before we too become preoccupied with the more sophisticated motive power units, we should pause to remember that in many underdeveloped countries animal and wind power are still very important. Bullock carts and horse and donkey carts are still used extensively in some of the poorer countries, and pack animals still persist in countries where poor roads, or absence of them, make wheeled transport difficult. Although their numbers have diminished in recent years, many sailing vessels still operate in the Middle and Far Eastern areas.

Types of Prime Mover

The term 'prime mover' is used to describe fundamental units of propulsion. Whatever variations of motion are achieved by gearing, belting, frictional contact or other means there must be a primary source of power to generate the original motion. The chief types of prime mover may be listed as follows:

(a) the steam engine;

(b) electric motors, which are of two types, series wound and shunt wound;

(c) internal combustion engines, driven by petrol or liquefied petroleum gas (propane and butane);

(d) diesel engines, or oil engines;

(e) turbines;

(f) jet engines.

Steam Engines

The first prime mover was the steam engine, which for 100 years dominated both transport and production as the main source of power. Stationary steam engines drove the machines in the mills of the eighteenth and nineteenth centuries, pumped out the mines and even wound trains up hills on cables.

Steam locomotives dominated the railways for more than a century from 1825 onwards. The steam roller was the most powerful road vehicle for the best part of a century too, though badly hampered by controls over its speed. The durability of steam engines gave them great 'inertia' as a form of prime mover. While nations less highly capitalised in steam than the United Kingdom turned readily to electrical and other forms of motive power, the United Kingdom hesitated to change because its steam engines continued to give good service. A further point is that the steam engine burned an indigenous fuel, coal, while the petrol and diesel engines required a foreign fuel supply.

Electric Motors

The work of Michael Faraday in the years 1830–67 formed the basis of the modern electrical industry and when applied to transport gave us the series motor and the tramway, trolleybus and electric railway. The diesel electric motor operates on the same principles but uses power generated by a diesel engine instead of power from an external source of supply. There are also battery-operated vehicles like milk floats and forklift trucks, while a battery-operated motorcar and battery buses have recently appeared.

The series motor has the merit of a very high-powered starting torque, which overcomes the initial inertia of a stationary vehicle. As the inertia is overcome the acceleration is extremely rapid under the enormous power of the series motor. As a safe operating speed is approached the power to the motor has to be reduced to conform with the reduced effective load now that the vehicle is moving.

Battery-powered vehicles have several disadvantages. They are not suitable for heavy work, or continuous work, and their rate of acceleration is low. The batteries have to be recharged at intervals, a slow process which means the machine cannot be used continuously unless a change of batteries is carried out. The renewable battery—one where the plates can be replaced by a new set for a further period of work—is being actively sought, especially as it would reduce the pollution problems inseparable from petrol and diesel prime movers. Such a development would influence very greatly the use of battery-operated electric vehicles.

The sodium-sulphur battery, which has as many as 49 cells using a sodium electrolyte, has enormous potential in this field. It lasts four times as long as a lead-acid battery, giving vehicles a range of about 100–140 miles, and should operate more efficiently and at lower capital cost than a lead-acid battery-driven bus or van.

Internal Combustion Engines

Internal combustion engines are more numerous than any other type of prime mover today. They are susceptible to mass production and are therefore relatively cheap. They are easily understood, suitable for small family vehicles, and relatively economical to run. They give good acceleration, high speed and are adaptable to many different types of transport. The range is convenient for most ordinary household or business purposes, and the capital cost is not great. Even the poorest families can advance up the trade-in range to the possession of a vehicle of reasonable quality.

Diesel engines operate on a slightly different basis from the internal combustion engine. The ignition is spontaneous once the engine is hot, and there are therefore no sparking plugs in use. There will be some device to start the engine from cold, but once warm the compression of the air in the cylinders heats it to the point where an injected jet of oil fires by itself. The diesel engine is very powerful, and best suited to heavy vehicles. It is an extremely efficient engine and converts about 40 per cent of heat energy to useful work. A steam locomotive by contrast would not convert more than about 5 per cent.

Turbines

A turbine may be one of two types: impulse turbines and reactor turbines—or a combination of both. The circular motion is achieved in the impulse turbine by a ready-made stream of air or steam which pushes the blades round. A reaction turbine has blades which are shaped so as to accelerate the flow, which results in a reaction which kicks the blades round. The refinements and developments of these basic systems are numerous, some applications being more suited to one mode of transport than others.

Jet Engines

A jet engine consists of a shaft with a compressor at the front and a reaction turbine at the rear. There are a number of combustion chambers between. Air is drawn in at the front in huge quantities, compressed and fed into the combustion chambers where it is mixed with fuel vapour and fired. The gases produced are fed into the turbine, which operates the compressor, and pass from there into the jet pipe. The expansion that takes place then expels the gases at great speed, causing a forward thrust which propels the unit of carriage.

A later development, the by-pass engine, only passes about half the compressed air through the combustion chambers. The rest by-passes the high-pressure compressor and combustion chambers. It is cooler and moving at a slower speed than the hot exhaust gases with which it mingles in the tailpipe. The resulting jet stream is more efficient, less noisy and more economical of fuel. The Rolls-Royce Conway engine incorporating the by-pass principle powers the V.C.10 and the Boeing 707.

The introduction of the wide-bodied jet aircraft, such as the Boeing 747, the original Jumbo jet, was made possible by the introduction of the turbo-fan engine of high by-pass ratio. The JT9D engine which powers the Boeing 747 incorporates a fan with a diameter almost as great as the length of the engine. This giant fan handles many times more airflow than that passing through the 'core' engine. As a result the engine develops many times more thrust than its predecessors and makes much larger aircraft possible, yet at the same time it is quieter and more economical than earlier engines.

Motive Power and Road Haulage

Diesel engines are most appropriate for heavy haulage duties and a modern 4, 6 or 8-cylinder diesel with a 5-, 6- or even 10-speed gearbox is a powerful unit well able to move the plated weight it is designed to carry, with power to spare. Reliability and economy are a feature of the diesel engine, and developments like direct fuel injection and advanced piston combustion chambers mean clean combustion, free of fumes. Flame pre-heaters give starting from cold down to −19 °C. Transmission from the engine is sophisticated, to give a smooth flow of engine power through the gearbox, dynamically balanced prop shafts and differentials to the wheel drive.

Typical power units for 32-ton trucks give between 192 b.h.p. (the legal minimum necessary) and 335 b.h.p. for really heavy sustained motorway working.

By contrast the light vans on the market are usually petrol driven, and have engines which generate between 30 and 60 b.h.p.

Accessibility of power units for maintenance purposes is an important aspect, and many large vehicles have forward-tilting cabs to leave the engine clearly accessible.

Motive Power and Railways

In the United Kingdom the 1950s saw the beginning of the end of steam power and the switch to diesel power and electrified lines. Compared with the diesel, the electric traction unit offers greater power, greater acceleration, greater reliability and cheaper operations. However, the capital costs of electrification are enormous, whereas a diesel locomotive operates on the traditional lines without major alterations. The modernisation of British Railways which took place between 1955 and 1965 required a very considerable measure of dieselisation, since the supply of capital equipment for electrification was inadequate to push modernisation ahead at the rate envisaged in the plan.

There are two types of diesel: the diesel electric and the hydraulic diesel. The diesel electric uses the diesel engine to generate electricity, which is then used to drive the wheels through ordinary electric motors similar to those used by the electric traction unit operating on electricity from the national grid. The transmission to the wheels is thus an electrical transmission.

The hydraulic diesel, by contrast, transmits the drive to the wheels through a device called a torque-convertor which carries out the same function as a gearbox. An ordinary gearbox is unable to stand up to the high loads and fast speeds of railway traffic, but the torque convertor transmits the motion through a fluid mechanism, much more smoothly and with greater power.

While it is true that the use of diesels was inevitable if fast, accurately timed services were to be offered in the modernisation years, the long-run aim of British Rail is to electrify all main lines. The electric traction unit is cheaper, it is available for almost continuous use, it is susceptible to computerised planning and control because of its predictable performance, and its high speed makes the return on capital invested very satisfactory. The exception to this rule is the advanced passenger train (A.P.T.), which is to be powered by a gas turbine. This gives a very favourable power/weight ratio and consequent rapid acceleration.

Aircraft Power Units

The design of motive power units for aircraft, more than with any other unit of carriage, depends upon economic considerations. The performance of an engine is one thing; its performance as an economic unit is another. This means that before design begins a clear picture of the background to the design must be built up. This picture is not easy to bring into focus, for many of the aims of the airlines who may eventually operate an aircraft are imprecisely stated, but as a rough guide we may mention three:

(*a*) Safety and reliability are very important.

(*b*) The economics of the power unit should be as good as possible.

(*c*) The complete unit of carriage must be socially and environmentally acceptable.

By a series of optimisation studies the design engineer evaluates traditional ideas and well-established mechanisms against more recent ideas and proposals for turning them into practical reality. In the long run he must tell the manufacturer what to make and the airline what it can have and at what price.

Today, while petrol-driven piston engines are still important for club flying and small aircraft of many sorts, the jet engine reigns supreme for passenger and cargo aircraft. It is faster, quieter and more economical than any other type of engine, and its general performance has increased both the size and the economy of operation of commercial aircraft out of all recognition compared with other power units.

STOL and VTOL Technology

Two aspects of aircraft design which are of great interest are the Short Take-Off and Landing (STOL) and the Vertical Take-Off and Landing (VTOL) techniques. The high capital cost of airports for major civil airline operations is prohibitive in many parts of the world where the aircraft is a vital link in the national life yet the traffic to be carried is limited. Examples are the Canadian North and the Australian Outback. For these areas the STOL aircraft is the ideal type of aircraft. Canada in particular has developed a range of STOL aircraft: the Beaver, Otter, Buffalo and Caribou and its latest De Havilland Canada 7 aircraft. These aircraft will operate from small airports in remote areas—even from frozen lakes (kept frozen all the year round by artificial refrigeration in some cases). They will also operate in and out of city centre airports without giving offence on noise levels. The Canadian Authorities say of the DHC-7:

The DHC-7's main attraction for travellers is its ability to take off and land in busy city centres and designers have concentrated heavily on public reaction to this innovation. The craft is quieter than conventional planes. It is estimated that occupants of buildings will have difficulty detecting it flying overhead at 750 feet (228 metres), and in ascent and descent, the airplane's steeper angles will expose a much smaller area of land to noise. On a mile-to-mile basis, emission of pollutants will be one half that of the average automobile.

The DHC-7's speed of 300 miles (480 km) an hour is slow by current standards but by eliminating time-consuming trips to outlying air terminals, it will deliver passengers to their destinations faster than more powerful planes. Frequent departures that will eliminate the need for reservations and reduce traffic bottle-necks in and around terminal buildings, are also expected to heighten the DHC-7's appeal.

STOL promises even more important benefits for terminal authorities and carriers, particularly in countries where the public opposes expansion of existing terminal facilities and construction of new airports. Studies show that STOLports capable of handling five to ten million passengers annually—complete with runway and all necessary buildings and parking lots—can be built on approximately 40 acres, or less than one per cent the area required by jetports.

STOL runways can also be incorporated into existing facilities, thus delaying or eliminating new construction of conventional terminals. The shorter runways do not even require additional land acquisition and STOL's low noise output and steep flight profile permit greater activity without further disturbance to nearby communities.

The STOL principle does not of course depend only on the power unit—the whole design of the aircraft is vital—but the power units clearly have to be appropriate to the design.

With vertical take-off and landing aircraft the power unit is crucial. The ability of the engines to change their alignment so as to point downwards and thus give direct lift from the ground is an essential feature. As their fore and aft alignment is restored, the forward movement begins and ordinary lift from the aerofoils replaces the lift from the engines. This makes take-off from a landing pad a practical possibility but the chief use for VTOL aircraft at present is for military aircraft.

Motive Power at Sea

For centuries ships depended upon the wind for their motive power. Then came the steam engine, which transformed marine transport and spelled the death of sail except for leisure purposes. At the end of the nineteenth century Charles Parsons took the principle of the steam turbine, which had been known to the ancient Greeks, and converted it to practical use. By allowing hot, high-pressure steam to escape past the curved blades of turbine wheels he created an engine far smaller but infinitely more powerful than the existing reciprocating engines.

Today only the biggest merchant ships are powered by steam turbines, because for small and medium-sized vessels marine diesel engines are more efficient and more economical.

Finally, there has been the development of nuclear power for ship propulsion. The advantage of this form of propulsion is that very little space is required for fuel and ships can have a very long range, and high cruising speed. Despite the fact that nuclear-powered merchant vessels have been operational since the late fifties, there has been no rush to switch to this form of propulsion and in many countries these vessels are regarded with suspicion and distrust and are refused entry to many ports for fear of nuclear hazards. However, there seems little doubt in the face of a world energy crisis that nuclear power will become a most important form of marine propulsion in the years to come.

Motive Power and Pipelines

Piped products have to be driven along the pipeline by some sort of pump. The variety of pumps in use is very great, as is the variety of prime movers driving them. Reciprocating pumps and single-stage or multi-stage centrifugal pumps are the main types, driven by electric motors, diesel engines, gas engines and steam or gas turbines. The particular situation, the product to be pumped, the fuel available, and the size of the installation are major factors in determining the responses of the engineer to the problems he faces.

To double the volume of a fluid passing through a pipeline requires four times the pressure. Therefore a pipeline installed some time ago which, due to changes of demand, needs to take a bigger volume of traffic will need very much greater pumping power if it is to carry the load. Four times the volume would require sixteen times the pressure. It is better to install a number of pumping houses at intervals along the line and spread the increased work among them. In many cases pumping stations can be remotely controlled by an automatic sequence of operations, and sensing devices will shut down a pump which for some reason is malfunctioning.

Suggested Further Reading

Danforth, P. M., *Transport Control*, Aldus Books Ltd, 1970.
Gunston, W., *Transport Technology*, Geoffrey Chapman, 1972.

CHAPTER EIGHT

PHYSICAL DISTRIBUTION: INTRODUCTION

Definition

'Physical distribution' is a term that has gained general currency in the last decade as a convenient description of a wide range of activities which take place after goods have been produced and before they reach the consumer, or the next stage of production if they are part of a continuing process. These activities include materials handling, storage and warehousing, packaging and unitisation and freight transportation by all modes of transport. Related activities such as vehicle routing and scheduling and vehicle maintenance are also included. The purpose of these activities is the bridging of gaps between the producer and consumer. They ensure the safe passage of goods from the point of production to the point of consumption, so that they arrive in perfect condition where they are wanted when they are wanted.

In performing such a wide range of activities in a world where specialisation is a major feature of the method of production, long geographical journeys will be inevitable. Vast quantities of raw materials and finished products move restlessly along the major trade routes, subject to attack by climatic changes, insect pests, dessication, humidity, pilfering and theft. To counter such influences strategies must be developed and plans prepared. At the same time these plans must be economically viable, because safe arrival over the geographical and time barriers will be fruitless if the final cost to the consumer is greater than he can afford. Goods must reach the consumer not only in the right quantity, the right condition, the right place and the right time, but also at the right price. A chief function of physical distribution therefore is to ensure economic operations.

Planning Physical Distribution—the Total Distribution Concept

A company involved in distribution will be wise to draw up a strategic plan after examining the detailed requirements of its own or its customers' activities. The aim of this strategy is to achieve the most economic operations possible in the circumstances. The costs of moving goods about and of their storage are clearly inter-related, so that they must be viewed as complementary costs. Greater efficiency in movement will reduce storage, while greater warehousing efficiency will enable the goods to wait safely and economically while transport is organised. The plan must weigh up the total distribution problem from start to finish, and devise a system of operations which will achieve the desired result at the least possible cost. Factors such as market forecasting, materials handling, space utilisation, inventory control, natural wastage, damage during handling or storage, employee fatigue, employee motivation, safety, protective packaging, security, speed of transit, depot location, intermodal handling, order processing and documentation and customer service will become part of the overall strategy, and the plan will aim to overcome the difficulties envisaged.

Physical distribution is concerned with demand satisfaction, whereas marketing seeks to create demand. In satisfying demand the aim will be to reduce the time between the receipt of an order and its actual completion by delivery. To reduce this time—called the *lead-time*—we must examine the procedures necessary to document the order, process and perhaps transmit it, pick out the goods at the warehouse (perhaps with a sophisticated computer selection system or order picking lift trucks), pack, load and deliver it to the customer. Once each of these processes has been improved as much as possible we are left with a basic lead-time for the earlier activities plus the transit time for actual delivery which will reflect the distance to be travelled. However, one further factor—reflecting the company's policy on stocks—is the *percentage satisfaction* possible. Any item which we are unable to supply at once from stock necessarily generates a back-order. To attempt to fulfil orders completely is to offer the perfect service, but at an increasing cost as we approach perfection. Most firms will settle for something less than this—say, 95 per cent satisfaction. This rate of satisfaction is usually based upon the goods ordered, i.e. it tells us what percentage of goods ordered we were able to supply from stock.

Total Distribution Costs

Total distribution costs are the aggregate of the following costs:

(*a*) In-plant movement and storage
(*b*) Plant-to-depot transport
(*c*) Depot operating costs
(*d*) Depot inventory costs
(*e*) Depot-to-customer costs

The first of these—in-plant movement and storage costs—will be fairly uniform, however many depots are used, so long as there is no undue delay and storage in the plant. The rest will reflect very considerably the company's depot policy. A few large depots will be internally large-scale and efficient, but situated some distance from customers. A greater number of depots implies more sites and less economies of scale, but reduced distances to customers. The problem is to establish the best configuration of depots to achieve the least combined cost. Transport, warehousing and inventory costs will all vary with the policy, and trade-offs of one against the other will have to be estimated as the alternative policies are envisaged.

The range of costs envisaged under each of the headings (*a*)–(*e*) above will vary with other factors besides the depot policy. For example, the channels of distribution to be employed vary from own-account road transport through privately operated haulage services to nationalised road, rail or air transport. The number of lines to be offered, the degree of customer satisfaction aimed at and the minimum order size are other factors to be considered, while constraints such as warehouse space, inventory cost, vehicle utilisation and labour supply may require modifications in any plan.

Distribution is essentially a flow, and the preparation of a *flow chart* showing the distribution process will enable the centres of activity within the flow process to be isolated and costed. The contribution made by each activity within the overall process can be assessed, and the total system compared with alternative proposals envisaged along different lines. A new activity will be envisaged from different angles and viewpoints to ensure that the total distribution solution is the most economical possible under the circumstances.

In assessing cost, and seeking cost reductions, it is essential to review the activities carried on at present; quantify them in the light of current costs and volumes; consider viable alternative systems; cost them and select the best alternative; and finally compare this best alternative with the present system. A word about each of these aspects is desirable.

Evaluation of the Present System

The following questions need to be answered:

(*a*) What is the present pattern of distribution?

(*b*) What are the centres of activity and what costs do they involve, including hidden costs such as stock deterioration, pilfering, etc.?

(*c*) What is the present pattern of order size, order frequency, lead-time, percentage satisfaction from stock, etc.?

(*d*) What is the pattern of demand for each item, and are there any seasonal fluctuations? If so, what is their nature, their duration and the volume required to meet the boom when it arrives—including growth trends?

(*e*) Are there any marked geographical characteristics in the present pattern; if so, what is the cause of the disparities?

(*f*) What are the existing management objectives; are they the proper objectives today, and to what extent have they been met?

Costs of the Present System

(*a*) Quantify the costs of each centre of activity in the present system, under such headings as packaging costs, handling costs, transport costs, storage costs, operating costs, documentation costs, personnel costs, capital costs, overhead costs, etc.

(*b*) Integrate these cost-centre figures into total cost figures under each heading.

(*c*) Analyse by finding average order-processing cost, rate of stock turn, storage cost per unit, handling cost per unit, etc.

What Alternatives Are Available?

Here it is necessary to think carefully about the present system, posing questions which indicate weaknesses in it that could be solved by alternative systems.

(*a*) Is the tonnage carried in each centre the most appropriate and economical? If not, what would the cost savings be by other methods?

(*b*) What double-handling occurs, and what savings could be made by its elimination? Large cost savings can sometimes be made by the provision of materials handling equipment of a new type, which may also increase the utilisation of warehouse space, freeing accommodation for other purposes and releasing capital by the disposal of properties no longer required. Often double-handling can be eliminated by the use of through-transport or inter-modal transport.

(*c*) Can customer service be reduced without loss of business? If the small order is disproportionately costly can a contribution towards it be compelled from the customer?

(*d*) Will high-speed but expensive transport save more money than its extra costs? For example, a decision to air-freight components may mean the closure of dispatch centres previously concerned with the provision of timber cases for transits by sea, or might eliminate the need for warehouse facilities at local plants now to be supplied with daily requirements by regular air transits.

All the above costing exercises come under the heading of *differential cost analysis*, in which we seek to analyse the differences of cost involved when various ranges of goods are distributed in different ways, i.e. different order sizes, different modes of transport, different depot locations, etc.

The answers to many of the questions given above may result at once in the implementation of improvements which save costs. The best solution to the problem may be obvious, but comparison must now be made with the present system.

Comparison with the Present System

Today computer simulations of proposed distribution systems can be tried out under a representative range of operating conditions. These techniques enable management to make decisions about future activities on a much sounder basis than formerly. These techniques should enable decisions to be made for effecting the greatest cost savings over the total distribution network.

An Outline of the Distribution Process

There are a number of functions in the distribution process, not all of which will appear in every distribution system, but most of which will be present in any system. As management moves into a fully sophisticated control of physical distribution it embraces activities previously thought to be separate functions from physical distribution so that a full list now includes the following:

(*a*) A purchasing function
(*b*) An 'assembly' activity
(*c*) A packaging and unitisation activity
(*d*) A storage function (warehousing)
(*e*) Inventory management
(*f*) A transport function
(*g*) A depot activity
(*h*) A marketing function

While the particular circumstances of a firm may be such that some of these functions may not be necessary, most of them will be necessary in all firms. A brief description of each is given here and a fuller account of some, and other related matters, is given in the succeeding chapters.

The Purchasing Function

This function procures for the business those items that it requires for the successful prosecution of its activities. For manufacturing concerns it will be raw materials, components and capital items like machinery. For wholesale businesses the purchase of stock for re-sale will be the major requirement. Haphazard and intuitive purchasing has probably led to more failures in business than any other weakness, and the purchasing function must be fully reviewed at regular intervals.

An 'Assembly' Activity

This will be less apparent in a factory manufacturing situation than in a farming or market gardening system. With many types of produce—fruit, vegetables, milk, poultry, etc.—there will be a process of collection to take place. Fruit does not all ripen on the same day, for example, and a succession of collections will be necessary during the season. The assembly function leads into a packaging and unitisation function.

Packaging and Unitisation

This is a major feature of modern distribution. More than anything else the selling of pre-packaged, often perishable products has transformed the retail trade in recent years, breaking down barriers between retailers that have existed for centuries. The skilled tradesman who understood his merchandise and how to market it has been replaced by the self-service trader, whose sole function is to display and sell. The pre-packaging function is of great importance, and greatly simplifies distribution. Its compact units lend themselves to palletisation and modern mechanised handling, while bulk haulage by containerisation makes for economic transport over long distances.

Storage and Warehousing

Storage is inseparable from distribution for a variety of reasons. Goods are often produced seasonally but consumed continuously. A notable example is wheat, and the bread we make from it. Others are consumed seasonally, but produced throughout the year, like Christmas decorations and fireworks. Others may be produced in batches—because the demand for a period can be produced in a few days. Almost any product may require storage at a particular time for reasons quite external to the product itself—a strike, or a dislocation of transport, or a minor depression reducing demand temporarily. The storage function may involve many types of expertise, often referred to as 'merchandising' knowledge. Every product has its peculiar properties, its own inherent vice which must be controlled by appropriate treatment.

Inventory Management

Related to the purchasing function, but most obvious in the warehousing situation, is the question of inventory management. Stocks which are not turned over represent capital tied up without return. It must be a management function to control stock levels, in the interests of shareholders to ensure a good return on capital invested. It involves decisions about 'assortments', optimum ordering, maximum and minimum stock levels, etc. 'Assortment' is a term which refers to the variety of stock available. It is a matter of policy how wide a variety of stock shall be handled and what limitations shall be placed on the range of sizes, colours and qualities available.

The Transport Function

Transport alters the geographical position of the goods from the production point to the point of consumption. They can rarely go the entire journey in a single trip, because the economic load for the major part of the journey is usually greater than any single customer can use. In rare cases they might do so: for example, a road tanker might leave an oil refinery with a full load of petroleum for a single customer's garage. More usually some sort of depot network will be used as a buffer where the uneven nature of supply and demand can be accommodated. Sometimes a wholesaler will perform this function as an intermediary at whose premises bulk can be broken. A large organisation will use its depots as bulk-breaking centres.

Depot Activity

The depot constitutes a local warehouse for temporary storage where merchandise is secure and properly cared for by staff who understand its characteristics. The depot acts as a buffer to accommodate excess of supply over demand, and a source of reserve for emergency requirements. It often provides an area stock of slow moving items to reduce stocks held in branches, the slow-moving item being ordered up when required.

The Marketing Function

Marketing is the final link in the distribution chain. It puts the product into the hands of the consumer, or perhaps the retailer who serves the consumer. It is of enormous importance, bringing to fruition the activity commenced long ago when the production process started.

Each of these functions is dealt with in the short chapters which follow, and there are also other chapters dealing with related activities such as materials handling.

Suggested Further Reading

Management of the Physical Distribution Function, American Management Association, 1960.
Wentworth, F. R. L. (Ed.), *Physical Distribution Management*, Gower Press, 1970.

CHAPTER NINE

PHYSICAL DISTRIBUTION: PACKAGING, UNITISATION AND CONTAINERISATION

Introduction

No single aspect of physical distribution has had more effect on modern life than the change to pre-packaged commodities which lend themselves to self-service marketing by 'non-expert' retail staff. This is not to suggest that retail staff today are less knowledgeable than those of former generations, but their skills are marketing skills rather than merchandising skills. A supermarket manager is not an expert grocer, knowledgeable about produce, but an expert in shop organisation, display and stock turnover.

This revolution began with the packaging of produce, which is a developing technique in its own right, and proceeded by unitisation (the conversion of many small packets into a single unit lift) to containerisation. We must examine these three types of activity in detail.

Packaging

Most manufactured articles require some form of packaging. The word 'container' was formerly used for these specialised packages, but it has now come to mean a standard-sized unit for major transport activities. To save confusion we will use the word 'carton' to describe the individual package in which such articles as motor vehicle components, household articles, etc., are sold.

The carton serves three purposes. It *contains* the object, altering its shape to a convenient packaging shape, a cube or cuboid. Internal packaging, either of corrugated cardboard or moulded polystyrene, assists in this modification of the real shape of the packaged object, and plays a large part in the second function of packaging, to *protect* the object packaged. This protection is against breakage, distortion and contamination. Finally the carton is a vehicle for the marketing organisation, which uses it for advertisement and *communication*, enabling the packaged article to be identified, and to appeal to the customer, while instructions and information can also be printed appropriately.

With many cartons the product has no intrinsic shape—beef suet, for example. These products are packaged in cartons designed to hold an appropriate quantity. The package is easily handled and stored, the product is free from contamination, the cube size is the minimum necessary—thus saving on transport costs—and pilfering is easily observed (one packet missing from an array leaves an obvious gap).

The packaging proceeds to a further level by the use of cardboard cartons which aggregate the small packs into a unit load of standard proportions. Many considerations enter into the use of cardboard boxes, and a packaging policy must be devised to take account of them. For example, protection should not be greater than is really necessary, since it requires thicker board and adds weight to the consignment. Strength may be necessary if boxes are to be piled one upon another, shrink wrapping may be appropriate to protect goods from moisture, insects and atmospheric pollution, and opaque wrapping which hides what is inside reduces pilfering.

Some major considerations in formulating a packaging policy include:

(*a*) The nature of the goods; their fragility, their dangerous nature, their susceptibility to damp or other contamination, their pilferability and perishability.

(*b*) The nature and duration of the transit, the mode to be employed and the constraints imposed as a consequence.

(*c*) The value of the goods, and the relation between value and packaging cost. Clearly we cannot afford expensive packaging of very cheap goods.

(*d*) Statutory or other regulations relating to the transit of particular goods, or to their inspection en route for customs, insurance or other reasons.

Even when packaging has been designed to suit the product and its proposed journey, it does not follow that the load is convenient to handle. Traditional movements by road, rail and sea tended to be movements of a haphazard collection of packets, crates and loose objects. Such goods cannot be handled cheaply or easily; they must be dealt with in a non-specialist way using small-scale methods. The docker with his hook for bagged goods and for easing crates on to hand barrows is a non-specialist, low-productivity jack-of-all-trades. Only in recent years has the professional approach of the physical distribution manager begun to improve handling activities. The first step in any such analysis is the unitisation of cargo.

The Unit Load Concept

The concept of the unit load is that a collection of items is moved as a single unit. Thus if fifty tins of baked beans are put into a cardboard carton that is a small unit load. If twenty such cardboard cartons are put on a pallet in five rows of four cartons each, the forklift truck which lifts them as a unit load is lifting 1,000 tins. If twenty pallet loads are deposited in a container the gantry crane which lifts it on to a rail wagon is lifting 20,000 tins as a unit load. This will be a very economical lifting operation.

Unit loads may be of the following types:

(*a*) *Work Boxes*. This type of unit load is suitable for handling small components, such as metal castings, angle joints, bolts, washers, etc. Metal or plastic boxes designed to stack easily can be moved manually, or on conveyors or by forklift trucks.

(*b*) *Cardboard Cartons*. These are a protective packaging unit which can be stored on pallets or racks. If the contents have intrinsic strength, i.e. canned goods, light cardboard cartons will be enough. Stronger cartons will be needed for contents which might crush in transit.

(*c*) *Sacks*. Sacks are made in a variety of materials: paper, jute and plastic being the commonest types. When properly filled and dry, paper sacks have considerable strength and can be easily piled one upon the other. They will not stand excessive amounts of handling in transit, but otherwise are cheap and appropriate for many goods such as cement, animal feedstuffs, fertilisers, etc. Designed to hold a designated quantity of product, they are easily tallied by storekeepers at both ends of a journey, and unlike some bulk powder transport do not suffer losses due to blowing away.

(*d*) *Stillages*. A stillage is a base-plate, usually of wood, with bearers to give a clearance between the platform and the floor. The clearance enables the forks of a truck—most probably of the 'ground-clearance' only type—to enter below the stillage, raise it clear of the floor and re-position it where required. Stillages cannot be stacked one on top of the other.

(*e*) *Pallets*. The most versatile unit load system is the pallet, which is a wood or metal framework which can be picked up by a forklift truck or other mechanical device. Fig. 9.1 illustrates several different types of pallets. Two-way-entry pallets can be picked up from front and rear, a clear passage for the forks of the truck being left between the bearers. Four-way-entry pallets, instead of bearers, merely have short blocks of wood to separate the top and bottom decks of the pallet, so that whatever angle the forklift truck approaches the pallet it can secure a sound lift from all four sides. There is also an eight-way pallet which can be lifted from all four sides and from all four diagonals. This is sometimes a convenience in restricted areas—for example, in container stuffing—but the extra expense hardly makes them worthwhile for most firms.

The component parts of a pallet, as illustrated in Fig. 9.1, are thus as follows:

(*a*) A top deck, on which the load rests.

(*b*) Three bearers, usually of 3×2 in. wood, or smaller metal strips, which in the case of two-way pallets run the full length of the pallet, but with four-way pallets are reduced to nine mere cubes of wood to permit entry from all sides.

(*c*) Stringers, which are horizontal members to join up the cubes of wood in four-way and eight-way pallets.

(*d*) A lower deck (not always included). It gives extra strength and also is useful in stacking, since the lower deck spreads the weight of the goods above over the full area of the goods below. This lower deck is, however, an inconvenience when the pallet truck (as distinct from the forklift truck) is being used, since these ground-clearance only trucks carry the weight of the pallet on 'load-wheels' which have to be introduced between the upper and lower decks, and positioned on the floor on the far side.

There are many other types of pallet which have their particular uses. A brief mention of each is desirable.

(i) *Wing pallets*. These have the decks extending out beyond the bearers to facilitate the use of spreader bar slings for crane hoisting.

(ii) *Skeleton pallets*. These have slatted decks for cheapness, where goods are lightweight.

(iii) *Stevedores' pallets*. These are very strongly built, reinforced with steel, and with steel lifting-eyes for use with slings in crane lifting.

(iv) *Expendable pallets*. Pallets are expensive, and securing their return is a great problem. Expendable pallets are used for goods which are travelling a long way, and where the return of the pallet is unlikely. They are as cheap as the activity they are to perform will permit and the recipient puts them to any use he can.

(v) *Post pallets*. Post pallets are pallets used for carrying fragile, awkwardly

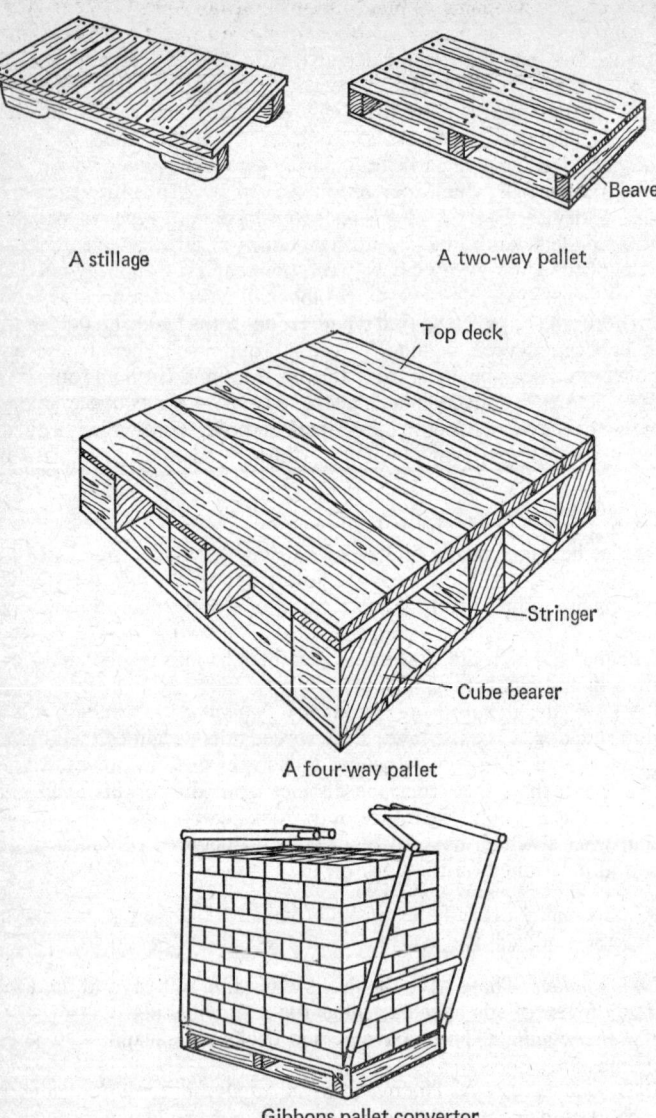

A stillage

A two-way pallet

Beaver

Top deck

Stringer

Cube bearer

A four-way pallet

Gibbons pallet convertor

Fig. 9.1. Some typical pallets
(courtesy of Gibbons Bros. and Gush and Dent Ltd.)

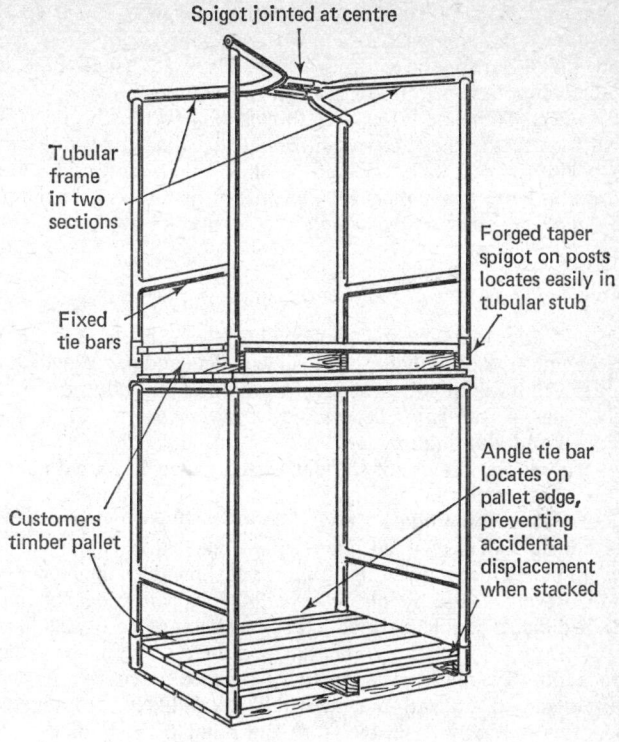

Spigot jointed at centre

Tubular frame in two sections

Fixed tie bars

Customers timber pallet

Forged taper spigot on posts locates easily in tubular stub

Angle tie bar locates on pallet edge, preventing accidental displacement when stacked

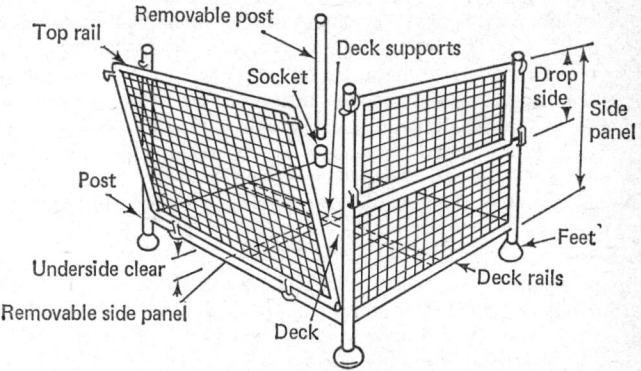

Top rail

Removable post

Socket

Deck supports

Drop side

Side panel

Post

Underside clear

Removable side panel

Deck

Feet

Deck rails

(top) Gibbons pallet convertor
(bottom) Gush and Dent collapsible pallet

shaped or crushable items which for economy reasons need to be stacked. The posts provide a solid framework to support the pallet above. The posts usually have feet to locate on the pallet post below them, and thus form a solid, rigid stack. Similar devices, called convertors, can be removed from the pallets and folded flat for the return journey. These are usually patented by the firm which supplies them (see Fig. 9.1).

(vi) *Box pallets.* These are boxes with three sides or a fourth side which can be dropped for access. They are useful for safeguarding small objects which would otherwise fall out, or be pilfered perhaps. Wire netting sides are quite common, while many box pallets have drop bottoms to enable them to be used in production processes releasing the contents as free-flowing materials or parts.

Other interesting aspects of pallets are as follows:

(i) *Materials.* Most pallets are wooden, but steel pallets and aluminium pallets are common, especially for collapsible pallets and pallets which have a very long life. Aluminium pallets are rustproof and light, but more expensive than steel pallets. A wooden pallet will cost between £1 and £3, with higher prices for steel and aluminium.

(ii) *Standardisation.* The use of standard-sized pallets has great advantages in many ways, especially if racking, vehicles, cartons and even warehouses were designed to accommodate them. The 40×48 in. pallet is popularly suggested, but no firm agreement has yet been reached.

(iii) *Pallet Pools.* Once a pallet has been made, how does the owner compel its return or prevent its use by 'pirate' organisations who use it for their own ends? It is a difficult problem which led some time ago to suggestions for a national pallet pool. Regrettably, this has presented some major difficulties, but where a number of firms agree to co-operate and use one another's pallets, an increased utilisation rate would seem likely. Any increase in utilisation rates is highly desirable from the point of view of the physical distribution industry.

(*f*) *Pallet-less Unit Loads.* The latest development in unit loading is the pallet-less unit load. This is achieved by special machines called 'load formers' which form unit loads automatically on the pallet principle but without the use of pallets. Layers of the desired pattern are formed either automatically or manually on a marshalling table, and are then moved on to a stripper apron from which they can be picked up by a lift section of the machine. This receives successive layers without the use of any pallet. A clamp-lift truck can collect as many layers as it requires from the stack using its squeeze clamps.

Containerisation—Intermodal Transport

Although containers were first used as long ago as the 1920s, the container revolution may be said to have started in April, 1963, when the first 'Sea Land' service opened from Puerto Rico to Baltimore, U.S.A. Two ships, the *Mobile* and the *New Orleans*, operated this service so successfully that Sea Land began construction of the first container terminal at Baltimore. Since then the use of containers has increased enormously, and the variety now available to freight forwarders demonstrates their versatility and popularity. Their use has had repercussions on the designs of ships, on the operation of the ports, on rail and road haulage and on warehousing. It has necessitated new attitudes on the part of both management and labour. It has led to the development of integrated transport systems offering depot-to-depot (or door-to-door) services on world-wide routes for both refrigerated and general cargo.

The revolution was essentially the provision of a door-to-door service from the point of inland origin to the point of inland distribution at destination, utilising more than one mode of transport, without having to break bulk. It is the *intermodal* nature of the transit that is so important. Instead of traffic meeting delays at every interface, where rail or road reaches the sea, or where the sea transit again changes back to inland transport at the port of destination, the containers move easily off one unit of transport and on to another. The port ceases to be a bottleneck, and becomes a smooth linking mechanism between the different modes of transport.

The enthusiasts for container transport confidently predict that eventually 80 per cent of all traffic will be containerised. Estimates of 50 per cent by the mid-seventies seem likely to be fulfilled, while at the time of writing the change to containers is so rapid that container manufacturers are finding it difficult to meet all needs. The initial stage of containerisation, from 1963 to 1970, was a period of trial and error with individuals experimenting with the new system and eventual international agreement on a standard range of sizes. The second leg of the race to containerise was run between 1971 and 1975, with approximately 100,000 containers in circulation in Britain alone by the end of that period. What exactly is a container, and what are its advantages?

What is a Container?

A container is a steel-framed box, with a strong floor and panelled sides, end and roof. The doors at the open end can be secured and sealed giving good protection against pilferage. The steel frame must be strong enough to support other containers stacked above it, since in some ships they are stacked seven high. The I.S.O. (International Standards Organisation) containers have hollow castings at each corner with holes which engage with special T-headed twist locks on vehicles, whether lorries or rail freight wagons. These twist locks can be turned through 90° to clamp the container securely to the vehicle. They can also be used to clamp adjacent containers together for added security. The same hollow castings on the top of the container engage with lifting platforms lowered on to the container by container cranes and straddle carriers, so that the container can be lifted cleanly by all four corners at once to transfer it from road vehicle to rail, or from ship to shore and vice versa. The bottom frame also has hollow sections in the sides of the framework, which permit giant forklift trucks to operate, lifting it on to road and rail vehicles. Fig. 9.2. illustrates these features.

The side, end and roof panels may be made of a variety of materials. Stainless steel is best, being rustproof and strong, but it is more expensive than aluminium, plastic or plywood. All these are more vulnerable than steel to damage or deliberate attack by thieves. Whatever the material, panels should be smooth rather than corrugated, thus facilitating their use for promotional advertisements. In some containers where full access to side-loading is desired, side panels can be demountable, slotting into position after loading to give weather protection and to restrain the load for greater security. The floor must be strong enough to take the weight of a fully loaded forklift truck. Many

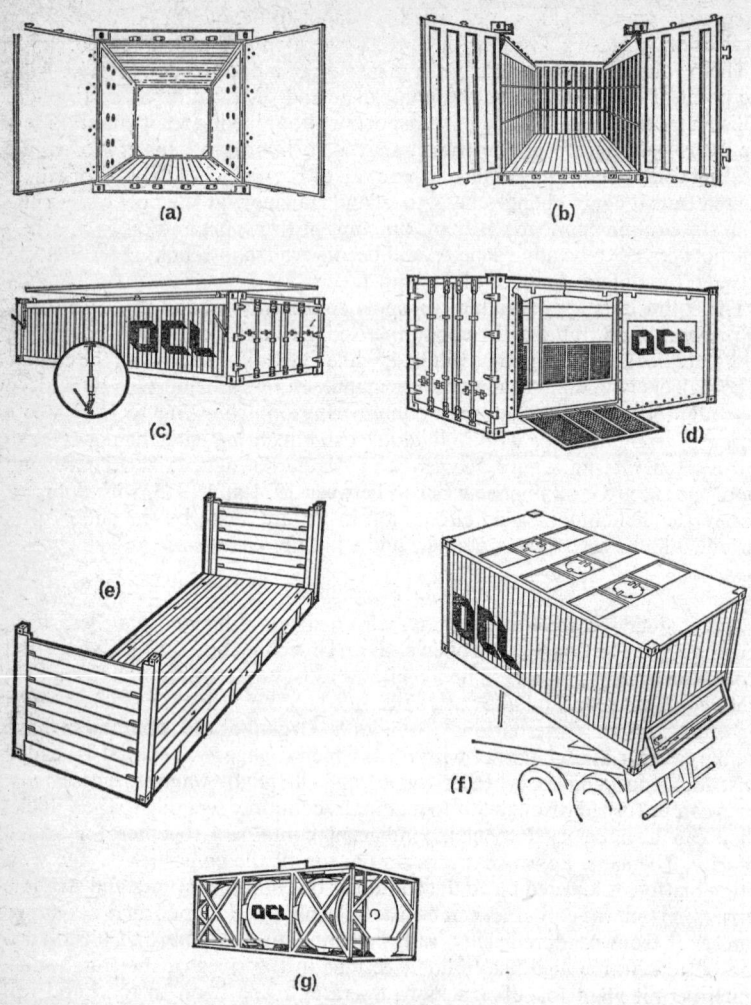

Fig. 9.2. Types of container in common use: (a) 20-ft. general cargo container showing position of fixing points; (b) 20-ft. top-loading container showing header bar removed; (c) half-height container with solid removable top; (d) open-sided containers; (e) 20-ft. flat-rack container; (f) dry bulk container on a tipping trailer; (g) a tank container.

(courtesy of Overseas Containers Ltd.)

types of specialised fitting to suit the requirements of regular consignors are offered by the manufacturers, but of course their installation inhibits the use of the container for other traffic and makes it specific to the class of goods for which it has been designed.

I.S.O. Containers

The standard size of I.S.O. containers is 8 × 8 ft. cross-section, though there are half-size containers for heavy goods. These are 8 × 4 ft. cross-section, and reduce the weight of, and space occupied by, a container carrying dense material—for example, steel rod or steel plate. Lengths are 10 ft., 20 ft., 30 ft. and 40 ft., but the 20-ft. size is the most popular. Besides having standard dimensions, the I.S.O. containers must be strong enough to be stacked four high fully laden, and meet stringent requirements about roof, wall and door strengths, and watertightness. Tare weight (the weight of the empty container) and maximum gross weight must be marked on the right-hand door and side walls. The owner's identification has to be marked on the front and on the roof, while on the sides a code indicates the type, size and country of origin. Exact details of I.S.O. requirements may be found in *Specifications for Freight Containers*, published by the British Standards Institution (see Further Reading List).

Types of Container

Apart from the I.S.O. standards for containers, manufacturers are free to supply whatever types of containers they like, with whatever fittings are most appropriate bearing in mind the need to keep the container versatile. From the standpoint of thickness of skin—an important factor for some cargoes—there are three main types:

(*a*) Thin-skinned containers of the general type already described. These give no real insulating effect as far as temperature is concerned, and merely protect against weather and pilfering.

(*b*) Insulated containers. These have no system of temperature control but are thick-skinned, having some sort of fibre glass or other material which reduces heat losses and heat gains, thus protecting cargoes which sweat, or dry out, or become frosted in cold conditions.

(*c*) Refrigerated containers, with or without an integral refrigeration plant. Some containers are connected to the ship's refrigerator system, or on land to small refrigeration clip-on units. Others are self-contained refrigerated containers, needing only a supply of electricity to operate. This may be supplied from the ship, or from a diesel generator in the container park. The refrigeration unit reduces the internal dimensions of the container, and may give rise to difficulties in restraining cargo.

The following other types of container are in use:

(i) *General cargo containers*. These have access through the end doors, with internal securing points at appropriate places.

(ii) *Top-loading containers*. These are for use with large, heavy or awkward cargoes. The roof, and the header bar above the door, can be removed to allow cargo to be swung in through the door opening as well as through the roof.

(iii) *Half-height containers*. These are for use with heavy, dense cargoes such as steel pipes and tubes. A full-height container stuffed with these dense materials would exceed the normal weight of a container.

(iv) *Open-sided containers*. Especially suited for hazardous cargo, this type of container is fitted with a fixed roof and there are open sides fitted with wire mesh.

(v) *Flat rack containers*. These are basic 'flats' with removable slatted boards at each end. They are used to assist the movement of heavy and awkward pieces of cargo. There are lashing points for strapping down the goods in transit.

(vi) *Dry bulk containers*. These are for the carriage of granular cargo and dry powders. There are three loading hatches and a discharge door at the front end, which is used to empty the container by tipping it on a tipping trailer.

(vii) *Tank containers*. These enclose a tank within a standard frame of similar dimensions to a standard container.

(viii) *Igloo containers*. These are specially designed to fit into the hulls of aircraft. They are not intermodal containers, but are designed for air transport operation only (see Plate 11).

These types of containers are illustrated in Fig. 9.2 (page 118).

The Advantages of Containers

These may be listed as follows:

(*a*) They consolidate cargo, bringing into a unit load what was previously a number of smaller packages or crates.

(*b*) This unitised cargo is handled more quickly and more easily, thus reducing loading and unloading time.

(*c*) A very important advantage is that usually much less packing is required —the cost of timber to make cases, and the labour involved can be very expensive. Less packing often makes possible the stowage of a greater quantity of actual goods as opposed to goods plus cases in the same space. It is important, however, to ensure that containers are carefully stowed, otherwise extensive damage can occur to lightly packed goods if excessive movement occurs within the container.

(*d*) The goods are carried more easily, since they are better restrained than loose cargo. Of course, container vehicles do turn over if driven round bends at excessive speeds, but the traditional problems of shifting loads are not met with in a well-stuffed container.

(*e*) The carriage itself is economic, since a fully loaded container represents an economic utilisation of that volume of cargo space, whether in a ship, or on a railway wagon or road haulage vehicle.

(*f*) Pilfering is reduced. The sneak thief cannot pick up and walk off with a container, as he can with loose cargo. Theft of containers is of necessity a large-scale operation, requiring conspiracy by a group of thieves. As conspiracy is more severely punished than mere theft, this is in itself a deterrent.

(*g*) Simpler documentation can be achieved. A given volume of cargo requires much less documentation, even if it is going to a large number of eventual consignees. The groupage firm which specialises in unitising cargo from a number of small consignors will prepare documentation for the container as a single unit. It then assumes the responsibility of de-stuffing the container at the far end of the journey so that individual items reach the ultimate consignee safely.

(*h*) Insurance costs are reduced, because of the reduction in pilfering. While insurance companies are not entirely happy that their rates for container traffic are realistic, recent trial periods have enabled them to adjust loss rates in the light of experience. The average container is worth about £7,500 fully loaded.

(*i*) Containers make through-transit the logical and economic way to forward cargo. We thus see the development of integrated door-to-door or depot-to-depot services by rail–sea–rail, rail–sea–road, road–air–road, etc. We also see the development of documentation devices such as T.I.R. carnets to speed goods through customs without examination.

Taken together, the points listed above present a formidable argument in favour of containerisation. Despite the problems inseparable from their use, the response of freight forwarding and shipping firms to their introduction is evidence that these advantages reduce costs and are reflected in cheaper freight rates. Let us now consider the problems involved.

Problems of Containerisation

Any new mode of transport brings its problems. These are of many kinds: technical, operational and financial. Some of the more important may be listed as follows:

(*a*) *Technical problems*. These have largely been solved in the ten or so years that have elapsed since containers began to be widely used. The chief technical problems, which involved international agreement on standard strengths and sizes, were solved by the I.S.O. agreements described above (see page 119). The responses of engineers and design staff to the needs of the freight-forwarding industry have been varied and interesting, yet new uses are being found every year for these versatile components. One shipping firm has now built containers into a permanent feature of the superstructure of its vessels, to give replaceable ship's galley facilities for each ship. The entire galley requirements for each voyage are collected into two refrigerated containers occupying a regular position on the deck of each vessel. On arrival in port the remaining supplies and all waste products are removed in the old containers, to be replaced by two new containers fully provisioned for the new voyage.

An important aspect of container operations is the need to design special ships, berths, container parks, handling facilities and vehicles. These have presented formidable technical and financial problems. Some of these units are dealt with more appropriately elsewhere in this book. Others are described on pages 123–5.

(*b*) *Operational problems* have been numerous and varied, particularly in the early days when containers were used on vehicles not specially designed for them. The overall problem is to provide an integrated system, based on standard I.S.O. containers, and maximising the advantages accruing to their use. Improvements in performance have been achieved with services such as the Seatrain land-bridge service from the United Kingdom and Europe to the United States East Coast, which goes over the land-bridge to the Pacific Coast of the U.S.A. by special unit train and catches container ships for Japan. This type of intermodal transport offers very considerable economies in operation to both European and Japanese shippers. Similarly, the opening up of the trans-Siberian routes has reduced the journey time from London to Japan by about three weeks—a very considerable saving.

While these types of integrated operation illustrate the economies of container transportation the capital costs of the facilities required are enormous, and many areas of the world must of necessity handle containers by less satisfactory methods. Typical problems concern the difficulties of unloading containers at ports which are without special cranes. The problem is best solved by putting the crane on the ship, making it independent of shore-based facilities. Such gantry cranes are of course very expensive; they are large and offer considerable wind resistance in passage, but they are of great service in many ports. The ship can actually be trimmed by positioning the gantry crane at the best point to assist the ship's stability.

Another operational problem faced by rail and road hauliers using non-specialised equipment is how to secure the container to vehicles not equipped with appropriate twist-lock devices. The essential features here are the friction between the container and the vehicle platform and the securing arrangements. Packing material (dunnage) between the container and the vehicle platform is usually undesirable since it reduces friction. Some containers, however, have the corner units raised proud of the main framework of the base. This reduces the friction very considerably and thin packing material fitted to increase the area of contact in these cases will increase the friction. Ropes are undesirable for securing containers; one-inch chain should be used with a safe working load of two tons. Two chains each side should be used to restrict forward movement and one each side to prevent rearward movement. This precaution ensures that when braking from high speeds the container will not move forward and crush the driver in his cab.

Getting back empty containers or getting as many as possible reloaded for the return journey is a major problem. Unfortunately world trade is not evenly balanced: containerised cargo from Europe may be used to pay for oil from the Middle East which is shipped in bulk. There is then no return cargo for the container, and it makes an uneconomic return journey. Skilled traffic organisation is required to minimise 'empty-leg' journeys, and the growth in specialist forwarding agencies and specialist transport companies reflects their greater ability to fill containers on return journeys.

Who Provides Containers?

One operational aspect is the actual provision of the containers. They are expensive to build, costing between £1,000 and £2,000 each. The most obvious providers are the carriers, who in the early years built the majority of containers, leasing them out to shippers and other consignors. Before a major breakthrough was made in convincing shippers of the practicality of the containers as a transport method, rates were very competitive. Container builders were forced to offer a wide variety of styles of container, and even to cater for special requirements. This was not a bad thing, since it finally convinced all sections of the freight market that this system was adaptable to their particular needs, but it was scarcely a profitable period.

In addition to leasing of containers by carriers, there are container leasing firms who are not transport operators. Even in 1970 one of these firms had

25,000 containers in operation, and a world-wide network of depots, agents, etc. In this system empty containers are returned to the nearest depot, and are then available for use on any shipping line's vessels on any route.

With the development of the specialist freight forwarder, particularly the groupage firms, the shippers began to provide their own containers, if only to bring the containers under their personal control. Later still, large manufacturers shipping regular consignments found it practical to have their own containers. These could then be specially adapted to suit their own products, or even designed and constructed for their personal use. Containers became analogous to, but more flexible than, the 'own-account' fleets (owner-operated vehicles), with promotional advertising on the sides and ends, and standard packaging and dispatch procedures. Special contractual relations with other firms, often at very cheap rates, for return loads, helped to reduce 'empty-leg' journeys.

Financial Aspects of Containerisation

The container revolution has required enormous capital expenditure by all branches of the distribution industry. The port authorities have had to provide special terminals, cranage and other facilities. Shipping firms have had to design new ships. The railways and road hauliers have had to develop new terminals and vehicles to handle the new mode of transportation, while at every stage modifications in procedure, documentation, communication, etc., have been required. The total capital expenditure must exceed the cost of any previous transport revolution, but of course the modern world is able to afford this capital cost more easily. Some idea of the costs borne by individual firms can be gathered from two examples: one firm in 1972 received delivery of its 20,000th container from a single supplier—a capital expenditure over ten years of £30 million on containers alone. Another international firm negotiated in early 1974 a credit of $60 million just to finance the leasing of containers to other users. This firm, by spring 1975, had 100,000 × 20 ft. equivalents, or £150 million of containers.

The high cost of port facilities in particular has required the establishment in many countries of strict control over development finance. In Britain— with over eighty major ports—the National Ports Council has been used to control the capital invested in container berths, which otherwise might have been too numerous and fractionated for real efficiency. Even so, the latest figures reveal that in seven years £130 million was spent on 148 specialised unit load berths, including 22 deep-sea gantry berths. For this expenditure the movement of 21·9 million tons of cargo was achieved in a single year over quays which averaged 1,107 tonnes per metre of quay per annum. This rate of berth utilisation was exceeded only by the Netherlands, which has but a small number of ports.

Special Facilities for Containerisation

(*a*) *Specialised ships.* These include cellular ships, roll-on roll-off ships and barge-carrying ships. They are described fully in a separate chapter (see pages 85–8).

(*b*) *Gantry cranes.* The essential feature of a gantry crane is that, having picked up its load, it can traverse with it to a suitable position for lowering the load on to another vehicle or vehicle route. Thus a container may be lifted from a road vehicle or railway wagon and traversed over the hold of the ship.

At the same time the gantry crane can move on its own tracks, under its own power, so as to line up with the precise 'slot' or 'cell' in the vessel. Here the container is lowered into the hold and secured. The gantry crane then picks up a container for off-loading from the ship, traverses with it back to the road vehicle or railway wagon and places it on the vehicle. If a vehicle is not being used it will off-load it on to the ground, where it will be collected by a straddle carrier. A container crane costs about £300,000 and can carry out a typical on–off loading cycle in about three minutes.

(*c*) *Scotch derricks.* Scotch derricks are heavy lift derricks with a very long jib, able to reach out and cover the holds of a ship to handle unit loads weighing as much as fifty tons. They are very useful in container operations, and commonly handle as much as 200,000 tons of cargo per year.

(*d*) *Forklift trucks.* Very heavy forklift trucks, capable of lifting a fully loaded container, are now available to load containers on to road and rail vehicles. The forklift engages with special apertures in the bottom frame of the container. The whole container can then be lifted to the required vehicle height and can be positioned on the vehicle. The forklift truck then backs away and the prongs disengage from the container. Special frames can be fitted over the forks to enable top-lifting where required. These are especially suitable for side-loaders, i.e. forklift trucks with the forks at the side instead of in front of the vehicle.

(*e*) *Container parks.* Traditionally quays have only needed to be big enough to enable road and rail vehicles to come alongside the ship to receive cargo. Container working requires much larger working areas, for the speed at which containers are landed is so great that other transport cannot be called forward fast enough. The protection formerly given by the transit shed is now provided by the containers themselves, which are parked upon open aprons surrounding the quay apron. Part of the modernisation of an existing port usually involves the provision of huge parking areas, where containers can be stored, marshalled and sorted. Customs inspection may also take place there, or at special inland clearance depots.

(*f*) *Inland Clearance Depots (I.C.D.s).* An Inland Clearance Depot is a depot approved by Customs where goods may be packed in containers and sealed, or on arrival from foreign ports may be opened, examined and cleared. The use of an I.C.D. ensures that the working of a ship is not delayed by the need for Customs' inspection of cargo. The sealed containers leaving the ship are transferred to the I.C.D., and sealed containers for export are received from the I.C.D. Approval depends upon certain requirements; convenient size to make the depot an economic Customs control point; non-discriminating behaviour so that the depot is available to all firms in an area and evidence of co-operation between commercial firms, port authorities and other interested parties. The concept of containerisation rests on the basic idea that goods should be containerised as close as possible to the point of origin, and de-containerised as close as possible to the point of destination. I.C.D.s situated within major conurbations achieve these ends more effectively than container bases elsewhere. They are usually open for 16 hours daily, on a double shift basis, and may offer a wide range of groupage facilities.

(*g*) *Groupage facilities.* Groupage is a system of container operations which groups together goods in such a way that maximum advantage is taken of containerisation. It can operate in several ways:

(i) A manufacturer shipping full container loads (F.C.L.s) to foreign countries can have these full container loads broken up at destination by the groupage firm, which then transports the part loads to the individual consignees.

(ii) A manufacturer shipping small quantities only, less than container loads (L.C.L.s), may hand them over to the groupage firm who will then containerise them with the goods of other firms, issuing a 'house bill of lading' as proof of shipment. The goods will be de-containerised by the groupage firm at the I.C.D. in the country of destination, and distributed by traditional methods to the ultimate consignees.

(iii) A consolidation of a multiplicity of cargo for a single consignee may be effected by the grouper in the exporting country. Thus a department store in Chicago buying European goods from countless European suppliers may have these goods grouped in London or Rotterdam for export to the U.S.A. as full container loads.

Groupage firms are able to take advantage of intermodal world-wide operations in great detail, using services such as the Manchester Liners 'Flying Fish' service. Air freight from Europe to Manchester is put upon the company's fast trans-Atlantic container ship service with continued air freighting across the American land mass if required. Similarly the use of the ice-free port of Halifax, Nova Scotia, as a link in the chain that joins the United Kingdom, Europe and the Mediterranean on one side of the Atlantic via the Canadian National Railway network and Vancouver, to Japan, Korea, Hong Kong, New Zealand and Australia is a typical world-wide example of intermodal initiative.

Conclusion About Unit Loads

There is no doubt that unitisation has revolutionised physical distribution over the last fifteen years, and made the whole distribution and forwarding industry aware of the economic advantages that accrue when many small lifts are converted to one big lift. In the fifteen years since trans-ocean containerisation began, the non-fuel container and roll-on roll-off traffic passing through United Kingdom ports has increased by about 20 million tons, while other non-fuel traffic has fallen by about 9 million tons. About 50 per cent of this unit load increase has been with Europe, so that the short-sea routes have become very important. The development of unitisation has brought a significant growth in the understanding of exporters and importers of the need to choose least-cost methods for the movement of their goods. The ingenuity of the physical distribution and transport industries in finding cost-saving solutions to their problems has been remarkable. It has been one of the greatest periods in transportation history.

Suggested Further Reading

Basic Economies of Containerisation and its Significance for Freight Transport, McKinsey & Co., Institute of Materials Handling, 1968.
Container and Roll-on Roll-off Port Statistics, National Ports Council, 1974.
Containerisation—the Key to Low Cost Transport, McKinsey & Co., The British Transport Docks Board, 1967.
Finlay, P. (Ed.), *Jane's Freight Containers*, S. Low, 1971–2.
Specifications for Freight Containers, B.S. 3951, British Standards Institution, 1967.
Wentworth, F. R. L. (Ed.), *Physical Distribution Management*, Gower Press, 1970.

CHAPTER TEN

PHYSICAL DISTRIBUTION: MATERIALS HANDLING

Introduction

The total distribution concept assumes that management will seek the cheapest and most efficient solutions to their physical distribution problems. It is therefore axiomatic that they should investigate rigorously all devices suggested or developed by design staff in the materials handling industry, so as to obtain the equipment most suitable for the handling of their products. The materials handling industry has shown enormous ingenuity in the last thirty years, and has provided many interesting and economic pieces of equipment. They come under five main headings, which may be listed as follows:

(*a*) Lift trucks
(*b*) Mobile cranes and lorry loaders
(*c*) Conveyors
(*d*) Holding aids
(*e*) Ancillary equipment

A full understanding of the range of facilities available cannot possibly be given in this book. Many firms specialise in the analysis of storage and distribution requirements, and will design and install layouts of complete warehousing and distribution systems. Without partiality towards any particular manufacturer's equipment they will seek the solution that gives maximum efficiency of operation, tailoring the systems to meet the needs of the firm they are serving. The great advantage of using the services of such specialist firms is that a team of experts has been built up with the necessary types of expertise, able to deal with the varied aspects of the work involved, from nuts and bolts assemblies to sophisticated computerised control engineering. They will invariably be members of the professional body, the Institute of Materials Handling, which exists to foster and encourage the fullest development of this important science, and holds regular exhibitions in pursuit of these aims. The reader is strongly advised to visit such an exhibition and see the equipment for himself. Here it is only possible to outline the chief types of equipment.

Lift Trucks

The handling of many small items individually is a tedious and time-wasting process. Wherever possible such cargo should be unitised. The effect of this process is to make one big lift of a number of little lifts. The problem then arises: can the warehouseman or stevedore lift them? The solution to the problem is the lift truck. Most lift trucks have forks to raise the load. Others use platforms or clamps. A brief description of the characteristics of a forklift truck is helpful at this point.

Characteristics of the Forklift Truck

In size the forklift truck may vary from the manually propelled truck, through the battery-driven truck with a lifting capacity of a few tons, to the very large, heavy duty vehicles powered by internal combustion engines and capable of lifting loaded containers weighing up to 30 tons.

The forked platform can be raised (*a*) to free the goods from the floor for transit and (*b*) to place them on shelves or vehicles.

Most trucks—the so-called counterbalanced trucks—can move with the forked platform raised to any height, provided that basic aspects of stability are borne in mind. The centre of gravity of the load must be kept within the

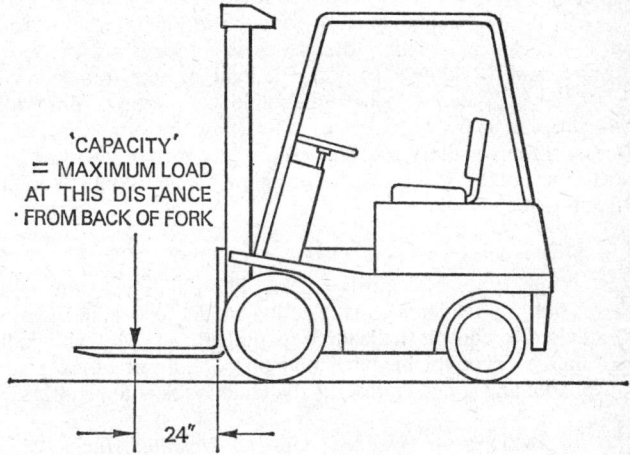

'CAPACITY' = MAXIMUM LOAD AT THIS DISTANCE FROM BACK OF FORK

24"

Fig. 10.1. The 'capacity' feature of a counterbalanced forklift truck.

(courtesy of Lansing-Bagnall Ltd.)

specified number of inches of the heels of the fork, i.e. a '2 tons 24 inches' truck will be stable with a load of 2 tons if the centre of gravity is within 24 inches of the heels of the truck. The higher the truck is to lift loads the more tilt-back there must be on the fork ramps, and the lifting of heavy loads is made more difficult. The capacity of the truck is illustrated in Fig. 10.1.

The small wheel base makes them very manoeuvrable.

If operating into and out of sheds or departments problems arise with (i) fumes, (ii) doors, (iii) draughts, (iv) door frames. These difficulties are explained below.

Trucks may be manually operated (i.e. you push it yourself), electrically operated by a battery-powered motor, or driven by an internal combustion engine, driven by either petrol, diesel or liquefied petroleum gas. Battery-driven trucks have the advantage that the battery is heavy and provides much of the counterbalance weight required to counterbalance the load. They take 8–12 hours to recharge, and thus are less economic for shift working unless a battery change is undertaken. Changing batteries is an inconvenient operation due to their weight, and it is usually preferable to plug them in for re-charging while still on the vehicle, at purpose-built re-charging stations. Where many vehicles are required spare vehicles may be provided to give an overlap while others are being recharged. Petrol engines give off poisonous carbon mon-oxide fumes and are therefore only suitable for outdoor use, in countries where petrol prices are low enough to make them economic. Diesel engines give off less toxic fumes than any other internal combustion engine, but when badly maintained they do give off very unpleasant fumes, the unpleasantness arising from unburnt hydrocarbons. Sheds where diesel lift trucks are used must therefore be well ventilated and trucks should be well maintained. Liquefied petroleum gas is conveniently bottled, and the exhaust from gas engines is less toxic than exhaust from petrol engines. More importantly, engine wear is re-duced and the servicing costs are therefore lower than for diesel engines.

When forklift trucks are used it is obvious that door frames must be flush with the floor; trucks cannot jump over steps. Also, loads are likely to catch on door frames and do damage to both the load and the framework of the building. If draughts are not to be unbearable some type of door must be devised which opens as the truck drives at it. These are often of overlapping rubber, but even then a safety problem arises. Any member of staff standing in the doorway is liable to be hit by a door giving way before a loaded truck entering from the other side.

Types of Forklift Truck

There are many types of forklift trucks. The chief types are described briefly below, but any reader who is selecting trucks for use in his own firm is strongly advised to consult the leading manufacturers, who will gladly give guidance in the best type for his particular purpose. Some of these are illus-trated in Fig. 10.2 and a description of the chief types is appropriate at this point.

(*a*) *Pallet trucks.* These are usually pedestrian-operated trucks, which roll under the pallet or stillage and raise it sufficiently to free the load from the floor. It can then be moved to a new warehouse position, but the load cannot be raised for stacking. These are essentially load-transporting trucks. Another type of pedestrian truck is the pedestrian high lift truck, which can raise loads as high as 10 ft.

(*b*) *Counterbalanced trucks.* The characteristics of these have already been described above. They are the types of truck most commonly seen by the ordinary public, for much of their work is done in the open air. They can lift, raise and stack palletised loads, and a variety of attachments (see Fig. 10.4) is available for specialised handling.

(*c*) *Narrow-aisle trucks* (*reach trucks and turret trucks*). Narrow-aisle trucks are either reach trucks, which can move the load forward of the truck to place it upon shelving either side of the aisle, or turret trucks, which travel over a guide-rail down very narrow aisles but have the facility to turn the turret head to left or right to place pallets on racking. Special models can reach as high as 68 ft. which gives many rows of shelving in a warehouse, and consequent capital saving on warehouse space. The reach trucks may operate either by a scissors-like motion of the forklift pantograph, or by moving the whole mast-assembly forwards.

(*d*) *Side-loaders.* Side-loading forklift trucks are used for picking up long

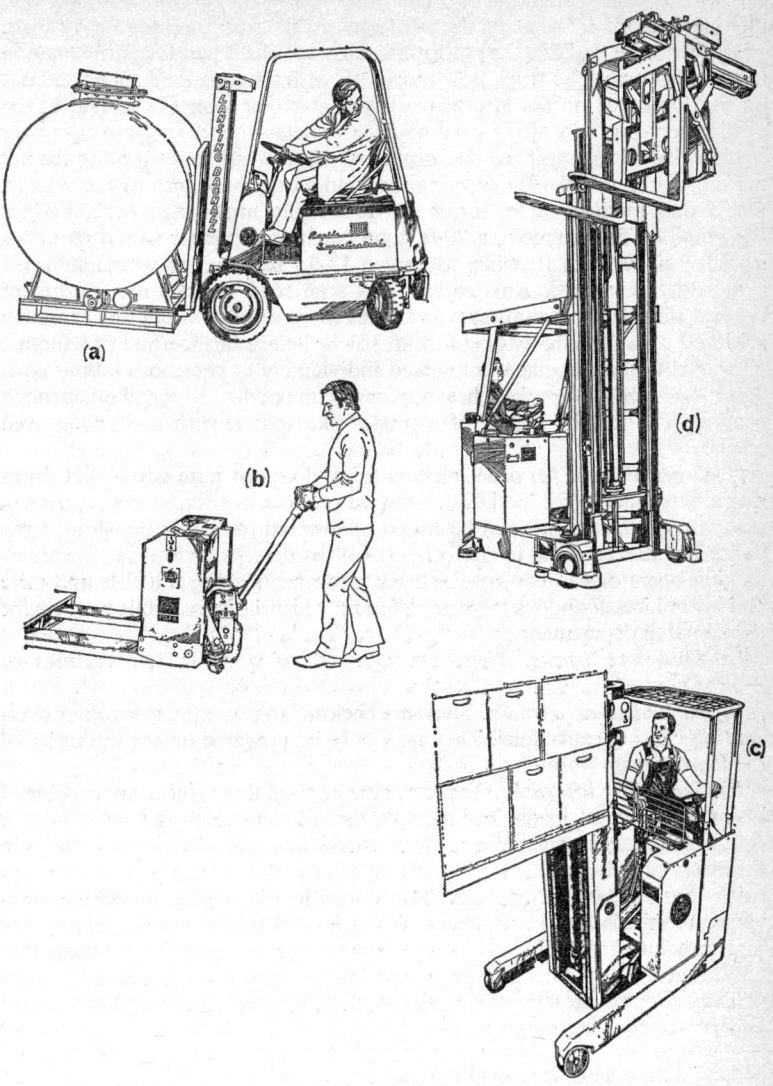

Fig. 10.2. Types of lift truck: (a) a counterbalanced battery-driven truck; (b) a pallet truck; (c) a narrow aisle reach truck; (d) a turret truck.

(courtesy of Lansing-Bagnall Ltd.)

loads such as packaged timber or containers. The forks are positioned at the side of the vehicle, between two solid platforms. They have a reach-action, moving forward in front of the platforms to pick up the long heavy load. They then raise it above the platforms, retract inwards and lower the load on to the platforms. The truck now moves off with the long load supported not on the forks but on the strong platforms at either side. On arrival at the destination—say, a waiting road haulage vehicle—the forks again take over the load by raising it off the platforms, move it out and lower it on to the flat surface of the vehicle. By carrying the load along the length of the vehicle, rather than at right angles across the front forks, much narrower gangways are possible. For example, a 20-ft. long package of timber would require a gangway at least 25 ft. wide, whereas a 12–15 ft. gangway would suffice if side-loaders are used. Anyone who has seen road vehicles moving timber stacked three high, two abreast and three long, will appreciate the economy achieved with the side-loading forklift truck. Before this method of handling packaged timber, planks were moved individually at enormous labour cost.

(e) *Rough-ground trucks*. These are for use on building sites and other rough ground. The forklift is part of a tractor-like vehicle with large wide-tyred wheels.

(f) *Order pickers*. An order-picking truck does not raise goods, but raises stores personnel to the level of the stacked produce in a warehouse. A control platform on the forklift can be raised or lowered to enable the storekeeper to reach and select items from storage to fulfil orders for customers. The order-picking operator can control the truck movements along the aisle and raise and lower himself and his trays or pallets on which he is assembling orders for the dispatch department.

(g) *Cold-store trucks*. These are adapted to work in temperatures of $-30°$ C.

(h) *Hazardous-area trucks*. These are enclosed to prevent any spark or over-heating causing explosions. They may only be prepared on the authority of the factory inspectorate.

(i) *Heavy-duty lift trucks*. As their name implies, these trucks are capable of lifting the heaviest loads. The most celebrated name here is Lancer Boss, a firm which makes a complete range of trucks but is particularly successful in the heavy lift truck field. Their latest model, the world's biggest ever front-lift truck, has 130,000 lb. capacity. For duties in steelworks, foundries, ship-yards, terminals and ports, the K130/48 has 20 tons more lifting capacity than previous trucks in the range. Features include a braking system that automatically applies the inner service brakes during a full-lock turn, independent fork positioning, hydraulic sideshift, a six-cylinder diesel power unit and powershift transmission.

Special Attachments for Forklift Trucks

There are a number of attachments which enable a forklift truck to deal with loads which would otherwise be inconvenient. Some of these are illustrated in Fig. 10.4. The commonest attachments are:

(a) *Drum tines*. This attachment slips over the forks and replaces them by three drum tines. The drums, which must have been stacked horizontally, settle between the tines.

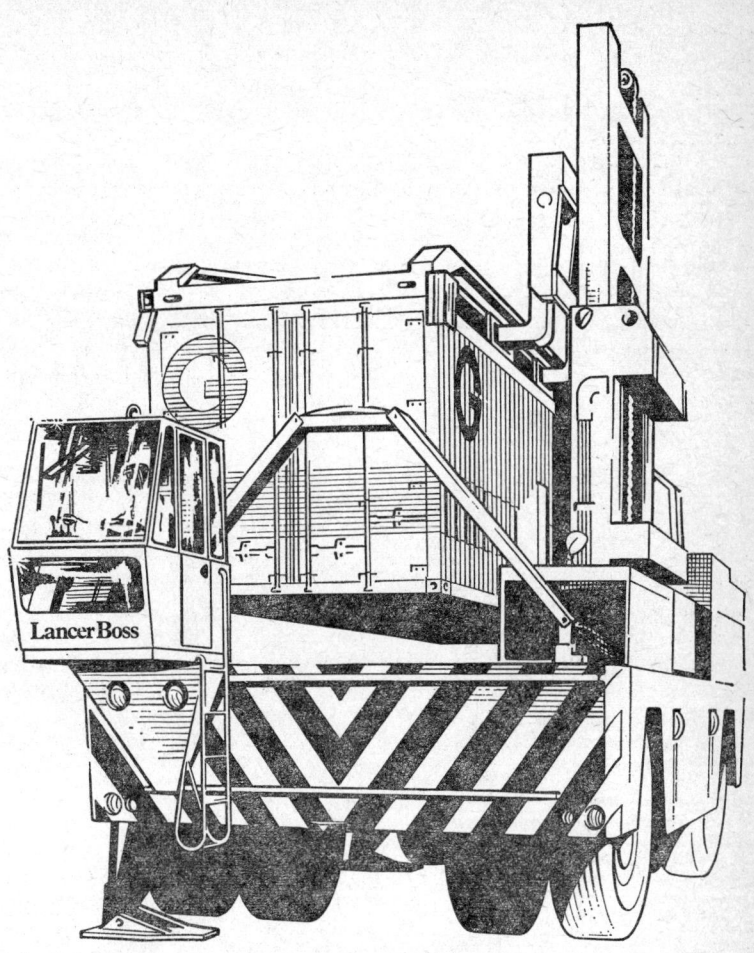

Fig. 10.3. A heavy-duty side-loader.

(courtesy of Lancer Boss Ltd.

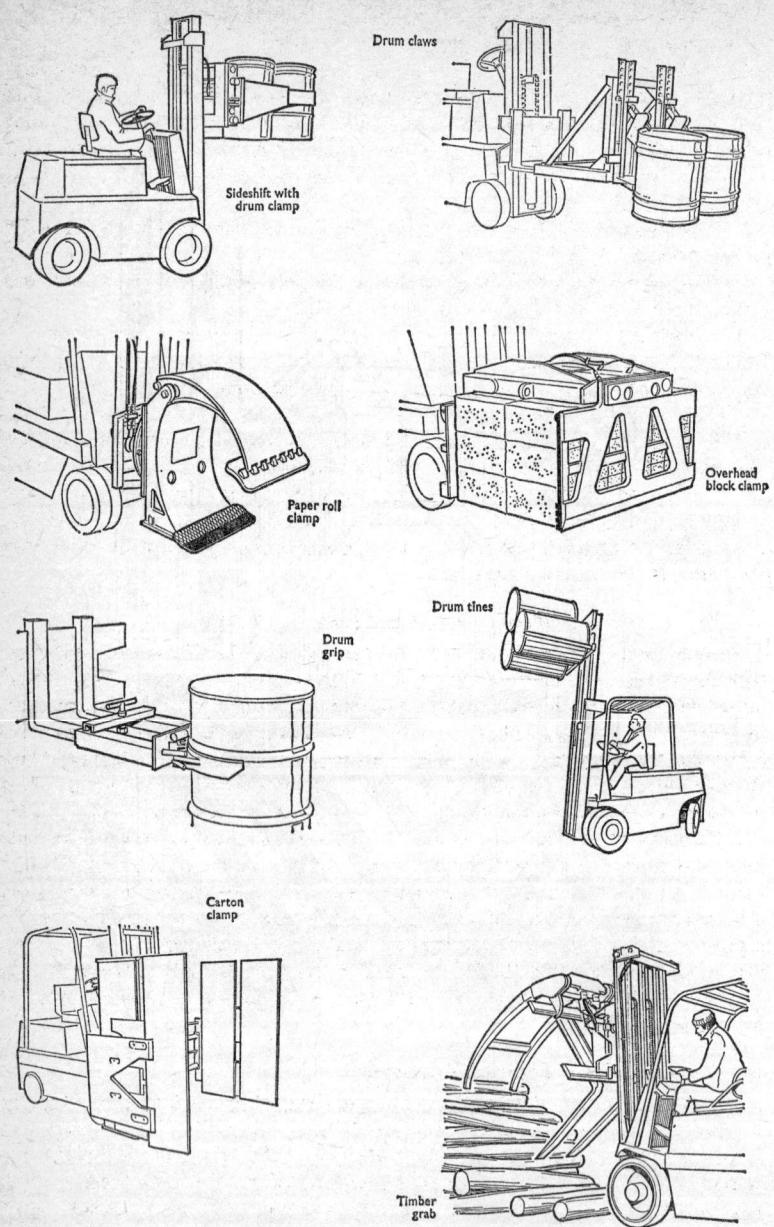

Fig. 10.4. Special attachments for forklift trucks.
(courtesy of Lansing-Bagnall Ltd.)

(*b*) *Drum claws.* These are used for drums stacked vertically.

(*c*) *Drum grips* are also used for vertical drums.

(*d*) *Side clamps* are used for picking up baled cotton, cartons, drums, etc., the particular type of clamp being designed to suit the object to be lifted. Side clamps do not need pallets, since the object itself is picked up, and hence recently developed methods of pallet-less lifting use this kind of attachment.

(*e*) *Timber grabs* are able to embrace logs and lift them with an arm-encircling action.

(*f*) *Overhead block clamps* fit down over the top of a stack of blocks and embrace them firmly from above.

(*g*) *Paper roll clamps* similarly embrace the roll of paper from above and are contoured to give a good grip on the roll.

(*h*) *Crane attachments.* These give a gallows-like structure which enables the forklift truck to pick up members hung on the gallows by a hook. It is convenient for lifting heavy members of constructional platforms, etc.

Attachments are a mixed blessing. They tend to be more specific in their use than the forklift, and consequently reduce the truck's versatility. On the other hand, a firm which has a full-time use for a particular type of attachment can gain enormous benefits from a truck specially adapted to its needs. Once again the industry is keen to supply, and discuss the design of, special attachments for particular purposes.

Mobile Cranes and Lorry Loaders

Besides the wide variety of lifts made possible by the lift trucks, materials handling firms have need of cranes able to lift materials both on sites and in industrial premises. A wide range of mobile cranes is now available with an impressive range of mountings, reaches and attachments. Many of these are hydraulically operated, with fully slewing superstructures, mounted on vehicles ranging from small solid-tyred manoeuvrable platforms for in-plant use to four-wheel drive vehicles with broad tyres for site operations.

Perhaps the most useful of all are the lorry loaders, which render a vehicle independent of lifting capacity at either end of a transit. The HIAB lorry loaders reproduced in Plate 3 and Fig. 10.5 illustrate the reach, variety of attachment and neat stowage of this type of crane. A co-operative driver of such a vehicle will place site materials in convenient packs exactly where they are required on the site, thus eliminating much post-delivery movement. It is just as easy to deliver materials on a scaffold 10 ft. up as to leave them at ground level.

Pallet Loaders for Lorries and Containers

A pallet loader is a device which fits into channel tracks laid in the floor of lorries, containers or ordinary premises. Once a forklift truck or tailboard lifting device has placed a pallet on the tail of a vehicle it can be raised off the floor by the pallet loaders through the action of simple tommy bars. Once free of the floor, the load can be rolled forward to the head of the vehicle. It cannot crash the headboard because a safety device operates, nor can it over-run the tailboard on the return journey when unloading or de-stuffing the container. Each pair of pallet loaders can lift $1\frac{1}{2}$ tons, and is rustproof, rugged and portable for transfer from one vehicle to another. On reaching its final

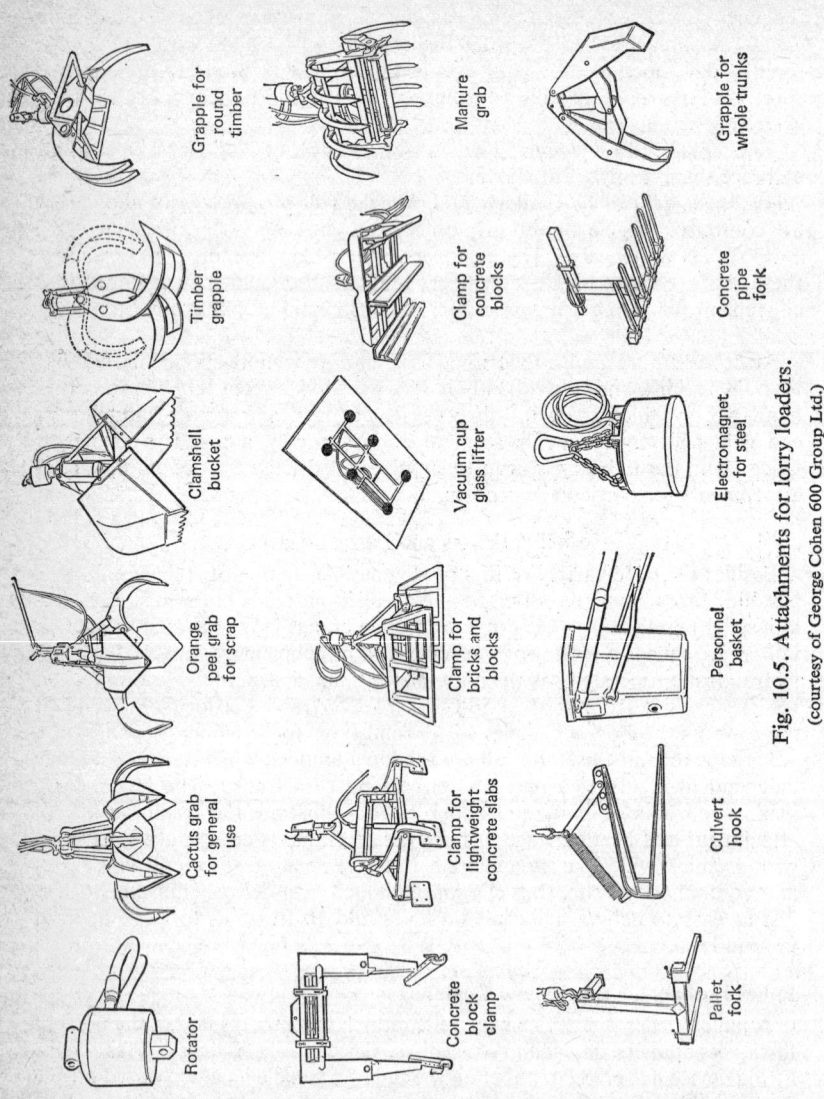

Fig. 10.5. Attachments for lorry loaders.
(courtesy of George Cohen 600 Group Ltd.)

Grapple for round timber

Manure grab

Grapple for whole trunks

Timber grapple

Clamp for concrete blocks

Concrete pipe fork

Clamshell bucket

Vacuum cup glass lifter

Electromagnet for steel

Orange peel grab for scrap

Clamp for bricks and blocks

Personnel basket

Cactus grab for general use

Clamp for lightweight concrete slabs

Culvert hook

Rotator

Concrete block clamp

Pallet fork

position the tommy bar is turned to the lowered position, leaving the pallet firmly positioned on the floor. The pallet loaders are now below floor level in their channel tracks and can be rolled back to pick up the next pallet.

Conveyors and Elevators

Conveyors are used for a wide variety of activities, from manufacturing projects to luggage conveyance at busy airports. The essential feature of a conveyor is that a product is moved from A to B either on a continuous belt or in a continuous tube impelled either by friction with the belt itself, or by the force of gravity or by compressed air. Conveyors frequently include some element of elevation to raise products to floors or levels where they are required. Some have lifts which automatically tip up at the top of their travel to tilt products on to a further conveyor.

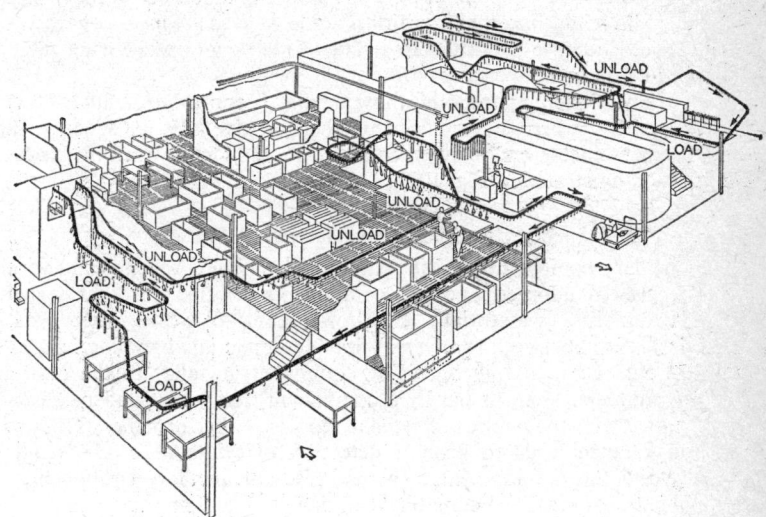

Fig. 10.6. An overhead conveyor system.
(courtesy of Finspa Engineering Co. Ltd.)

Conveying equipment has become very sophisticated with electronic and on-line computer control. Horizontal transporter units will bring up unit loads for order picking; transfer back-up stock to active stock; discharge empty pallets from the system; deliver documents to correct work stations and store; accumulate, rearrange and group carriers as desired. Many carriers will move horizontally, vertically up or down and across inclined planes. Many conveyors for granular materials and powders have bucket-type transit vessels which can be automatically tipped into hoppers or on to belt conveyors. Other conveying equipment uses gravity or powered rollers and tubs into which orders can be picked manually or automatically on the larger volume lines. Others have screw conveyors. Conveyors for food products may be of stainless steel and incorporate hose-proof motors and switchgear to facilitate cleaning. Fig. 10.6 shows a zig-zag overhead conveyor of a type used in manufacturing. It is made from standard parts which can be assembled into complete conveyors to customers' specifications.

A wide variety of *elevators* is available, both for integral installation in a conveyor system or as free units which can be moved into position to suit the materials handling situation and capable of handling a variety of goods, including boxes, packages, bags, cartons and bottle crates.

Holding Aids

Modern materials handling requires that warehouse shelving space shall be available as cheaply as possible, yet it must be strong and adaptable. There are many types of angle iron and interlocking racking which give adjustable storage, often in combination with pallets, tote trays, bins or containers, assembly benches, shelving, order-picking stepladders and elevators. Dense storage is possible in mechanised bins and drawers, mounted on roller bearings and with variable internal partitions. Some systems are mobile, gangways being reduced because hydraulically operated racks can open a gangway up at a speed of six inches per second.

The variety of racking and other holding aids is enormous, many of them boltless systems where parts click together to give strong, space-saving installations to customers' requirements. A typical system, which in this case is boltless, is illustrated in Fig. 10.7.

Ancillary Equipment for Materials Handling

The ancillary equipment used in materials handling is diverse, and varies with the system adopted and the components selected for that system. Materials handling is essentially a 'better mousetrap' world, where established firms, firms wishing to diversify into the materials handling field and countless engineers actually operating equipment are alert to the need to improve products. There is hardly a component that is not under constant consideration and the subject of regular reports on performance. This constant surveillance leads to prompt detection of faults, research into the difficulty and the development of a new piece of ancillary equipment, or optional extra or standard component in due course. Some of the available equipment is described in the following paragraphs.

Automatic Battery Chargers

Electric forklift trucks need fully charged batteries for each shift. They take 8–12 hours to charge up, and are discharged in about the same period. This constant charging and discharging is a great strain on any battery, but the strain can be reduced if the charging is carefully done. Automatic battery chargers allow the battery itself to dictate the rate of charge. The battery charge controllers automatically monitor the requirements of the battery, which when fully charged will not need to be immediately disconnected, but simply shuts down and is ready for use when required.

Tyre Protectors

Lift trucks and other mobile plant operating in industrial conditions are prone to high puncture rates. Tyre protectors are cord reinforced rubber interlays which fit between the outer casing and the tube. Any sharp object

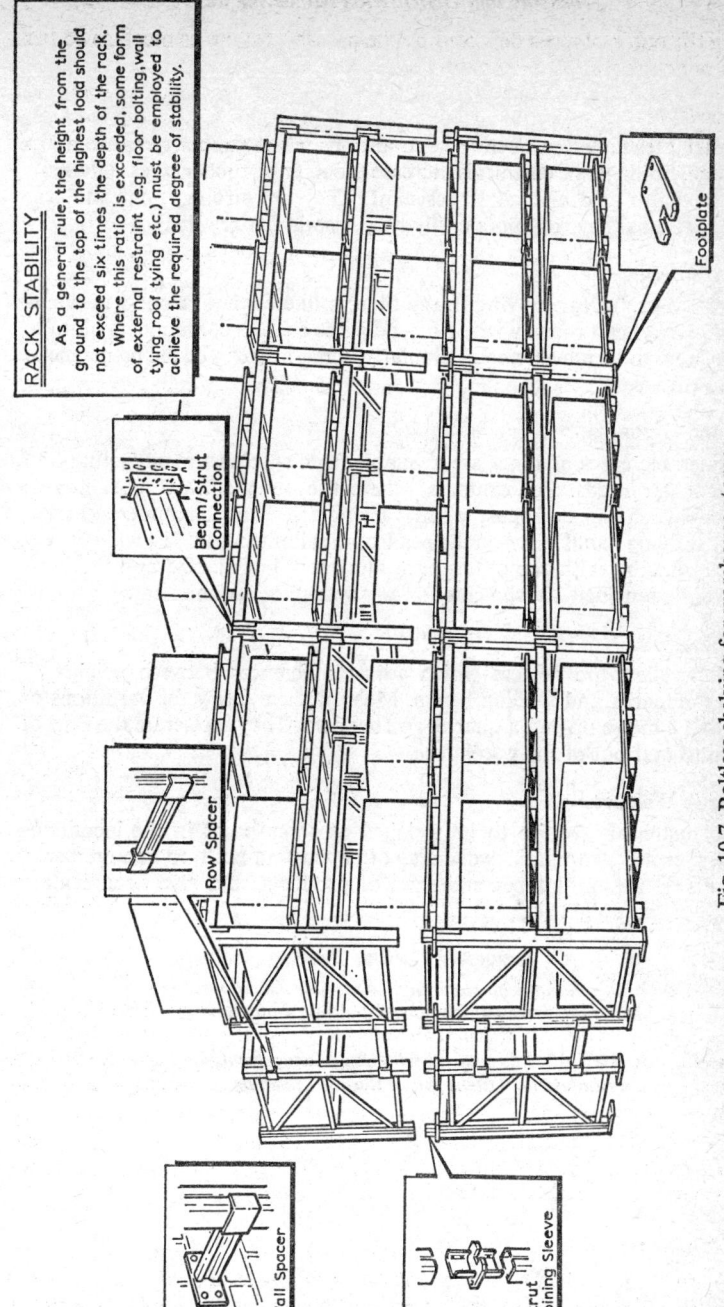

RACK STABILITY

As a general rule, the height from the ground to the top of the highest load should not exceed six times the depth of the rack.
Where this ratio is exceeded, some form of external restraint (e.g. floor bolting, wall tying, roof tying etc.) must be employed to achieve the required degree of stability.

Footplate

Beam/Strut Connection

Row Spacer

Wall Spacer

Strut Joining Sleeve

Fig. 10.7. Boltless shelving for warehouse storage.
(courtesy of Boltless Systems Link 51 Ltd.)

piercing the outer cover is deflected by the interlay, saving as much as 85 per cent of punctures.

Urethane Tyres

Industrial trucks often operate in conditions where rubber tyres are a disadvantage. Spillages of chemicals increase the wear of rubber tyres. Urethane tyres are dilute acid and alkali resistant. They are stronger, cut and tear resistant, and as they roll more easily they sustain battery life.

Runway Systems

These are useful for moving heavy objects like engines around in workshops. An overhead runway with lifting devices enables components of up to a ton or more to be moved about. Similarly, scrap iron can be fed by magnetic lifts into furnaces.

Slings and Grabs

Innumerable types of slings are available from specialist manufacturers to suit particular needs. For example, where the outer surface must not be damaged by chains or ropes; when varying sizes and circumferences are constantly being handled; when the headroom is limited, etc. The wide variety of grabs available with cranes has been illustrated in Fig. 10.5 and specialist firms will design such attachments for any system or requirement.

Dock Levellers

Dock levellers are devices which adjust differences between heights of vehicle tailboards and loading banks. Most of them allow for variations of about half a metre up and a quarter metre down. They accelerate the flow of goods into and out of the warehouse.

Automatic Weighers

Many materials require to be weighed at some point in the incoming–outgoing cycle. Automatic weighers, often custom-built to requirements, are available for most types and sizes of products, and give documentary evidence of the weight registered.

Suggested Further Reading

Magazines such as *Mechanical Handling*, *Materials Handling News* and *Storage Handling Distribution*, are available and should be studied as they appear.

Wentworth, F.R. L. (Ed.), *Physical Distribution Management*, Gower Press, 1970.
Williams, I., *Using Industrial Trucks for Materials Handling*, Hutchinson, 1974.

CHAPTER ELEVEN

PHYSICAL DISTRIBUTION: WAREHOUSING

The Function of the Warehouse

The warehouse exists chiefly as a storehouse where goods not currently required can be safely stored and cared for until required. It thus smoothes out fluctuations in supply and demand. These fluctuations may be influenced by natural events, political events, commercial practicalities, etc. For example, at times of political uncertainty a good deal of stockpiling of raw materials takes place in anticipation of possible interruptions of supply. Seasonal demand means that production must be stored until required. Batch production is often necessary to secure economic operations—perhaps a three-month supply of a particular component can be made in two weeks. The batch must be stored until required. Similarly, optimum order sizes often dictate a certain amount of storage of goods purchased at a cheap rate for a large quantity. Stockpiling against a possible interruption of production will ensure that sales can continue during the shutdown. We may therefore list the functions of the warehouse as follows:

(a) To store flows of materials which are not in phase with production.
(b) To store flows of finished products which are not immediately being demanded.
(c) To build up stocks against possible interruptions in production.
(d) To cater for seasonal demands, and seasonal supplies.
(e) To assist economic batch production.
(f) To assist economic purchasing.
(g) To promote displays to customers.

Warehouses exist at many points in the distribution flow. Some form assembly points in agricultural areas where produce is consolidated for shipment to distant markets. Others are located at factory premises where they receive finished goods for storage until distribution can be arranged. Unless journey distances are small to the final markets, manufacturers usually find the factory warehouse an inconvenient arrangement, and establish strategically placed depots to supply areas of the country.

This is too expensive for the small-scale manufacturer, who must rely on wholesalers to take his product and store, display and distribute it to retailers. The traditional pattern of three activities—manufacturing, wholesaling and retailing—has been considerably modified in recent years but is still commonly found operating alongside the direct selling by manufacturers and direct buying by multiple shops, chain stores, supermarkets, hypermarkets and consumer co-operatives. The wholesalers survive best in large countries where the depot system, if too widespread, places unbearable strains on managements of manufacturing enterprises, who therefore find that the specialist wholesaler still has a useful part to play.

As a general principle the rule 'first-in, first-out' applies to the storage of most items. To carry goods over time requires considerable skill; deterioration of some sort is almost inevitable. It is only prudent to remove and sell (or use) the item that has been in store longest. This rule is often called F.I.F.O. (first in, first out) as distinct from L.I.F.O. (last in, first out).

Warehouse Layout

For many years the typical warehouse was a single-storey structure of vast extent which enabled internal transport to operate horizontally at a single level. The multi-floor warehouse, with its need for expensive lifts or access ramps, strong construction and extra handling costs was deemed impracticable. In recent years the higher cost of sites and the development of specialist materials handling techniques has transformed warehouse design. By using standard turret trucks capable of reaching as high as 27 ft. and turning the load at right-angles to the direction of motion down the aisle, it is possible to stack up to seven racks high from a single ground floor. The actual racks can be used to strengthen the building and support the roof if necessary.

One constraint upon excessively high racking is the difficulty of order picking. Although order pickers are available which will raise staff to pick orders from high racking, the raising and lowering speed is slow compared with the movement horizontally. It is therefore better, if space is no object, to limit racking to about three racks high and have more order pickers at work.

In designing a warehouse it is necessary to conceive the whole storage function as a handling system for particular commodities: the use of standard pallets; loads of uniform heights; racks of correct strength for the type of load being handled; aisle widths which are adequate for the reach trucks or turret trucks being used; order-picking trucks to take men up to the height of the racks to select items required and computerised installations for the selection of the most popular items means that all these items are interdependent and part of a total warehousing concept. This concept seeks to ensure economy, system and security.

The warehouse is in many ways a terminal, where goods arrive and depart, but the interval between arrival and departure is a time of storage. While in storage the goods occupy non-selling space, and it may be possible to reduce this if design takes into account the need for customers to inspect merchandise. With many town centre sites space is at such a premium that shop display goods are not sold to customers, the order being fulfilled from storage stocks at some out-of-town depot. In others there is a shading-off between display and storage, some goods which are really in store being accessible to salesmen or even to persistent customers who are strong-minded enough to insist.

The layout of the warehouse must be such as to ensure location of any item that is in the warehouse when it is wanted. To this end we may have *fixed locations* for any item—perhaps in stock number order or alphabetical order. This fixed location system may be wasteful, in that it means the permanent provision of a certain fixed capacity of space for each item. At times when we have less than the normal stock, space is being wasted, while at times when for some reason we are carrying more than normal stock, space is inadequate. Some firms therefore adopt *random location* with goods being stored in the next available space. This is more economic in use of space but requires a check to be kept of location. Direct links to a computer facilitate this type of system. The computer is informed by electric keyboard of the arrival of goods.

It then feeds back a location tag giving the goods a three-part location number, the first part giving the floor level, the second an aisle letter and the third a bin number. The goods are then stored in that location. When required an enquiry to the computer will trace the stock in seconds and feed back its location number.

Automated Warehouses

In the last decade automated warehousing has made great strides, and the sceptical attitudes common when the idea was first proposed have been overcome. Specialist firms are now supplying complete and integrated services, from storage racks, stacking units and infeed systems to control equipment and programs to suit the needs of customers. The major cost savings are two: in the field of inventory control, so that capital tied up in stock is reduced; and in land use. One warehouse for a major motor manufacturer has racking 110 ft. high, at more than twenty levels, making a very economic use of space.

Horizontal transporters operate automatically at each level to store and retrieve unit loads. Pallets are often divided into two main sections, active stock and back-up stock. Active stock simply consists of a single pallet of each line in stock. This pallet will be called up to the order picker as required, until it is empty, when the empty pallet will be expelled from the system and a full pallet brought forward from the back-up stock to the active stock. Transporters can also marshall pallets in correct sequence.

Many retrieval systems operate in three dimensions and have a two-command facility, which instructs the retriever to store one pallet and retrieve another by the shortest route in a cycle. Safety devices to prevent incorrect positioning, misalignment of the load and free-fall protection for the vertical carriage are incorporated in the retrieval system.

Direct on-line control of the system by a computer gives largely automated order picking for high-user lines. This includes automatic keying to the computer of all goods on arrival. When demanded, the goods are retrieved and routed to a carousel or to a vertical closed-loop conveyor, where operators can select the number of items required for the order. One of the advantages the computer gives is in its choice of storage for particular lines. If a line is fast-moving it will be stored in a location close to the order picking point; slow movers will be routed to more remote locations.

Warehouse Equipment

Much has already been said in Chapter Ten about materials handling and the equipment used in modern distribution. Basically a warehouse requires racking of some sort to hold the goods; aisles between the racks in which lift trucks and order pickers can operate; the necessary trucks and order pickers; loose steps and ladders as required; and an internal transport of some sort. A few words about each of these is required:

(*a*) *Racking.* Racking may be of several types, and many manufacturers make similar equipment, so that evaluation of the types available is essential. The chief types of rack are *shelf racks*, *pigeon-hole racks*, *pallet racks* and *line storage racks*. Shelf racks are usually adjustable, and serviced by low steps or ladders. Pigeon-hole racks accommodate work-boxes of small parts or components, and are serviced by steps or small order-picking trucks incorporating different working levels and a main storage area where orders can be prepared. Pallet racks are skeleton frameworks serviced by turret trucks, and often as high as the building itself. Line storage consists of channelling with rollers to permit the movement of boxed or palletised materials, often under the influence of gravity.

(*b*) *Trucks and order pickers*. These have been fully described in Chapter Ten.

(*c*) *Steps and ladders*. Steps and ladders are likely to be the cause of accidents if they are not carefully designed. Strength and stability are vital; so is a good tread and, where possible, a container to receive the order being picked. Step-trucks are devices which not only provide steps for access to higher levels but also carry devices for the orders picked.

(*d*) *Internal transport systems*. A circulating transport system which incorporates clip-on trolleys or trucks and some sort of sensing device which follows automatically a magnetic guide laid in the floor is essential for large warehouses. Control panels on the truck can direct it to off-load the truck at certain destinations.

Suggested Further Reading

Foster, D. (Ed.), *The Automatic Warehouse*, Iliffe Books, 1970.

Kaylin, S. O., *Food Warehousing and Transportation*, Chain Store Publishing Corporation, 1968.

Wentworth, F. R. L. (Ed.), *Physical Distribution Management*, Gower Press, 1970.

Williams, I., *Using Industrial Tracks for Materials Handling*, Hutchinson, 1974.

CHAPTER TWELVE

PHYSICAL DISTRIBUTION: BULK TRANSPORT

Introduction

Containerisation apart, the increase in bulk transport is the most significant development in land and sea transport in the last twenty-five years. During the Second World War, American Class T.2 tankers of 16,500 dwt. were regarded as outsize giants. Today the 477,000-ton tanker is sailing and the million tonner is on the drawing boards. Oil is a natural choice for bulk physical distribution, but the significant advance is not only in the size of bulk carrier of the V.L.C.C. (very large crude carriers) type. The variety of products now carried in bulk is also important. At sea we have bulk carriers for oil, methane, ores, grain, chemicals and other specialised carriers. On land we have petroleum, liquid gases, powders, chemicals, milk and countless other products moved in bulk. What are the advantages of bulk transport?

The Advantages of Bulk Transport

Transport is peculiarly susceptible to the achievement of *economies of scale*; great benefits can be derived from large size. Although at very large sizes certain diseconomies do begin to creep in they do not arise until certain critical sizes have been reached. Thus the million-ton ship will face operating problems not faced by the 250,000 tonner and the 44-ton lorry is environmentally less acceptable than the 32 tonner. Below these critical sizes there are strong arguments for increasing the size of ships and vehicles to achieve economies of scale.

Obvious examples of operating economies are the capital cost per unit carried, the crewing costs per unit carried, and maintenance and servicing costs per unit carried. If we double the size of a V.L.C.C. we do not have to double the number of radar units or double the crew, or to service the ship twice as frequently. Most important of all, we do not have to double the amount of motive power and the quantity of fuel used. In road haulage, where for congestion reasons the number of possible journeys between depots is necessarily few in a day, it makes good sense to increase the size of the tanker and thus achieve a maximum advantage from each completed journey.

Other economies are in the safety and training fields. If we move products in bulk the number of transport units required is reduced; so are the chances of collisions or incidents at sea or on land. Many products moved in bulk are dangerous; such as petroleum, liquid gases, acids and alkalis. Not only will the number of incidents be reduced but the reduced number of personnel required can be specially trained to meet the increasingly stringent requirements of a pollution conscious world. Yet another economy is achieved in the administration field. The documentation for a large consignment is much less than for many small consignments, while it also becomes worthwhile to fit a large vehicle with sophisticated measuring equipment and other devices which promote administrative control.

Another major factor in the growth of bulk transport is the political stability of advanced nations compared with developing nations. In earlier times industrial complexes were built close to the sources of raw materials, and only the finished manufactured products were actually moved. This was clearly more economic than moving the crude material including all the impurities. This was certainly the case with the early iron industry. However, where political instability means that plants or oil refineries are likely to be expropriated—as in Iran and Indonesia in the years following the Second World War—it becomes more economic to move the raw material, however crude, and refine it in the advanced country. It is also true to say that the more intensive industrial exploitation of the crude reduced the waste to a very small proportion of the total crude.

Where ores are concerned, sometimes partial refining takes place to produce pellets of concentrate, which makes more economic use of the bulk carrier. Thus bulk carriage by sea tends to be of unrefined, untreated products, while bulk carriage on land by road or rail tends to consist of internal movements within a country of refined and processed products or semi-manufactured products on their way to factories where manufacture will be completed. Hard and fast lines cannot be drawn, however, and within a group of nations of similar development many bulk movements will occur as if only a single politically stable unit existed. Only the severest political stress is likely to interrupt such movements.

Bulk Transport by Sea

Bulk transport by sea has been the major development in maritime transport in the last quarter of a century. In one recent day Port Hedland, a previously little-known Australian port serving the grazing industry, loaded four bulk ore carriers with 417,213 tons of iron ore and pellets. The port had been developed during the 1960s to take ships up to 160,000 tons, at a cost of $A75 million. The ore carriers using the port are fed by ore trains from Mount Newman and Goldsworthy Mining. These ore trains are themselves one of the most spectacular examples of bulk rail haulage in the world.

Bulk carriers by sea tend to be specialised ships, owned by particular international companies or chartered to them for long periods. The chief types are V.L.C.C. vessels (very large crude carriers), O.B.O. (ore-bulk-oil) vessels, grain carriers, methane carriers and specialised carriers for such cargoes as caustic soda and bananas. The container ship is considered separately in this book.

All these ships incorporate special design features to suit their purposes. Oil tanks have extensive bulkheads to divide the ship into separate compartments which prevent surging of the liquid cargo as the ship rolls and pitches. Engines are at the rear of the vessel so that the propellor shaft is short and need not pass below the cargo as it would do with engines in the amidships position. Tankers suffer from the great disadvantage that crude oil is essentially a one-way traffic, and the tanker must spend much of its time in ballast. It is also specific to one product. The ore-bulk-oil ship is more versatile, though slightly more expensive to build. It has alternative uses so that it is more likely to be chartered at times when there is surplus tanker capacity available. On the other hand, most other bulk products tend to move from primary producing countries to advanced secondary producing countries so that the problem of the return load has not been entirely eliminated.

Bulk carriers now include a very wide range of ships that are not necessarily of enormous size. While the V.L.C.C. ranges up to 500,000 tons, many products benefit from shipping in rather smaller ships. Thus bulk carriage of refined petroleum products is very economical in 20,000 ton ships, and products such as solvents, agricultural products, fishmeal, caustic soda, etc., are often carried in mini-bulk carriers ranging from 2,000 to 26,000 dwt. Specialist ships are even in use today for carrying indivisible heavy loads, both on deck and below deck.

Bulk Haulage by Rail

Railways are particularly effective for bulk haulage. A fully loaded bulk haulage train manned by a crew of three is a very economic form of transport. We therefore find trainloads of tank wagons leaving oil refineries at regular intervals with motor spirit, and bulk ore trains delivering ore to ports for shipment. A thousand tons is easily moved in this way, compared with a maximum 44 tons by road haulage. Safety is much greater, speeds are higher, regularity of service to industrial customers is excellent and the cost is low per ton of product carried. The usual criticisms of railways, that there are delays in terminals, do not affect bulk movements which go from door to door in their service to major industrial customers.

The types of wagon available in a modern railway system are numerous, and designs are available for all sorts of traffic. Often these are built by the railway company to customers' specifications so that they are specific to the product concerned. Such tailor-made wagons can be purchased outright, leased over long periods or hired as and when required. The 'angle of repose' of the bulk commodity is vital if it is to be unloaded easily, and steep valley sides within the vehicle prevent materials sticking. Linings are designed to suit the product—for example, where corrosion is a possibility stainless steel, or coated steel, or aluminium may be used. Internal fittings can be supplied to prevent packages shifting, overall dimensions adjusted to suit palletised cargo exactly, heat shields can be provided for refrigerated cargo and fibre-glass coatings reduce heat losses or protect low-temperature cargoes. The list below gives some idea of the versatility of the transport engineers in designing specialised units of carriage. These include:

(*a*) Tank wagons for petroleum products, petrochemicals, carbon dioxide, ammonia, china clay slurry, cement powder, acids, alkalis, molasses, etc.

(*b*) Tipping ore wagons for iron ore, coke, coal, limestone, clay, aggregate, etc.

(*c*) Side-discharge vehicles for aggregates, wheat, fishmeal pellets, etc., with gravity loading and discharge.

(*d*) Side-loading vans for bagged and other products, such as fertilizer, cement, zinc blocks, palletised cargo, etc.

(*e*) Hopper wagons for salt, lime, wheat, aggregates, etc,

(*f*) Insulated and refrigerated vehicles for meat, frozen foods, ice-cream, etc.

Typical capacities of these units of carriage would be from 25 tonnes to 100 tonnes. Filling can be by gravity, pressure or forklift truck; emptying by bottom door, side door, pressure or forklift truck. Speeds of 60 m.p.h. are normal and transits are usually by special train or liner train with guaranteed delivery times so that factory schedules can be met.

Company Trains and Freightliner Services

The wide variety of rail wagons described above has created a large 'company train' traffic, rail freighting bulk requirements on a regular daily basis without terminal losses except loading and unloading at specialist terminals. The chief traffics are petroleum products, iron ore, limestone, cement, petrochemicals, chemicals and steel. The routing of such trains has been made simpler by the completion of the rapid transit Freightliner network.

The Freightliner concept is the use of high-capacity containers carried on high-speed wagons run as fixed-formation trains. They give fast, reliable services at low cost over medium and long distances. A network of lines links twenty-four terminals in all parts of the country, where containers are accumulated in trainloads, being transferred from road to rail or ship to rail by gantry cranes. This enables a national and international intermodal service to be offered to customers.

Freightliners Limited is a subsidiary of the National Freight Corporation and British Rail, who own 51 and 49 per cent respectively of its capital. The service runs 175 trains daily, over 75 routes and handles over 600,000 containers a year.

As shown in Fig. 12.1, the network includes twenty-four terminals and four port terminals. These are Holyhead, Parkeston Quay Harwich, Felixstowe and Tilbury. The largest cities have more than one Freightliner terminal. These are:

> London: Willesden, Kings Cross, Stratford, Barking
> Birmingham: Birmingham, Landore Street, Dudley
> Southampton: Millbrook, Maritime
> Manchester: Trafford Park, Longsight
> Glasgow: Gushetfaulds, Coatbridge

The advantages claimed for the Freightliner system are as follows:

(*a*) Fast transits and reliable scheduled deliveries enable stocks to be minimised, i.e. the amount of money tied up in distribution is minimised especially where intermediate warehousing can be reduced. This is clearly of great importance to those interested in physical distribution management.

(*b*) Complete container trains with high payloads running to fast schedules over medium and long distances give scope for competitive trunk haul charges to hauliers and traders and to shippers a rapid accumulation or dispersal capacity at container ports.

(*c*) Complete door-to-door prices over medium and long distances for the transport buyer who requires an overall service.

(*d*) Flexible charging policy based upon customers' requirements, designed to encourage a regular pattern of business, making possible high utilisation of equipment.

(*e*) The container offers a high degree of security against pilferage as well as freedom from damage associated with shunting and transshipping piece by piece in a depot shipping shed, or ship loading in a similar manner. Containers carry no labels and, therefore, their contents are known only by a few people.

(*f*) Freightliner containers are designed for easy loading and the majority are to world I.S.O. standards.

(*g*) The system is simple, as is the documentation, which is minimal.

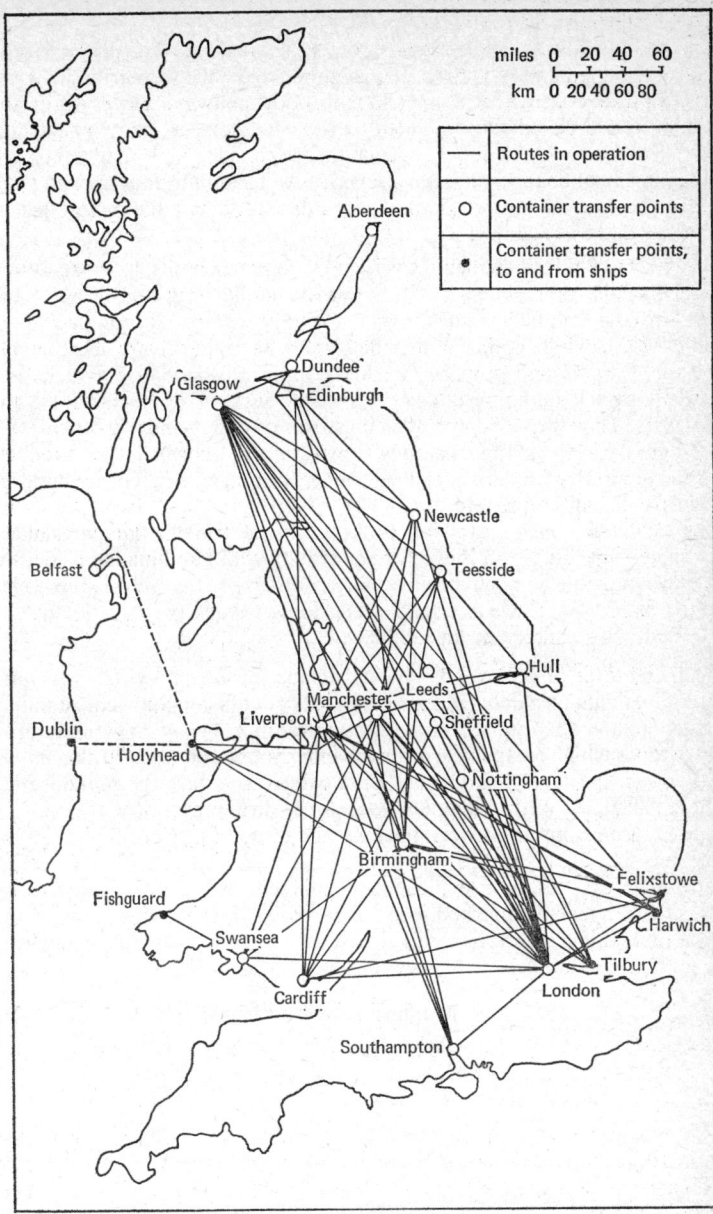

Fig. 12.1. The Freightliner network.

Bulk Haulage by Road

Bulk haulage by road gives some of the advantages accruing to bulk haulage generally as well as the usual road haulage advantages, i.e. personal control of the consignment and door-to-door delivery. Once again the responses of motor vehicle designers to the needs of customers and traffic have resulted in a wide variety of specialised vehicles for bulk road transport. The movement of containers is a special class of road bulk movements, dealt with elsewhere (see Chapter Nine). Apart from containers the main types of vehicles used are as follows:

(*a*) *Tankers* carrying petroleum spirit and hydrocarbon oils, latex, acids and other chemicals, beer, wine, spirits, molasses, milk, eggs and other liquid foodstuffs. Powders such as flour, sugar, fertilisers, cement, lime and sand are major cargoes, while grains and pellets such as fishmeal are increasingly important. Liquids and powders are loaded and off-loaded by a variety of methods. Gravity, pumping under pressure or sucking by vacuum are the chief means. They move easily under pressures of about one atmosphere.

(*b*) *Flats* (vehicles or trailers simply providing a flat base). The commonest goods moved in this way are packaged timber, bricks, tiles and other building materials, steel rod, pipes, etc.

(*c*) *Articulated vehicles* drawing tankers or flat trailers are particularly useful since they combine a low centre of gravity with good manoeuvrability. To achieve the same manoeuvrability with a non-articulated vehicle the design must give as short a vehicle as possible. This tends to raise the centre of gravity of the load, with consequent instability.

Special features of bulk road vehicles include those complying with statutory requirements on safety. Since the chances of collision and vehicle failure are much greater than in rail haulage, and pollution problems (for example, liquid cargoes which escape nearly always enter water courses) are also potentially serious, special legislation has been passed to ensure the minimisation of these hazards. With inflammable cargoes fire prevention precautions include fireproof screens between the cabs and tank units, transverse exhausts on the cab side of this screen, marking of the vehicle with a 'flame' symbol and training of staff in fire prevention and control. Similarly, corrosive products are specially marked with a corrosive symbol. Some countries exclude tankers from certain roads where particular hazards to the environment exist; for example, water reservoirs nearby might lead to such a ban.

Bulk Movements by Pipeline

Pipeline transport has already been referred to (see Chapter Four) as a unique form of transport in which the way, the unit of carriage and the propulsion unit are combined. The result is a bulk movement of unwrapped product. The chief points about pipelines are most conveniently made in this chapter.

Advantages of Pipeline Transport

The advantages of pipeline transport may be listed as follows:

(*a*) Low operating cost
(*b*) No packaging or return of empty containers

(c) No return-journey load problems
(d) No transshipment problems
(e) No congestion
(f) High speed
(g) 24-hour operation
(h) Indifference to terrain

A word of explanation of some of these is necessary.

(a) *Low operating cost.* Once constructed the pipeline has low operating costs relative to other methods of transport. Many booster stations can be made fully automatic, with safety cut-out devices controlled by sensors able to detect excessive pressures in the pipelines, or abnormal temperature changes. The sequence of activities of starting up pumps, etc., can be remotely controlled, or self-monitoring and adjusting feed-back systems can be incorporated. The cost of these systems is offset by the reduced labour cost of employing staff, whose presence at booster stations in unpleasant Arctic or desert conditions can be expensive. Apart from these costs the chief operating costs are way-leave rentals negotiated during the capital construction stage and renewable at intervals, inspection and maintenance of the pipeline and the labour and fuel charges for the pumping stations.

(b) *No packaging or return of empty containers.* Clearly a product which is piped to its destination requires no packaging. Only the product itself moves, the pipeline providing the necessary protection of the product. There are no empty containers to be returned and no packing or unpacking problems at the start and finish of the journey.

(c), (d) and (e). These points are self-explanatory.

(f) *and* (g). *High speed for 24 hours per day.* Speeds of 100–150 km/h are quite common in pipelines. As they operate for 24 hours per day the speed is quite extraordinary compared with other forms of transport. For example in railway transits 300 km per day is regarded as fast transit: 3,000 km per day is quite possible by pipeline.

(h) *Indifference to terrain.* Overland transport is usually bedevilled by terrain. Railways face particular problems in mountainous territory; road vehicles suffer abnormal wear and tear in hilly country and ever-present possibilities of accidents. Pipeline engineers of course face problems in constructing pipelines in difficult country, but once these constructional problems have been overcome and the pumping stations have been designed to deal adequately with the volumes to be transported the actual transport of products is relatively free from difficulties. This is a great advantage over the life of any particular pipeline.

The Uses of Pipelines

Pipelines are only suitable for the delivery of particular materials from one point to another on a long-term basis. The demand for the good must be steady and enduring if pipelines are to be economic. They have long been used for water supply, town gas supply and sewage disposal. In recent years the chief use of pipelines has been for supplying crude oil and natural gas, and two million kilometres of pipeline are already in use for these purposes. A notable development of the system is the proposal of an Arctic gas pipeline to bring Canadian and Alaskan gas down the Mackenzie River Route to join up with the Trans-Canada pipeline. Other major pipelines are the Trans-Arabian pipeline from the Arabian Gulf to the Mediterranean; the dense network of gas and oil pipelines in the U.S.A. and Canada; the Soviet pipelines from the Urals to the Comecon countries in north-eastern and south-eastern Europe; the Trans-Siberian pipeline and the south European pipelines taking Mediterranean oil from France and Italy to refineries in eastern France, Switzerland, south Germany and western Austria.

Besides crude oil and natural gas, pipelines are used extensively, particularly in the U.S.A. and Canada, to distribute processed products to major centres. Refined motor spirit, aviation spirit, liquefied petroleum gases (propane and butane), paraffin, diesel oil and other products are sent to depots in major centres by multi-user pipelines. The products are separated by one or two 'pigs'—piston-like objects of steel with rubber plunger ends—which are inserted into the pipeline at the point where products change. A special device removes the 'pig' when it comes to a pumping station and short-circuits it round the pump, re-inserting it at the same point in the supply after the pump has been passed.

Solids are being moved increasingly by pipeline, usually in the form of a slurry with 40 per cent liquid to 60 per cent solid. Coal is moved in this way in America over distances of 100 miles or more. It is particularly useful where the liquid used is water (because water is cheap) and where this water does not interfere with the subsequent processing of the product. For example, cement is manufactured in kilns from a slurry of limestone and clay. Huge tanks are used for mixing the slurry at the clay, limestone or chalk sites. It is then pumped to the kilns in slurry form. While this type of pipeline is for the sole use of a particular owner, and highly specific, it will be very economic as cement works themselves have a long life and the demand is continuing. Also the solid products, clay and chalk or limestone, are difficult to scrape out of road vehicles or rail trucks, and travel much more readily in slurry form.

Pipelines are extensively used for transporting hot, molten products over short distances, and special problems have to be faced. One of the main ones is the 'freezing' of the product in the pipe due to heat losses. This is even a problem in ordinary pipelines in winter time with some products like diesel fuel, and pipelines are often provided with electrical heating which can be switched on in cold weather.

Suggested Further Reading

National Ports Council, *Research and Technical Bulletin*, 1969.
Webb, M., *Transporting Goods by Road*, Weidenfeld & Nicolson, 1972.
Wentworth, F. R. L. (Ed.), *Physical Distribution Management*, Gower Press, 1970.

CHAPTER THIRTEEN

PHYSICAL DISTRIBUTION: INVENTORY CONTROL

The Nature of Stocks

The physical distribution concept is a wide-viewing continuous appraisal of the sum total of movements through time and space, from the first producer to the final consumer. It takes account of the distribution flow from raw materials to final sale. In the panorama the physical distribution manager sees many places where stages of production are out of phase with one another, and notes the accumulation of stocks to act as buffer zones adjusting for the uneven behaviour of supply and demand. Thus raw materials arrive in batches rather than daily requirements. When the ship comes in, or the lorry arrives, or the rail train shunts its trucks into the company siding, the stocks build up, only to run down steadily as production proceeds in the days and weeks that follow. These stocks are sometimes known as *replenishment quantity stocks*, ordered in optimum order sizes but used up as the cycle of production proceeds. A second type of stocks, known as *anticipation inventories*, are produced at steady rates in anticipation of a seasonal demand. *Safety stocks* are stocks accumulated to allow for sudden surges in demand, to prevent customer dissatisfaction. *Buffer stocks* are stocks of finished goods which pile up awaiting demand from wholesalers or depots. Rates of production cannot be varied easily, and a temporary fall in demand must be stockpiled if the complex production pattern is not to be disturbed. The time may come when everything is full to overflowing and we shall have to cut back, but until then the inventory, like a buffer, takes the strain. We thus have stocks at all stages of the distribution network. What attitudes exist to stock?

There are three chief attitudes to stock: the accountant's attitude, the salesman's attitude and the production attitude.

The Accountant's Attitude to Stock

To the accountant stock is only capital tied up to little effect. Profit can only be earned when stock turns over, and the ideal arrangement is to hold only enough stock to meet the demands of customers, replenishing it as and when required. The accountant is therefore interested in the rate of stock turnover, which may be found by either of the formulae given below.

$$(1)\ \text{Rate of Stock Turn} = \frac{\text{Cost of Stock Sold}}{\text{Average Stock at Cost Price}}$$

$$(2)\ \text{Rate of Stock Turn} = \frac{\text{Sales}}{\text{Average Stock at Selling Price}}$$

These formulae are more helpful in wholesale and retail trade than they are in other areas—for example, inventories of partially finished goods waiting to be completed do not throw up any helpful figures to calculate a rate of stock turn, but in general the accountant's attitude is to keep stock to a

151

minimum wherever possible. This is the very reverse of the salesman's idea of stocks.

The Salesman's Attitude to Stock

To the salesman, with his eye on commission, the unpardonable thing is to be out of stock. If there are no stocks customers must be kept waiting, the lead-time between order and customer satisfaction increases and he may even lose customers to other firms. The salesman therefore likes full shelves irrespective of the capital tied up. Between the accountant's viewpoint and the salesman's viewpoint comes the viewpoint of the production staff.

The Production Manager's Attitude to Stock

The production manager regards stocks as an incidental aspect of the general production problem. He will generally seek the optimum production from his own point of view, which means that 'batches' of parts will be produced with fairly long production runs to cut down other costs such as re-jigging machines too frequently. These batches must be stored, so that inventories are inseparable from production, but the idea of cost centres is such a natural one for the production engineer that he is generally aware of inventory costs and will not produce excessive batches if it is clearly uneconomic. He therefore comes closer to the accountant's viewpoint than the marketing viewpoint.

To reconcile these conflicting viewpoints in a dynamic situation is not easy. The dynamic nature of modern business life presents an endless variety of situations. Communication these days is instantaneous; a president sneezes and bankruptcies follow; natural disasters, political upheavals, military coups and guerrilla activities immediately affect inventory calculations. It is a lucky distribution manager who can keep ahead of the field in the daily assessment of requirements. However, the acknowledged techniques of inventory management can do much to assist in the decisions which must be made, and can significantly reduce inventories to the satisfaction of the accountant, without significantly reducing sales or raising production costs.

Inventory Management by Objectives

A management will achieve the best control over inventories if it has set appropriate inventory objectives. These will usually include the following aims:

(a) A balanced inventory, operating at minimum costs within an inventory budget appropriate to the company's level of activity.

(b) A prescribed level of customer satisfaction, say at 95 per cent of popular lines and rather less than this with other lines.

(c) Secure control of stock positions by the adoption of a quantitative approach to inventory problems, which lays down clear guidelines to action in re-ordering, and in the alerting of management to exceptional situations.

(d) The development of an adequate body of expertise by a training programme for both administrative and operative staff in the techniques of inventory control, so that there is the fullest understanding of, and sympathy for, the management's objectives.

We must now examine these techniques.

The Techniques of Inventory Management
Deciding What is Important, or ABC Analysis

Sometimes called volume analysis, this technique consists of arranging the various products handled in an ABC order, with A allocated to that product which represents the highest contribution to sales turnover, B to that product which comes next, etc. Having arranged items in this way, we can immediately see the items which should represent the major part of our inventory and those items of less importance. Thus the following figures might be discovered.

	Units sold	Unit price	Total sales figures	Percentage of total sales figure
A	1,000	£48	£48,000	48
B	500	£72	£36,000	36
C	200	£50	£10,000	10
D	50	£40	£2,000	2
E	50	£40	£2,000	2
F	50	£20	£1,000	1
G	4,000	£0.25	£1,000	1

It is clear that there is no point in spending time and effort upon items which have a negligible effect upon profits earned, and it might even be desirable to discontinue certain lines altogether.

Deciding How Much to Order—or E.O.Q. Analysis

E.O.Q. stands for economic order quantity. Any order involves certain costs, called acquisition costs, and once acquired the order gives rise to certain further costs called possession costs. It can be shown that the formula for calculating economic order quantities is

$$\text{E.O.Q.} = \sqrt{\frac{2400 \, R_m S}{CI}}$$

In this formula R_m stands for the monthly rate of sale in units, S stands for the fixed cost per order, C stands for the cost per unit, and I for the inventory carrying cost percentage.

Using an example of 100 units per month, at a fixed cost per order of £10, and a £2 cost per unit with inventory carrying costs of 25 per cent we have

$$\text{E.O.Q.} = \sqrt{\frac{2400 \times 100 \times £10}{£2 \times 25}}$$

$$= \sqrt{48000}$$

$$= 219 \text{ units}$$

Actually the inventory service costs are not very sensitive to changes in E.O.Q., and purchasing somewhere above or below the economic order will not add a lot to inventory costs. Once the E.O.Q. is known, so long as the actual orders are within 35 per cent of the E.O.Q., the inventory costs will only vary by about 6 per cent. It may therefore pay—at times when stocks are cheap—to buy more, or at times when stocks are dear, to buy less, and thus realise other, more valuable, economies.

Deciding When to Order

A common method is to designate a fixed re-order point based upon the lead-time—the time between the placing of an order and its satisfaction. This period will require a certain stock, based upon the weekly sales. Thus a four-week lead-time requires us to have a four-week stock in hand. In practice a safety margin would also be allowed—say, a further week's stock—and when stock fell to a five-week stock we will order the E.O.Q.

Depot Replenishment

When depots or branches are delivering stock to customers their inventories fall day by day. How shall we ensure that they do not run out of stock? The answer is to replenish supplies in some economic way, and often replacement on a one-for-one basis is adopted. Data supplied to head office of invoices to customers notifies them of the quantities delivered. These can then be integrated into economic loads, preferably full container loads, and stock will be replenished when this point is reached.

Conclusion

Inventory control is a sophisticated process today, and computerised refinements of the basic concepts described in this chapter give modifications to take account of variations in the rate of usage; adjustment of replenishment procedures to take account of slow-moving items which are not very influential contributions to sales; alterations in lead-times, etc. The reader is urged to seek in-company advice if inventory control is important to him. Only in an in-plant situation can a really detailed answer be given to the question 'How does this company control inventories and ensure replenishment of stock for re-sale?'

Suggested Further Reading

Hadley, G., and Whitin, T. M., *Analysis of Inventory Systems*, Prentice Hall, 1963.
Report by National Materials Handling Centre on Costs in the Distribution Industry, National Economic Development Office, 1974.
Thomas, A. B., *Stock Control in Manufacturing Industries*, Gower Press, 1968.
Wentworth, F. R. L. (Ed.), *Physical Distribution Management*, Gower Press, 1970.

CHAPTER FOURTEEN

PHYSICAL DISTRIBUTION: TRANSPORT ASPECTS AND CASE STUDIES

Introduction—The Choice of Transport

An important part of the transport or transport and distribution manager's job is to decide which mode or modes of transport is best suited for moving the traffic for which he is responsible. He will be guided in his decision by a knowledge of the advantages and disadvantages of the various modes. At times his original choice will need to be altered to take into account changes in circumstances, e.g. larger or smaller quantities to be transported, and the degree of urgency of a particular transit. The following are some of the characteristics he will need to bear in mind in inland and international transport. We have thought it best to include an account of the advantages and disadvantages of each mode of transport, since the choice available is very wide, but no account can be complete because of the improvements being implemented month by month in this dynamic and restless field.

Inland Transport

Road Transport

Advantages

(a) Flexibility. Collection and delivery can be arranged without transshipment wherever a motor vehicle can travel. It is this characteristic more than any other that accounts for the pre-eminence of road transport over all other forms of inland transport: for example, in the United Kingdom there are 200,000 miles of roads compared with only 12,000 miles of railway, giving direct delivery advantage over rail in the vast majority of cases.

(b) Promptness and controlled delivery. Fairly precise times for collection and delivery can be arranged. This is important where labour must be arranged for loading and unloading and where the arrival of goods must be arranged to suit the needs of manufacturers, construction work and consumers. Delivery can be specified for a particular time of day or at a specified rate, e.g. *x* tons per day.

(c) Packaging. Frequently, less packing (or even no packing at all) is required, as compared with other forms of transport.

Disadvantages

(a) Prompt discharge essential. Vehicles must be discharged promptly. Unexpected arrivals of vehicles may mean that labour for loading or unloading must be diverted from other work, or alternatively the vehicle and driver must stand idle until labour is available.

(b) Expenses. For less than full loads a minimum charge related to vehicle capacity will usually have to be paid, irrespective of the weight or quality of goods carried.

(c) Misdeliveries. Where a number of part-loads are sent by the same

155

vehicle, crossed deliveries may occur unless careful attention is paid to labelling, etc.

(*d*) Pilfering and theft. Road vehicles are liable to pilfering and hijacking if they are left unattended.

(*e*) Low capacity. Compared with rail or road transport capacity is low. This may render it uncompetitive in situations where there are good rail or canal connections.

The Merits of a Self-owned Fleet compared with Alternative Methods

Because of its inherent advantages, and its rôle as a link with other modes of transport, all transport managers will employ road transport to a greater or lesser degree. At some time it may be necessary to decide whether or not to rely on public hauliers for all road transport needs, whether to hire on a contract basis, whether to operate a company owned fleet or to what extent a combination of two or more alternatives is desirable. The lists that follow demonstrate that economics alone may not be the sole factor in reaching the decision.

Public Hauliers

Advantages

(*a*) By 'shopping around' the lowest haulage rate may be secured for each delivery.

(*b*) A wider choice of vehicle sizes and types is available, so that the vehicle best suited for a specific delivery can be obtained.

(*c*) Deliveries can be arranged without reference to return loads.

(*d*) The problems of idle vehicles during slack time and shortage of vehicles during peak periods are avoided.

Disadvantages

(*a*) A user who is known to 'shop around' generates no loyalty from hauliers, and if his peaks coincide with those of other users in the area, he may find his transport needs unfulfilled or subject to delay.

(*b*) For similar reasons, urgent loads may not always be easily catered for, since the haulier will satisfy the needs of his regular customers first.

(*c*) The user has little control over the driver, and should a conflict of interests arise he is likely to put his employer's interests first.

(*d*) No advertising value accrues from vehicles not in the firm's livery and diseconomies may result from shabby vehicles and unco-operative drivers.

Contract Hire Fleet

Advantages

(*a*) Gives complete control over drivers and the operation of vehicles.

(*b*) Vehicles painted in the company's livery provide valuable advertising.

(*c*) No garage or maintenance facilities have to be provided by the company —these are the responsibility of the haulier.

(*d*) Costs are known. There are no hidden costs, as can happen with own-account operations, and except where provided for in the contract, will not be subject to fluctuation according to market demand, inflation, etc., during the term of the contract.

Disadvantages

(*a*) Return loads are difficult to organise; hence a high proportion of light running will occur.

(*b*) The hired fleet must be fully employed for the currency of the contract.

(*c*) More expensive than running an 'own fleet' or using public hauliers (but remember there are no hidden costs).

Self-owned Fleet (Own-account Operation)

Advantages

(*a*) Complete control over drivers and operations.

(*b*) Valuable advertising from smartly turned-out vehicles in company's livery.

Disadvantages

(*a*) Return loads are difficult to organise; hence a high proportion of light running will occur.

(*b*) Garaging and maintenance facilities must be installed.

(*c*) It is expensive to provide a fleet big enough to cover peak periods and this means that hiring must be done at busy periods.

(*d*) It often happens that the full capital cost, overheads and operating costs are not debited and a false impression of transport costs results.

(*e*) Unless very carefully controlled by the transport department, other departments will make uneconomic demands on the fleet 'since it is there to be used'.

It is most likely that no single selection will be made, but that a flexible system will be selected. Depending upon circumstances, this could result, for example, in a small own-account fleet, a contract fleet and occasional hirings to meet peak demands. The contract fleet operator is likely to have vehicles other than those operating on contract, and the provision of extra vehicles is unlikely to prove difficult.

Whatever decision is finally reached, the following factors will need to have been taken into account.

1. Is there a regular flow of traffic, and does it follow a particular pattern?
2. Can return loads be arranged for many of the journeys?
3. To what extent is the advertising value of vehicles important?
4. Can garage and maintenance facilities be provided without heavy capital cost?
5. Does the company possess or can it attract administrative and operational staff of the right calibre to ensure efficient operation?

Rail Transport

Advantages

(*a*) Quick delivery over long distances between important towns and cities, e.g. London and Glasgow. This characteristic, true even for conventional rail traffic, has been accentuated by the development of the Freightliner system.

(*b*) Convenient where the receiving point has a private siding; even more so where both ends have private sidings.

(*c*) Demurrage. Goods can be left under load for one day exclusive of the day of arrival, without payment of demurrage. This is most useful for the economic development of labour for discharging purposes, as unloading can be performed at slack periods for other work, or between arrivals of road vehicles.

(*d*) Large capacity. Rail transport is convenient for the regular receipt of large quantities because of the much greater capacity compared with road transport. Company trains, i.e. those specifically allocated to one company, have become increasingly important in recent years, and special rates and 'tailor-made' services can be negotiated with British Rail.

(*e*) Nationwide. A countrywide service is available for 'smalls' traffic.

Disadvantages

(*a*) Slow delivery. Away from main lines, services are infrequent and traffic has to wait in sidings.

(*b*) Transshipment. Except with private sidings, the beginning and end of transit must involve road transport. This can result in increased damage due to extra handling, loss of time in the transshipment process and greater overall transit times, where road and rail schedules do not coincide.

(*c*) Packaging. Except for Freightliner services, heavier packing is required to compensate for higher level of 'shocks' due to shunting.

(*d*) Pilferage. Greater susceptibility to pilferage, especially where boxes or cartons are small and portable, and sent in less than truck loads. These require multiple handling, and goods are not constantly under the control of one person as with a road transport driver.

Water Transport—Inland Waterways

Advantages

(*a*) Convenience. Where loading and discharging points are on canal sites and wharf facilities are available.

(*b*) Cheapness. Large capacity makes the mode of transport particularly cheap for bulk low-value goods.

(*c*) Environmental. Inland waterways avoid congestion of roads and built-up areas and may be suitable for hazardous goods such as petroleum, fragile goods such as glass and pollutants as with the transport of toxic waste through urban areas. Also arrivals do not congest factory sidings or roads.

Disadvantages

(*a*) Slow delivery. Speeds in inland waterways must be kept low.

(*b*) Limited mileage of way. The inland waterway has limited application due to very small mileage of canals available (350 miles in the United Kingdom).

(*c*) Specialised terminals and equipment. Cranes, etc., are necessary for loading and discharging.

Estuarial Transport

Advantages

(*a*) Uncongested transit between points on the same estuary.

(*b*) High capacity. This means low-cost transport.

(*c*) Dock dues. Dock dues are not payable on deliveries to and from import and export vessels in enclosed docks.

(*d*) Demurrage. Free time is allowed before the incidence of demurrage and this permits economical use of labour.

(*e*) Intermodal transits. Where estuarial transport forms part of an international transit, advantage can be taken of through systems such as Lash, Seabee and Bacat.

Disadvantages

(*a*) Minimum tonnage. High minimum tonnage per barge may have to be paid for, making it unsuitable for small lots.

(*b*) Specialised terminal equipment. Unless wharf facilities and equipment exist, high capital costs may preclude their provision unless regular traffic makes it worthwhile in order to take advantage of much lower transport costs.

Coastwise Transport
Advantages

(*a*) Low cost. The low cost of bulk transport by water makes this a cheap form of transport for lots of over 100 tons for journeys in excess of 150 miles, where loading and discharging points have access to or are near water.

(*b*) Awkward loads. For very heavy or large indivisible loads coastwise heavy-lift vessels may provide a better alternative to road or rail, providing loading and discharging points are convenient to a port.

Disadvantages

(*a*) Specialised terminal facilities must be available.

(*b*) Slow. Compared with road or rail, coastal transport is slow, except perhaps for heavy or indivisible loads.

(*c*) Additional transport costs may be incurred unless private access to a waterway is available.

(*d*) Weather. Coastal transits are subject to delays due to bad weather.

Air Transport

Air transport is unlikely to be relevant except for very high priority transits, e.g. emergency drugs and plasma; vital parts during breakdowns, etc. (see International Transport).

International Transport
Sea Transport

Because of its very high capacity relative to the motive power employed, water transport—in particular deep-sea transport, which can benefit most from economies of scale—can offer cheaper transport rates per ton/mile than any other form of transport. It will almost always, though not invariably, be cheaper than its competitor, air transport.

Advantages

(*a*) Low freight rates.

(*b*) Very high capacity.

(*c*) Continuous operation on 24-hour basis, partly affecting the speed advantage of air transport over shorter distances.

(*d*) Less susceptible to adverse weather conditions, particularly fog.

Disadvantages

(*a*) Relatively slow speeds.

(*b*) Possibly less frequent services.

(*c*) Because of high capacity, time spent in loading and discharging may cause a disproportionate increase in transit times in view of the distances involved.

(*d*) Usually more packing required than with air transport.

Deep-sea Transport

On long voyages, the greatest economy can be achieved by chartering a vessel, which will be at the sole disposal of the charterer at freight rates agreed between the charterer and the shipowner. This kind of operation is only available to those users who have very large quantities of goods to move, usually of a bulk nature. The majority of users will be best served by liner companies where the goods of many forwarders are carried in the same vessel, at a published freight rates, on a regularly scheduled service.

On the most densely used routes, container vessels have supplanted conventional break-bulk vessels; on some others the two forms of deep-sea transport continue to operate in competition. The transport manager must decide between the advantages offered by container shipment (see Chapter Nine) at high rates, and the cheaper, but less efficient conventional services. The development of Lash has added a further dimension to the choice, with the following characteristics making these vessels particularly suitable for some forms of traffic.

(*a*) Overall transit times much faster than break-bulk vessels, though not as fast as all-container services.

(*b*) Much larger transport units, i.e. barges capable of carrying many times more cargo than the largest I.S.O. container.

(*c*) Especially suitable for inland penetration via navigable rivers and canals, where destinations are water-served.

Land Bridges

Where land masses make sea routes very much longer than direct distances, combined sea–land services have been developed with the object of providing faster services. Although land transport is more expensive than sea transport on a ton/mile basis, the reduced distance may bring the total freight charges closer together. This, combined with the time saving, may make the service very competitive: for example, the route over the United States land bridge to Japan. Careful comparison of freight rates, times and the needs of the cargo must be made to determine correct choice.

'Flying Fish' Services

Combined sea–air services known as flying-fish services are designed to realise as far as possible the benefits of fast air transits linked with the economies of scale derived from sea transport. The effect is to produce a total transit time somewhat lower than that which could be achieved by an all-air transit, but much faster than land–sea services, and at a much lower freight rate than all-air services. Examples are the consignments, suited to air transport, which are flown from many European airports to Manchester, where they are consolidated and sent by fast container ship on the long sea leg to Canada.

Short-sea Routes

The choice on short-sea routes, i.e. to Europe, becomes more complicated. Older transport managers will remember when the conventional break-bulk vessel was the only form of sea transport available. Now to some European destinations he must choose among conventional vessels, road ferry (Ro-Ro), rail/container ships, car ferry (with Freightliner links), Bacat and short-sea container services.

Break-bulk Vessels

Still the most suitable for bulk cargoes and for low-value cargoes between ports without specialised services or equipment, where additional transport to and from specialised services from alternative ports is uneconomic because of increased transport costs. (The development of more Bacat services may further limit this type of operation.)

Ro-Ro

Especially suitable for loads which would not benefit from or are unsuitable for containerisation, or for containerised goods originating from or destined for locations not well served by the Freightliner system or Interfreight (the Continental counterpart of the Freightliner network). Ro-Ro is also appropriate where it is desirable for the driver to accompany the goods from origin to destination, or for a driver belonging to an associated European company to complete the transit.

Short-sea Container Services

Suitable for container traffic as in Ro-Ro above and for transshipment traffic to and from feeder ports and ocean-going vessels calling at major ports. Also used for traffic to and from ports not used by Ro-Ro or rail/container ship services.

Rail/Container Ships

Especially suitable for containerised traffic that can benefit by Freightliner/Interfreight networks. Precisely scheduled arrival times can be determined in accordance with rail timetables.

Bacat

Especially suitable where inland penetration by navigable rivers or canals is possible and for low-valued bulk goods for which containers are not suited. Economies can be gained from the use of the large barge units.

The choice is limited to a few services as yet, but these will undoubtedly be increased in future years.

The Channel Tunnel

Despite the recent decision not to proceed at present with the Tunnel project, it may still be that in future years the Channel Tunnel will provide a direct rail or road/rail link with Europe and this would involve further reappraisal of existing physical distribution activities.

Air Transport

Advantages

(*a*) Speed: much higher than any other mode of transport.

(*b*) Lighter packing may be possible than for other forms of transport.

(*c*) Cheaper insurance because goods are at risk for a shorter period and there is a good 'freedom from damage' record of this mode.

Disadvantages

(*a*) High freight rates, but note that savings on packing, insurance, inventory costs, etc., may cancel this out, and that some goods charged at ad valorem rates by sea may be carried at weight rates by air, and actually incur lower freight charges.

(*b*) Gains from high airspeed may be lost on journeys to and from airports.

(*c*) Susceptible to delays due to bad weather, particularly fog.

(*d*) Restrictions on size and weight may operate, but larger all-freight aircraft are making this less important.

Whatever transport mode is selected for particular transport purposes, the Transport Manager must never be content to regard that as a final choice, to be followed slavishly on future occasions. Competition among modes and individual carriers is keen, new developments occur with almost bewildering rapidity, new services are initiated, old services are improved, new motorways and links are opened—all of these things make it essential for the Transport Manager and his staff to keep themselves up to date by assiduously reading the technical and trade publications, and by maintaining contact with the marketing services of transport agencies of all modes, so that as far as possible they can be sure that a wrong choice is not made through ignorance or inadequate information.

Introduction to Distribution Case Studies

To conclude this section on distribution, we thought it would be helpful to include brief outlines of some actual solutions to distribution problems. We are very grateful to Western British Road Services Ltd., Boots Ltd., Shell-Mex and B.P. Ltd. and Jeyes Ltd. for permission to use their operations as illustrations.

Case Study No. 1: Boots (The Chemists) Ltd.

The problem. In the Hampshire and Dorset area, the company has seventy-one retail outlets, located on 'High Street' sites. The high rental value of such sites makes it imperative to utilise the maximum amount of space for the selling function, and keep storage space to a minimum. This in turn necessitates frequent replacement of stock. Apart from Boots' own products, those of many other manufacturers are carried as standard items among the many hundreds of lines sold by even their smallest stores. Storage space apart, direct delivery from each of the manufacturers would be impractical, and direct delivery by Boots after central consolidation would be uneconomic.

The solution. Boots and other manufacturers deliver in bulk to one Western B.R.S. transshipment point in the area. Here, vehicles are unloaded and the various items placed in racking in coded order. Daily orders for individual shops can be 'picked' from the racks in code sequence and placed in special nesting bins for delivery. Most of the daily deliveries to the shops are transferred directly from the bins to the selling space, avoiding double handling via the stockroom. Each store receives only one vehicle per day, with the whole of its intake. This scheme, which has been in operation since 1966, currently handles some 4 million packages annually.

Case Study No. 2: Shell-Mex and B.P. Ltd.

The problem. The company is involved in selling lubricants and grease, totalling approximately 750 product lines in a highly competitive market. Quality of service, and efficient stock control are essential requirements. The area to be covered consists of part of South Wales and the South-West. Deliveries are mainly to garage forecourts, with some deliveries to industrial users. The former are frequently limited in storage space and require stock replacement at short notice.

The solution. Bulk deliveries are made to the Western B.R.S. depot at Avonmouth. On arrival the vehicles are unloaded by forklift trucks, some fitted with specially designed rim clamps enabling large drums to be handled two at a time. Slower moving products in large drums are stored in purpose-built drum racks, while faster moving products in large drums are stored in pallet stocks. Products in retail packaging are kept in multi-tier racking, palletised for forklift handling. As orders are received, delivery rounds are compiled for local deliveries. Two night trunk deliveries are made to two other depots, where again local delivery rounds are compiled. Any point in the area covered can receive deliveries within 24 hours. Thirteen vehicles are used, all fitted with tail-lifts, for ease of handling the products at customers' premises.

Case Study No. 3: Jeyes Ltd.

The problem. This company and its subsidiaries manufacture disinfectants and other sanitary products, amounting to several hundred product lines (taking into account different sizes of the same product). Deliveries are mainly to 'cash and carry' wholesalers and to supermarkets. Direct delivery by Jeyes would be uneconomic, much of it involving empty or light running.

The solution. Bulk deliveries are made to Avonmouth from various sources, and stored in multi-tier racking. While many vehicle loads consist solely of Jeyes products, deliveries which on their own would be uneconomic can frequently be made in combination with the lubricants and greases mentioned above. Basing distribution schemes for compatible products on one depot provides a neat solution to a situation where the delivery of one company's products on their own would be a very unprofitable undertaking.

Other Solutions to Transport Problems

These case studies are typical of the types of distribution service offered to manufacturers. Basically B.R.S. schemes are of two types, which may be modified to meet the customer's particular requirements. These are illustrated diagrammatically in Fig. 14.1.

Basic Scheme 1 (see Fig. 14.1)

(*a*) The regional stock depot, maintained by the customer, is replaced by a regional B.R.S. vehicle base.

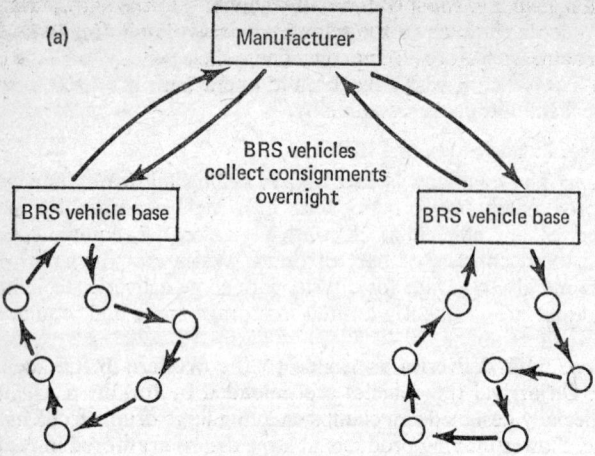

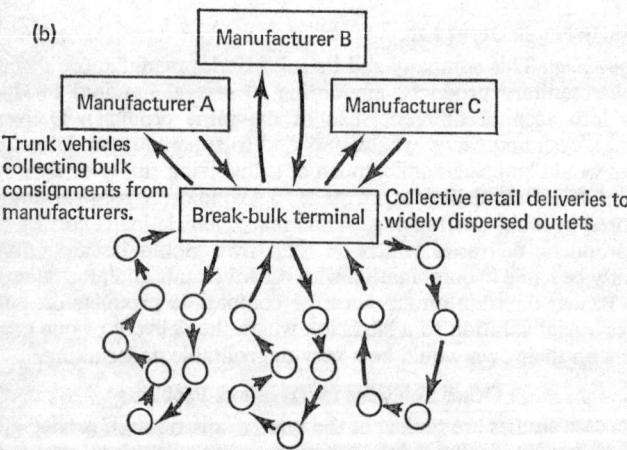

Fig. 14.1. Two B.R.S. solutions to the transport problem: (a) replacing regional stock depots by direct delivery through a B.R.S. vehicle base; (b) delivery in remote areas direct from the manufacturer via a B.R.S. break-bulk terminal.

(courtesy of British Road Services Ltd)

(*b*) Overnight trunk deliveries to the base from the manufacturer's premises bring full loads of the manufacturer's products into the region for distribution.

(*c*) Without transshipment the trunk vehicles are taken over by daytime drivers who deliver the goods to customers in the area.

Basic Scheme 2 (see Fig. 14.1)

This is particularly suitable for remote or scattered delivery areas, where no manufacturer has sufficient orders to merit the use of Scheme 1.

(*a*) Bulk delivery to a break-bulk B.R.S. terminal—from several manufacturers.

(*b*) Consolidation of various products from various manufacturers into loads for local delivery. The loads on any vehicle must be compatible.

(*c*) Local delivery by B.R.S. drivers.

It must not be thought that B.R.S. are alone in providing these sorts of services. Other hauliers, large and small, are providing distribution schemes to firms whose products are distributed on a national or regional basis, but B.R.S., because of its nationwide network, was selected as ideal for illustrative purposes.

Suggested Further Reading

Wentworth, F. R. L. (Ed.), *Physical Distribution Management*, Gower Press, 1970.

The current literature on motor transport, port operations, air freight, container transport, rail freight, etc., must be read regularly by transport staff. Particularly relevant articles should be drawn to their attention through house magazines, etc.

CHAPTER FIFTEEN

FINANCIAL ASPECTS OF TRANSPORT

Business Finance and Transport

The field of business finance is wide, and the problems for management in successfully launching, developing and controlling any firm are very numerous and complex. We live in an era of sophisticated financial techniques, where extremely rapid evaluations of alternative projects can be made. To convince investors of the merits of his transport firm the private entrepreneur must prepare conclusive evidence that the prospects of profitability he envisages are in fact real enough. The managers of public corporations do not face the same tests, but the scrutiny of auditors, the Public Accounts Committee or other scrutinising body, and the legislature itself are daunting. Whatever the results achieved by public bodies, criticism can be expected from one quarter or another.

Financial problems come under the following headings, each of which will be examined later in this chapter in detail:

(a) The risks involved, and the sources of finance available.

(b) The flow of income and expenditure, and the management of these funds by budgetary control.

(c) Depreciation and obsolescence of transport facilities.

(d) The control of costs by budgets and control procedures.

(e) The return on capital invested in private enterprise firms, and the allocation of profits.

It is difficult in a general book of this type to deal with the financial problems of the huge range of firms and institutions to be found in transport, and more specialised reading from books suggested in the reading list should be undertaken by those particularly concerned with finance. They should also read the current literature, trade journals, etc., in their own special field, with particular attention to anything likely to affect the financial plans of their own firms.

Risks Involved in Transport

There are as many types of 'uncertainty' which have to be faced in the conduct of a transport firm, as there are in life itself. These risks can be divided into 'insurable risks' and 'non-insurable risks'. Insurable risks are those where it is possible to calculate the probability that the risk will occur, so that a fair premium can be proposed which will enable a pool to be set up for compensating unfortunate contributors. Non-insurable risks are those which are not susceptible to calculation, so that insurance companies are unwilling to attempt to set up a pool for compensation. Even where a risk is insurable it does not follow that the businessman can afford the necessary cover. Certain insurances—for example the insurance of road vehicles against damage to third parties—are compulsory, and the transport firm will *have* to afford them, but many other forms of cover available to him may be so expensive that he

Table 15.1. Uncertainties in Transport

Type of Uncertainty	Examples in Transport	Insurable or Non-insurable	Avoidance Action
1. Natural hazard	Flood, fire, frost, storms, gales, subsidences, rockfalls, static electricity.	Insurable	(a) Insure (b) Lay down clear guidelines to staff about behaviour in these circumstances.
2. Human uncertainty	(a) Death of key staff. (b) Transfer of employment by key staff. (c) Vandalism, theft, embezzlement, etc. (d) Lack of capacity in the owner or entrepreneur.	(a) Insurable (b) Non-insurable (c) Insurable (d) Non-insurable	(a) Insure (b) Train up substitutes with good staff training programme. (c) Insure (d) Be cautious before embarking.
3. Economic risks	(a) The risk that conditions of demand may change so that demand at the price envisaged is smaller than expected. (b) The risk that conditions of supply may change so that supply at the price envisaged proves to be impossible.	Both non-insurable	None—the uncertainty must be borne by the businessman.
4. Technical risks	Risks that the project may prove technically more difficult than anticipated. The more technical the project the more risky it is. Premature obsolescence is a feature of transport.	Non-insurable	Careful preparatory work with built-in safeguards as to price and delivery dates. Adequate provision for obsolescence.
5. Political risks	Risks that the project may prove politically unpopular or that pressure from environmental, domestic or foreign political interference, wars and riots may render it impossible.	Mostly non-insurable	Careful cost-benefit analysis. Caution in international arrangements. ECGD insurance where available.
6. Monetary risks	Risk that inflation/deflation, etc., may adversely affect calculations.	Non-insurable	Caution in preparatory work (use of inflation accounting).

has no alternative but to carry the risk himself. A table of uncertainties is given in Table 15.1.

Sources of Finance Available

The sources of finance available to transport firms—as to other firms—may be listed as follows:

(a) Personal savings.

(b) Ploughing back of profits from a previous period.

(c) Private borrowing from friends, banks or other institutions.

(d) Partnerships.

(e) By issuing debentures, either privately or publicly.

(f) By issuing shares, either as a private company or as a public company.

(g) By public loans, or state loans, to bodies set up by Act of Parliament as statutory bodies, municipalities or nationalised undertakings.

Only a brief look at each of these is possible in this book, and the reader with a particular interest should consult the reading list suggested.

Personal Savings

In those fields of transport where it is possible to enter the field with relatively little capital, the personal savings of the proprietor make the most important contribution to the start of the enterprise. The purchase of a first vehicle from savings, or partly from savings and partly by 'Hire Purchase', has brought many a firm into existence. It is difficult to borrow money unless security can be offered, but banks will often lend relatively small sums without security, and slightly larger sums against a life insurance policy. Thus a business project which appears to a bank to offer prospects of profitability provided the future owner keeps living may lead a banker into suggesting to the would-be borrower that if he goes away and insures his life the bank will then lend against the security of the life assurance policy. This is a risk to the bank, since life assurance policies of the type described only pay out at death, and the venture may fail for other reasons. Illness may prevent the success of the business but the bank will not get compensation apart from any small surrender value. It is therefore vital for the would-be transport entrepreneur to save the maximum sum possible before embarking on his venture.

Ploughing Back Profits from a Previous Trading Period

Once a business has begun, the ploughing-back of profits by the owner is the best source of finance for the expansion of the firm. The more profitable a firm is, and the more frugal the standard of living of the proprietor, the more it is likely to grow, to the eventual enrichment of the owner. Even with a public company, whose shares are owned by the general public, the ploughing-back of profits is a major source of new capital for the firm. Of course the shareholders in such cases do not receive such a large dividend, since the profits are being retained in the business, but the price of the shares on the Stock Exchange will rise because the value of the business is increasing. An individual shareholder wishing to enjoy the extra value as income can usually sell his shares and take his profits at the expense of losing his stake in the company.

Private Borrowing from Friends, Banks and Other Institutions

Borrowing is often helpful when a firm for some reason hits a patch of illiquidity (i.e. it has little cash available). If the illiquidity is foreseen, and can be justified to the person or firm making the loan, then it can usually be arranged to borrow the money on reasonable terms. For example, a firm purchasing new vehicles which will make it more competitive, or able to tender for a new class of work, will be sympathetically listened to when it asks for an overdraft. A firm which is in financial difficulties because its trade is declining or because incompetence has led it into financial difficulties is less likely to be able to borrow at reasonable rates.

Most lenders of money require some safeguard from the borrower, and the most usual form this takes is a mortgage on the title deeds of the land and buildings. This type of security is not available to businessmen who do not own the freehold or leasehold of their properties, but are in rented accommodation. It is also possible to borrow against the security of other assets: vehicles, for example, or plant and machinery. The paradox arises that it is easiest to borrow money when you have plenty of assets and can offer good security. This is usually the very time that you do not need to borrow money. This paradox is a sad fact of life which would-be entrepreneurs must bear in mind.

Second mortgages are sometimes available. Here the firm which has already borrowed money on a mortgage of its landed property, borrows a further sum, usually from a different source, as a 'second' mortgage. The second mortgagor cannot get any benefit from his mortgage until the first mortgage has been settled and consequently is running a bigger risk. The rate of interest is therefore higher, and businessmen are well advised to keep away from such borrowing if possible. Legislation is in preparation to control the worst abuses of second mortgages, but even this legislation envisages a true interest rate of 20 per cent or more as a 'fair' rate of interest—a sobering thought for any borrower.

Second mortgages apart, more than one businessman has found that a generous lender of funds has, in the end, replaced him as the owner of the business. The astute lender, seeing a business which is viable but which is in difficulties due to the inexperience of the owner, uses his funds to secure control by helping the original owner to get into debt at higher rates of interest than the business can afford. By creaming off the top 15–20 per cent of profit he leaves so little for the original owner that the enterprise ceases to be worthwhile and falls an early prey to the big fish waiting to swallow it.

Small businesses experiencing real difficulties in finding finance from the normal institutions such as banks and finance houses may find the specialised institutions set up by governments for this purpose more sympathetic. Examples from the United Kingdom are the Finance Corporation for Industry Limited (F.C.I.); the Industrial and Commercial Finance Corporation Limited (I.C.F.C.); and Technical Development Capital Limited (T.D.C.).

Partnerships

Partnerships are formed for a variety of reasons, but the provision of the necessary finance almost always enters into the partnership agreement. A partnership agreement is best expressed in a formal *partnership deed*, in which the parties lay down the terms on which the business will be conducted. It is not essential to have such an agreement, but where it exists the provision of the capital, the proportions in which profits will be shared, the rate to be paid on capital, if any, and the rate of interest to be charged on drawings, if any, will be specified in the agreement. A full description of partnership arrangements is given in a companion volume to this: *Book-keeping Made Simple*.

Debentures

Companies, if permitted to do so by their articles of association, may borrow money by the issue of debentures. Debentures are a charge on the assets of the company, and give debenture holders a trust deed which entitles them to step in and seize either the general assets or specific assets should the company appear likely to be unable to pay the interest on the due date. They are therefore a very safe form of investment, and are popular with the more timid type of investor unwilling to risk the loss of his savings. They may be of three types:

1. *Fixed Debentures*, secured on the fixed assets of the company, i.e. the land, buildings, plant and motor vehicles.

2. *Floating Debentures*, secured on the stock in trade. Some firms have few fixed assets, but much stock in trade. This type of debenture might be issued, for example, by a motor trade parts dealer, but would not be issued by a road haulage firm providing services.

3. *Naked Debentures*, issued without security, and therefore, as the name implies, more exposed. They could only be issued by firms with excellent reputations.

Debentures have a prior claim upon the assets of a company, ranking for repayment before the shareholders and before other unsecured creditors should the firm get into difficulties. For this reason it would be most undesirable for debentures to be issued secretively, so that shareholders and creditors did not know that they had come into existence. Therefore companies are required under the Companies Acts to register their debentures, i.e. record them on a 'Register of Charges' in their company records at Company House. Since these records are open to the public for a very nominal charge anyone doing business with a company can inspect the register and see whether there are 'secured creditors' likely to step in and seize all or part of the assets should the firm get into difficulties.

Debentures earn a fixed rate of interest which is lower than other investments because the lender is running little risk of losing his money. Many of them are redeemable either at a specific time, or at the discretion of the company, whose directors may repay the loan when they feel its usefulness has declined and profits in cash form are available to repay it.

The Issue of Shares

Every limited company issues shares since the shares represent ownership of the company, but for many private companies the capital is very small. The issue of shares as a means of raising capital is chiefly confined to the public companies who are granted a quotation by the Stock Exchange Council so that their shares may be dealt in on the Exchange. The issue of shares, and the dealings on the Stock Exchange, are fully discussed in a companion volume to this, *Commerce Made Simple*.

New issues of shares and debentures are usually made with the assistance of specialised banking houses called Issuing Houses, who are usually members of the Issuing Houses Committee. These houses may 'place' the shares privately with institutional investors such as insurance companies and trade unions. With issues of shares in private companies there is often an understanding that the company will apply for quotation at a later date, when a favourable opportunity arises. With publicly quoted shares the issuing house will assist in the preparation of the application to the Stock Exchange Council, and arrange the necessary publication of the prospectus of the company. Discussion of the variety of rules and procedures required is inappropriate here. The final result will be the availability of the capital required, after deduction of expenses, underwriting fees for the issue, etc.

Finance for Statutory Bodies

Many transport organisations are set up not as limited companies registered under the Companies Acts but as public corporations authorised by an Act of Parliament to perform certain transport activities. Often this involves the nationalisation of firms currently offering services to the public. In other cases the process stops short of nationalisation. For example, with the Port of London Authority, in 1908 Parliament thought fit to solve the problems of the port by taking over the activities of the various enclosed docks and placing them in the hands of a public body established for the purpose. While not actually run as a nationalised enterprise, the autonomous port authority acts in the interests of all parties using the port: shippers, shipowners, lighterage firms, trade unions, etc. The finance is arranged for autonomous bodies by the issue to the public of stock, which entitles them to interest at an agreed rate and to redemption of capital at a future date. Clearly, different terms of issue of such stock are possible, and the range is too wide to discuss here.

The Provision of Capital by Government Agencies

In transport economics, as in all economic activities, we are faced with the problem of scarcity. There is never enough of any resource available to satisfy all demands, and this is true of capital more than most resources. Generally speaking, the flow of capital will be controlled by market forces, where certainty of return on capital invested and security of the capital itself are the chief influences at work. This means that capital will flow most readily to those industries which are certain to be successful. Unfortunately, the rich and powerful multi-national firm is most likely to meet this requirement, while the inventor struggling to produce a revolutionary product or the innovator endeavouring to launch a new service is starved of capital. Such growth points in industry often need to be helped from official sources, where a longer-term view of profitability can be taken. In this way the more serious risks of new enterprises can be carried partly by society as a whole.

The specialist bodies available to finance this type of project include the following:

(*a*) *The Finance Corporation for Industry Limited.* This institution assists firms with a fixed capital of more than £200,000, when normal sources of finance are not available. Its team of experts appraises the project or product in the course of development and if the case is strong enough makes funds available.

(*b*) *The Industrial and Commercial Finance Corporation Limited.* This body performs a similar function for firms with capital less than £200,000. Once again, projects are judged on their merits and are rigorously appraised.

(*c*) *Technical Development Capital.* This body provides help with technical innovations in their early development stages.

(*d*) *The National Research Development Corporation.* This body also exists to help new projects in their early stages of development and follows their progress by regular reviews.

While these bodies make capital available to projects which would otherwise be starved of capital, it is also necessary to conserve capital in the national interest. Although it might be thought that in a free-enterprise society a person or group should be entitled to press ahead with any project it envisaged as desirable, this might lead to waste of capital by the over-provision of resources. During the nineteenth century this happened in a great many cases; canals were dug where there was insufficient traffic to justify the expenditure, railway lines were laid which could never be profitable, and docks and wharfs proliferated in estuaries until the competition was cut-throat and all faced bankruptcy. We therefore find bodies being set up by the legislature to control capital development and restrict it to a level which is desirable and to those areas that are in the optimum position.

Such a body is the National Ports Council (see page 260). It has the task of approving all port projects costing more than £1 million. It considers the plans submitted by port authorities for developments they deem desirable, and views them in the widest context of the national interest. Britain has, if anything, too many ports, and modern shipping operates in such a way that fewer ports are needed. No longer do ships move from port to port around the coast to collect whatever traffic is available. The modern container ship makes a single call at a designated port, and then makes for the high seas to earn its living. To allow every port in Britain to become a container port would be a great waste of capital, which is in short supply. The National Ports Council approves only those projects which it deems desirable. It then, by powers conferred upon it under the Harbours Acts, ensures, subject to the Minister's approval, that these projects go ahead by recommending loans from the Department of the Environment. The port authority does not need to approach a fickle public for the capital it requires, since the money is available from official sources. There is no doubt that the National Ports Council has done excellent work in preventing excessive development of port facilities, which would undoubtedly have occurred had an entirely free-enterprise climate prevailed in the port industry in Britain.

The Calculation of Initial Capital Requirements

The capital requirement of a new firm is often underestimated by the promoter of the enterprise. It is easy to forget that the return of funds as payment for services rendered is often delayed for some considerable time. It is quite usual not to render accounts until the end of a month, and then to give 30 days for payment. This may mean that as much as two months elapses before payment is received. Many larger firms demand much longer, often three months, and will not take on a transport contractor who cannot wait for this period. Such major firms are valuable customers, and absolutely reliable if you can meet their conditions, but the initial waiting period can be difficult for the contractor. The authors know of one firm, handling a major contract for a reputable manufacturer, which had done £9 million worth of forwarding before the first payment arrived. This had only been possible because of firm backing by a merchant bank.

The following imaginary example will illustrate the initial capital requirements of a small firm.

Example

1. The Wills Brothers will set up in business as road hauliers using three vehicles which will cost, second-hand, on January 1, 19.., £2,800, £2,000 and £500 respectively.

2. It is hoped to do £3,000 of business a month for the first two months and £4,000 thereafter: 20 per cent of this is expected to be for cash, 40 per cent payable in 30 days and 40 per cent in 3 months.

3. Apart from the cost of vehicles, outgoings will include rent of £120 a month, other fixed expenses of £400 per month and variable expenses of 50 per cent of the business done.

4. The three brothers expect to draw £120 a month each.

The cash budget over the first six months looks like this:

Summary of Cash Position

	Jan. £	Feb. £	Mar. £	Apr. £	May £	Jun. £
Receipts (from services rendered)						
Cash	600	600	800	800	800	800
Monthly credit	—	1,200	1,200	1,600	1,600	1,600
3-monthly credit	—	—	—	1,200	1,200	1,600
Total (A)	600	1,800	2,000	3,600	3,600	4,000
Expenditure						
Motor vehicles	5,300					
Rent	120	120	120	120	120	120
Other fixed expenses	400	400	400	400	400	400
Variable expenses	1,500	1,500	2,000	2,000	2,000	2,000
Total (B)	7,320	2,020	2,520	2,520	2,520	2,520
Drawings	360	360	360	360	360	360
Total outgoings	7,680	2,380	2,880	2,880	2,880	2,880
Net cash flow						
In + (A–B)				+720	+720	+720
Out − (B–A)	−7,080	−580	−880			

Clearly the total finance required before the cash flows into the business make the firm viable is £8,540, far more than the original cost of the vehicles, which was only £5,300. A bank manager approached for a loan with which to buy three vehicles, costing £5,300, will react coolly to the idea until he knows more facts. A bank manager presented with the cash budget shown in this example will have a greatly improved view of the likely situation of the business in the months ahead. He will still ask astute questions. The reader should consider what questions he would ask were he the bank manager. Likely questions might be:

(*a*) What customers have you sounded out to make these estimates of £3,000 business in the first two months and £4,000 thereafter?

(*b*) What items do you include under fixed expenses?

(*c*) What grounds have you for believing that one fifth of your work will be for cash, and two fifths for firms prepared to pay within 30 days?

(*d*) Do you consider that these second-hand vehicles can be kept serviceable, so that business is not interfered with by maintenance activities? How many days per month do you think a vehicle can be on the roads?

(*e*) When your cash flow eventually turns favourable (in April), what proportion of the balance are you prepared to use to repay the loan and interest?

Budgets of this sort are clear plans for the future activities of the firm. No one is going to get into too difficult a situation if he watches the firm's activities from month to month and compares the actual achievements with the budgeted achievements. The budget 'rolls forward' ahead of the business, being adjusted as experience shows. If, in fact, three fifths of the customers pay within 30 days the cash flow position will improve and the budget will be adjusted to account for this change. Management must keep an open mind, exploiting favourable situations as they arise and getting the best results possible in the circumstances from adverse situations.

Keeping Capital Intact—Depreciation and Obsolescence

Any transport firm must be at pains to preserve the assets it creates or buys in as good a condition as possible. Inevitably vehicles, equipment, installations and buildings decline in efficiency with the passage of time. To fail to renew and repair as and when necessary is to consume one's capital. Every accounting period must provide not only the reward to the investor but sufficient funds to keep his original investment in good heart. This is done by charging all repairs and renewals to the Profit and Loss Account so that the profit available for distribution is reduced. Where an asset declines in value over a period of years, it is usual to provide for this by a process known as depreciation. Special account must also be taken of obsolescence.

A more difficult problem arises in times of inflation, when the cost of new assets rises year after year. To put away a sum of profit each year which is based on the cost price of the present facilities means that when the replacement time arrives there will be insufficient funds available to purchase the new asset at its higher price. This leads us into considerations of what is known as 'inflation accounting'. We shall now consider these three problems: depreciation, obsolescence and inflation accounting.

Depreciation

Depreciation is the reduction in value of an asset as a result of fair wear and tear. As an asset loses value we reduce the book valuation of it in line with our estimate of the loss. There are several ways in which depreciation can be calculated. The accounting principle which motivates accountants to try different methods of depreciation is that they are seeking in their accounting to achieve a 'true and fair view' of the position of the business. As far as limited companies are concerned in Great Britain, this is positively required by law. The Companies Act requires all businesses to keep accounts in such a way as to give a 'true and fair view' of the company's affairs. This requires two things:

(*a*) The assets must be valued on the books at a fair value so far as we can estimate it.

(*b*) If a loss has been suffered it must be charged against the profits—to do otherwise would overstate the profitability of the business.

Applying these two rules to the problem of depreciation, we see that if an asset wears out the loss suffered as a result of wear and tear must be written off the profits. At the same time the asset will be reduced in value to show only its present value now that it has been partly worn out.

A common method adopted in transport firms is the 'Straight Line Method', which has the merit of being simple to understand. In any case, whatever system is used assets wear out or become obsolete for so many reasons that no method can be exact.

The Straight Line Method of Depreciation

The accountant first calculates the amount of the annual charge for depreciation necessary to reduce the asset to its scrap value, or residual value, over the lifetime of the asset. To do this we use the following formula:

$$\text{Annual charge} = \frac{\text{Cost price less Scrap value}}{\text{Estimated lifetime in years}}$$

Example: A motor vehicle is purchased from Roadworthy Limited for £2,800 on January 1st. It is estimated that it will need replacing in four years, and will then fetch £800. Using the formula, we have

$$\text{Annual charge} = \frac{£2,800 - £800}{4}$$
$$= £500$$

The asset will be depreciated by four equal instalments of £500 each. Each year the sum of £500 will be written off the Profit and Loss Account as a loss due to depreciation, and this will be collected into a special 'Provision for Depreciation on Motor Vehicles Account', as shown in Fig. 15.1.

The value of the asset at any given time is therefore the book-value (i.e. cost price), less the accumulated depreciation to date.

In this case it would be:

	£
Cost price	2,800
Less depreciation	1,500
Present value of asset	1,300

Motor Vehicles Account

19..		£	
Jan. 1 To Roadworthy Ltd. J. 1		2,800	

Provision for Depreciation on Motor Vehicles Account

			£
	19..		
	Dec. 31 By Profit & Loss A/C		500
	19..		
	Dec. 31 By Profit & Loss A/C		500
	19..		
	Dec. 31 By Profit & Loss A/C		500

Fig. 15.1. Leaving the asset on the books at cost price.

Obsolescence

Obsolescence occurs when technical developments render an asset un-economic in use, and it has to be prematurely replaced. It effectively reduces the life-time of the asset, and represents an abnormal loss in value. Such abnormal losses have been particularly common in the aviation industry, where rapid advances in technology have made aircraft obsolete before their full working life has elapsed. For example, the introduction of the 747 Jumbo Jet has caused the premature retirement of smaller aircraft. When such abnormal losses are likely to occur it is common to establish a Provision for Obsolescence Account, where sums written off the profits can be retained to meet any abnormal decline in value which may occur in the years ahead.

If proper allowance is made for depreciation and obsolescence the capital will be preserved at its original value and the business will be kept in good heart.

Inflation Accounting and Historical Cost Accounting

The Company Acts of 1948 and 1967 require companies to publish accounts for their shareholders annually. These accounts must give a 'true and fair view' of the affairs of the business. This has traditionally meant that the original cost of assets must be shown, less the total depreciation to date, to give their present value on the books. At the same time, in the Profit and Loss Account, the total receipts must be shown, set against the total expenditure incurred in earning these receipts. The difference will be the profit, or loss, of the venture. In times of stable prices this picture does give a 'true and fair view' of the affairs of the business. In inflationary times the picture may be far from true, and even absolutely misleading. This is because the sums of money spent over the years, i.e. the 'historical costs', are in fact sums of money of different values. The reader will understand this most easily if a simple example is taken.

Imagine a road haulier who has purchased four similar lorries over the years, one of them ten years ago, one six years ago, one four years ago and one this year. The historical costs and 'current purchasing power' costs are roughly shown in Table 15.2.

The difficulty here is that the historical costs, added together as a total of £11,435, are in fact additions of different things. The pounds of ten years ago were not the same as the pounds of today. To get a clear picture we ought to adjust all our prices to 'current purchasing power' prices.

Table 15.2. Costs of Vehicles

	Historical cost (£)	Purchasing power of £1	Cost at present-day prices
10-year-old vehicle	2,000	1	4,000
6-year-old vehicle	2,360	0·85	4,000
4-year-old vehicle	3,075	0·65	4,000
New vehicle	4,000	0·50	4,000
	11,435		16,000

Every transport firm is faced by the problems of inflation. These problems may be listed as follows:

(*a*) Prices are always rising, so that both running costs and the costs of new assets to replace old worn-out assets increase all the time.

(*b*) £1 put away for future use in purchasing new assets will, by the time it is put to use, have declined in value so that it buys less. This means that in depreciating our assets we need to put away more than the ordinary fraction of its original cost; we need to put away the same fraction of its eventual new cost. It is not easy to guess what this will be.

(*c*) If we do not use inflation accounting the following results follow:

(i) Profits will be overstated, and hence will give a false appearance of well-being to the firm.

(ii) This false appearance will lead investors to expect a distribution of dividends in excess of what is really desirable, since in fact the profits were overstated.

(iii) Labour will demand a higher share of the rewards available to the industry; that is, pressure for wage increases will follow higher profits, although in fact these profits are illusory.

There is plenty of evidence to show that all these results have followed the continued use of 'historical accounting' in the last few years. The 'true and fair view' given by historical cost accounting is used to justify higher dividends and higher wages although in fact it is not 'true', and not 'fair'. The higher the rate of inflation the more the distortion of the true position, and the higher demands of both labour and investors, leaving firms short of finance for the replacement of assets.

The Capital is Not Being Kept Intact

The solution is to change over to '*current purchasing power*' *accounting* or *C.P.P.* The 'true and fair view' we need the auditors to certify is the fact that the capital has been kept intact in real terms, before profits have been declared. The final accounts which are to be published need simply to be revalued in terms of current purchasing power. If this was done then the following desirable effects would follow:

(*a*) Profits would be reduced to their true level, and this would reduce demands for distribution of dividends.

(*b*) Trade union pressure would be reduced and wage negotiations would be pursued on a more realistic basis.

(*c*) Changes in the valuation of shares would occur as Stock Exchanges took account of the true profitability of firms.

(*d*) Amalgamations and takeovers would be reduced, since the number of firms getting into financial difficulties would be reduced.

There is some danger that prices might rise as managements, now forced to recognise their true situation, might adjust prices to restore profits to the incorrect levels of former years.

Cash Flow and Depreciation

One interesting aspect of depreciation is its effect upon cash flow. Cash flow is the generation of cash by profitable activities over a period of time. If services are provided at a profit the profits become available in cash form and are available for the use of the proprietor either to consume as his 'income' or to plough back into the business as 'growth'. Depreciation is deducted from the profits in the same way as running expenses, but unlike the running expenses no outside individual or firm is taking the payments. Wages deducted from the profits have been paid to employees. Depreciation allowances deducted from the profits are not paid to anyone—instead they generate cash flow. This cash becomes available to the business. Management must be careful to recognise its existence and decide how to use it in the interval between its creation and its requirement to replace the assets wearing out. It is frequently invested outside the business to provide funds eventually from an external source for the replacement of the assets. If this is not done it must certainly not be enjoyed by the proprietor as 'income'. It may be used to promote growth, but the management must then make special plans to replace the assets when necessary.

The Financial Statements of an Established Enterprise

It is now appropriate to consider the accounts of an established enterprise. Before looking at the actual accounts of an important transport body we must consider the principles governing the accounting records of such an enterprise. Every enterprise has two aspects of finance to consider: the capital aspect and the revenue aspect. Let us examine these two aspects in some detail.

Capital Receipts and Capital Expenditure

Capital receipts and capital expenditure refer to the following matters:

(*a*) The collection of the original capital necessary to start the enterprise.

(*b*) The provision of additional capital during the course of its activities, whenever expansion of the firm or institution requires it.

(*c*) The expenditure of this capital in creating the capital assets of the firm, from the purchase of the geographical site or sites, the erection of buildings, installations and plant to the provision of furniture and equipment, motor vehicles, etc.

An annual presentation of the current capital position is made in the Balance Sheet, a document which lists the assets and liabilities in some simple format to present a true and fair view of the affairs of the enterprise, for the benefit of interested parties. This document always shows the Capital Employed and the sources from which it was obtained. Against this, under a heading 'Represented By', are listed all the assets of the business which have been purchased with the capital made available by investors and creditors. These assets represent the capital in actual physical form and can be viewed, valued and appraised by interested parties. Such a Balance Sheet for the Port of London Authority is shown on page 181.

Revenue Receipts and Revenue Expenditure

Revenue receipts and revenue expenditure refer to the following matters:

(*a*) The revenues earned by the firm's activities, from all sources such as sales of trade goods; sales of manufactured articles; payments for services rendered and for facilities provided; fees for professional advice; commissions and other profits; rents from land or premises; leasing of facilities, premises and plant and other revenues such as licensing of other firms to use patents, etc.

(*b*) The expenditures incurred in earning the revenues listed above, including wages and salaries; running expenses of every kind; fixed charges such as rent, rates and taxes on vehicles; losses such as bad debts, insurance premiums, loan interest, etc. Depreciation charges are also included in these expenses and make possible the purchase of new assets to replace worn-out or obsolete capital items.

The difference between revenue receipts and expenditure will be the profit or loss of the firm or institution. Profits will be used to pay the dividends to which shareholders are entitled. Alternatively they will be ploughed back into the firm for expansion purposes and will appear on the Balance Sheet as reserves. Losses will represent a decline in the total value of the capital and will appear as such on the Balance Sheet.

Financial Statements

At one time when enterprises were small and the proprietor conducted his own affairs, financial statements were not necessary to the conduct of an enterprise. Today they are essential. Not only are they required to satisfy the Inland Revenue authorities who wish to levy income tax or corporation tax on the business, but business is so competitive that the proprietor who does not have some regular and effective check on expenditures and incomes will find himself in difficulties. For limited companies they represent an opportunity for the shareholders to review the activities of the directors and for public corporations they present a similar opportunity to Parliament to review the industry's work.

The reader is urged to consider the final accounts of the Port of London Authority, reproduced here by kind permission of the Director General (Figs. 15.2 and 15.3). The explanatory notes included in brackets in the presentation bring out the chief points about each heading shown. Some minor adjustments from the actual published accounts have been made to simplify the presentation.

Costing Transport Activities

Definition of Costing

Costing is an accounting process which allocates expenditure to particular activities or operations, so that their likely or true cost can be discovered. If

PORT OF LONDON AUTHORITY

REVENUE ACCOUNT
for the year ended 31st December, 1972

	£000	£000
OPERATING REVENUE RECEIPTS		
Dock and conservancy charges on ships (for use of the river and facilities)		5,935
Port rates on goods (charges made to cargo owners)		4,432
Passenger dues		36
		10,403
Cargo handling		18,342
Cranes and plant (charges made for use of facilities)		1,685
Warehousing and storage charges		1,145
Sundry services and facilities		1,842
Rents		1,067
Other miscellaneous revenue		459
TOTAL OPERATING REVENUE		34,943
EXPENDITURE		
Operating and maintenance	7,011	
Dredging	609	
Handling costs	13,826	
Administrative and other general expenditure	6,280	
TOTAL EXPENDITURE		27,726
OPERATING PROFIT BEFORE DEPRECIATION		7,217
Provision for depreciation (straight-line basis)	2,381	
Less Proportion of official port modernisation and investment grants	273	2,108
OPERATING PROFIT		5,109
Investment income (from reserves loaned out or invested)		1,114
PROFIT BEFORE INTEREST		6,223
Less Interest charges (payable on short-term and long-term loans)		4,881
PROFIT for year		1,342
EXCEPTIONAL ITEMS		
Add profits on sale of surplus assets, including docks, offices, plant and investments	5,122	
Deduct severance pay (paid to dockers and other staff agreeing to leave the industry)	3,433	
		1,689
		£3,031

Fig. 15.2. Revenue Account of an established enterprise.

(courtesy of Port of London Authority)

BALANCE SHEET
at 31st December, 1972

	£000	£000	£000
CAPITAL EMPLOYED			
CAPITAL LIABILITIES (Port of London Stock and borrowing from official bodies)			68,442
RESERVES (including profit of £3,031)			52,361
PORT MODERNISATION AND INVESTMENT GRANTS not yet credited to revenue			7,023
INSURANCE FUND			1,200
			129,026
Less DISCOUNT AND EXPENSES ON ISSUE OF PORT STOCK at cost, less amounts written off			245
			128,781
REPRESENTED BY			
FIXED ASSETS less depreciation			118,077
INVESTMENTS			
Held for insurance fund		1,200	
Trade investments in certain port firms		49	
Held for stock and loan redemption in years to come		8,921	
			10,170
CURRENT ASSETS			
Stores and materials at cost		617	
Port modernisation and investment grants receivable		1	
Debtors, accrued income and payment in advance		7,648	
Short-term loans, deposits and investments		2,295	
Bank and cash balances		27	
		10,588	
Less CURRENT LIABILITIES			
Bank overdraft	27		
Short-term bills of exchange	2,000		
Interest accrued due	1,333		
Creditors and other accrued liabilities	6,694		
		10,054	
NET CURRENT ASSETS			534
Net assets of the Port			£128,781

Fig. 15.3. The Balance Sheet of an established enterprise.

(courtesy of Port of London Authority)

the costs are being forecast, then the cost accountant is said to be preparing a budget for future activities. If the costs have already occurred, and they are simply being allocated to the particular activities which caused them, we say that the accountant is preparing 'historical' costs. In most firms both processes will be carried out. The budgets represent an intelligent and informed forecast of the expenditure to be incurred and the revenues to be earned. As the operations get under way and 'actual' costs are incurred, it becomes possible to compare the actual costs with the budgeted costs. Any 'variance' between actual costs and budgeted costs will be analysed to discover the reason. This process is called 'variance analysis'. It may reveal price trends which would otherwise be overlooked; errors in calculations; even dishonesty, embezzlement or theft of fuel and spare parts. The resulting action varies from dismissal of the dishonest employee to corrective action to make the budget more realistic in view of current trends in prices of supplies, labour and other resources.

Budgets

A *capital budget* is a forecast of capital expenditure under particular headings for a forthcoming period, and the sources of finance available. The

Table 15.3. Budget for Road Haulage Operations (January–June 19 . .)

Details	Costs & Revenue Vehicle No. 1 for period		Costs & Revenue Vehicle No. 1 per working day	Vehicle No. 2 Costs, etc.	Total Fleet
Vehicle No.	XYT 997 H				
Date of purchase	1/1/19..			*Notes*	
Capacity	16 tons			(a) Since tyres are regarded as a	
Cost	£4,650			running expense it is usual to	
Less tyres	850	(a)		deduct these from the value of any vehicle purchased.	
	£3,800				
Running costs per mile in pence.		(b)			
Fuel and oil	3.069				
Tyres	0.965			(b) These costs are based on current prices at the time the budget is prepared	
Repairs and Maintenance	2.266				
	6.300 pence				
Estimated mileage	25,000	(c)	200	(c) This estimate is based on previous experience, and 125 days' operations.	
Estimated revenue	£4,875	(d)	£39	(d) As above	
Deduct Estimated costs					
Wages	£1,250	(e)	£10.00	(e) As above	
Licence/insurance	240	(f)	1.92	(f) Factual at the time the estimate is prepared.	
Depreciation	360	(g)	2.88	(g) Straight line method.	
Overheads	640	(h)	5.12	(h) Allocated on vehicle tonnage basis.	
Running costs	1,575	(i)	12.60	(i) Based on estimates above.	
	4,065		32.52	Note on (h) above:	
Profit	810		6.48	Total vehicle tonnage = 200 tons	
	£4,875		£39.00	Total overheads = £8,000 This vehicle = 16 tons $\frac{16}{200} \times £8,000 = £640$	

a

b

Plate 9. (a) Fred Olsen berth, side-loading fruit. (b) Roll-on roll-off ship discharging at Felixstowe.

(courtesy of the Port of London Authority (a), and Transport Ferry Services Ltd. (b))

Plate 10. The container ship *Discovery Bay* passing Tilbury grain terminal.

(courtesy of Overseas Containers Ltd.)

Plate 11. Loading igloo containers from a roller pallet van, via a scissors-lift.

(courtesy of Lufthansa)

Plate 12. A luggage carousel at Edmonton Airport, Alberta (**a**), and a Cres-Flight baggage claim conveyor at Perth (**b**).

(courtesy of Mathews Conveyor Co. Ltd., Canada)

a

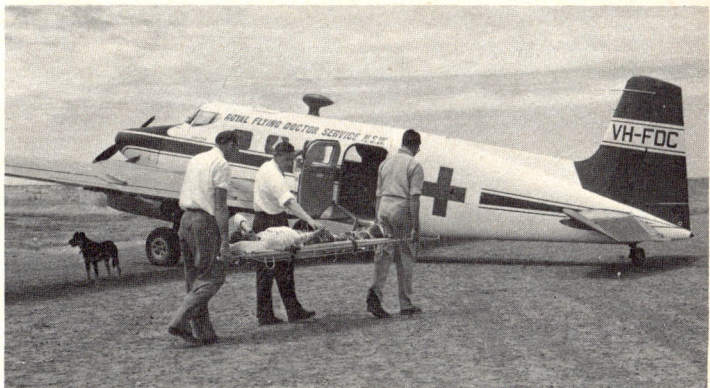

b

c

Plate 13. (a) Concorde 02 touching down. (b) Australia's Flying Doctor
Service. (c) Rushing a human kidney for transplant.

(courtesy of British Aircraft Corporation (a), the Australia High Commission (b), and St. John
Ambulance Brigade (c))

Plate 14. (a) The Goodyear Airship *Europa*. **(b)** Seaspeed
Hovercraft *Princess Margaret* arriving at Dover.

(courtesy of the Goodyear Tyre and Rubber Co. (Gt. Britain) Ltd. (a), and British Rail
Hovercraft Ltd (b))

Plate 15. A 'Skyfotos' picture of a Lykes Line Seabee barge-carrying ship.

a

b

c

Plate 16. (a) Oil pipelines crossing hilly country in Iran.
(b) and (c) Pumps at work boosting pressures on the crude oil pipelines
at Fahud.

(courtesy of Shell International Petroleum Co. Ltd.)

budget will be scaled down to what seems possible in view of the current financial position, postponing until a later date those projects which are least necessary. These marginal projects will usually be those with smaller prospects of profitability.

A *revenue budget* is a forecast of expenditure and receipts from a particular activity. By adding together the budgets for all these activities we can arrive at a total budget for the firm. Help in the preparation of budgets can often be obtained from trade associations which make available tables of costs, updated from time to time. For many industries specialist accounting firms have devised special systems of cost records. These can be very useful to firms in the industry.

The road haulage revenue budget given in Table 15.3 refers to a single vehicle, but in practice would be prepared in columnar form for all vehicles to give a budget for the total fleet.

The total budget for the whole fleet per week would then be compared with the actual weekly costing statement shown in Table 15.4. This statement would be produced as soon as the figures became available. Actual figures would be used for the revenue earned and the wages, while the running expenses would be based on the budget for the actual mileage run. The rest of the figures would be based upon the budgeted figures.

Table 15.4. Weekly Costing Statement for 5-Day Week Ending . . . .

Revenue earned (actual)	£ —
Expenses	
Wages (actual)	—
Running costs (based on actual mileage)	—
Licences/Insurance (as per budget)	—
Depreciation (as per budget)	—
Overhead expenses (as per budget)	—
Total Expenses	—
Profit for Week	£ —

The Return on Capital Invested

Every enterprise can be judged according to the return it brings to the investor. Such returns are best calculated as a percentage return on capital employed. The formula is

$$\frac{\text{Net profit}}{\text{Capital employed}} \times 100$$

Unfortunately, as with all formulae, we must define our terms carefully or we shall arrive at different answers, or answers which are less useful than they might be. Let us consider limited companies first.

The Return on Capital Employed—Companies

With limited companies the true capital employed is found as follows (some imaginary figures have been inserted):

		£
1. Ordinary shares issued at the start of the year	=	25,000
2. Reserves retained in previous years	=	8,000
Ordinary shareholders' interest in the company	=	33,000
3. Preference shares issued at the start of the year (7%)	=	7,000
4. Debentures issued at start of the year (6½%)	=	10,000
		£50,000

		£
True profit figures are:	Net profit (say)	7,800
	Debenture interest paid	650
		£8,450

$$\therefore \text{ Return on Capital Employed} = \frac{8,450}{50,000} \times 100$$

$$= 16\cdot9\%$$

Notice that although this return on capital was earned by all the capital employed, some of it was rewarded with a much smaller figure than 16·9%. The debenture holders only received 6½% and the preference shareholders only received 7%, so that in fact the ordinary shareholders received rather more than 16·9%. Of course it does not follow that they actually received anything like this percentage in actual dividend, since it is up to the directors how much is actually given away as dividends to the shareholders. A board which is expanding the affairs of the company may retain most of the profits to finance expansion.

The Return on Capital Employed—Sole Traders and Partnerships

With sole traders and partnerships there is a modification required if correct ideas are to be formed about the profitability of the firm. Since the proprietors are usually working in the business, it would not be right to regard the net profit earned as being entirely 'profit'. Some of it should be regarded as wages of the proprietor. The reader who has studied Economics will know about 'opportunity cost': the cost of any resource is the value of the lost opportunity we sacrificed of employing it in the next best situation. If the proprietor had not been running his transport firm he might instead have been employed elsewhere, perhaps as a manager in some other firm. We must therefore deduct from the net profit earned the probable wage he could have been earning elsewhere. The return on capital employed will therefore be found by the formula

$$\frac{\text{Net profit} - \text{Estimated wage elsewhere}}{\text{Capital at the start of the year}} \times 100$$

Imagining a firm of the same general size as the company referred to earlier, whose proprietor could have earned £2,800 elsewhere, we have

$$\frac{£8,450 - £2,800}{£50,000} \times 100$$

$$= \frac{£5,650}{£50,000} \times 100$$

$$= \underline{\underline{11 \cdot 3\%}}$$

This return may be compared with the return obtainable on alternative investments.

Costs in Distribution—Analysis and Control

In distribution, as distinct from transport, there has been insufficient thought given in the past to the true analysis of costs. A full analysis may therefore result in salutary decisions affecting the performance of the company. These may include alterations to the product range, re-siting of depots, new intermodal handling methods, etc. A complete reappraisal starts with the preparation of a list of distribution centres of activity and cost. These may be listed as follows, but an individual firm may not have all of them in its organisation.

Distribution Cost Centres

(*a*) Collection and storage of raw materials.
(*b*) Collection and storage of components from sub-contractors.
(*c*) Finished goods storage at the factory.
(*d*) Dispatch centre costs at the factory.
(*e*) Transport to the depot.
(*f*) Depot handling and inventory costs.
(*g*) Inter-depot transfer costs.
(*h*) Depot dispatch costs.
(*i*) Depot to customer transport costs.
(*j*) Administration and documentation costs at each of the above cost centres.

Many of the true costs of distribution are hidden away in the accounts of many companies, disguised in other costs. Thus costs (*a*) and (*b*) above will often be found included in manufacturing costs, and costs (*h*) and (*i*) will often be included in sales costs. The true distribution costs are often therefore much greater than at first thought, due to poor definition and analysis. A true estimate of distribution costs is likely to be about 30 per cent or even 40 per cent of total costs. The chief difficulty in controlling costs is that the only true guide to the performance of a company is the return on capital invested, so that a simple procedure of always reducing costs as much as possible will not necessarily produce the best result. This is why the concept of minimum total distribution cost is so important—it alone brings the best return on capital invested. To cut out a distribution process simply because it was expensive might result in greater total costs if the expensive item was more effective, and therefore should be increased rather than curtailed.

Allocating Costs to Products or Activities

Very often existing costing systems list costs under expense categories, such as labour, fuel, light and heat, occupation, administration, etc. This system of allocation lends itself to the examination of variances in expense categories—we can see whether fuel costs rose this month and do something about investigating them. What it does not help us to do is to evaluate the worthwhile nature of a particular product in its contribution to the return on capital invested. If these costs are allocated to products—so that occupancy reflects the time goods are in storage—we shall soon see whether it is worthwhile keeping a slow-moving item in stock. If the return on that item is less than the cost of storage and handling we can either raise our margin of profit on it or phase it out as a line of stock.

Having identified the true costs of distribution, and allocated them to particular products or services, the accountant can examine them with a view to reducing total distribution costs. Streamlining of many activities may be immediately highlighted, particularly in the administrative field. It may become apparent that certain customers are given services which are uneconomic, while others are given services, which, while uneconomic viewed on their own, are marginally profitable because they are make-weight services thrown in in the course of serving other customers who are profitable to trade with. Some simulation of these activities on a computer may be very helpful here in analysing ultimate profitability.

Unfortunately this introductory textbook cannot deal adequately with the analysis and control of distribution costs, but the subject is of great importance and readers concerned with this particular field are urged to pursue its study.

Suggested Further Reading

Baggott, J., *Cost and Management Accounting Made Simple*, W. H. Allen, 1973.
Distributive Industry Training Board, *Mind Your Own Business*, 1972.
Lee, G. A., *Transport Finance and Accounting*, 1969, Pitman.
Midgley, K., and Burns, R. G., *Business Finance and the Capital Market*, Macmillan, 1972.
Wentworth, F. R. L. (Ed.), *Physical Distribution Management*, Gower Press, 1970.
Whitehead, G., *Book-Keeping Made Simple*, W. H. Allen, 1975.
Whitehead, G., *Commerce Made Simple*, W. H. Allen, 1975.
Whitehead, G., *Economics Made Simple*, W. H. Allen, 1975.

CHAPTER SIXTEEN

LEGAL ASPECTS OF TRANSPORT

Transport as a Contractual Arrangement

Transport and distribution are such ancient activities that they have a very old legal background. The origins of *charter-parties* and *bills of lading* can be found in Greek and Roman times, while in the United Kingdom the concept of the common carrier, carrying by the *ancient custom of the realm* is still basic to the law of carriage. Another enduring feature of transport is its international character, so that a *'conflict of laws'* is inseparable from transport activities, especially today where nations are dependent on one another for so many basic requirements. In recent years these legal conflicts have tended to be resolved by *international conventions*, which have laid down mutually agreed rules for the carriage of goods and passengers by air, sea, rail and road. The most recent of these—concerned with the *law of combined transport*—has not yet been adopted by nations. This chapter can do little more than outline the general thinking behind the legal relationships in transport, but the reader is urged to pursue his study of transport law as rigorously as he pursues his study of transport itself.

The Common Carrier

A common carrier in English law is anyone who holds himself out as willing to carry for reward. He must do it as a regular business, not as a casual operation. He may limit the extent to which he is willing to carry, both as to the type of goods and as to the distance and direction he is prepared to go. If he holds himself out as a carrier, by announcing the fact on public notice boards, advertisements in the press, stationery, etc., then the law regards him as a common carrier, with a legal duty to carry.

Ancient custom of the realm regards the carrier as prima facie suspect for does he not go 'over the hills and far away' with other people's property? Who can tell what tricks the carrier is up to when out of sight? English law therefore very early on placed a very onerous responsibility on carriers, that they were liable for every loss that occurred. This is often expressed as 'the liability of an insurer', but the idea precedes the idea of insurance by many centuries. The common carrier bore the heavy responsibility of compensating anyone who suffered loss, irrespective of whether or not he was at fault. If A's cart was overturned by B's cart whose horse had bolted, A must compensate the owners of any goods in his cart which were damaged, seeking indemnity from B, the owner of the other vehicle. Gradually the courts developed some 'common law exceptions' to the severity of this rule, and a common carrier who could prove that the loss occurred through one of these common law exceptions could escape responsibility. They were:

(*a*) Act of God
(*b*) Act of the Queen's enemies
(*c*) Inherent vice

(*d*) Fault of the consignor (usually faulty packaging, addressing, etc.)
(*e*) Fraud of the consignor

The enduring nature of the concept of the common carrier is best illustrated by the railways. These were held to be common carriers right down to 1962, when the Transport Act of 1962—recognising that the heavy losses on railway operations were partly caused by the railways' status as common carriers—declared them to be private carriers from that time on.

The Private Carrier

A private carrier is anyone who is not a common carrier. He only holds himself out as being a private carrier. That is to say he announces in his public notices, advertisements, etc., that he is not a common carrier, but only carries under private 'Conditions of Carriage', which form a contract between him and his customers. These sets of conditions of carriage are often in practice drawn up by the trade associations, such as the Road Haulage Association, or the Institute of Freight Forwarders, and readers are urged to obtain such a set of Conditions of Carriage and read them carefully. They form part of a body of contracts called 'Standard Form Contracts'. A word about the abuse of standard form contracts is desirable.

Standard Form Contracts and the Privity of Contract

Standard form contracts are to be found in every area of commercial activity, in Sale of Goods, in Hire Purchase, and especially in Carriage. Typical examples are the conditions of carriage issued by the Road Haulage Association (the 1967 rules), the British Railways Conditions of Carriage (B.R.18793), and the Conditions of Carriage of the Institute of Freight Forwarders. Naturally these bodies issue such Conditions of Carriage as a protection for their members, and embody in them the considered advice of their lawyers. Irrespective of the area they cover these documents can be criticised from one point of view: they make the contractual agreement very one-sided. English law holds that a contract is a private arrangement between two parties, both of whom are deemed to be equally knowledgeable, equally sophisticated, equally alert to the implications of the contract. The use of standard form contracts makes a mockery of this concept, for the housewife who asks a carrier to take goods from one part of the country to another has little knowledge of the law, or of contracts, and is forced to accept the terms and conditions offered. In many cases the carrier is a monopolist, perhaps even having a statutory monopoly, and no alternative mode of transport is available to the customer. In these circumstances, in years gone by, carriers have abused their position by having onerous clauses inserted into their standard terms and conditions. Conflicts between customers and carriers have frequently arisen; Parliament itself has intervened—sometimes to little effect—and even today the protection of the consumer in carriage matters gives some cause for concern.

The ability of a carrier to advertise himself as a private carrier, and thus escape the rigorous position of a common carrier liable for every loss that occurs, has meant that a contractual arrangement is now the normal relationship between the carrier and his customers. These contracts are based on standard terms and conditions drawn up by the carrier's trade association, giving him the best protection their lawyers can devise. Every student of transport should make a point of studying such a set of Conditions of Carriage carefully. One of the best is the Road Haulage Conditions of Carriage (1967 rules), which embody most of the modern ideas of what is fair to both parties. Reading these rules carefully it might seem that they are unduly biased in favour of the road haulier, but careful thought will let the reader see that in fact the carrier under these rules does accept responsibility (see Clause XI) for things which are his fault, while rejecting responsibility for all things which are not his fault (such as strikes, acts of foreign governments, etc.). At the same time, the carriage of goods and passengers is a competitive industry in many ways, and the severity of terms in the contract is often reduced by the need to maintain goodwill. It is perhaps not insignificant that in international carriage, where competition is most fierce, the severity of these contracts has been reduced by international agreement.

Inland Carriage and International Carriage

Within the boundaries of any state or territory carriage of goods and passengers will be governed by the laws of the state concerned. It follows that a 'conflict of laws' can easily arise where goods and passengers cross frontiers, as they inevitably do in sea carriage and often do in carriage by air, carriage by road via roll-on roll-off ships, and continental rail carriage. The 'conflict of laws' arises because the parties concerned, living in different countries, are free to bring their complaints in the courts of their own countries. Of course the courts of both countries may reach the same conclusion about a particular matter, so that no conflict arises; the case is more difficult where the laws of the countries are different. What is permissible in one country may be illegal in another, and hence a 'conflict of laws' is inevitable. How shall such conflicts be resolved?

The answer to this problem has been found in the 'convention' system. An international convention is held at which the representatives of both sides in each nation are present. The two sides referred to are the 'carriers' on the one hand, i.e. the ship-owners, airlines, road hauliers and railways, and the 'consignors' or 'passengers' on the other hand. The consignors are chiefly the shippers or forwarders of goods, represented by their Chambers of Commerce. Passengers, a less well-organised group, tend to be represented at these conventions by their respective governments in some official way. The first of these international conventions was the *Convention Internationale Merchandises*, which was originally signed in 1914. This was a railway convention, signed at a time when all merchandise travelling internationally went either by sea or railway. It was designed to provide a body of rules for European rail carriage. These rules are known as the *C.I.M. rules*.

Later conventions were the International Conference on Maritime Law, held in Brussels in October, 1922. This convention drew up a set of rules which became known as the *Hague Rules*. The nations which ratified this convention then enacted statutes in their own countries embodying the convention in their own national laws. Thus the convention became law in all the leading maritime countries. In the United Kingdom the relevant statute is the Carriage of Goods by Sea Act 1924, shortly to be replaced by the Carriage of Goods by Sea Act 1971, which embodies modern amendments to the original convention. In 1929 a Warsaw Convention laid down rules for international

Table 16.1. Legal Points Covered in English Law

	Body of rules	Nature of carrier's liability	Basis of legal relationships	Official document in use
1.	Common Law (Common carriers)	Liable for every loss that occurs	Ancient custom of the realm	No specific document
2.	Contract Law (Private carrier)	Liable for negligence only	Oral or written contract	No specific document
3.	Road Haulage (1967 Rules)	Contractual—liable for negligence	Standard contract based on the Conditions	R.H.A. 1967 rules
4.	British Railways Standard Conditions (B.R.18793)	Contractual—Two scales of charges: Owner's risk and Company risk	Standard contract based on the Conditions	Railway Consignment Note
5.	Hague Rules (International Carriage by Sea)	Statutory. Inter alia: He is bound to exercise due diligence to provide a seaworthy and cargoworthy ship	Carriage of Goods by Sea Act 1924 (or 1971 Act when implemented)	Bill of Lading
6.	Warsaw Rules (International Carriage by Air)	Statutory. He is liable under the convention for those losses which are his fault	Carriage of Goods by Air Act 1961 (although repealed the 1932 Act still has effect in some cases)	Air Waybill (1961 Act). Air Consignment Note (1932 Act)
7.	C.I.M. Rules (International Carriage by Rail)	Contractual. England has not enacted the convention but contractually impounds it by the Rail Consignment Note	C.I.M. Convention contractually adopted	Rail Consignment Note
8.	C.M.R. Rules (International Carriage by Road)	Statutory	Carriage of Goods by Road Act 1965	International C.M.R. Consignment Note

and in the International Carriage Conventions

Jurisdiction of the courts	Limitation of liability of carrier	Time limit on legal actions	Special notes
County Court or High Court	None	6 years (Limitations Act 1939)	Common Law exceptions apply to liability
As above	As specified in the contract	6 years as above	—
As above	£800 per ton (or per 80 cubic feet)	6 years as above	Read the Rules for full information
As above	£800 per ton (or per 80 cubic feet)	6 years as above	There are special rules for live-stock, coal and coke and carriage by water
The convention is silent on this matter. It is for the parties to decide	£100 per package under 1924 Act. Under 1971 Act 10,000 francs per package or 30 francs per kg, whichever is higher	One year under 1924 Act. Under the 1971 Act this time limit may be extended by mutual agreement	The implementa-tion of the 1971 Act depends upon the Queen issuing an Order in Council
A case may be heard in the court where the carrier is resident, or has a place of business, or at the destination of the goods	1932 Act Passengers, 125,000 francs. Goods, 250 gold francs per kg 1961 Act Passengers, 250,000 francs. Goods, 250 gold francs per kg	Two years	Domestic flights are governed by the Non-International Carriage Rules
A case may normally be brought by any party against the carrier from whom he is claiming, in the courts of the country where the carrier resides. This will usually be the claimant's country too	100 gold francs per kg, converted to currency at the rate prevailing on the day the claim is settled	Usually one year, but three years is allowed if wilful misconduct is alleged.	The British Rail Through Consignment Note contractu-ally impounds the C.I.M. Rules into the conditions of carriage
Action may be brought anywhere agreed or in one of the countries concerned	25 gold francs per kg	One year (three years if wilful misconduct is alleged)	The decisions of foreign courts become matters of record in the U.K. and hence precedents

carriage by air. The relevant statute in the United Kingdom was the Carriage by Air Act 1932, subsequently replaced by the Carriage by Air Act 1961. These rules for the settlement of disputes about air carriage are called the *Warsaw Rules*. Finally, road haulage was the subject of a convention, the *Convention de Merchandises per Route*. When enacted into British law this convention became the Carriage of Goods by Road Act 1965. The rules are known as the *C.M.R. Rules*.

One further draft convention, the T.C.M. convention, drawn up by the Institute of Unification of Private Law (Unidroit) at Rome, and the Comité Maritime International, is about the legal rules on combined transport; that is, transport using more than one mode, e.g. road–sea–road, or rail–sea–road transits. It is unlikely at present that this convention will be generally adopted.

This is not a law book, and the reader must turn elsewhere for full details of these conventions, but Table 16.1 shows the main points made in the conventions in tabular form.

Suggested Further Reading

Ivamy, H., *Payne's Carriage of Goods by Sea*, Butterworths, 1972 (or later editions).

Kahn-Freund, O., *The Law of Carriage by Inland Transport* (most recent edition), Stevens & Sons Ltd.

Lord McNair, A. C., *The Law of the Air*, Stevens & Sons Ltd., 1973.

Ridley, J., *The Law of Carriage of Goods by Land, Sea and Air*, Shaw & Sons Ltd., 1975.

CHAPTER SEVENTEEN

THE TRANSPORT ACT, 1968

Introduction

The British transport industry could legitimately claim in the last quarter of a century that it had been repeatedly placed in a position where it was attempting to carry out the provisions of a Transport Act recently passed by Parliament, in a climate of discussion which was considering the dismantling or re-shaping of the Act. Thus the 1947 Transport Act, which set up the British Transport Commission, was barely able to carry out the major nationalisation proposals when discussions were afoot to denationalise some sections of the industry. The 1953 Act attempted to denationalise road haulage, but the climate of opinion against this was so strong in some sectors of industry that it proved impossible to find buyers for the long-haul lorries. Interested parties were fearful of renationalisation without compensation. The 1962 Act made a further attempt to get things right, but was overshadowed by the Labour Government's determination to produce a major piece of legislation rectifying those sections of the 1962 Act which it regarded as unsatisfactory. Fortunately the 1968 Act, despite its controversial solutions to many problems, has proved to be less contentious than the earlier Acts. This is perhaps partly because it has not tried to repeat the mistakes of the 1947 Act, and has been assisted by environmental factors which have tended to show that there is a limit to the total expansion of free enterprise road haulage, however economic it may appear to be.

This major Act of Parliament should be studied seriously by every student of transport, for it illustrates the far-reaching impact of legislation upon the transport industry. To assist the student, a brief paraphrase of most of the sections is included here, under major headings.

Part I: The Act's Provisions with Respect to the Integration of Freight Services

Section 1.   A National Freight Corporation to be set up which will provide properly integrated services for the carriage of goods by road or rail—rail to be used whenever such carriage is efficient and economic, and bearing in mind the nature of the goods and the needs of the customer. The essence of the provision of all services is to be efficiency, economy and safety.

The Railways and the National Freight Corporation are to co-operate with each other to provide the services needed. It is not the Railways' *duty* any longer to provide freight services but they *may* still do so.

Section 2.   The Freight Corporation may carry goods by road, make arrangements with the railways to carry by rail, carry by sea or hovercraft, consign, warehouse, co-operate with any other carrier in through-deliveries, operate depots, harbours, or hire vehicles, vessels, etc.

The Freight Corporation is *not* a Common Carrier.

193

Section 3. It will take over capital debt up to £200–300 million.

Section 4. It will take over certain securities, rights and liabilities of the Transport Holding Company, the British Road Services Federation Limited, etc.

Section 5. The British Railways are to set up as separate companies a Freightliner Company and a Freight Sundries Company so that these sections of their activities could be transferred to the National Freight Corporation.

Up to £60 million losses over 5 years may be covered by Ministry of Transport grants.

Section 6. A Freight Integration Council to be set up to which any matters concerning an integrated service may be referred. The Council is to have a Chairman and four other members appointed by the Minister, plus the Chairman of the National Freight Corporation, the Chairman of the Railways Board and two trade union members.

Section 7. Powers are given to redistribute any activity between the Railways, the National Freight Corporation and any of its wholly owned subsidiaries.

The commencing structure of the National Freight Corporation is:

(*a*) A Chairman appointed by the Minister.
(*b*) Not more than twelve or less than six others appointed by the Minister in consultation with the Chairman.

Part II: The Act's Provisions with Respect to Passenger Transport

Section 9. (*a*) In any area outside London where the Minister feels that a properly integrated and efficient system of passenger transport requires it, he may designate the area a Passenger Transport Area. He may then establish:

(*b*) A Passenger Transport Authority (P.T.A.) consisting of:

(i) Local councillors from the councils in the area.
(ii) One sixth of the members (at most) to be appointed by the Minister from among interested and knowledgeable people.
(iii) A Chairman chosen by the others.

(*c*) A Passenger Transport Executive consisting of:

(i) A Director General
(ii) At least two and up to eight other members.

The Passenger Transport Authority is to be in charge of general policy, the Passenger Transport Executive is to provide the actual services of a fully integrated and efficient system of public passenger transport.

Section 10. Powers of the Executive

(*a*) To carry passengers by road within, to and from that area.
(*b*) To carry passengers by *any other form of inland transport*, or waterway up to 25 miles outside the area.
(*c*) To pay the Railway Boards for any services used.

    (*d*) To make arrangements with air services where necessary.

    (*e*) To hire passenger vehicles.

    (*f*) To provide refreshments and other services.

    (*g*) To sell petrol; repair and service vehicles; supply spares, etc., to anyone.

    (*h*) To construct, manufacture, produce, purchase, maintain or repair anything needed for their businesses.

    (*i*) To make arrangements with outsiders for any purposes, but especially for such matters as through-fares or through-passages on combined services.

    (*j*) To acquire land, property, businesses, etc.

    (*k*) To provide houses, hostels, training facilities, etc.

Section 11. The Executive's Financial Duties

    (*a*) The Executive has a duty not to show a deficit at the end of any period (so far as is practicable).

    (*b*) To submit its capital budget to the Minister, who may restrict it.

Section 12. Powers are given to borrow money for a variety of purposes, chiefly of a capital nature.

Section 13. Powers are given to the Passenger Transport Authority to require the local councils to levy rates to make up any deficit on the Current Account.

Sections 14–23. Deal with sundry other matters with regard to the powers of the Authorities and the Executives.

Part III: Bus and Ferry Services

Section 24. Two public authorities are to be established, the *National Bus Company* and the *Scottish Transport Group*. When an area has been designated a Passenger Transport Area, the Passenger Transport Executive of the Area and the National Bus Company (or Scottish Transport Group) must co-operate together, and with the Railways, to co-ordinate the transport of the area.

Sections 25 & 26. These two public authorities have the following powers:

    (*a*) to carry passengers by road, vessel or hovercraft

    (*b*) to carry and store luggage and goods

    (*c*) to hire vehicles, act as travel agents and co-operate with all persons or companies engaged in passenger transport.

Section 27. The powers of the Passenger Transport Authorities and the Passenger Transport Executives to run services without incurring a deficit, to borrow funds, etc., are also to apply to these two authorities.

Section 28. The securities, etc., held by the Transport Holding Company under the 1962 Act are to be transferred to the Bus Company or the Scottish Group.

Section 29. The Railway Boards are to transfer to the Bus Company or the Scottish Group their assets in Sheffield, Halifax, Huddersfield and Todmorden, and the Caledonian Steam Packet Company and the ferry to the Kyle of Lochalsh and Kyleakin.

Section 30. In certain cases the traffic commissioners for an area may grant licences to run bus services (12-seater maximum), particularly to get children to school, provided there is no convenient bus service.

Section 32. The Minister may, with Treasury approval, make grants to service operators who buy new buses or public service vehicles and to defray fuel duty charge on fuel used.

Section 34. Councils of rural areas may make grants to help keep open any vital ferry service.

Section 35. Any person applying for a Public Service Vehicle licence must be prepared to justify past records on maintenance, treatment of staff, etc., before the Commissioners, who may hear any interested party who wishes to oppose the application.

Section 36. Local authorities may run public service vehicles on contract services provided they receive Ministry approval of their plans for co-ordination with other persons providing such transport, but they must return accounts to the Minister showing to what extent this contributed to—or relieved—a deficit.

Section 37. Local authorities may acquire or dispose of public service vehicle undertakings.

Part IV: The Authorities and Boards

Section 38. The Railway Boards' composition is reduced by one and the requirement to set up Regional Railway Boards imposed in the 1962 Act is abolished.

Section 39. If services are continued which would be discontinued on economic operation grounds but are retained on social grounds then grants to cover the deficiencies are to be made to the Boards.

Section 40. If necessary the Government may make grants up to £50 million in the 5-year period (1969–74) to cover the cost of operating track and signalling gear excess to requirements.

Section 41. All the Boards are to ensure that the revenues are sufficient to cover costs when all charges proper to Revenue Account have been so charged—taking one year with another.

Section 42. The Railways Board is to have its capital debt reduced to £300 million, and its capital and interest debt reduced to £550 million.

Section 43. The Waterways Board original capital debt to be reduced to £3,750,000 and its subsequent borrowings to £12 million.

Section 44. The Minister and the Secretary of State for Scotland are to account in a proper manner for any sums received from the National Loans Fund, or from the Boards as surpluses for the Consolidated Fund.

Section 45. It is a duty of the Freight Corporation and the Railways Board to review their operations to ensure efficiency and to report to the Minister.

Section 46. All Boards have a duty to carry out research and development.

Section 47. The functions of Boards in the 1962 Act with respect to many items like development of land, pipelines, etc., are carried over to the new Boards and Authorities.

Section 48. All Authorities and Boards to have the power to manufacture and sell and repair for *outside* persons; to buy similar items to ones they already use for sale to outside persons; to repair motor vehicles and sell petrol, oil, etc., to anyone where they operate a car park. The Waterways Board has power to sell goods to anyone from shops or premises operated by them. (But these activities are not to be developed so much that they interfere with the Boards' ordinary activities under the 1962 or 1968 Acts.)

Section 49. The Boards' powers to develop land subject to the Minister's approval are defined.

Section 50. The Boards are given powers to operate hotels and some other amenities.

Section 51. Subsidiaries and Joint Subsidiaries are deemed to be part of the Authorities.

Sections 52–58. A number of minor powers on a variety of subjects are dealt with in these sections, i.e. the right to close down railway lines.

Part V: The Licensing of Road Transport

Section 59. The Licensing Authority for Road Haulage
The chairman of the traffic commissioners for each area laid down in the 1960 Road Traffic Act (or his deputy) shall be known as the Licensing Authority. He acts under the general supervision of the Minister and makes an annual report to him.

Section 60. Operators' Licences
All users of road vehicles for carriage of goods either for hire or reward or for their own purposes must have an operator's licence issued by the Authority.

But this does not apply to small goods vehicles of less than $3\frac{1}{2}$ tons plated weight or 30 cwt. unladen, or to vehicles of any class specified in the regulations. Penalty £200 for contravention.

Section 61. What does the Operator's Licence Do?
  (*a*) It lets the operator use any vehicles specified in the licence, and any trailers and motor cars he likes up to the limit set in the licence if any.
  (*b*) It only authorises vehicles to operate if the vehicle's operating base is in the authority's area, or the vehicle has not operated for at least 3 months from its home base if that is outside the area.
  (*c*) If new vehicles are acquired they must be, within one month, included in the licence by giving a formal notice to the licensing authority—who may also remove vehicles from the licence if he discovers they have left the operator's service.

Section 62. Applying for an Operator's Licence
  (*a*) The operators apply to the licensing authority for each area where they operate a depot. Only one licence is permitted for each authority.
  (*b*) They detail what vehicles or trailers they intend to use.
  (*c*) They detail the person or persons to be transport managers under Section 65.
  (*d*) They state anything else the Authority may require as to the purpose for which vehicles are required, driving hours, loading limits, maintenance, convictions in the last five years, financial resources and names and addresses of the directors if they are a company.

Section 63. The Power to Object to the Licensing Authority granting a Licence
The Licensing Authority shall publish notice of any application for a licence—except where it is for an operation in another area and does not involve a substantial increase in his fleet—and any trade association or trade union or the police or local government may object provided they do so: (*a*) in the prescribed time; (*b*) in the prescribed manner; (*c*) stating the grounds, and (*d*) are prepared to justify them.

Section 64. The licence will be granted if:
(*a*) The applicant is a fit person.
(*b*) The proposals about points in Section 62 are satisfactory.
(*c*) The provisions about drivers' hours are likely to be complied with.
(*d*) The provisions about overloading are likely to be complied with.
(*e*) The provisions about maintenance are likely to be complied with.
(*f*) That adequate finance is available.

Section 65. (1) The licence will specifically name a person to be responsible for the operation and maintenance of the vehicles and such a person shall be: (*a*) the holder of a Transport Manager's Licence of the prescribed class; (*b*) employed in a position of responsibility.
(2) Where a firm has more than one centre it shall have more than one Transport Manager. A firm may also designate more than one person to be Transport Manager.
(3) The Transport Manager is to carry *direct* responsibility for the operation and maintenance of vehicles.
(4) In the event of the death of a Transport Manager three months is allowed for the licence to be amended. Penalty for not having a Transport Manager is £200.

Section 66. If a Licensing Authority requires it, it may order information about changes in the use of vehicles, directors of companies, etc., to be laid before it.

Section 67. Licences last for 5 years, unless the Authority varies this.

Section 68. Licences may be varied by application to the Authority.

Section 69. Licences may be revoked, suspended or curtailed if:
(*a*) The holder contravenes Section 65.
(*b*) The holder is convicted of a breach of Section 64 or any breach of licensing, wages, hours, maintenance, loading, etc., regulations.
(*c*) The holder made false statements.
(*d*) The holder is bankrupt.
(*e*) The holder employs a disqualified person (i.e. one suspended by the Authority from operating vehicles).

Section 70. Appeal on all these matters lies to the Transport Tribunal.

Special Authorisations (see Note below Section 94)

Section 71. The Act controls the use of large goods vehicles (*a*) if they are going more than 100 miles, (*b*) if the goods weigh over 11 tons. To move such goods you must have a special authorisation. A large goods vehicle is one having a plated weight of 16 tons or an unladen weight of 5 tons. The fine for using a vehicle of this size in the way described without a special authorisation is £200.

Section 72. The authorisation is obtained by applying to the Licensing Authority for the area containing the operating centre and stating:

(*a*) the vehicles proposed to do the job
(*b*) the goods to be carried
(*c*) the places of destination
(*d*) for whom and on what occasions or in what circumstances.

Section 73. The Licensing Authority will (unless a signed statement is enclosed saying that these Authorities have no objection) send to the Railways Board and the National Freight Corporation a copy of the application. They then have 14 days to object and show how the service could be offered either partly or completely by rail. This then becomes either wholly or partly a disputed service under the Act. The Licensing Authority will then send copies of these objections to the applicant and an enquiry will be held if necessary.

Section 74. The granting of the special authorisation will be automatic if (*a*) no objection is raised, or (*b*) the proposed railway service or part-service would be disadvantageous to the applicant, (*c*) it would not be disadvantageous to him but would represent a serious detriment either to him or some other person because of some other services that would be interfered with. Otherwise the authorisation will not be granted.

Section 75. In certain circumstances where an unexpected service has to be provided, the urgency of the case may entitle the Licensing Authority to dispense with formalities, but such a licence expires after three months.

Section 76. Special conditions may be attached by the Licensing Authority to any authorisations it makes.

Section 77. Every special authorisation shall state the date it comes into effect and it shall then run until the Minister's regulations say it shall expire, except in special circumstances (as in Section 75 for example).

Section 78. A Special Authorisation may be varied on application to the Licensing Authority.

Section 79. Special Authorisations may be revoked on the grounds of:

(*a*) contravention of the rules
(*b*) use of the vehicle without a consignment note
(*c*) false statements
(*d*) material change of circumstances

The revocation may be accompanied by disqualification.

Section 80. Appeal lies to the Transport Tribunal.

Section 81. All vehicles shall carry a consignment note in the prescribed form and signed in the prescribed manner. They must be prescribed for the required period.

Section 82. Officers may require the production of drivers' documents or of past records that are required to be preserved. They may retain them if they suspect an offence.

Section 83. For falsification of documents the punishment is a £200 fine or two years' imprisonment.

Section 84. The Licensing Authority need not appear to give evidence which is sufficiently acceptable if a certificate is made out which an officer may produce in court, i.e. as to whether a person did or did not have a licence, etc.

Section 85. The Minister may make orders enabling a Holding Company or subsidiaries to have operating licences and special authorisations.

Section 86. Operators' licences and Special Authorisations are not transferable.

Section 87. The Licensing Authority may hold such enquiries as he thinks necessary.

Section 88. Appeals to the Transport Tribunal will result in an order which shall be binding on the Licensing Authority. The composition of the Tribunal is laid down. Fees may be remitted if poverty is proved.

Section 89. The Licensing Authority may stipulate such fees as are reasonable and they are to be paid into the Consolidated Fund.

Sections 90–92. These Sections deal with the making of orders and appointment of staff.

Section 93. Users of goods vehicles of 30 cwt. or less do not now need a carriers' licence.

Section 94. This Section is about transitional arrangements.

Note. In fact the Special Authorisations procedure has not, in practice, been used.

Part VI: The Control of Drivers' Hours

Section 95.   This Section declares that in the interests of public safety drivers' hours are to be controlled on both passenger and goods vehicles, whether the driver is an employee-driver or an owner-driver.

Section 96.   Says that no driver may drive for more than 10 hours a day, or be on duty for more than $5\frac{1}{2}$ hours without a half-hour for rest and refreshment. No driver's day may exceed 11 hours, unless extra rest periods are provided when the day may be extended to $12\frac{1}{2}$ hours ($1\frac{1}{2}$ hours' extra rest) or 14 hours (4 hours' rest). The latter applies to contract hire and express carriages only. (For international travel the drivers' hours are now restricted to 8.)

Section 97.   This Section provides for the installation of tachographs in vehicles. (This is currently envisaged as commencing on new vehicles in 1976 and existing vehicles in 1978.)

Section 98.   Requires written records of drivers' hours to be kept (and many specialist record books are now available for such records—see page 222).

Section 99.   This requires that all such records and documents shall be produced as and when required, to the Licensing Authority, and that spot checks may be carried out on vehicles for the purpose of inspecting the driver's log book.

Section 100. Empowers the Minister to implement all international agreements to which the United Kingdom becomes a party, by making such modifications as he thinks fit in the provisions of the Act.

Section 101. Lays down rules about the delegated legislation required under this Section of the Act.

Section 102. States that the rules about drivers' hours do apply to vehicles and persons in the public service of the Crown, but do not apply to the police or fire brigade authorities.

Section 103. Refers to the definitions of words and their interpretation under the Part VII rules.

Part VII: Inland Waterways

Section 104. The Act divides inland waterways into three groups: commercial waterways, cruising waterways and other waterways.

Section 105. The British Waterways Board has a duty to maintain the first two groups of waterways in a suitable condition for commercial craft and cruising craft respectively, but there is no duty to widen or deepen the waterways, unless the Minister specifically directs the Board, because of changes in the types of vessel desiring to use the waterway.

Section 106. Certain Courts may require the Waterways Board to remedy any serious or persistent failure to discharge its duties.

Section 107. With regard to 'other waterways' the Board's duty shall be to see that each individual waterway is dealt with in the most economical way, either by being disposed of, or if retained, by being managed with a view to amenity, public health and safety.

Section 108. Any 'other waterway' may be deemed a watercourse, or a vacant site, and shall be dealt with as such to prevent any nuisance arising.

Section 109. Empowers the Waterways Board to make arrangements with any other appropriate body to take over an 'other waterway'. Appropriate bodies are local authorities, river authorities, highway authority, gas, electricity and hydro-electric authorities and any statutory or regional water board or water development board.

Section 110. An Inland Waterways Amenity Advisory Council is to be set up consisting of not less than 12 members appointed by the Minister to advise the Waterways Board and the Minister on any proposal to add to or reduce the cruising waterways or any use of waterways for amenity purposes.

Sections 111–115. Make certain other powers clear, particularly regarding access and right of way to canals and land adjoining canals.

Part VIII: Bridges, Level Crossings, etc.

Sections 116–125. These Sections change certain rules about the repair of roads and bridges over canals and railways and allocate powers to the Highway Authorities and the various Boards to ensure the proper construction and maintenance of bridges and level crossings.

Part IX: Regulation of Road Traffic

Sections 126–133. Contain minor amendments to the Road Traffic Regulation Act 1967.

Suggested Further Reading

The Transport Act 1968, H.M.S.O.

CHAPTER EIGHTEEN

THE DOCUMENTATION OF TRANSPORT

Introduction—Aligned Documentation

The amount of documentation required whenever goods or passengers move is considerable, and in recent years some hard looks have been taken at documentation procedure, so that wherever possible documents are *aligned*. This means that the information required by various parties is placed in the same position on a standard-shaped piece of paper, often of A4 size. For example, nearly everyone—consignor, carrier, Customs, consular officials, chambers of commerce, port authorities and the consignee—will wish to know the address to which the goods are to be sent. There is no reason why this unit of information, the consignee's name and address, should not be placed on the same spot on each document—the invoice, shipping note, bill of lading, air waybill or whatever document is in use. If this is done, and if all similar pieces of information are similarly placed in a standard spot on the page, then a master form can be prepared giving all the required information in the correct positions. From this master document, *once it has been thoroughly checked to ensure complete accuracy*, we can then run off copies of any document required, using the techniques of spirit duplication, dyeline, ink duplication, offset litho or electrostatic copying (see *Office Practice Made Simple*).

In running off the various documents little expense is involved. The usual procedure is for a list of the required documents to be drawn up, perhaps like the list shown below:

Invoice	5 copies
Consular invoice	12 copies
Bill of Lading	4 copies
Certificate of Origin	3 copies
Customs Form 273(4)	3 copies

Blank forms for the required documents are then placed in a file with the checked master copy, and passed to the duplication clerk. She fixes the master copy on to the duplicator machine, and positions the various blanks accurately one after the other so that the copies are speedily run off. A system of masking sheets enables her to exclude from any particular document information on the master which is not required on that document. For example, it is unwise to let the lorry driver know the value of the goods he is delivering, and the invoice copy which is used as a delivery note would be masked off at the point where the value was shown. The whole set of documents will be as accurate as the master, and need not be checked in any way, since only the information on the master can possibly come out on the documents; they have not been individually prepared so there is no danger that figures have been copied incorrectly. Also every copy will be as good a print as the next. Before aligned documentation was developed, a typist producing several copies of a document using carbon paper could not fail to have fainter and fainter copies at the

Appendix 6

(reproduced by courtesy of Her Majesty's Stationery Office)

Master Document

Exporter		Air WB (or B/L) No.	
		Exporter's Ref.	Export Division
		F/Agent's Ref.	C.D.6.No./N.A.
Consignee (if 'Order' state Notify Party)	Name & Address of Exporter's Bank in U.K.		
Forwarding Agent/Merchant	Export Licence No.	Ship's Nationality	
	Country of Origin of Goods	Country to which Goods Consigned	
Date of Clearance	Dock / Wharf / Station	Terms of Delivery and Payment	
Local Vessel	From (Local port of loading).	CD6: Amount Due:	
		Insured Value:	
		(In words)	
		Currency:	
Ocean vessel / Aircraft, etc.	Sea / Air Port of Loading		
Sea/Air Port of Discharge	Final Destination	Freight. payable at	Figs: Number of original Bs/L
Marks & Numbers	Number and kind of packages; description of goods	Export List Code No.	Gross Weight T C Q L Cube Ft. In.

Machine Grip and Filing.

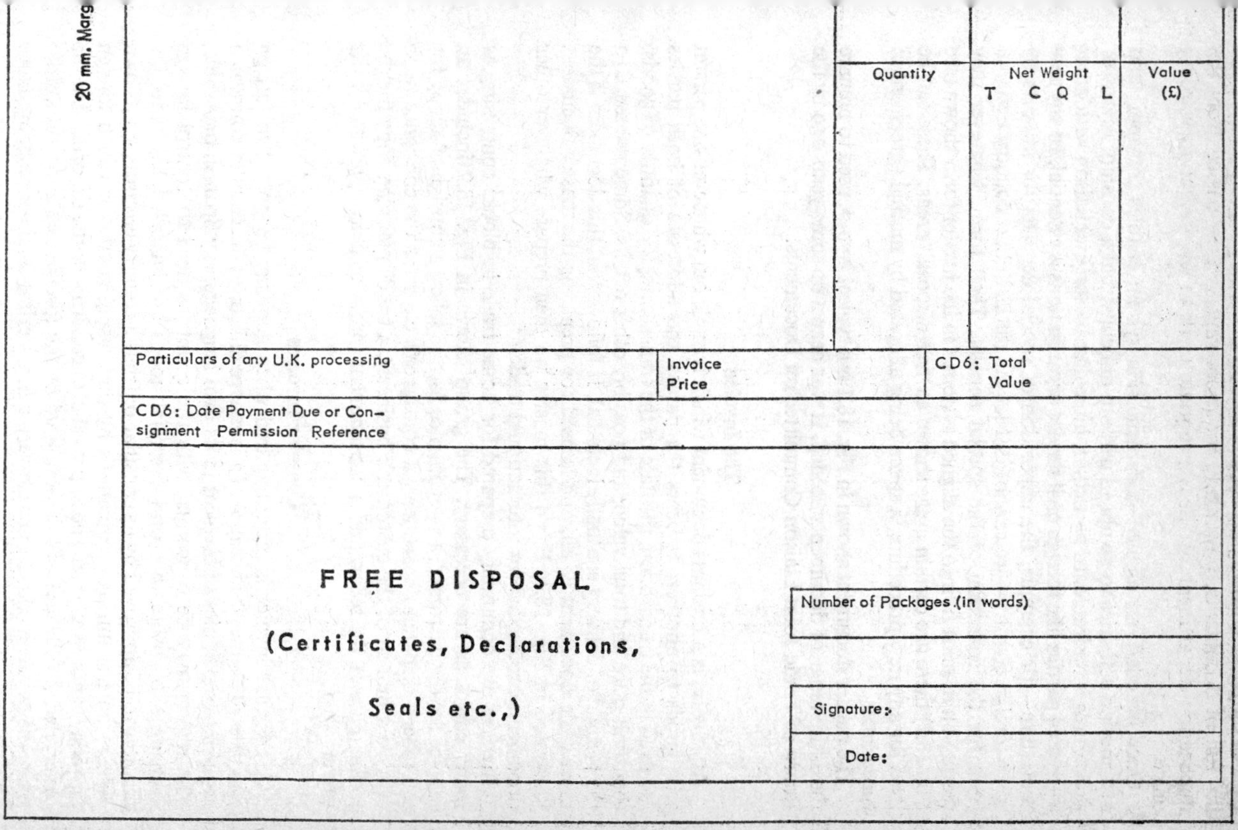

Quantity	Net Weight T C Q L	Value (£)

Particulars of any U.K. processing

Invoice Price

CD6: Total Value

CD6: Date Payment Due or Con-signment Permission Reference

Number of Packages (in words)

FREE DISPOSAL

(Certificates, Declarations, Seals etc.,)

Signature:

Date:

20 mm. Marg

Fig. 18.1. A master document for an aligned series.

back of the pack. With aligned documentation all copies are equally clear. The file full of documents, now ready for processing, is then passed from the duplication department to the appropriate clerk in the freight forwarding office.

Once installed, an aligned documentation system enables transport and distribution activities to go ahead without difficulty, but a constant review of procedures is desirable. In particular, inter-firm liaison and liaison with other interested parties like foreign civil service organisations is essential. In any new procedure—for example, the imposition of special deposits for imports by some foreign country—we cannot just let the clerks in that country design a form for the collection of the special deposit. Their form, whatever they require on it, must fit into the aligned system. On the master form shown (see Fig. 18.1) there are certain areas shown as 'free disposal' areas. These can be used for any new procedure, a space being allocated by mutual agreement in those areas.

The master document shown in Fig. 18.1 is a typical layout, used to prepare the entire range of documents needed. It was drawn up some years ago by the Board of Trade Joint Liaison Committee on Documents.

The Invoice

An invoice is a business document which is made out whenever one person sells goods to another. It bears the names and addresses of both parties involved in the transaction, the date of the transaction, the quantity of goods, their unit price and total value, and possibly other details. Some reference to the method of delivery is usually included. It follows that this document is the most basic document of all, and is used for preparing the master document illustrated in Fig. 18.1. From this master we then prepare whatever other documents are needed for international trade.

Invoices are commonly prepared for home trade in blocks containing as many copies as are necessary. The group shown in Fig. 18.2 includes an invoice for the customer, a copy invoice for the seller, a consignor's copy for the seller's dispatch department, a consignee's copy for the consignee (who may be a branch of the customer's business), a traffic planning copy for the traffic office of the seller, and a consignment (proof of delivery) note for the driver.

Consular Invoices

A consular invoice is often required when goods are exported to foreign countries. This may be because of a language difficulty; the country concerned requiring true copies of invoices in its own language, say Spanish or Arabic. The reason may be concerned with the country's need to control foreign exchange, to ensure that only essential goods are imported. By requiring invoices to be approved by its consular officials a country ensures that its own citizens do not infringe regulations by purchasing goods for which foreign currency is not available. The approval also confirms to the exporter that the order placed with him will be honoured by the foreign exchange authorities when the payment comes to be converted into sterling on the foreign exchange market.

CONSIGNOR'S COPY	TIBBETT & BRITTEN LTD	DEPOT:
INVOICE	TIBBETT & BRITTEN LTD	DEPOT:
COPY INVOICE	TIBBETT & BRITTEN LTD	DEPOT:
TRAFFIC PLANNING	TIBBETT & BRITTEN LTD	DEPOT:
CONSIGNEE'S COPY	TIBBETT & BRITTEN LTD	DEPOT:
PROOF OF DELIVERY	TIBBETT & BRITTEN LTD	DEPOT:

The International Clothing Trade Transport Specialists
Head Office: 691-697 High Road, TOTTENHAM, LONDON, N.17

LONDON 01-808 5371/6
STOCKPORT 061-483 9595/6
GLASGOW 035-52 34461/2
DURHAM 0385 780672/3

LEICESTER 0533 874751/2/3
BRISTOL 0272 76324
BELFAST 746184
DUBLIN 507812 & 507756

No. A1616652

DATE 7th October, 1974

PLEASE INSERT ALL NAMES & ADDRESSES IN FULL & IN BLOCK LETTERS

NAME & ADDRESS OF SENDER	INVOICE ADDRESS (if different from Senders)	CONSIGNEE'S NAME & ADDRESS
A.B.C. Limited, Frith Street, London, W.1.		X.Y.Z. Limited, 286 Duke Street, Bradford,

ENTER ONLY **ONE** DELIVERY ON EACH CONSIGNMENT NOTE

ROUTE CODE

QTY.		DESCRIPTION
	STD. Sets	
10	Short Sets	mens two piece suits
	Long Sets	
	½ STD. Sets	
	½ Short Sets	
	½ Long Sets	
1	PACKAGES	

SENDER'S SIGNATURE	RECEIVING DRIVER'S SIGNATURE	COLLECTING DEPOT	TRANSFER OUT	TRANSFER IN	DELIVERING DEPOT	RECEIVED THE ABOVE-MENTIONED GOODS CONSIGNEE'S SIGNATURE

THIS CONSIGNMENT NOTE IS THE ONLY OFFICIALLY RECOGNISED RECEIPT
All goods are carried under the Company's current printed Conditions of Carriage, copies of which may be obtained on application.

Fig. 18.2. An invoice pack with transport copies included.

(courtesy of Tibbett and Britten Ltd.)

Certificates of Origin

A Certificate of Origin is a document required in certain circumstances where preferential tariff arrangements are made between countries. For example, if British goods may enter Germany free of tariff, but U.S. goods may not, attempts to evade the tariff might be made by American firms if they could ship the goods to Britain first.

Under an international convention of 1923 it was agreed that in order to simplify Customs formalities each nation should nominate certain official bodies who should have the sole right to issue Certificates of Origin. In Britain the bodies nominated are the Chambers of Commerce affiliated to the Association of British Chambers of Commerce. For a fairly nominal sum they will certify the origin of goods declared to be of British origin, provided evidence of their manufacture in the United Kingdom is available and a suitable declaration to that effect is made and signed by an appropriate person in the applicant firm. This declaration reads: 'I declare that the goods specified in the Schedule are of United Kingdom origin, production or manufacture.' The certification by the Chamber of Commerce reads: 'The undersigned, duly authorised by the . . . Chamber of Commerce (incorporated) hereby verifies the declaration made below by the Exporter specified above, in respect of the goods to be dispatched to the Consignee specified above.' Generally the Certificate of Origin will be a separate document, but where the regulations of a country require the commercial invoices to be certified, the Chamber of Commerce will certify the actual invoices.

The Bill of Lading

A Bill of Lading is a document prepared usually in the exporter's office or in the office of his freight forwarding agent. These days it is run off from the master document described above, from basic information based on the invoice, or perhaps a pro-forma invoice issued earlier during the original

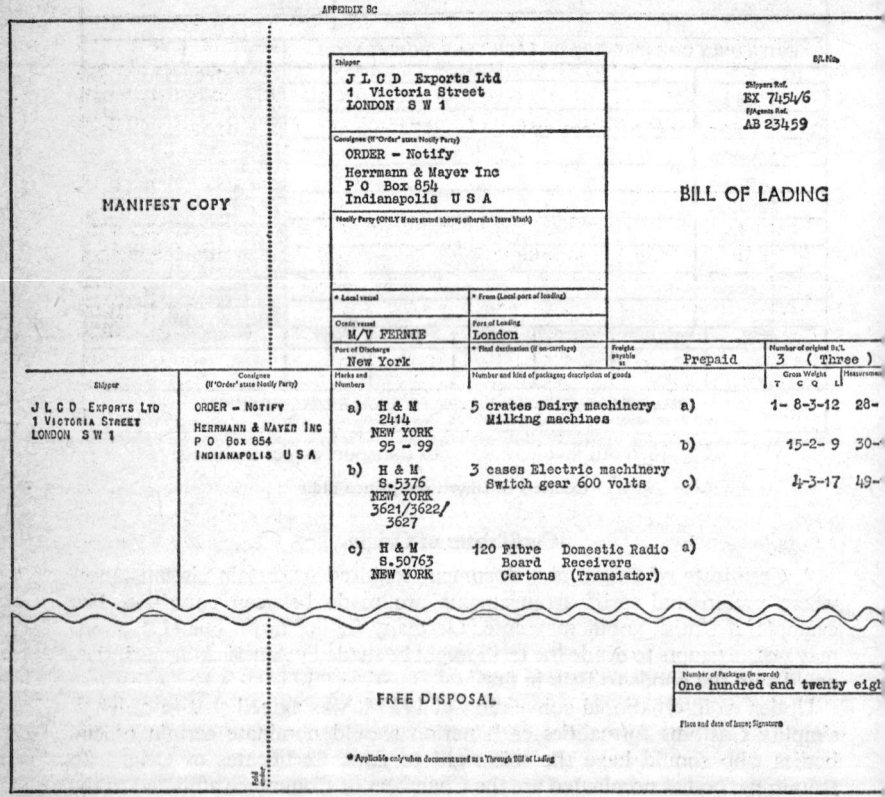

Fig. 18.3. A Bill of Lading.

(courtesy of Her Majesty's Stationery Office)

negotiation of the bargain concerning the goods to be shipped. It concerns the arrangements for moving goods by sea, and will include the name of the vessel or vessels to be used in the carriage. The important point is that no matter where the document is prepared, the actual point of issue, at which the document acquires legal significance, is the ship's office. Here it is signed by the master of the vessel, or his agent, as evidence that the goods have been shipped. At that moment the bill acquires its three attributes, which are:

(*a*) It is a receipt for the goods shipped.

(*b*) It is strong evidence of the terms of the contract of carriage, although the actual contract may have been made some time before, and possibly even orally over the telephone.

(*c*) It is a document of title, which may be assigned from one person to another, and the holder of the bill will need to present it to the master of the vessel at the destination port before he can remove the goods from the ship.

The bill of lading has been the subject of major legal enactments, the purpose of the Acts being to ensure that purchasers of bills of lading who imagine they are buying a cargo already on the high seas, are not disappointed in their expectations. The reader should study the Bills of Lading Act 1855 and the Carriage of Goods by Sea Acts 1924 and 1971 to obtain a clear picture of the legal position. The conditions of carriage, usually printed in very small print on the back of the bill, are very interesting too, and should be studied closely.

House Bills of Lading

Where a consolidator takes small consignments from exporters and consolidates them into a full container load for a single destination, the carrier will expect the bill of lading to refer to the container and not to the individual packages contained therein. The exporter of a single package is thus reduced to a position where he has no bill of lading, and must be content with something less. The practice has grown up in recent years of issuing House Bills of Lading which act as Certificates of Shipment. By a custom of the trade—confidence in which increases annually—these house bills of lading are acquiring in practice many of the attributes of a true bill of lading, but they do not have the same position legally, and are positively forbidden in some letters of credit. (A letter of credit is a document issued on behalf of an overseas customer by a banker, agreeing to pay the purchase price of an article provided it is exported to him in the way specified in the letter of credit. If these instructions specifically reject the use of house bills of lading, the exporter must avoid the use of a consolidator. If in doubt he should seek the approval of the customer to send goods via a consolidator.)

The forwarding Agent's Certificate of Transport shown in Fig. 18.4 is a document which combines the function of a receipt for the goods with a negotiable function. It is a negotiable document of control; the Forwarder is responsible for delivering the goods at destination against presentation of the original document properly endorsed.

Through Bills of Lading

Many consignors and consignees have no facilities for handling goods at one end or the other of a sea journey. They will prefer the goods to be dis-

DK	N
S	SF

FCT

**Forwarding Agents
Certificate of Transport**

Ref. No.

SPEDITOR
FÖRBUND

ORIGINAL

Suppliers or Forwarding Agents' Principals

Consigned to order of

for delivery of these goods apply to

Notify address

Conveyance	from/via

Destination

Marks and numbers	Number and kind of packages and description of goods	Number of original FCT documents		
			Gross weight	Measurement

with subject to the General Conditions printed overleaf.

SPECIMEN

Contents, weight and measurement according to senders declaration

Acceptance of this document or the invocation of rights arising therefrom acknowledges the validity of the following conditions, regulations and exceptions also of the trading conditions printed overleaf, except where the latter conflict with conditions 1-6 below.

1. The undersigned are authorized to enter into contracts with carriers and others involved in the execution of the transport subject to the latter's usual terms and conditions.
2. The undersigned do not act as Carriers but as Forwarding Agents. In consequence they are only responsible for the careful selection of third parties, instructed by them, subject to the conditions of Clause 3 hereunder.
3. The undersigned are responsible for delivery of the goods to the holder of this document through the intermediary of a delivery agent of their choice. They are not responsible for acts or omissions of Carriers involved in the execution of the transport or of other third parties. The undersigned Forwarding Agents will, on request, subrogate their claims against Carriers and other parties.
4. Insurance of the goods will only be effected upon express instructions in writing.
5. Unforeseen and/or unforeseeable circumstances entitle the undersigned to deviate from the envisaged route and/or method of transport.
6. Unforeseen and/or unforeseeable disbursements and charges are for the account of the goods.

We, the Undersigned Forwarding Agents, in accordance with the instructions of our Principals, have taken charge of the abovementioned goods in good external condition at

for despatch and delivery as stated above or order against surrender of this document properly endorsed.

In witness thereof the Undersigned Forwarding Agents have signed the original FCT documents, which are of this tenor and bear the same date. When one of these has been accomplished, the others will lose their validity.

Place and date of issue

Stamp and authorized signature

Insurance through the intermediary of the undersigned agents:

☐ Not covered

☐ Covered according to the attached Insurance Policy/Certificate.

All disputes shall be governed by the law and within the exclusive jurisdiction of the courts at the place of issue.

For delivery of the goods please apply to:

Freight and charges prepaid to

thence for account of goods, lost or not lost.

Fig. 18.4. A forwarding agent's Certificate of Transport.
(courtesy of FIATA)

patched from start to finish without any responsibility on their part. In these circumstances a *through bill of lading*, involving pre-carriage to the port of departure and on-carriage to the place of destination from the port of arrival, will be used.

The Shipping Note

A shipping note is a document prepared when goods are sent to the port for shipment. It contains details of the consignment, the marks and numbers of packages, the name of the ship, and of the supplier and the port of discharge. The National Standard Shipping Note reproduced in Fig. 18.5 was introduced on April 1, 1975. It is used to deliver export cargo to the Receiving Authority at any British port, container base or freight depot. Produced by the Sitpro Board (Simplification of International Trade Procedures Board), it

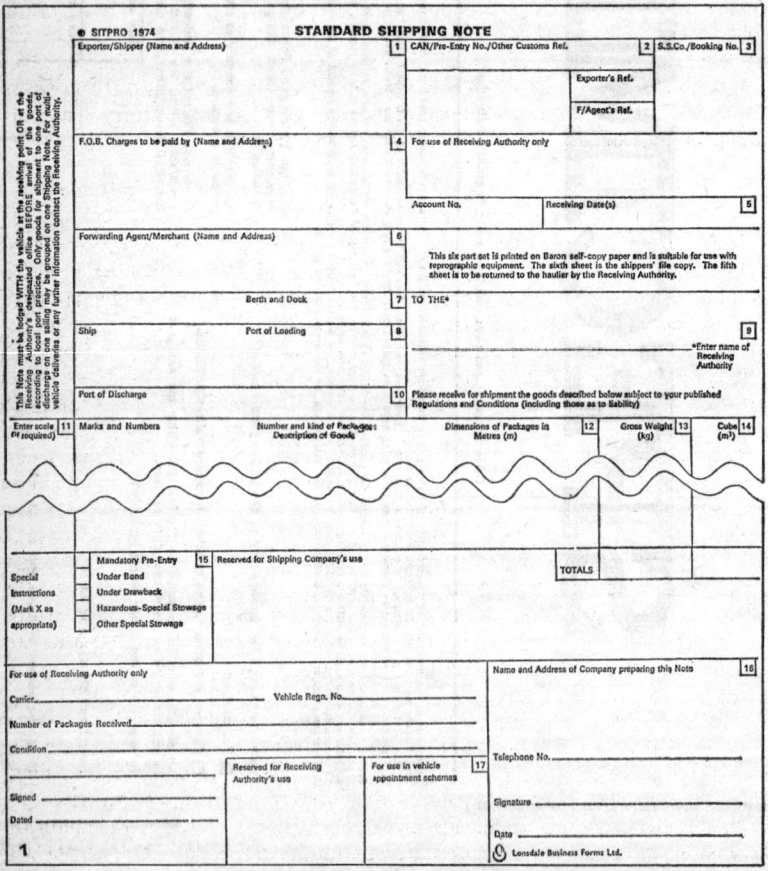

Fig. 18.5. National Standard Shipping Note.

(courtesy U.K. SITPRO Board—Simplification of International Trade Procedures Board) is the first new document produced as a result of their review of international documents.

The C.M.R. Consignment Note

The C.M.R. consignment note conforms with the requirements of the international convention on road haulage, the *Convention de Merchandises per Routes*, held in Geneva in 1956. This was embodied in British law by the Carriage of Goods by Road Act 1965 (see page 192) and incorporates the fair conditions of carriage agreed at that convention. It contains the names and addresses of all three parties concerned in the movement of goods, the consignor, the carrier and the consignee, as well as a space for a second or third carrier if necessary. The description, weight, measurements, number and marks of the packages are given, together with a list of documents attached, and sender's instructions for Customs and other formalities. A tabular presentation enables carriage charges to be recorded and indicates to whom they should be charged, while a section is provided for the carrier's observations and any reservations he may have about the condition of the packages taken over. The note also contains a clause clearly stating that it is subject to the C.M.R. Convention notwithstanding any clause to the contrary. The note is reproduced in Fig. 18.6 and warrants careful study.

The T.I.R. Carnet

Vehicles on international road haulage may sometimes experience considerable delay when crossing frontiers because of Customs formalities. To ease this problem a Customs Convention on the International Transport of Goods held in 1959 set up a system of carnets. The idea is that the carnet (or pad of forms) contains enough copies of a Customs declaration to provide two copies for each country through which the vehicle is to pass. The carnets are sold in three sizes, of 6, 14 or 20 pages. Thus they can be used for three countries, seven countries or ten countries. The lorry must be of approved design, and if a tilt is used to cover the goods it must comply with stringent requirements. The load is sealed by Customs at the commencement of its journey. On arrival at the first frontier the seals are inspected, a copy of the carnet is detached from the pad and given to the Customs authorities and the lorry proceeds on its way. At the next frontier, where the lorry leaves country A and enters country B, a second copy of the carnet is surrendered to the Customs of country A and a first copy to country B. When sent back to the central control, the matching up by country A of an entry form and an exit form proves that the goods were not unloaded in the country and as a result no duty is payable.

Clearly this is a very sensible system. If any tampering with seals occurs, or if there is any tear in a tarpaulin, a special procedure is followed under the rules, and severe penalties can follow if a good explanation is not forthcoming. Even accidental damage is the subject of special procedures, and the loss of a carnet is regarded as a very serious matter indeed and may lead to the exclusion of a careless haulier from future participation in the scheme. The carnet will also serve as a bond, guaranteed by the Trade Association which issued it. This Trade Association will pay the duty assessed by the country of destination, and will recover it from the operator. The use of these carnets for

1 Expéditeur (nom, adresse, pays)
Sender (name, address, country)

LETTRE DE VOITURE INTERNATIONALE
INTERNATIONAL CONSIGNME IOTE № 1004

Ce transport est soumis, nonobstant toute clause contraire, à la Convention relative au contrat de transport international de marchandises par route (CMR).

This carriage is subject, notwithstanding any clause to the contrary, to the Convention on the Contract for the International Carriage of goods by road (CMR).

2 Destinataire (nom, adresse, pays)
Consignee (name, address, country)

16 Transporteur (nom, adresse, pays)
Carrier (name, address, country)

3 Lieu prévu pour la livraison de la marchandise
Place of delivery of the goods
Lieu / Place
Pays / Country

17 Transporteurs successifs (nom, adresse, pays)
Successive carriers (name, address, country)

4 Lieu et date de la prise en charge de la marchandise
Place and date of taking over the goods
Lieu / Place
Pays / Country
Date / Date

18 Réserves et observations du transporteur
Carrier's reservations and observations

5 Documents annexés
Documents attached

6 Marques et numéros / Marks and Nos	7 Nombre des colis / Number of packages	8 Mode d'emballage / Method of packing	9 Nature de la marchandise* / Nature of the goods*	10 No statistique / Statistical number	11 Poids brut, kg / Gross weight in kg	12 Cubage m3 / Volume in m3

Classe / Class   Chiffre / Number   Lettre / Letter   (ADR)

13 Instructions de l'expéditeur (formalités douanières et autres)
Sender's instructions (Customs and other formalities)

19 A payer par: / To be paid by:	l'expéditeur / Sender	Monnaie / Currency	le destinataire / Consignee
Prix de transport / Carriage charges			
Réductions / Deductions –			
Solde / Balance			
Suppléments / Supplem. charges			
Frais accessoires / Other charges			
Divers / Miscellaneous +			
Total à payer / Total to be paid			

14 Remboursement
Cash on delivery

15 Prescription d'affranchissement
Instructions as to payment for carriage
Franco / Carriage paid
Non Franco / Carriage forward

20 Conventions particulières
Special agreements

21 Etablie à / Established in   le / on   19

24 Réception des marchandises / Goods received   Date / Date
le / on ________ 19__

22 (Signature et timbre de l'expéditeur) (Signature and stamp of the sender)

23 (Signature et timbre du transporteur) (Signature and stamp of the carrier)

(Signature et timbre du destinataire) (Signature and stamp of the consignee)

A remplir sous la responsabilité de l'expéditeur 1 – 15 y compris et 21 + 22. Les parties encadrées de lignes grasses doivent être remplies par le transporteur.
To be completed on the sender's responsibility including 1 – 15 21 + 22. The spaces framed with heavy lines must be filled in by the carrier.

* En cas de marchandises dangereuses indiquer, outre la certification éventuelle, à la dernière ligne du cadre: la classe, le chiffre et le cas échéant, la lettre.
* In case of dangerous goods mention, besides the possible certification, on the last line of the column the particulars of the class, the number and the letter, if any.

CMR

Fig. 18.6. A C.M.R. Consignment Note.

journeys within the European Economic Community will probably be super-seded after 1975 by new Common Market procedures.

Rail Consignment Notes

The standard railway document is a rail consignment note. There are a variety of these notes, ranging from a simple inland transit consignment note to a more sophisticated document called a C.I.M. consignment note, which embodies the C.I.M. Convention (the *Convention Internationale Merchandises*) for the carriage of goods by rail. This consignment note is also used in conjunction with a T.I.F. International Customs Declaration. This is similar to the T.I.R. carnet system for road haulage, permitting railway wagons to pass through a country unopened on surrender of a copy of the declaration at entry and exit. A C.I.M. consignment note from British Rail is shown in Fig. 18.7. It is a comprehensive document with a great many details which can only be fully understood by those who read the Convention, but a careful perusal of both will leave the reader with a very clear understanding of international rail movements.

The Air Waybill

The name 'air waybill' was introduced in the Amended Warsaw Convention embodied in English law by the Carriage by Air Act 1961. Previously the document was called an 'air consignment note', and the same form is usually used whether or not a country has ratified the Amended Convention. The form is very detailed, and requires careful study, but it may be said to contain all the data required by the parties to any movement of goods by air. It has the names and addresses of the consignee, the consignor and the carrier, with a space for the consignor to sign to certify the accuracy of the particulars included on the waybill, and another for the carrier to sign as receiving the goods for carriage. The number, weight, description, dimension and marks of the packages are recorded, together with special handling instructions, declared value for carriage and particulars of the charges payable and by whom.

The air waybill is very similar to the bill of lading in many respects, but it is not a document of title in quite the same way, since it is not normally negotiable to third parties. However, in certain cases it does appear that the air waybill may, by custom of a particular trade, develop this negotiable character and we may find in the near future that a negotiable air waybill has *de facto* recognition.

The reader is urged to study carefully the air waybill reproduced in Fig. 18.8.

Charterparties

A charterparty is a contract for the hire of a vessel or part of a vessel by a shipper of goods. Such a contract is usually negotiated on the Baltic Exchange, although charterparties can be negotiated privately. There are several types of charterparty, and some typical standard charterparties are published by BIMCO (the Baltic and International Maritime Conference—Copenhagen). A typical uniform General Charter is reproduced in Fig. 18.9. Other BIMCO charterparties are the Gas Voyage Charterparty (code name Gasvoy), the Uniform Time Charter (code name Baltime 1939), and the Standard Bareboat Charter (code name Barecon 'A').

(36) Invoiced - Enregistré - Abgefertigt

from - de - von ....

to - à - nach ....

(39) Routes - Itinéraires - Leitungswege

(42) To be cleared through Customs at - A dédouaner à - Zu verzollen in

(44) Reforwarded from/to - Réexpédié de/pour - Neu aufgegeben von/nach

(37)
(38)
(40)
(41)
(43)
(45)
(48)
(49)
(50)

(46) Load Limit - Lim. de charge - Lastgrenze ↑

(47) Axles - Essieux - Achsen

(16) Wagons - Wagons - Wagen No.

(17) Tare - Tare - Tara

(2) Eigengewicht kg

(18) Exchangeable pallets - Palettes échangeables - Austauschpaletten
No. Nombre Anzahl

Description of goods - Désignation de la marchandise - Bezeichnung des Gutes

(51) Goods - Marchandises - Waren

(20) Wagon Load - Wagon complet - Wagenladung
Part Load - Detail - Stückgut

(21) Charge par - Verladen durch:
Loaded by:
Sender - Expéditeur - Absender
Railway - Chemin de fer - Eisenbahn

(26) Weight Poids kg

(12) Sender, firm - Expéditeur, raison sociale - Absender, Firma

(13) Consignee, address (town and country)
Destinataire, adresse (ville et pays) - Empfänger, Adresse (Ort und Land)

Loading Tackle-Containers - Agrès-Containers - Lademittel-Behälter
(15) Mark & Number - Marque et No - Eigentums merkmal und Nr.

(14) Category - Catégorie - Art

(15) Mark & Number - Marque et No - Eigentums merkmal und Nr.

(14) Category - Catégorie - Art

(19) Declarations - Déclarations - Erklärungen (CIM Art. 6, 12, 15, etc)

(25)

(24) Nature of packing - Nature de l'emballage - Art der Verpackung

(23) No. of packages - Nombre - Anzahl

(22) Address-marks-numbers - Adresse-marques-nos - Adresse-Zeichen-Nr.

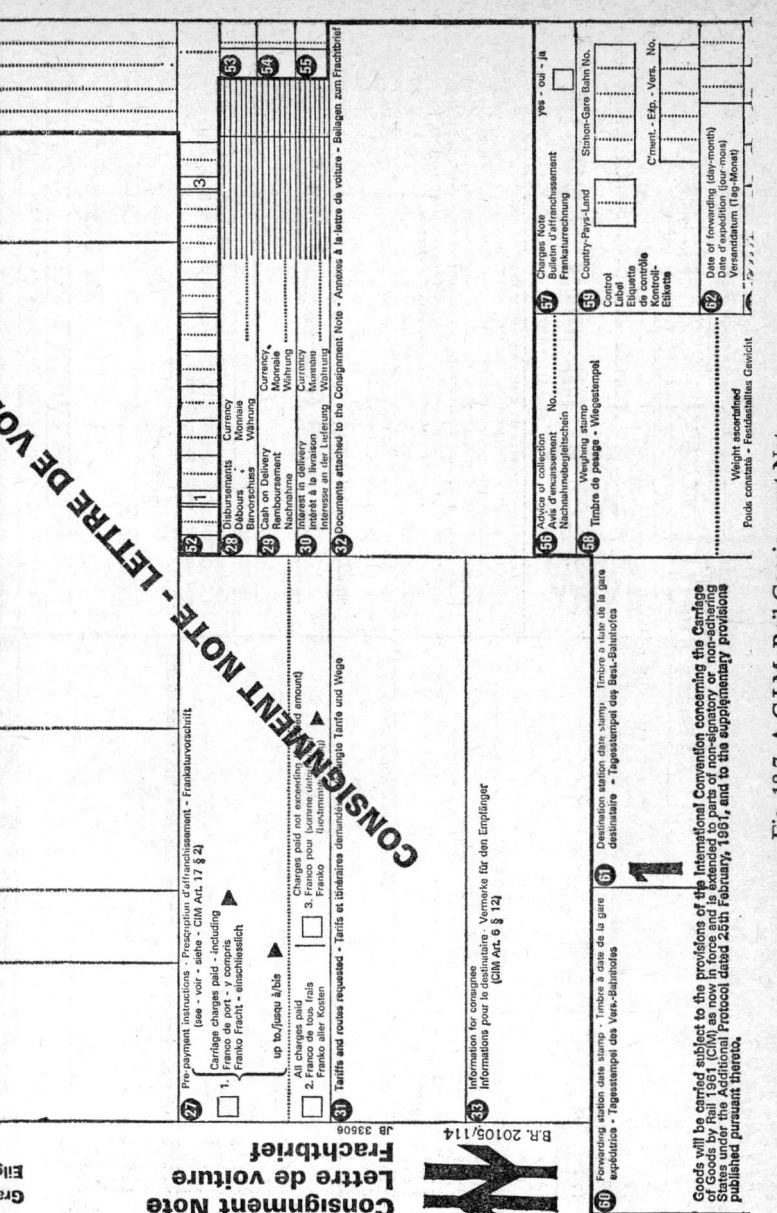

Fig. 18.7. A C.I.M. Rail Consignment Note.

(courtesy of British Railways Board)

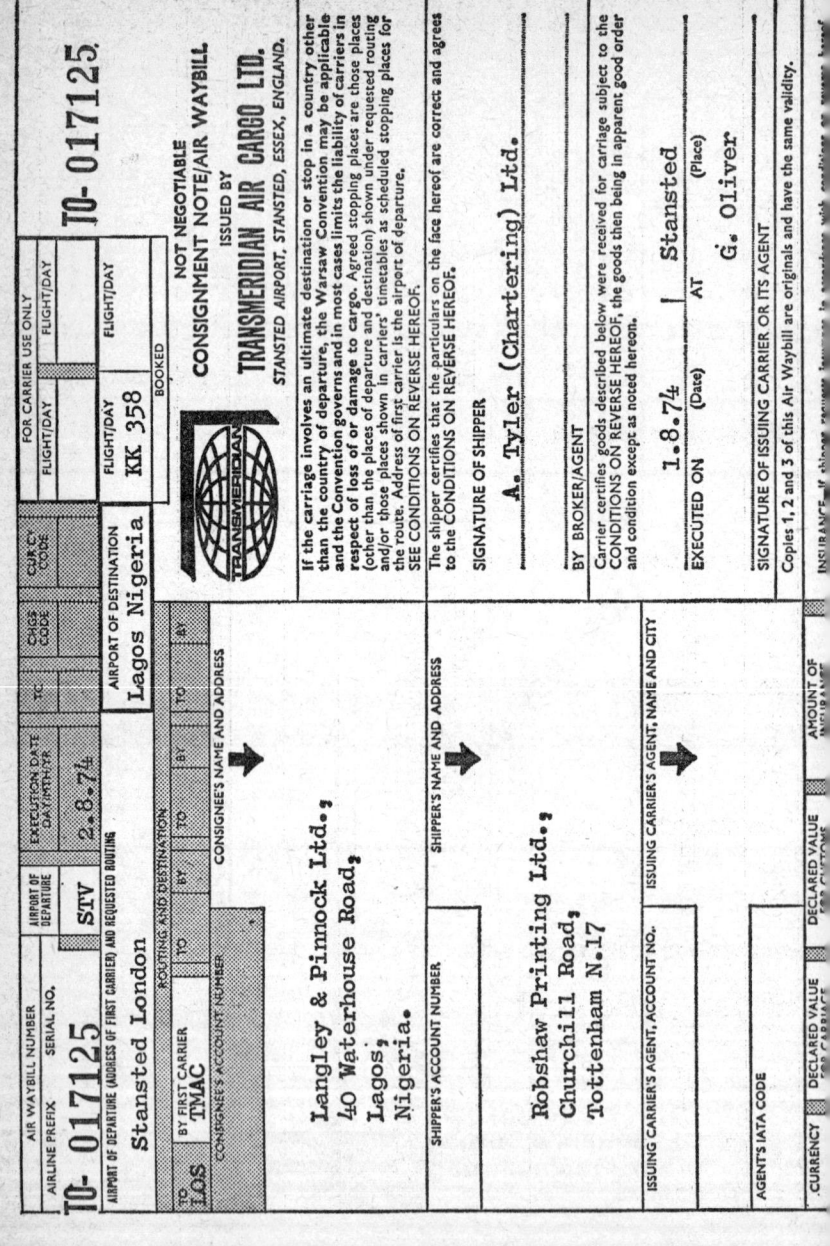

AIR WAYBILL NUMBER		EXECUTION DATE DAY/MTH/YR	AIRPORT OF DEPARTURE	TC	CHG CODE	CUR.C CODE		FOR CARRIER USE ONLY	
AIRLINE PREFIX	SERIAL NO.							FLIGHT/DAY	FLIGHT/DAY

TO- 017125

2.8.74

STV

AIRPORT OF DEPARTURE (ADDRESS OF FIRST CARRIED) AND REQUESTED ROUTING

Stansted London

AIRPORT OF DESTINATION

Lagos Nigeria

FLIGHT/DAY **KK 358**   BOOKED

TO- 017125

ROUTING AND DESTINATION

TO	BY FIRST CARRIER	TO	BY	TO	BY	TO	BY
IOS	TMAC						

NOT NEGOTIABLE
CONSIGNMENT NOTE/AIR WAYBILL
ISSUED BY
TRANSMERIDIAN AIR CARGO LTD.
STANSTED AIRPORT, STANSTED, ESSEX, ENGLAND.

CONSIGNEE'S ACCOUNT NUMBER   CONSIGNEE'S NAME AND ADDRESS

Langley & Pinnock Ltd.,
40 Waterhouse Road,
Lagos,
Nigeria.

SHIPPER'S ACCOUNT NUMBER   SHIPPER'S NAME AND ADDRESS

Robshaw Printing Ltd.,
Churchill Road,
Tottenham N.17

ISSUING CARRIER'S AGENT, ACCOUNT NO.   ISSUING CARRIER'S AGENT, NAME AND CITY

AGENT'S IATA CODE

If the carriage involves an ultimate destination or stop in a country other than the country of departure, the Warsaw Convention may be applicable and the Convention governs and in most cases limits the liability of carriers in respect of loss of or damage to cargo. Agreed stopping places are those places (other than the places of departure and destination) shown under requested routing and/or those places shown in carriers' timetables as scheduled stopping places for the route. Address of first carrier is the airport of departure.
SEE CONDITIONS ON REVERSE HEREOF.

The shipper certifies that the particulars on the face hereof are correct and agrees to the CONDITIONS ON REVERSE HEREOF.

SIGNATURE OF SHIPPER

A. Tyler (Chartering) Ltd.

BY BROKER/AGENT

Carrier certifies goods described below were received for carriage subject to the CONDITIONS ON REVERSE HEREOF, the goods then being in apparent good order and condition except as noted hereon.

EXECUTED ON   **1.8.74**   AT   **Stansted**
          (Date)   (Place)

          G. Oliver

SIGNATURE OF ISSUING CARRIER OR ITS AGENT

Copies 1, 2 and 3 of this Air Waybill are originals and have the same validity.

CURRENCY	DECLARED VALUE FOR CARRIAGE	DECLARED VALUE FOR CUSTOMS	AMOUNT OF INSURANCE

INSURANCE

NO. OF PACKAGES RCP	ACTUAL GROSS WEIGHT	Kg./lb.	RATE CLASS	COMMODITY ITEM NO.	CHARGEABLE WEIGHT	RATE/CHARGE	TOTAL	NATURE AND QUANTITY OF GOODS (INCL. DIMENSIONS OR VOLUME)
59	1424	K		AS PER CHARTER AGREEMENT				Printing Ink CAN 10342

	PREPAID WEIGHT CHARGE	PREPAID VALUATION CHARGE		TOTAL OTHER PREPAID CHARGES		TOTAL PREPAID	FOR CARRIER'S USE ONLY AT DESTINATION
PRE-PAID	As agreed		DUE CARRIER	DUE AGENT			COLLECT CHARGES IN DESTINATION CURRENCY

OTHER CHARGES (EXCEPT WEIGHT CHARGE AND VALUATION CHARGE)

To be advised

COD AMOUNT

TOTAL CHARGES

	COLLECT WEIGHT CHARGE	COLLECT VALUATION CHARGE	TOTAL OTHER COLLECT CHARGES		COD AMOUNT	TOTAL COLLECT
COL-LECT			DUE CARRIER	DUE AGENT		

HANDLING INFORMATION

Printed in U.K.   IAL/AERAD

ORIGINAL 3 (FOR SHIPPER)

Fig. 18.8. An Air Waybill.
(courtesy of Transmeridian Air Cargo Ltd.)

A

RECOMMENDED
THE BALTIC AND INTERNATIONAL MARITIME CONFERENCE
UNIFORM GENERAL CHARTER (AS REVISED 1922) – BOX LAYOUT 1974
(Only to be used for trades for which no approved form is in force)
CODE NAME: "GENCON"

PART I

Adopted by
the Documentary Committee of the Chamber
of Shipping of the United Kingdom
and the Documentary Committee of The Japan
Shipping Exchange, Inc.

1. Shipbroker	2. Place and date
3. Owners/Place of business (Cl. 1)	4. Charterers/Place of business (Cl. 1)
5. Vessel's name (Cl. 1)	6. GRT/NRT (Cl. 1)
7. Deadweight cargo carrying capacity in tons (abt.) (Cl. 1)	8. Present position (Cl. 1)
9. Expected ready to load (abt.) (Cl. 1)	
10. Loading port or place (Cl. 1)	11. Discharging port or place (Cl. 1)
12. Cargo (also state quantity and margin in Owners' option, if agreed; if full and complete cargo not agreed state "part cargo") (Cl. 1)	
13. Freight rate (also state if payable on delivered or intaken quantity) (Cl. 1)	14. Freight payment (state currency and method of payment; also beneficiary and bank account) (Cl. 4)

15. Laytime allowed for loading (Cl. 5)	16. Shippers (state name and address) (Cl. 5)
17. Laytime allowed for discharging (Cl. 6)	18. Demurrage rate (load. and disch.) (Cl. 7)
19. Cancelling date (Cl. 11)	20. Brokerage commission and to whom payable (Cl. 15)
21. Additional clauses covering special provisions, if agreed	

It is mutually agreed that this Contract shall be performed subject to the conditions contained in this Charter which shall include Part I as well as Part II. In the event of a conflict of conditions, the provisions of Part I shall prevail over those of Part II to the extent of such conflict.

Signature (Owners)	Signature (Charterers)

Printed and sold by Fr. G. Knudtzon Ltd., 57, Toldbodgade, Copenhagen, by authority of The Baltic and International Maritime Conference, Copenhagen.

Fig. 18.9. The BIMCO uniform general charter.

(courtesy of BIMCO, Copenhagen)

Documents for Road Haulage Operations

The documents required to maintain adequate supervision of road haulage vehicles are numerous, and it is impossible to give a full account of them here. Apart from statutory requirements about licences to operate, plating and testing of vehicles, insurance of vehicles and drivers' record books, any firm will have a complex system of documents for keeping track of vehicles and their utilisation.

Generally a programme of transport operations will be in existence to meet customers' requirements. This schedule of operations will then have to be planned against the vehicles that are available, bearing in mind their position, maintenance schedules and fitness for particular purposes. They will also need to be planned against the drivers' availability, bearing in mind the variety of the work, the journey frequency, individual driver preferences, etc. From a

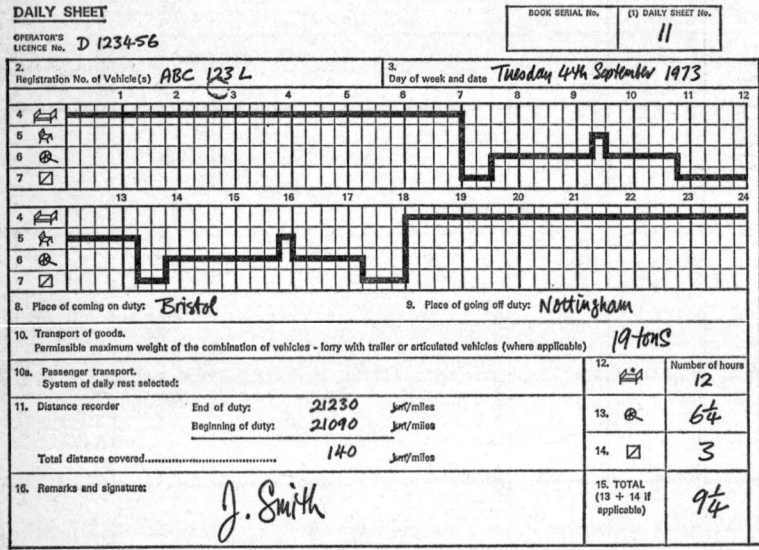

Fig. 18.10. Pictorial driver's record book.

(courtesy of Eversheds Ltd., St. Albans)

rough planning sheet the decisions made will be transferred to a destination sheet, and the foreman in charge will then see that the loads actually go. Before they can do so the dispatch office will prepare delivery notes, in sets, giving a copy for each party. A typical set would be something like the set shown in Fig. 18.2.

The Transport Act 1968 requires records of drivers' hours of work to be kept for all goods vehicles exceeding 30 cwt. unladen weight or 3½ tons gross

MOVEMENT CERTIFICATE

| 1 Exporter (Name, full address, country) | **EUR 1 No.** F 233 893 |

See notes overleaf before completing this form

2 Certificate used in preferential trade between

THE EUROPEAN ECONOMIC COMMUNITY

and

(insert appropriate countries or groups of countries or territories)

| 3 Consignee (Name, full address, country) (Optional) |
| 4 Country, group of countries or territory of exportation **EEC** | 5 Country, group of countries or territory of destination |
| 6 Transport details (Optional) | 7 Remarks |

(1) If goods are not packed, indicate number of articles, or state "in bulk" as appropriate.

| 8 Item number: marks and numbers   Number and kind of packages (1) : description of goods | 9 Gross weight (kg) or other measure (litres, cu.m, etc.) | 10 Invoices (Optional) |

SPECIMEN

11 CUSTOMS ENDORSEMENT

Declaration certified.   Stamp

Export document (2) :

(2) Complete only where the regulations of the exporting country or territory require.

Form_____No_____

Customs office_____

Issuing country or territory:
UNITED KINGDOM

Date_____

(Signature)

C.1299

12 DECLARATION BY THE EXPORTER

I, the undersigned, declare that the goods described above meet the conditions required for the issue of this certificate.

_____
(Place and date)

_____
(Signature)

1   F-4265 (Dec. 1973)

Fig. 18.11. A European Community Movement Certificate.

(courtesy of The Controller, Her Majesty's Stationery Office)

E.C. E.F. E.G. C.E.

A 073 80

T3L

INTERNAL COMMUNITY TRANSIT DOCUMENT FOR ESTABLISHING THE COMMUNITY NATURE OF GOODS

See notes overleaf

Document issued on under No.

10. DECLARATION: ....

represented by ....

hereby declares that the goods described below are Community goods

At .... on ....
(place of signature) *(date)*

Signature ....

30. Number, kind, marks and numbers of packages	31. Description of goods

CANCELLED

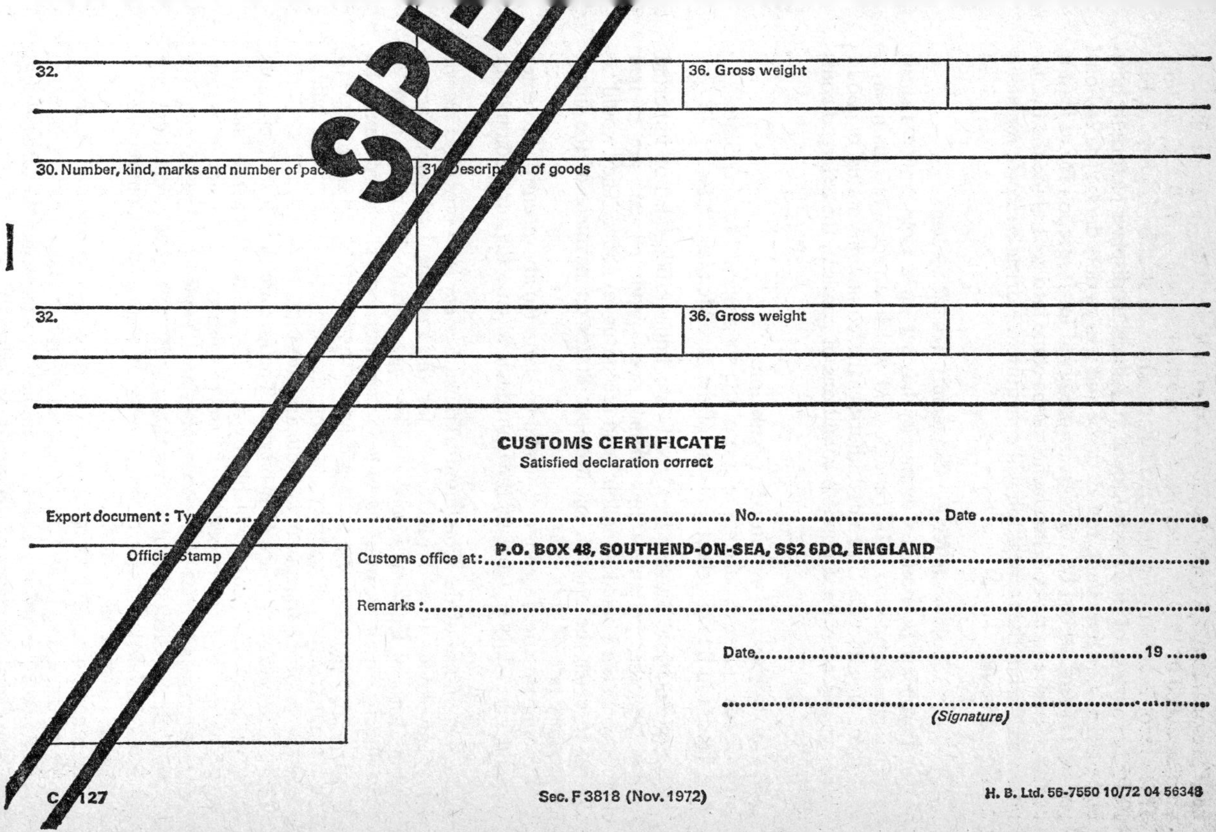

Fig. 18.12. An E.E.C. Transit Document.
(courtesy of Her Majesty's Stationery Office)

32.

36. Gross weight

30. Number, kind, marks and number of packages

31. Description of goods

36. Gross weight

32.

CUSTOMS CERTIFICATE
Satisfied declaration correct

No.......................... Date..........................

Customs office at: **P.O. BOX 48, SOUTHEND-ON-SEA, SS2 6DQ, ENGLAND**

Remarks:

Export document: Ty..........................

Official Stamp

Date.........................., 19..........

....
(Signature)

Sec. F 3818 (Nov. 1972)

H. B. Ltd. 56-7550 10/72 04 56348

C 127

plated weight. Regulations issued in 1970 make it obligatory for drivers to keep personal logbooks covering a period of at least 14 days. The regulations were extended in 1973 to cover the Continental regulations in E.E.C. 543/69. These records are in diagrammatic form and an illustration is given in Fig. 18.10 by courtesy of Eversheds Ltd. of St. Albans. It displays pictorially how many hours the driver slept, rested, drove and was on duty during the 24-hour period. Drivers' record books must be preserved for inspection for at least a period of twelve months. When tachographs come into general use the E.E.C. type record from the tachograph will constitute the driver's record, replacing the record book.

Documents for the Community Transit System

The European Economic Community has set up a Community Transit System under Regulation 542/69 as amended, which can act in two main ways. First it can signal to the Customs authorities the 'community status' of goods. This term describes three possible conditions of goods in the enlarged community:

(a) Goods which are not in free circulation.
(b) Goods in free circulation in one of the six original Member States.
(c) Goods in free circulation in one of the new Member States.

'Free circulation' implies that goods are home-produced, not imported from some other country. Thus British home-produced cars are in free circulation in the United Kingdom, and are status (c) above. They would be eligible to enter the original six Member States on payment of the intra-Community rate of duty.

German home-produced goods would be status (b) above, entitled to enter Holland free of duty and to enter the United Kingdom at the intra-Community rate.

The second use of the Community Transit System is to provide a transit document similar to a T.I.R. carnet for the movement of goods across frontiers without Customs inspection. The appropriate documents must be presented to an office of departure for certification. The goods must be available for inspection and sealing if necessary. Then the goods are free to move from country to country, passing through approved transit offices where copies of the transit advice note are given up.

The documents in use are of two types. The first are simplified documents called *movement certificates* which provide evidence that the goods and their packaging are in free circulation. These certificates do not act as transit documents across a series of frontiers. They are intended chiefly as documents to signal to the Customs authorities that goods are in free circulation, and hence may either be admitted free of duty or at the intra-Community rate during the transitional period.

The other types of document are known as 'full procedure' T forms, including Forms T1, T2 and T3. These act as transit documents, in the same way as T.I.R. carnets which they will eventually replace within the Community. They also signal the status of the goods, as follows:

Form T1. Goods not in free circulation and therefore not entitled to free entry or entry at the intra-Community rate.

Form T2. Goods in free circulation in the six original Member States. These signal free entry within the six, and intra-Community rates on entry to the other three States.

Form T3 will only be issued in the transitional period (up to July 1, 1977) and signals free circulation in the new Member States.

Suggested Further Reading

Reference Book for Exporters, current edition as revised monthly, Croner Publications Ltd.

Road Transport Operation, current edition as revised monthly, Croner Publications Ltd.

Simpler Export Documents, Board of Trade, London, 1965.

Walker, A. G., *Export Practice and Documentation,* Butterworth, 1970.

Whitehead, G., *Office Practice Made Simple,* W. H. Allen, 1974.

CHAPTER NINETEEN

TRANSPORT AND THE EUROPEAN ECONOMIC COMMUNITY

Introduction

The European Economic Community was founded by the Treaty of Rome, which originally had six signatories: France, Germany, Italy, the Netherlands, Belgium and Luxembourg. The intention was to establish a free trade area and eventually a political and monetary union. The Community was enlarged on January 1, 1973, by the accession of Britain, Denmark and Eire. The institutions of the European Economic Community are shown in a rather simplified form in Fig. 19.1. The emphasis has been placed on transport matters in this diagram, but the institutions of the Community study all aspects of the life of the community and attempt to harmonise them so far as possible. The reader is urged to study the chart, and note how the five major institutions are related to one another. These are: (a) the Council of Ministers, (b) the Commission, (c) the European Assembly, (d) the Court of Justice, and (e) the Committee of Permanent Representatives.

When the Treaty of Rome was signed in 1957 the parties agreed, by Articles 3e and 74 of the Treaty, to adopt a common policy in the field of transport. It was felt that a 'free trade' area, where goods were free to circulate within the Community boundaries, could only be developed if coherent Community transport arrangements were introduced. Accordingly, the Treaty required the progressive introduction of measures which reduced discrimination against carriers of other member states. In the early years fairly rapid progress in harmonisation was achieved, but this period ended in 1966, and since then the common transport policy has made slower progress. The objectives of the 'Transport' section of the Treaty (Articles 74–84) still remain the basis for action to achieve a common policy. Let us see what these provisions require.

The 'Transport' Provisions of the Treaty of Rome (Articles 74–84)

Article 74 provides that Member States shall pursue the objectives of the Treaty of Rome within the framework of a common transport policy.

Article 75. In order to implement Article 74 the Council of Ministers shall lay down common rules applicable to international transport between the territories of Member States, and the conditions under which non-resident carriers may operate transport services within Member States. These rules, and any other appropriate provisions, would be based upon proposals submitted to the Council of Ministers by the European Commission, and would be subject to unanimous agreement in the early years, and a qualified majority later. In fact, this use of a qualified majority to overrule a Member State is never used if the Member State makes it clear that it regards the matter as vital to its national interests.

Article 76 prohibits Member States from introducing legislation which

228

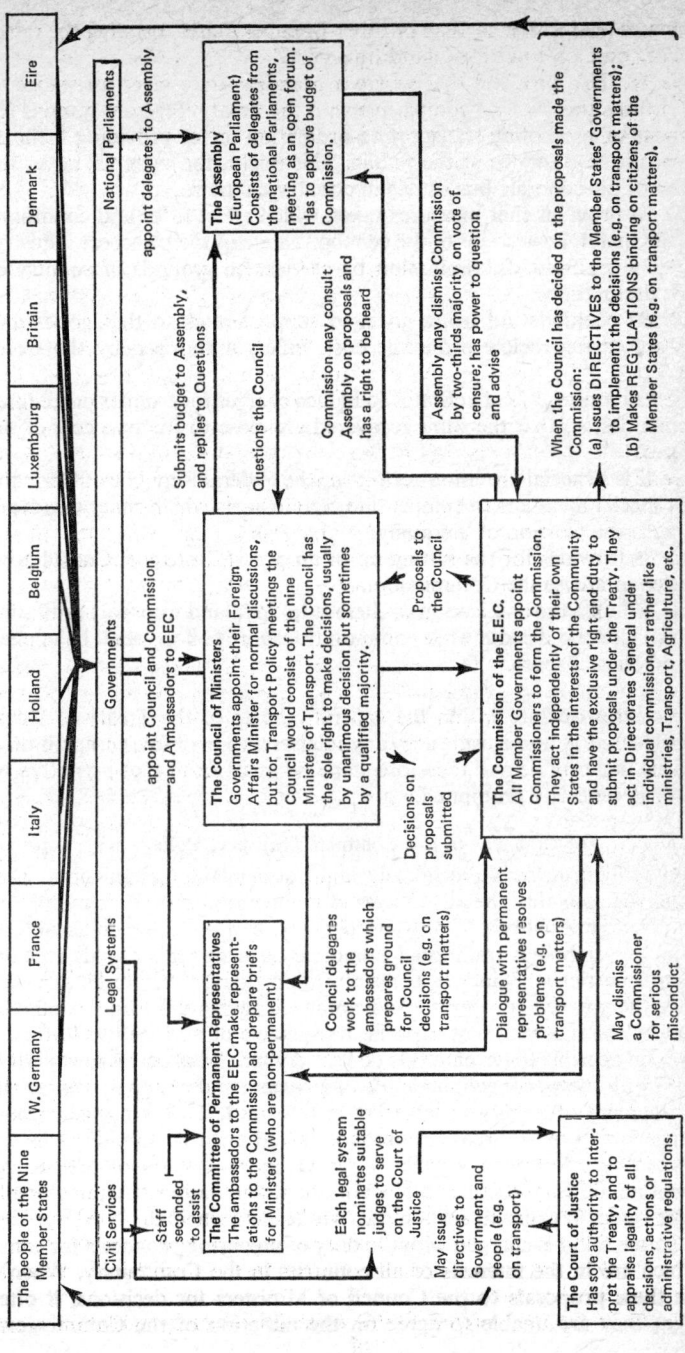

Fig. 19.1. Structure and organisation of the European Economic Community (with special reference to transport).

discriminates against the carriers of other Member States, pending the introduction of common rules for inland transport.

Article 77. This provides that where a Member State gives assistance to
transport firms this shall be compatible with the Treaty if the aid given is for
the purpose of promoting transport co-ordination or for providing facilities
which constitute a service to the public. This might, for example, cover the
operation of uneconomic bus routes in country districts.

Article 78 provides that measures taken which affect rates and conditions
of carriage shall take account of the economic state of the transport industry.

Article 79 prohibits discrimination by carriers on grounds of country of
origin or destination.

Article 80 prohibits aid being given to support rates so that goods and
services are carried below economic cost, unless authorised by the Commission.

Article 81 requires Member States to reduce charges for frontier procedures
and formalities, so that the sums recovered are close to the true cost of the
procedures.

Article 82 is a special provision permitting the Federal Republic of Germany
to adopt special measures to compensate certain areas which suffer disadvantages due to the division of Germany.

Article 83 provides for the setting up of an expert Transport Consultative
Committee to advise the Commission.

Article 84 limits the application of these rules to inland transport until such
time as the Council decides what common transport policies shall be applied
to sea and air transport.

These clauses operate within the general climate of the Treaty of Rome
which holds that in a free trade area any interference with free competition is
prima facie undesirable and therefore state aid apart from that permitted by
Article 77 is generally prohibited.

Development of the Common Transport Policy

The underlying principle, originally laid down in the Commission's proposals in 1961, was that the advantages of competition should be more fully
realised for the mutual benefit of transport users and transport undertakings.
This principle embodies traditional economic thinking which holds that the
'world' will be richer if nations concentrate on doing those tasks at which
they have the greatest comparative advantage. Transport facilities should be
provided by the most efficient carriers, irrespective of nationality. In fact, it
has not been possible to develop this policy very far. Transport is inextricably
bound up with the whole economic life of a nation, and nationalism prevents
the development of a truly free market in transport. This is not surprising,
since transport in many areas is uneconomic and must be subsidised in one
way or another. Although Article 77 recognises this, it is not easy to get
agreement on aid to particular services or areas, and nations are unwilling to
surrender rights in order to sustain the 'free trade' principle.

The Commission is charged with the duty of preparing proposals for transport which are in the interests of all countries in the Community. When it
submits these proposals to the Council of Ministers for decisions, it often
finds that they are unable to agree on the adoption of the Commission's

schemes. Instead they usually abstract certain parts of the proposals, and implement these more limited measures. This slows down the work of developing a meaningful transport system based on an overall approach to problems. A note of desperation can be found in some of the Commission's communications to the Council, appealing to that body to institute dialogues between itself and other institutions such as the European Parliament and the Economic and Social Committee to resolve the national differences which are delaying the Common Transport Policy.

There has been a marked expansion in transport in Europe since the Community began. The specialisation envisaged in the Treaty of Rome is only possible if more and more transport takes place. If all transport is included then it forms 15 per cent of the total gross national product of the Community; while it is 6 per cent if we leave out private cars and own-account transport. This compares with agriculture, which only creates 5 per cent of the total wealth. If such a large share of total wealth is to play its proper part in benefitting the European people the Common Transport Policy must be agreed. The Commission has therefore recently re-formulated the policy and re-defined its aims.

Objectives and Scope of the Common Transport Policy

The objectives of the Common Transport Policy may be listed as follows:

(a) To remove impediments to the free circulation of transport services.

(b) To harmonise the framework of laws and regulations within which the different modes and undertakings operate.

(c) To devise controls limiting extreme competition where this is found to be harmful.

(d) To devise guidelines which will enable transport to play its part in achieving the objectives of the Paris Summit of 1972. This conference attempted to put a more 'human' face on the Community, and the socio-economic aspirations of its people.

These objectives can only be achieved if transport plays a major rôle in other Community policies. Transport is an essential element in almost all aspects of community life, and the following particular cases illustrate its importance.

(a) *Regional Policy*. Regional policy is concerned with the solution of problems in particular regions which are either underdeveloped or are suffering from declining industrial activity. Transport can improve the accessibility of these areas; it can enable populations to move where necessary; it can develop their resources or promote schemes for their reclamation and rehabilitation.

(b) *Social Policy*. Social policies envisage the harmonisation of standards of living, working conditions, health and social security benefits, industrial safety, etc. Transport forms a large part of social life, and employs several million Europeans. It is desirable that employees in the same sort of transport services should have similar working conditions and rewards, while transport services to other citizens should be as uniform as possible in the different countries. Thus transport aspects of programmes of social action in environmental fields, in ambulance and similar services, and in education and training should be comparable.

(*c*) *Fiscal Policy*. Inevitably vehicles and their fuels attract taxation. The demand for transport is inelastic so that taxation levied on transport is inescapable and the yield to the Treasury is high. It is very desirable that taxation in this field should be harmonised, so that all operators face similar costs. Variations in tax could affect the relative competitiveness of operators, giving unfair advantages to countries which have less severe taxes.

(*d*) *Industrial Policy*. Transport bridges the gap between producers and consumers. It follows that industrial concentration and specialisation is increased when the transport system is efficient. The gaps can be bridged more easily, and the economies of large-scale operation are achieved.

(*e*) *Environmental Policy*. Transport is a major factor in environmental problems, especially those of noise, atmospheric pollution, traffic congestion and accidents: 60,000 people are killed and 1,500,000 injured every year in the Community. The Common Transport Policy aims at reducing these social costs.

(*f*) *Energy Policy*. A drastic re-thinking of energy policies has been taking place since the 1973 Middle East conflict. Transport policy must be influenced by energy policy and the utmost economy in energy must remain a feature of transport design for the conceivable future.

(*g*) *External Policy*. The Community is part of a greater world, on which it relies for resources, services and markets. The transport system has a major part to play in promoting international links, in developing the Third World, and in defence.

The Rôle of the Public Authorities in Transport

The public authorities are expected to play a much fuller part in future transport policy than they have in the past. This is because the creation, extension and continuous adaptation of the transport network is to take place within the framework of the Common Transport Policy. Such activities are best performed, and financed, by public bodies. This does not necessarily mean bodies of the E.E.C., but national authorities taking action along lines laid down in E.E.C. directives. The chief aim of such directives would be to harmonize transport policies along the lines described in paragraph (d), page 231. The public authorities would, in particular, be responsible for shaping the transport infrastructures. Firms, by contrast, would be responsible for planning their own investment in vehicles, installations and equipment.

The cost of the infrastructure must be calculated in such a way that each branch of transport can be charged with some appropriate share of the burden. These costs should be imputed with a view to achieving the best possible allocation of resources. Other public authority measures may also be used; priority for public transport, controls over routes, prohibitions of certain types of traffic, etc.

The public authorities charged with the implementation of the Common Transport Policy look carefully into the following matters:

(*a*) The preparation of forecasts of transport supply and demand.

(*b*) The preparation of a master plan for the infrastructure network which will best serve the whole community. This plan should promote the exploitation of the comparative advantages of each particular mode of transport, and the development of inter-modal systems.

(*c*) The development of committees to ensure co-operation about, and finance for, all projects which go beyond the national frame of reference.

(*d*) The allocation of costs, using the charging system proposed by the Commission. This charging system is based upon marginal social cost and the need to balance the transport budget. This means that charges for the use of the facilities provided would be greater if the social cost was great (for example, road use in town centres) but smaller if the social cost was small (for example, utilisation of an existing railway system in a depressed area). At the same time the overall cost of the facilities should fall upon the users of the facilities, i.e. the transport budget should balance. While the Commission expected some difficulty in costing out this system properly it was confident that the system would become more precise as knowledge of the true costs improved.

The Future of E.E.C. Transport

The history of transport gives many illustrations of transport systems appropriate to their own era but forming a vested interest resistant to future change. Examples are the canal system in Britain and the railway systems of almost every nation in the world. The Common Transport Policy, with its recurring review of the whole transport network and its clear principles, should ensure that the Community is served by a transport system which promotes the best interests of the transport users. A sound transport infra-structure serving the entire Community; a transport market operating in conditions of healthy competition; a well-trained and competent transport profession enjoying harmonised working conditions and rewards; these are the objectives of the Common Transport Policy. At the same time little progress has been made in defining a policy for sea and air transport. If the Community is to become an outward-looking body, rather than an intro-verted continental group, it must soon implement Article 84 and decide on a policy for shipping and air transport. The United Kingdom would presumably hope that such a policy would be a positive, vigorous one, based on the freedom of the seas and the air, enabling established transport firms to com-pete effectively in world transport.

At the time of writing (early 1975) attempts continue to devise an effective Common Transport Policy, against enduring difficulties over the dimensions and weights of heavy transport vehicles. Britain is being particularly difficult about these decisions. The slow progress made in developing a common road haulage policy since 1957 within the six nations seems to have persisted now that there are nine members. However, the agreement to increase by 20 per cent the licences that permit *cabotage*, i.e. the right to pick up and put down loads in another country, is a useful step to liberalisation. Cabotage is the right of a nation to reserve to its own nationals the right to carry on inland transport or coastal traffic. It seems inevitable that this ancient right must eventually be waived by E.E.C. countries as far as community transit is concerned and these licences are a part of the liberalisation process.

A Ports Study Group has been set up to study European ports, with a view to agreeing a Common Ports Policy, particularly over competition and subsidies. In the shipping field, with 25 per cent of the world's tonnage registered in E.E.C. countries and 40 per cent of the world's seaborne trade originating or ending in Community ports the need to use shipping effectively is very important. Crude flag discrimination, which puts cargo on to unsuitable half-empty ships, is an important problem which needs to be examined. One recent proposal by the T.U.C. that a national transport authority should be set up with the power to designate which type of goods should go by which mode of transport, has been strongly criticised by Chambers of Commerce and other bodies as premature and probably unnecessary in the light of the co-operative attitude displayed by most parties in securing efficiency in transport.

Suggested Further Reading

Communication from the European Commission to the European Council on the Development of a Common Transport Policy, Brussels, 1973.

Lasok, D., and Bridge, J. W., *Law and Institutions of the European Communities*, Butterworth, 1973.

Lowe, D., *Transport and Delivery to European Customers*, Kogan Page, 1974.

Notices No. 750, 751, 752 and 753, H.M. Customs, 1973.

CHAPTER TWENTY

THE CONTROL OF TRANSPORT

'Laisser faire' v. Control of Transport

The doctrine of 'laisser faire', which drew its force from the eighteenth-century activities of the early capitalists, holds that the state should not interfere with the activities of private individuals who are showing enterprise, but should 'leave them to act' as they see fit. It holds that in doing what is best for himself the entrepreneur will also do what is best for society at large, for his activities will utilise natural resources, give employment to his fellow men, create wealth, and—as far as transport is concerned—create the utilities of space which will be of great benefit to society.

It soon became apparent that in fact the doctrine was less applicable to transport than to other fields of enterprise. The entrepreneur, in aiming at the greatest personal profit, was likely to exploit the general public, especially in view of the monopolistic nature of many early transport enterprises. His pursuit of minimum business costs might result in excessive social costs, be it in pollution of the atmosphere, an excessive accident rate, dumping of unsightly or noxious waste material, etc. From the very earliest times therefore we find statutory regulation of transport, local bye-laws to control abuses and a running conflict between government and the transport industry.

There are a number of reasons why society must exercise control over transport. These may be listed as follows:

(a) The basic operations of any transport system need to be regulated in the interests of public safety.

(b) Transport is in many cases a natural monopoly.

(c) In other cases transport is so competitive that cut-throat price competition could lower standards of safety and service, and reduce wages to exploitation levels.

(d) Transport is not static but dynamic, and new transport modes developed alongside existing modes cause capital to be wasted and levels of service to be reduced on the outmoded transport network. The result is that some subsidy or encouragement may be necessary in the public interest.

(e) The social costs of transport are great and control must be exercised to keep them within reasonable limits.

(f) Transport often has international implications that require official agreements which are best conducted at governmental levels, and then imposed as a body of rules upon the operators of each particular nation.

Some illustrations of controls introduced over the years in the United Kingdom with regard to each of these aspects of transport may be appropriate at this point.

The Regulation of Basic Operations

Any transport system requires basic regulations in the interest of public safety. We may decide to drive on the left or on the right, but we cannot leave it to the general public to please themselves. A basic framework of rules must be laid down and enforced. We must agree on the types of sign to be used to signal hazards or notify compulsory regulations, and their exact meaning must be laid down. Offences must be delineated and punishments prescribed. These regulations may be of general application to the ordinary public or only known to the specialist operator, but the regulations will be numerous and far reaching in their effects.

Controlling Monopolies

Transport is a natural monopoly in many ways but particularly in the case of transport where very heavy capital costs are involved. The best examples are the canals of the eighteenth century and the railways of the nineteenth century, but the forerunners to both of these were the turnpikes built between 1663 and 1760 and on into the industrial era. It was found in all these cases that no entrepreneur was prepared to put up the capital for a project unless he could be assured of a return on the investment, and this required the granting of a monopoly for a period of years. Since any such transport undertaking required the use of other people's land, which had to be compulsorily acquired, and also needed the privilege of limited liability if it was to collect the capital, a private Act of Parliament was necessary to confer the requisite powers. The Act was also a convenient medium for conferring the monopoly, usually for a period of years. Even in recent times the same device has been adopted: for example, to build the Dartford–Purfleet Tunnel under the Thames.

When we say that transport is a natural monopoly we mean that it is obvious from the very nature of the project that it will be uneconomic to build two motorways, or two railways, or to cut two canals from A to B. If we confer upon one company the sole rights to build a facility we are giving it the opportunity to exploit a monopoly position. We will therefore incorporate as many safeguards or controls as we can. A common safeguard which does not always prove practicable is to say that anyone who wishes to do so may use the facility. Thus the early canal builders were required to accept other people's barges on their canals, and the early railways were forced to accept other people's trains. Frequent accidents soon put a stop to that, but even in the Pipelines Act of 1962 the Minister has the power to insist that other people may use any pipeline that is constructed to prevent a proliferation of applications to construct pipelines. Probably that is not a very practicable idea in many cases. A whole string of Railway Acts from 1845 to 1894 wrestled with the abuse by railway companies of monopoly powers. Such ideas as the 'Parliamentary Train', which required the railways to run at least one train in each direction every day which stopped at all the stations, ensured that the general public had at least a minimum service. The Cheap Trains Act required railways to offer cheap fares before 7.00 a.m. in the morning so that workers could travel cheaply to work. Above all the requirement that railways must not show any undue preference in offering their services was designed to give equal opportunity to all wishing to move goods by rail.

Controlling Excessive Competition

Cut-throat competition is a feature of those transport modes which do not have excessive capital costs. It was therefore most commonly encountered in the road haulage industry, but air transport has also suffered from it. The free enterprise system has much to recommend it and it might therefore seem unnecessary to control competition, but in fact cut-rate charges inevitably lead entrepreneurs whose profit margins are being reduced to cut back on costs.

The most likely costs to be cut are wages and maintenance costs. The first of these actions—cutting labour costs—will vary in its impact depending upon the economic climate at the time. During periods of high unemployment, when men are fearful of losing their jobs, it can result in reduced wage rates and excessive hours being worked. During periods of full employment only incompetent, less qualified staff would be prepared to accept such conditions. Better staff would soon seek work elsewhere and a deterioration in efficiency would result. Reduction in maintenance costs—highly desirable if the same standards can be maintained—could, where reduction of costs was the sole criterion, result in reduced safety standards, a higher incidence of breakdowns, and more frequent accidents.

There is a third type of waste: the waste of capital entailed when there are more than enough vehicles to carry the goods and passengers available, i.e. surplus capacity. This capital could have been used for alternative purposes and is therefore a squandering of the nation's resources. To solve such problems both quantity licensing and quality licensing have been used in the past. The term 'quantity licensing' implies a restriction of the quantity of transport made available, usually by the licensing of services. A licence is granted to an efficient operator, who is then given protection from competition. The licence is renewable at intervals provided the operator continues to conduct the service in a proper manner. Additions to existing services will only be sanctioned on clear proof of increased public need, and objections can be lodged by existing operators, while new applications will produce a similar response. This type of quantity licensing was used in the United Kingdom from 1930 to 1970 for controlling goods vehicles. It still applies to road passenger transport and air transport. 'Quality' licensing requires that the licensing authority shall be satisfied as to the ability of the licensee to maintain and service his vehicles or aircraft properly, and that he has proper staff adequately trained for whatever functions they are required to perform. There may also be particular controls over the operations of vehicles and aircraft. This type of licensing is the type used today in road haulage, where the 'operator's licence' certifies his ability to maintain and operate the vehicles, but not the number of vehicles he will operate, although he must declare how many he will use. Failure to continue to meet the required standards (for example, when spot checks disclose poor maintenance, overloading, and other infringements) may result in the licensing authority reducing the permitted number of vehicles.

Controls Necessitated by 'Structural' Changes in Transport

'Structural' changes refer to changes that come about due to changes in taste or fashion or as a result of technical innovation. Thus the petrol and diesel engines have changed the face of transport in the twentieth century, and rendered rail and inland water transport less attractive to many freight forwarders, although company trains are becoming more common and very attractive to some users. Similarly, air transport has practically killed off the seaborne passenger trade, except for the cruise trade and the car ferry. When such changes occur the pattern of influences at work is complex, and controls may be introduced which, though seemingly desirable in the short term, may have debatable long-term effects.

It is difficult for policy makers to extract the best policy from the welter of opinions, pressures from vested interests, etc. Old systems in decline rally their supporters to preserve the dying industry and the proponents of the new techniques, facing inevitable problems in proving their technology, may be less vocal and less politically active because of their involvement with those problems. The resulting policy may rivet an obsolete system on the nation for a considerable time, until inescapable economic pressures force the final rejection of the old system. The nationalisation of road haulage in 1947 was an example. Although this was largely undone in 1953, and no attempt has been made to renationalise the section of road haulage denationalised in that Act, the accelerated switch to road haulage from the railways which occurred between 1953 and 1962 would probably have come somewhat earlier had the 1947 Act not taken road haulage into public ownership and discouraged many transport users who had doubts about the new undertaking's ability to give an efficient service.

Nationalisation is an extreme form of control, but it represents a good solution to most problems of 'structural' change. Only a complete takeover of the obsolete facilities, and their replacement where necessary by up-to-date facilities and equipment, can achieve the streamlined operations which will produce a viable industry in the face of the changed demand situation.

Controlling Social Costs of Transport

Free enterprise activity aims at profitability. Profits can be achieved in three ways: by keeping costs low or by keeping prices high or by a combination of the two. The ability to impose high prices is limited by competition and the degree of flexibility of demand. This means that cost reduction probably offers the best solution to the problem of maintaining a high level of profitability. It has therefore been a common practice of entrepreneurs to avoid costs wherever possible, often without regard to the social consequences. Without positive legal sanctions to compel entrepreneurs to pay fair wages, contribute to training costs, install seat belts, insure third parties, eliminate noxious exhausts or pay fair contributions to road repairs, many would feel no obligation to do so. Unless these costs are compelled upon the transport operator he is likely to evade them and leave society to supplement the inadequate wages, subsidise training courses, bear the cost of accidents and workmen's compensation, hospital care and relief for the victims of accidents, endure the smogs and diseases inseparable from unclean air, pay for the repairs to roads, etc. To the extent that these increased costs are passed on to the consumer they must still be borne by society in general, but even so the costs are borne more fairly, for the average cost of safety devices is low and general, while the costs of injuries sustained by individuals are expensive and personal.

The development of a proper appraisal of social costs in recent years has done much to allocate the costs where they ought to fall, and has inevitably imposed many controls upon transport. These controls have increased the costs of transport firms, but have reduced costs overall and have shared them more fairly. They have also helped us to make wiser decisions about which forms of transport to develop and which to restrict.

International Implications of Transport

Transport is frequently international. Aircraft must fly over other countries if they are to utilise 'least time tracks' adequately. Ships finish their journeys in foreign ports and intermodal transits finish up on the roads and railways of foreign states. Countless problems arise as a result. There are 'conflicts of laws' inherent in national attitudes to what is and is not permissible or fair. There are problems of infestation, disease and virus control and quarantine. There are problems of liability for accidents in roadsteads, harbours, airport approaches, and on rivers and road and rail networks. All these matters are the subject of discussions at intergovernmental levels, and lead to conclusions embodied in 'Conventions', which have to be enacted as laws in the individual states. These laws are imposed upon and enforced among the citizens operating in the particular field concerned. This gives a very broad system of control.

For all these reasons the control of transport is an important aspect of the total transport scene. The reader who hopes to understand and participate in transport must know what the particular regulations are that affect him, and must observe them carefully.

The Development of Transport Control

Although the history of transport is too great a study to be dealt with fully in this book, a brief outline of the main policy threads over the years is worth a place here. In very early times the chief concerns of those seeking to control transport were twofold: (*a*) to control charges so that they reflected a fair price for the services rendered, and (*b*) to raise revenue from what was largely considered to be a luxury pastime for the well-to-do. In a nation which practised self-sufficiency to a very considerable degree, the movement of goods was largely confined to luxuries, furs, silks, wines, etc. Personal travel for pleasure was limited to the rich. Poor people walked.

Conditions have now changed. We are far from being self-sufficient, and transport is essential for the distribution of all those goods regarded as the necessities of our present mode of living and to enable people to go about their daily business. Yet transport is still regarded by governments as a lucrative source of revenue. Revenue is raised from transport in many ways, particularly from the private motor car, and severe criticisms could be made of the ways in which this revenue is levied. We do not usually regard this as a feature today of the control of transport. The problem is that the demand for transport is relatively inelastic with respect to price. This means that the demand for transport does not respond very easily to price increases, and the Chancellor who raises the road vehicle tax and the petrol tax with a view to reducing private motoring simply finishes up with a lot of revenue and very little reduction in the number of cars on the road. It is possible of course that the extraordinary rises in the price of petrol which have occurred recently, and others which it seems will inevitably follow, may have a greater effect on this apparent inelasticity than has hitherto been the case.

The mechanisation of transport made control much more necessary, and shifted the emphasis to control in the interests of public safety. This emphasis has endured down the years, and is still a major preoccupation of the Ministry of Transport and other transport bodies. Many of the controls to be looked at later in this chapter are controls designed to ensure the safety of the general public in their roles as transport users, transport employees and innocent third parties. There is a host of Acts of Parliament, E.E.C. Council Regulations and subordinate legislation to ensure the proper maintenance and operation of transport facilities, the proper training and fitness of staff and the adequacy of supervision.

A second aspect of control which developed alongside the mechanisation of transport was the drive to secure comprehensiveness and standardisation. This was not appreciated at first in the original Parliamentary sanctions given to those transport innovators, the Turnpike Trusts. Only when the miseries of a patchy road system made it obvious to all, did Parliament begin to insist upon a comprehensive road network rather than the making up of lucrative sections of road only. There was more awareness of the need to develop through-lines at the start of the railway era, and some Members of Parliament openly campaigned for Parliament to refuse to sanction piecemeal developments. It is true that their cries went unheeded to some extent, but Acts like the Gauge Act of 1846 did much to remedy the problem. The needs to secure standardised systems of working and co-ordination and even integration of the total transport system have been an enduring feature of control which is still of major importance.

The third thread in the control of transport was the control of charges to prevent the abuse of monopoly powers. This control is still an important aspect of the control of transport today, but it tends to be less a matter of setting maximum levels: such a policy is only effective in times of stable prices. Today it is more usual to find the control of charges consisting of a continuous, or at least frequent, monitoring of proposed price increases to ensure that the prices charged do reflect the increased costs incurred and conform to general government policy about prices.

The control of transport by nationalisation might seem at a first glance to be the ultimate form of control. In the United Kingdom this has not proved to be particularly rigid control, since the nationalised bodies have largely been left as autonomous units operating on a commercial basis with a duty to achieve a balanced budget taking one year with another. Included in this balance has been an element for a normal return on capital invested, and for the provision of capital for further expansion. Parliament, in attempting to achieve the best results from the nationalised industries, has modified its policies again and again, and has written off some heavy railway deficits. This has resulted in the original aims of a completely integrated transport system not being realised, and perhaps experience shows that they cannot in fact be realised without surrendering entirely traditional British ideas of what is desirable in terms of control. We have refrained from attempts to impose on transport any rigid system of operations which might only inhibit new developments in an extremely dynamic sector of the economy.

The pattern of control in transport is so complex and there are so many aspects to keep in mind that the authors have presented this section as a modal review of controls applicable to particular forms of transport. Where a full description has been given elsewhere in this book a cross-reference has been given, and the reader is urged to read the relevant pages.

The Control of Road Transport

The principal Acts of Parliament still in force relating to the control of road transport are as follows:

(*a*) The Road Traffic Acts 1960, and more importantly 1972.

(*b*) The Highways Acts 1959, 1961 and 1971.

(*c*) The Transport Act 1968.

(*d*) The Carriage of Goods by Road Act 1965.

(*e*) The Heavy Commercial Vehicles (Control and Regulations) Act 1973.

There are at least a dozen more amending or minor Acts and a host of pieces of delegated legislation, Ministerial Orders, etc. It is difficult for the transport manager to keep abreast of changes that occur. There are several firms which publish updating circulars in the transport field, at very reasonable prices. For his annual subscription, the transport manager receives a current loose-leaf folder containing the present situation on every aspect of the law affecting road-haulage operations. Each month he receives a packet of amended pages, designed so that the obsolete page may be removed and torn up, and the up-to-date page substituted for it. Perhaps the best system is the one by Croner's Publications Ltd.; readers who are in Road Transport are strongly recommended to become subscribers.

The implications of these Acts for the transport operator will be developed in the sections which follow.

The Regulation of Road Traffic in the Interests of Public Safety

Road traffic presents enormous problems of control to the police in their everyday affairs. The sheer volume of road transport and the relatively high speed at which it operates require clear directives to be given about the use of roads, early signalling of hazards and controlled areas, speed limits, the proper maintenance of vehicles and the fitness of drivers. These and many other directives are incorporated in the various Road Traffic Acts. The current Act is the Road Traffic Act 1972, but minor sections of earlier Acts are still in force. The main provisions of the Acts deal with driving offences, construction and use of vehicles, driving licences, etc. For the convenience of the ordinary public many of these rules are embodied in the Highway Code, a small pamphlet which lists several hundred rules, illustrates the chief signs used and the principles behind the design of signs, and gives a list of the enactments which confer powers upon the police in dealing with offenders. Every transport man should have a copy, and buy new editions as they appear.

Driving offences include causing death by reckless or dangerous driving, driving in a manner or at a speed dangerous to the general public, driving without due care and attention, and driving under the influence of alcoholic drink or drugs. More general offences include failure to obey a police officer directing traffic or in the performance of his duties, and parking a vehicle in a dangerous position. There are rules about accidents and what to do when one occurs, about the manning of certain vehicles, about the minimum age for driving and the licensing of vehicles and drivers.

Construction and Use Regulations

This body of rules is of very great importance to both the designer of road vehicles and operators, because vehicles must conform to the construction rules and be used in the manner laid down. The Secretary of State for the Department of the Environment has the power to make regulations about the width, height and length of motor vehicles and trailers, the diameter of wheels, the condition of tyres, the emission of smoke, fumes, sparks, etc., the weight, laden and unladen, the braking, steering and lighting and the loads to be carried.

Vehicles must be examined at an approved centre within one year of purchase to ensure that they conform with the construction and use regulations.

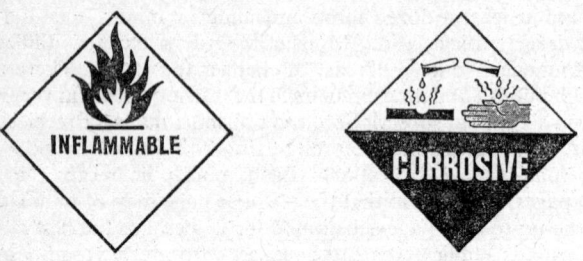

Fig. 20.1. The symbols for inflammable and corrosive loads.

If they do, the operator will be issued with a *goods vehicle test certificate* and a *plating certificate*. The former confirms that the vehicle has been inspected and is in accordance with the Construction and Use Regulations. The latter records the 'Plated Weights' at which the vehicle may be operated. This plate must be attached to the vehicle at all times and spot checks are held on the roads of any vehicle suspected of being operated at an excessive weight. This offence carries a fine of £50. A free *Guide for Vehicle Operators* is available from the Department of the Environment on the plating and testing of vehicles.

Certain vehicles carrying hazardous cargoes must be marked with internationally recognised symbols and with plates giving instructions on what to do in an accident. Two of these symbols are illustrated in Fig. 20.1 above.

The Licensing and Insuring of H.G.V. Drivers

It is an offence to drive or to employ a person to drive unless the driver has first passed a test conducted by an official supervisor to prove his competency to drive that particular class of vehicle, and has received the appropriate driving licence. Licences may be revoked or suspended in certain circumstances.

All users of motor vehicles must either be insured against third-party risks with an authorised insurer or alternatively they must deposit £15,000 with the Supreme Court as a security against claims made by aggrieved third parties.

Control of Heavy Commercial Vehicles

The Heavy Commercial Vehicles (Controls & Regulations) Act 1973 empowers local authorities to draw up proposals for lorry routes through their areas, and to restrict heavy vehicles to these routes. It may also prohibit them from entering certain roads or zones in their areas. These proposals must be published by January 1, 1977, in England and Wales and January 1, 1978, in

Scotland. It also prohibits parking of heavy commercial vehicles on verges, footpaths and land situated between two carriageways. There are exceptions in emergencies or with police consent, or for unloading purposes provided the vehicle is not left unattended.

Quality and Quantity Licensing

Under the 1968 Act, the quantity licensing which had existed in this country since the 1930s was abolished and the system of quality licensing by 'operator's licences' replaced it. This system has already been described above (see page 197) but an element of quantity licensing was retained to the extent that a maximum number of vehicles is usually stated in the licence. An operator purchasing extra vehicles is bound to notify the Licensing Authority of their purchase within one month, and must not exceed the limit set in his licence, which presumably reflects the Licensing Authority's opinion of the number of vehicles the operator's facilities can adequately maintain.

The Control of Road Haulage to achieve Co-ordination of Transport

Co-ordination and integration of transport are two ideas which have constantly recurred in the transport debate since 1945. The 1947 Act aimed at integration, bringing all inland transport under the control of a single organisation—the British Transport Commission. In the event it proved an unwieldy affair, particularly at that time when the nation was slowly recovering from the effects of the Second World War. The result was that measures to reduce the centralised control of transport began to be discussed before the industry had really had a chance to see what integration could achieve. The less centralised system—the co-ordination of transport arrangements by willing co-operation between the various branches of the industry—was pursued instead. Both the 1953 and the 1962 Acts reduced centralisation and the scale of the institutions, each mode becoming independent of the others. Finally the 1968 Act restored the emphasis to integration, particularly the integration of long-distance rail and road haulage (see Sections 1–8) and the establishment of Passenger Transport Authorities to integrate and develop transport services in their areas (see Sections 9–23). The 1968 Act is described fully in Chapter Seventeen, and the reader should read carefully the sections referred to above. The co-operation of road and rail operators has been reasonably successful under the new system, especially since the climate of solicitude for the environment coupled with economic stringencies has made all sides more reasonable.

The Act has also been influential in redressing to some extent the problems of structural changes in transport. Measures to subsidise uneconomic railway lines which are environmentally advantageous and country bus services which are socially desirable have been financed in an indirect way by the raising of goods vehicle taxation and fuel taxes. This indirect cross-subsidy, it may be argued, has required road haulage to carry a fairer share of the social costs it incurs.

The Control of Road Haulage to conform with International Requirements

The Carriage of Goods by Road Act 1965 requires that where road-haulage activities involve international carriage, the goods shall be carried under an international consignment note which conforms to the International Convention on the Carriage of Merchandise by Roadhauliers (the C.M.R. Convention). The consignment note automatically embodies the Convention as a part of the contract of carriage and overrides national laws on the carriage of goods. This means that a very much fairer contract exists between the parties than would be the case under many of the sets of conditions of carriage permitted by English contract law. Some brief details of this convention are given in Table 16.1 (see page 190), but a full study of the Act is the only way to gain a real understanding of its implications for the consignors and carriers of goods.

The European Agreement for the International Carriage of Dangerous Goods by Road (A.D.R.) came into force in July, 1969, and permits the carriage of dangerous goods provided that they are packed and labelled in accordance with the Agreement and carried in vehicles complying with the Agreement. Special tests of vehicles and tanks are conducted by the Department of the Environment inspectors at Heavy Goods Vehicle Testing Stations. They will be tested for corrosion, cracking of attachment points, valve connections, wiring and electrical connections, etc. Fire extinguishers and tool kits must be carried as well as flashing emergency lights independent of the vehicle to be placed 10 metres ahead and 10 metres behind the vehicle when it is halted on roads at night or in bad visibility.

The Control of Rail Transport

Apart from a few narrow-gauge railways, public railways in Britain today are owned and operated by a nationalised corporation, British Rail. During the nineteenth century Parliament sought to control the railway companies because they were powerful monopolies which did not hesitate to exploit their monopoly position. By the time Parliament had controlled the monopolists, the railways were beginning to face severe competition from the roads, and the monopoly was continuously eroded in the first four decades of the twentieth century.

A second reason for the control of railways was the overriding need for safety in rail operations; an insistence upon proper maintenance, signalling and manning was imperative. Many of the requirements imposed costs upon the railways, and repeated attempts were required by Parliament to monitor railway operations. Not that Parliament was always right. The drive by the railway companies to amalgamate lines in the interests of economic operations was opposed at every turn by a Parliament suspicious of such moves as a further tightening of the monopolists' grip. Only when the railways were taken over during the First World War and run as a unified group was it fully appreciated that the economies of amalgamation were indeed real and desirable.

Although the return of the railways to private enterprise in 1921 was achieved by forming four large-scale regional companies, the economic climate of the twenties and thirties was not one where they could expand and grow. Uncontrolled road haulage and road passenger transport in the 1920s and the severe depression of the thirties combined to depress the railways and reduce their share of the limited business available. Its strongly unionised labour force, whose syndicalist co-operation with the seamen and the miners in the first quarter of this century was finally defeated in the 1926 General Strike, believed strongly that only nationalisation could really solve the railways' problems, and was powerfully influential in the Labour Government which finally nationalised transport in 1947.

Since 1947 Parliament has enacted four major Transport Acts, the 1947, 1953, 1962 and 1968 Acts. It does seem that the 1968 Act may finally have got things just about right, for as yet no new proposed policy has appeared. The previous Acts have been implemented in an atmosphere where modified proposals were being actively canvassed. This has not happened in the six years since the 1968 Act appeared. Its provisions are fully described in Chapter Seventeen.

Parliamentary Control

Parliament has the right to introduce a new Act whenever it likes, and as the previous paragraph reminds us it has not hesitated to do so in the last twenty-five years. A revisionary Act is clearly the most far-reaching type of control that is possible of a nationalised industry. The general rule for day-to-day activities is that Parliament should not control or attempt to control such matters, since the industry is expected to operate generally on commercial lines. It should not be expected to undergo an Annual General Meeting every day at 'Question Time'. Theoretically Parliament debates these matters on 'Supply Days', which are traditionally at the disposal of the Opposition. As the Opposition often has more vital matters to debate it usually does not choose to use the Supply Days for these matters, and the Government has to make time available instead. The Railways therefore are usually debated in Government time as part of a general transport debate shortly after the Annual Report has been submitted to the Minister and the Accounts to the Public Accounts Committee. Even so this only happens about every other year as a full debate is rarely necessary more frequently.

The Railway Inspectorate was set up in the nineteenth century as part of governmental attempts to control the railways. It still functions as part of the Department of the Environment. Its investigations and formal enquiries into accidents are an important feature of its work, which also includes technical advice to the Secretary of State on railway affairs.

Under Section 55 of the 1968 Act the Transport Users' Consultative Committees were given amended powers which enabled them to discuss the services and facilities provided by the Railways Board, the Docks Board and the National Freight Corporation, but not those of the National Bus Company and the Passenger Transport Executives. Both the Central and the Area Committees have a duty to consider and report on any matters which appear to them to deserve consideration, especially where the public have made representations about them or the Secretary of State has referred the matters to them for consideration.

The controls exercised over the railways may thus be said to have declined in recent years rather than increased. The regulation of their fields of activity has been achieved by Parliamentary enactments laying down the general character of railway operations rather than by close control of what they actually do. The grants made under the 1968 Act for unremunerative passenger services have recognised the social nature of some of the transport services they provide and the part they play in preventing regional decay in some parts of the country, and reducing congestion in others.

Control of the Railways to conform with International Requirements

Although international agreements on railway transport have existed since 1914, Great Britain has never formally enacted the Convention on International Merchandise (C.I.M.) or the Convention on International Voyagers (C.I.V.). Instead British Rail, as the only British railway company engaged in international transport, has incorporated the C.I.M. convention in its Consignment Notes (see page 216). However, in 1972, by the Carriage by Railway Act, the Government did enact into law the extension of these conventions which refers to compensation to travellers whether as passengers or as persons accompanying freight, who are injured or lose their luggage in international rail journeys.

The Control of Sea Transport

Sea transport operates in the highly competitive field of international trade and is less susceptible to control by national governments than most other forms of transport because it operates over a way which is free to all, and beyond the control of a single nation. At the same time, most nations exert control over their own shipping, and in Britain this has taken the form of a series of enactments which tend generally to ensure that ships are operated safely and that crews are treated fairly.

The major Act is the Merchant Shipping Act 1894, which specifies what a British ship is and how it is to be surveyed, marked, registered and measured. It outlines the master's powers, duties and position, deals with crews, their payment, rights and duties, it provides for medical inspection and other health aspects, and it lays down rules on loadlines, wrecks, fire, the carriage of dangerous goods and the liability of shipowners. A subsequent minor Act, the Merchant Shipping Act of 1958, extends some of the protections given to shipowners to their crews.

To the extent that its sea transport is controlled by each nation as it thinks fit, a ship's competitiveness in world markets may be affected if governments impose strict manning requirements, safety standards, or prescribed levels of wages. This may encourage the use by shipowners of flags of convenience, which involves registering the ship with a foreign nation such as Panama, Liberia or Honduras. The chief advantage of such registration is in the tax field, for taxation in these countries is at very nominal rates. This is not particularly beneficial as far as the United Kingdom is concerned since the U.K. citizen is now taxed on all income received, whether earned at home or abroad. The other advantages, if they can truly be called advantages, of lower safety standards and lower wage scales may still give more competitive edge to shipowners adopting a flag of convenience. In general the system has little to recommend it apart from earning some foreign exchange for a few relatively undeveloped nations.

Voluntary Controls in Sea Transport

Shipowners and other interested parties have for many years joined together for their mutual advantage in Shipping Conferences. The conference system is partly a way of protecting the liner trade from unfair competition from tramp shipping at times when there is excess capacity in the tramp market. If liners are to provide regular services calling at scheduled ports and leaving at stated times irrespective of the cargo position, they must be assured of reasonable freight rates. Tramp freight rates fluctuate with supply and demand, but liner freight rates are held steady. At times when tramp rates are high the liners carry at their steady rates. When tramp rates are low there is a temptation for liner customers to transfer their cargoes to the cheaper tramps. If this happens the liners will suffer losses and may be driven out of business. To encourage regular support from traders, the conference system offers rebates which can be enjoyed only if the trader can prove that his goods have on every occasion in the previous trading period travelled by the conference liners. This conference 'tie' permits a trader to ship his goods by any line that is a member of the Shipping Conference. These liners charge similar rates, but it is unfair to regard them as price-fixing 'rings' since they have in no way a monopoly of shipping, which is international in character and highly competitive. The International Chamber of Commerce, which represents the liners' customers, itself approves the conference system because of the security and reliability of service that the liner owners give to businessmen.

In Appendix One the activities of many transport organisations are described. One of these is the Baltic and International Maritime Conference, an organisation of two thousand owners, brokers and club-members, with a registered tonnage of 100 million G.R.T. B.I.M.C.O. is perhaps the best example of a Shipping Conference where representatives of sea transport examine mutual problems.

Control of Sea Transport to Meet International Needs

There are no less than 83 international conventions on sea transport currently in operation. To give some idea of the range and variety of these conventions the list below includes those which have come into effect since 1960.

The International Convention for the Safety of Life at Sea	1960
International Convention for the Unification of Certain Rules Relating to the Carriage of Passengers by Sea	1961
International Agreement Regarding the Maintenance of Certain Lights in the Red Sea	1962
Convention on the Liability of Operators of Nuclear Ships	1962
Convention on Facilitation of International Maritime Traffic	1965
International Convention on Load Lines	1966
International Regulations for Preventing Collisions at Sea, Revised by the International Conference on Safety of Life at Sea, held in London in 1960, became applicable as from September 1st, 1965.	
International Convention Relating to Registration of Rights in Respect of Vessels under Construction	1967
International Convention for the Unification of Certain Rules as to Carriage of Passengers' Luggage by Sea	1967
International Convention for the Unification of Certain Rules Relating to Maritime Liens and Mortgages	1967
International Convention on Tonnage Measurement of Ships	1969
International Convention Relating to Intervention on the High Seas in cases of Oil Pollution Casualties	1969
International Convention on Civil Liability for Oil Pollution Damage	1969
Convention Relating to Civil Liability in the Field of Maritime Carriage of Nuclear Material	1971

International Convention on the Establishment of an International Fund for Compensation for Oil Pollution Damage	1971
Convention on the International Regulations for Preventing Collisions at Sea, 1972	1972
International Convention for Safe Containers (CSC)	1972
Customs Convention on Containers	1972

In most cases the Conventions become binding upon shipowners and shippers in one of three ways. They may be formally enacted by the legislatures of the countries adopting the convention, thus becoming laws of the countries concerned. They may be complied with as a result of a requirement for membership of some voluntary body such as a shipping conference or freight conference. Finally they may be required by the insurers, who will not offer cover unless the terms of the Convention are complied with.

I.M.C.O. (International Maritime Consultative Organisation), described in greater detail in Appendix One, acts as a forum for member nations to exchange information and discuss problems of control over maritime matters. As a specialised agency of the United Nations, it is frequently responsible for initiating International Conventions on Maritime Matters.

The Control of Air Transport

Air Transport in the United Kingdom is controlled by the Civil Aviation Authority, an independent public corporation, separate from the Government, which was given powers under the Civil Aviation Act 1971 to control almost all aspects of aviation. It consists of a Chairman, a Deputy Chairman, four full-time members and seven non-executive members. The Authority was set up as a direct result of the recommendation of the Edwards Report, 'British Air Transport in the Seventies'. It recommended that the new Authority should take over all the civil aviation functions previously undertaken by the Air Transport Licensing Board, the Air Registration Board, the Department of Trade and Industry and the National Air Traffic Services. The Authority is therefore directly responsible for:

(*a*) The economic regulation and well-being of the civil aviation industry, including air transport licensing.

b) Air safety, both operational safety and airworthiness.

(*c*) The air traffic control and telecommunications network.

(*d*) Airport planning.

(*e*) Advice to the Minister on all matters relating to civil aviation and its general well-being.

(*f*) Ownership of the Highlands and Islands aerodromes.

(*g*) The collection, analysis and publication of aviation information.

The organisation chart shown in Fig. 20.2 is helpful in understanding how such a public body organises its activities. Administratively it works through two principal committees: the Executive Committee and the Economic Policy and Licensing Committee.

Four broad objectives of Government policy for the British civil air transport industry are set out in the Act for the Authority to pursue. They are:

(*a*) To secure that British airlines provide air transport services which satisfy all substantial categories of public demand (so far as British airlines may

reasonably be expected to provide such services) at the lowest charges consistent with a high standard of safety in operating the services and an economic
return to efficient operators on the sums invested in providing the services and
with securing the sound development of the civil air transport industry of the
United Kingdom.

(*b*) To secure that at least one major British airline which is not controlled
by the British Airways Board has opportunities to participate in providing,
on charter and other terms, the air transport services mentioned in the
preceding paragraph.

(*c*) Subject to the preceding paragraphs, to encourage the civil air transport
industry of the United Kingdom to increase the contribution which it makes
towards a favourable balance of payments for the United Kingdom and
towards the prosperity of the economy of the United Kingdom.

(*d*) Subject to the preceding paragraph to further the reasonable interests
of the users of air transport services.

Economic Regulation of Air Transport

The economic regulation of the industry is carried out by the Economic
Policy and Licensing Committee with three primary objectives in mind. These
are:

(*a*) To provide maximum opportunities for the British air transport industry
to increase its share of world markets profitably and thus strengthen the
national balance of payments.

(*b*) To ensure that services are operated only by operators with the required
ability and resources (in continuance of established practices under the Air
Transport Licensing Board).

(*c*) To serve the public by maintaining and developing a network of
scheduled services.

The practical results of these objectives include the licensing of all service
operators and charter operators who comply with the requirements as to
financial adequacy, technical capacity, etc. The public can rest assured that the
safety of flights is not impaired by any financial weakness.

Another result is the fare structure, since the Authority approves all domestic
and international fares. It has also introduced Advance Booking Charters on
the North Atlantic, a system which has replaced the much abused system which
demanded bona fide membership of clubs by those using cheap fare charter
flights. The Authority took the lead internationally in proposing the new
system. The Authority has also instituted strict licensing of air travel organisers,
who are also required to enter into a bond that will make money available to
repatriate stranded passengers. The Authority publishes the C.A.A. Monthly
Statistics, a new series of civil aviation statistics, and C.A.A. Annual Statistics,
a more comprehensive selection of data.

Regulation of Air Transport in the Interests of Safety

The Authority develops and enforces safety standards applicable to every
aspect of civil aviation, from public air services to crop spraying. The
Controller, Safety is a member of the Authority, charged with responsibility
for airworthiness standards and operational safety. There is an Airworthiness
Requirements Board to advise the Authority on all aspects of design, con-

ORGANIZATION OF THE CIVIL AVIATION AUTHORITY

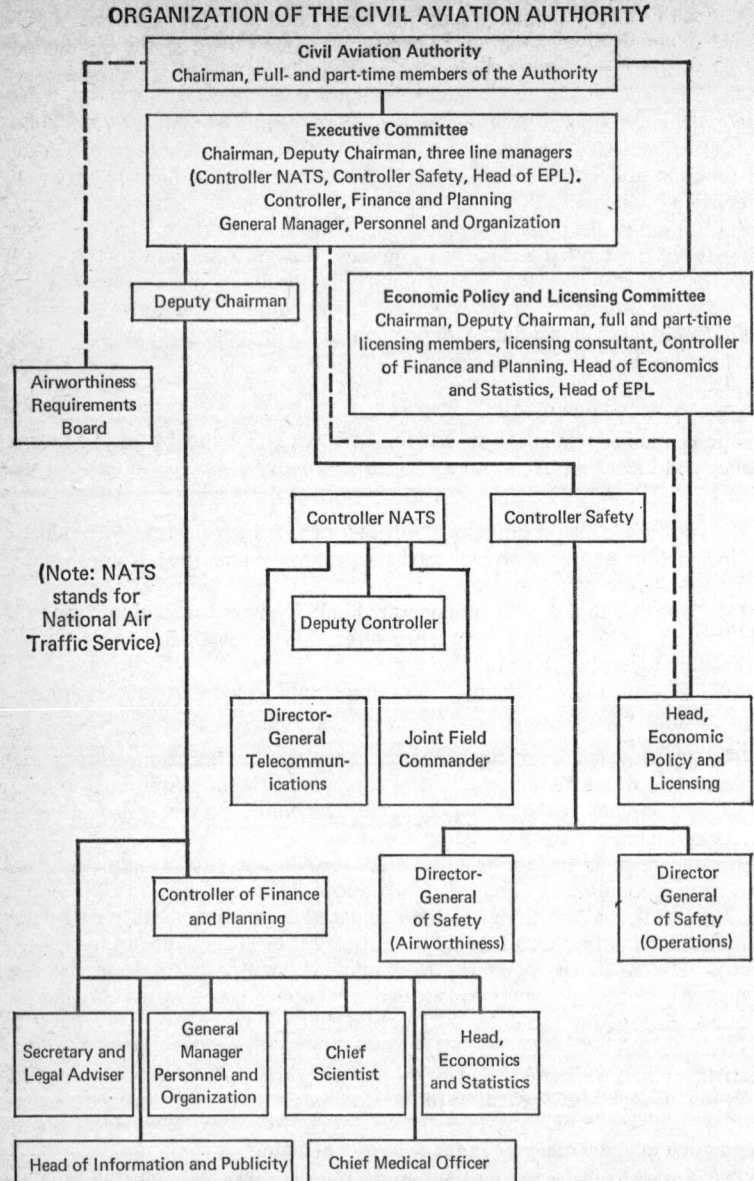

Fig. 20.2. Organisation of the Civil Aviation Authority.

(courtesy of the Authority)

struction and maintenance. No aircraft registered in the United Kingdom operating for public transport is permitted to fly unless it holds a current airworthiness certificate issued by the Airworthiness Division of the Authority. The Division is also responsible for the safety of hovercraft.

The operator of any aircraft must also hold an Air Operator's Certificate, which signifies competence to secure the safe operation of aircraft. The Authority's Flight Operations Inspectors investigate management structure, operational planning and control, training and testing of flight crews, operating instructions for pilots, premises, equipment and records. The Authority has a Civil Aviation Flying Unit (C.A.F.U.) which examines pilots for flying ability and tests navigational aids. All pilots have to be tested initially by C.A.F.U.—subsequent tests are delegated to suitable company pilots.

The National Air Traffic Services

The National Air Traffic Services is a joint civil and military body supervising Air Traffic Control. It reports to both the Civil Aviation Authority and the Ministry of Defence. It maintains a network of navigational aids, air traffic control centres at West Drayton, Preston and Prestwick, and operates the enormous telecommunications system. In 1972 more than one million flights were contacted and advised by the three traffic control centres.

I.C.A.O. and I.A.T.A. (described in detail in Appendix One) are the two international associations responsible for the control and regulation of international air transport. I.C.A.O. is an association of member states, while I.A.T.A. is an association of air transport operators. The former is concerned more with legal problems, safety, constructional problems, etc., while the latter has jurisdiction over more commercial matters.

The Control of Pipelines—The Pipelines Act 1962

Pipelines are of greatest importance to continental powers with large inland areas remote from ports. It follows that a system of control for pipelines is more necessary to continental powers than to countries like Britain.

A standard procedure for pipeline development in Britain was not introduced until fairly recently; the traditional system of legislation by private Act of Parliament being adequate for the pipelines laid down before the 1960s. Such private Acts gave authority for a particular project. The 1962 Act is a general Act, regulating and facilitating the construction of any pipeline, and ensuring that they are not unduly proliferated. The chief points covered by the Act may be listed as follows:

(*a*) No cross-country pipelines are to be constructed without the authority of the Minister of Power, who has discretion to grant an application or refuse it. Local pipelines do not normally require authority, but sixteen weeks' notice of the intention to construct a local pipeline must be given to the Minister, with plans and full particulars of the route, material to be conveyed, duration, maintenance procedures, etc. The Minister may then rule that authority is required if he deems it necessary. He may require the pipeline to be of such a size that others may use it too, to prevent the proliferation of pipelines by a multitude of applications.

(*b*) For safety reasons the Minister may impose certain methods of construction, use of appropriate materials, etc., on the constructors of pipelines.

He may order the performance of remedial work to protect a pipeline endangered by any building or other work, and in default he may even carry out the work at the expense of the parties concerned.

(*c*) The Minister has power to order enquiries into any accidents relating to pipelines. The owner of pipelines is bound to notify any explosions, collapses or the ignition of any substance in or from a pipeline.

(*d*) Owners of pipelines are required to keep local authorities and the Minister informed about changes of ownership, use and disuse of pipelines, and to inform police, fire brigades and other authorities of any escapes, fires, etc.

(*e*) Inspectors may be appointed by the Minister to test, inspect or take samples from any pipeline, and are vested with authority to inspect documents, enter upon land, etc.

(*f*) Certain powers are conferred upon the Minister to ensure the preservation of amenities, the prevention of water pollution and the restoration of agricultural land.

(*g*) The Act does not apply to drains, sewers, heating installations, refrigerating plants, domestic and many factory pipelines, gas, electricity or Atomic Energy Authority pipelines, and pneumatic dispatch tubes.

Suggested Further Reading

Birch, A. H., *The British System of Government*, Allen & Unwin, 1970.

British Air Transport in the Seventies, Report of the Committee of Enquiry, H.M.S.O., 1969.

Gwilliam, K. M., *Transport and Public Policy*, Allen & Unwin, 1964.

Lorries and the World We Live In, Department of the Environment, 1974.

Personal Mobility and Transport Policy, Political and Economic Planning, 1973.

Stanley, P. A., and White, P. R., *A review of medium-density inter-urban public transport*, Polytechnic of Central London, 1973.

Thompson, A. W. J., and Hunter, L. C., *The Transport Industries*, Heinemann, 1974.

PROFESSIONAL INSTITUTIONS AND OTHER BODIES

Introduction

The wide range of transport and physical distribution activities requires many types of knowledge and expertise. Firms and individuals have found it advantageous to join together in voluntary associations to pool experiences and ideas. Similarly, many official bodies set up to promote or control transport are broadly-based panels of knowledgeable people chosen for their experience and understanding of the needs of society and the problems of transport and distribution. This rich pattern of expertise is available to individuals and companies who wish to join, at fairly nominal expense, associations which can assist them with their problems.

Inevitably the authors' list of institutions and organisations is incomplete, and the references are brief. Every effort has been made to represent the activities of the institutions accurately. Readers interested in membership should apply to the addresses given.

List of Institutions

Airbrokers Association (The), Baltic Exchange Chambers, Bury Street, London EC3A 5BA.

Since 1744 the Baltic Exchange has been the Shipping Market of the world, where ships are found for cargoes and cargoes are arranged for ships. The new transport medium, the air freight industry, turned to the established expertise of the Baltic Exchange as the logical centre for fixing air charters. By 1949 an Airbrokers Association had been established to foster the young but flourishing Baltic Exchange Air Market.

The Airbrokers Association is a non-profit-making organisation. Its objects are to establish and maintain in London a world market for the charter of aircraft for the carriage of cargo and passengers; to promote uniformity in commercial transactions in the airbroking trade, especially with regard to contracts of Carriage of Air and Air Charterparties; to represent members in all negotiations with Government Departments, Chambers of Commerce and other public, mercantile or international bodies; and to offer arbitration machinery for the settlement of disputes between members where necessary. It promotes integrity in dealings, in conformity with the principle of the Baltic Exchange, 'Our Word is Our Bond'. A firm offer of aircraft space or cargo cannot be withdrawn once it has been made, until the time of expiry.

American Bureau of Shipping, Winchester House, 77 London Wall, London EC2N 1BU

The American Bureau of Shipping is a ship classification society which certifies the soundness and seaworthiness of merchant ships and other marine engineering structures. Its 640 'surveyors' include specialists in al aspects of the design, building and engineering operation of ships. They discuss original ideas, submit specific proposals for vessels, live with the ship throughout its construction and ensure that the Bureau's 'Rules' are carried out. The Bureau is authorised to assign Load Lines and Safety of Life at Sea Certificates.

The Baltic and International Maritime Conference (B.I.M.C.O.), 19 Kristianiagade, DK-2100, Copenhagen, Denmark

The Baltic and International Maritime Conference, known as B.I.M.C.O., is an Association of shipowners from all over the world. Originally founded in 1905, it has approximately 800 members owning 114·5 million Gross Register Tons. It also has about 1,200 Broker Members, and many Club Members such as Protection and Indemnity Associations, Freight, Demurrage and Defence Associations, etc.

B.I.M.C.O. exists to unite shipowners and other persons and organisations connected with the shipping industry in order to consider and take action on all matters affecting the industry. It communicates to members instances of unfair charges, freight speculation, unfair claims, etc. It reviews documents in use, issuing approved charterparties, bills of lading and other documents. It co-operates with all organisations working in the interests of the shipping industry, representing the industry in accordance with the spirit of its Rules.

The British Association of Removers, 279 Gray's Inn Road, London WC1X 8SY

The British Association of Removers is the only British organisation representing the views of the removing, storage and warehousing industry. It speaks for the industry at Government, local authority and European Community level.

British Industrial Truck Association, Glen House, Stag Place, London SW1E 5AT

The British Industrial Truck Association is an association of manufacturers of lift trucks. It exists to improve the status of industrial trucks as an essential tool of industry. Some measure of its success is to be found in the widespread use of trucks in industrial handling today, and the variety of design and performance offered.

British Ports Association, 3 Queen Square, London WC1N 3AR

The British Ports Association is an association formed to promote, further and protect the general interests of port authorities and conservancy authorities. I t constitutes a forum where discussion and consideration of general questions affecting the members can take place. It particularly designates in its rules that opportunities for discussion of matters affecting major ports, medium ports and small ports shall be created.

British Road Federation, 26 Manchester Square, London W1M 5RF

The British Road Federation is an association of firms and organisations who believe in the importance of roads and road transport to the life of Great Britain. They join together to put forward constructive policies for the development of an adequate road system and to rebut uninformed opposition to road transport.

British Ship Research Association, Wallsend Research Station, Wallsend, Tyne and Wear

The British Ship Research Association was founded in 1944 as the central research organisation of the British shipbuilding industry. It carries out a broad programme of research and development in all aspects of ship design, construction and operation, and has formed a model for several national ship research associations set up in Europe and elsewhere.

British Transport Docks Board, Melbury House, Melbury Terrace, London NW1 6JY

The British Transport Docks Board is a nationwide publicly owned authority operating 19 ports in England, Scotland and Wales. It was formed under the 1962 Transport Act when the port activities previously nationalised by the 1947 Transport Act became an independent entity. It owns and operates the ports, each of which is in charge of local managers vested with the maximum autonomous powers consistent with efficient group control. The Board controls overall policy including finance, and senior appointments. Its London headquarters is largely directive and advisory, encouraging enterprising local management within the framework of general policy.

Bureau Veritas, Ocean House, 24–5 Great Tower Street, London EC2R 5AQ

Bureau Veritas is an international organisation with offices in more than 100 countries. Established originally in 1828 at Antwerp, it exists to ensure that materials and equipment used in ships, buildings, industrial activities, electrical, electronic or nuclear projects, etc., reach the required standards. It periodically issues rules for the guidance of engineers and construction firms. These rules take into account the progress made in various fields and the experience of the Bureau's Inspection Department.

Chamber of Shipping of the U.K. British Shipping Federation, 30–32 St. Mary Axe, London EC3A 8ET

Three related organisations operate from this address:

Chamber of Shipping: The Chamber of Shipping was founded in 1878. Its objects and purposes, as defined in its Royal Charter, are 'to promote and protect the interests of British shipowners'. It deals with all policy aspects affecting the industry except personnel relations, which are handled by the British Shipping Federation (see below). The Chamber does not concern itself with commercial matters nor with the running of individual companies. Rather, it tries to set a climate, nationally and internationally, in which shipping can prosper and serve trade.

British Shipping Federation: The British Shipping Federation is a shipowners' organisation controlled entirely by shipowners, to co-ordinate and further their policy and activities with regard to the seafarers they employ. Its functions include recruitment selection; training; supply of crews to ships; welfare; accident prevention; health of seafarers; industrial negotiations and legislation affecting seafarers.

General Council of British Shipping: This is not a new name to the industry. From 1941 until 1963 when the Liverpool Steam Ship Owners' Association joined the Chamber of Shipping, it was the policy co-ordinating body for the whole industry associating these two bodies and also the Shipping Federation.

Chartered Institute of Transport, 80 Portland Place, London W1N 4DP

The Chartered Institute of Transport is the senior professional body for those engaged in transport and physical distribution. Members have passed rigorous examinations and acquired years of practical experience in the transport industry.

The Institute regards the body of knowledge concerning transport as falling broadly into six divisions: planning, operation and management, policy and financial control, technology, society and the environment, and finally research and education.

Chartered Shipbrokers' Protection and Indemnity Association Ltd., 15 St. Helen's Place, London EC3A 6DJ

The Chartered Shipbrokers' Protection and Indemnity Association Ltd. was founded in 1925 by a group of Chartered Shipbrokers and has developed since to provide a number of services for its members. These include two types of cover.

Class I. Protection: assistance in establishing or resisting claims by or against members in respect of brokerage and commission under a charterparty or freight contract or under a contract of sale and purchase of the vessel; fees under the Scale of Minimum Agency Charges; disbursements made in respect of any vessel; libel of a member in regard to his business as a Shipbroker; breach of warranty of authority where there has been no negligent act or omission on the part of the member and all claims, actions and disputes and matters against or in respect of which in the opinion of the Committee the members should be protected or assisted, including the giving of advice, legal or otherwise to members as to difficulties arising in the conduct of their business.

Class II. Indemnity: the Association indemnifies members against claims made against them by reason of any negligent act error or omission committed, or alleged to have been committed on the part of the member in the conduct of his business as a Chartered Shipbroker.

Its funds are obtained by a small annual subscription but members may be liable to calls should large sums be required for compensation purposes.

Civil Aviation Authority, Aviation House, 129 Kingsway, London WC2B 6NN

The Civil Aviation Authority was established by the Civil Aviation Act 1971, and came into full operation on the April 1, 1972. It is an independent public body, separate from the Government, with responsibilities for:

(1) The economic regulation and wellbeing of the civil aviation industry, including the air transport licensing duties formerly carried out by the Air Transport Licensing Board;

(2) Air safety, both airworthiness (formerly the responsibility of the Air Registration Board) and operational safety, including the licensing of pilots and flight engineers;

(3) The National Air Traffic Services, both air traffic control and telecommunications;

(4) Airport planning, as part of its general responsibility as the Government's adviser on civil aviation matters; the wellbeing of general aviation; research; consumer interests; the collection and publication of data relating to civil aviation; and a large number of miscellaneous functions such as the ownership and operation of the Highlands and Islands aerodromes.

Confederation of British Industry, 21 Tothill Street, London SW1H 9LP

The Confederation of British Industry is the premier organisation in Great Britain representing British management. It exists to represent industry in any discussions with Government, local government, international authorities or other bodies whose actions may affect its members. Its regular meetings with the Prime Minister over the state of the economy indicate its status and the high regard in which it is held.

Freight Transport Association, Sunley House, Bedford Park, Croydon CR9 1XU

This association is a United Kingdom trade association which exists solely to safeguard the interests of, and provide services for, trade and industry as operators and users of all forms of freight transport. It has two main spheres of activity. First, it provides a wide range of tangible benefits to members, assisting them with their day-to-day operations in the transport field. Such services include advice on technical, legal and practical problems, a costing service, advice on international operations, etc. Second, it seeks to influence the decisions of Government, local authorities, the European Economic Community, the providers of transport services and others.

Institute of Freight Forwarders Ltd., Suffield House, 9 Paradise Road, Richmond, Surrey, TW9 1SA

The Institute of Freight Forwarders was formed in 1944, and seeks to promote the highest standards of professional conduct in the freight forwarding industry. To this end it has two types of member: individual Associates or Fellows, qualified through its annual examinations and through experience in the industry to play a full professional part in the activities of their firms, and Company members, who employ a minimum number of professional members as a condition of membership. For these Company members the Institute acts as a Trade Association, representing the industry in discussions with official bodies about such matters as proposed legislation, documentation requirements, etc.

Institute of Materials Handling, St. Ives House, St. Ives Road, Maidenhead, Berkshire, SL6 1RB

The Institute of Materials Handling was founded in 1952 to promote the science of materials handling and to advance the knowledge and appreciation of that science among the public generally. Its membership consists of individuals who are experienced and trained in this field, and voluntarily associate to extend, increase and disseminate knowledge of materials handling.

Institute of Petroleum, 61 New Cavendish Street, London W1M 8AR

The Institute of Petroleum is concerned with all aspects of petroleum technology and distribution. In particular the Institute publishes *Model Codes of Safe Practice*, covering all aspects of the production of oil, its refining and the distribution of finished products.

Institute of Road Transport Engineers, 1 Cromwell Place, Kensington, London SW7 2JF

The Institute of Road Transport Engineers is an examining body which seeks to further skill, training and education in road transport engineering. Its members have reached a high standard in specialist education and training, and have acquired practical experience in the road transport industry. They seek to apply their specialist knowledge in the selection, modification, maintenance of mechanical condition and operation of wheeled, tracked and air-cushioned vehicles in the movement of goods and passengers.

Institute of Traffic Administration, 8 Cumberland Place, Southampton, SO1 2BH

The Institute of Traffic Administration is a leading professional body for transport managers and staff, running a broad programme of educational courses for the basic training and full professional qualification of members. It also provides regular meetings and conferences for the presentation and discussion of papers on all aspects of transport, to assist professional transport staff to keep abreast of the latest developments.

The Institute's network of centres at home and overseas meet regularly, enabling staff in particular regions to meet for the mutual discussion of problems, and for social occasions.

The Institute's officers serve on a variety of official bodies to express the point of view of the transport profession generally and advance the cause of traffic administration in the service of the nation.

Intergovernmental Maritime Consultative Organisation (I.M.C.O.), 101–104 Piccadilly, London W1V 0AE

The Inter-Governmental Maritime Consultative Organisation is the specialised agency of the United Nations concerned solely with maritime affairs. Its interest is mainly in ships used in international services. Eighty-six States are members of I.M.C.O. Its aims are to facilitate co-operation among governments on technical matters affecting shipping, and particularly safety of life at sea. The Council consists of representatives of eighteen Member States, elected by the assembly sessions. These normally take place in London every two years, the first session having been in 1959. The Assembly also chooses a Maritime Safety Committee and a Marine Environment Protection Committee.

I.M.C.O. is a forum where members can exchange information on, and endeavour to solve problems connected with, maritime technical, safety and legal problems. It administers the International Convention for the Safety of Life at Sea. Current developments include regulations on stability of passenger ships, fire safety, safety of fishing vessels, carriage of dangerous goods, carriage of bulk cargoes, etc. The list of conventions and instruments for which I.M.C.O. is responsible gives some idea of the wide influence it wields:

International Convention for the Safety of Life at Sea, 1948.
International Convention for the Safety of Life at Sea, 1960.
International Regulations for Preventing Collisions at Sea, 1960.
Convention on the International Regulations for Preventing Collisions at Sea, 1972.
International Convention for the Prevention of Pollution of the Sea by Oil, 1954.
International Convention for the Prevention of Pollution from Ships, 1973.
Convention on Facilitation of International Maritime Traffic, 1965.
International Convention on Load Lines, 1966.
International Convention on Tonnage Measurement of Ships, 1969.
International Convention Relating to Intervention on the High Seas in Cases of Oil Pollution Casualties, 1969.
Protocol Relating to Intervention on the High Seas in Cases of Maritime Pollution by Substances other than Oil, 1973.
International Convention on Civil Liability for Oil Pollution Damage, 1969.
Special Trade Passenger Ships Agreement, 1971.
Protocol on Space Requirements for Special Trade Passenger Ships, 1973.
International Convention Relating to Civil Liability in the Field of Maritime Carriage of Nuclear Material, 1971.
International Convention on the Establishment of an International Fund for Compensation for Oil Pollution Damage, 1971.
International Convention for Safe Containers, 1972.

International Air Transport Association (I.A.T.A.), P.O. Box 315, 1215 Geneva, 15 Airport, Switzerland

The International Air Transport Association is an association of air transport operators. Its members carry the bulk of the world's scheduled air traffic under the flags of some eighty-five nations. Its aims are to promote safe, regular and economical air transport for the benefit of the peoples of the world; to foster air commerce and to study its problems; to provide means for collaboration among the air transport enterprise and to co-operate with the International Civil Aviation Organisation and other international bodies. It has developed world air routes and traffic handling practices into a world-wide public service, despite barriers of language, currency, law and mensuration. It represents a medium for negotiation and consultation with governments, on matters of international co-operation, carriage of mails, etc. Originally founded in 1945 as the successor to the International Air Traffic Association of 1919, it draws its legal existence from a special Act of the Canadian Parliament. Once two governments have drawn up a bilateral air transport agreement, and have licensed the airlines selected to perform the service, I.A.T.A.'s activities commence. Its functions are to simplify and standardise documentation, procedures and operational devices so that airline costs are minimused and charges to the public are reduced as low as possible commensurate with safety.

International Cargo Handling Co-ordination Association (I.C.H.C.A.), Abford House, 15 Wilton Road, London SW1V 1LX

I.C.H.C.A. is a professional co-ordinating body unique in the international transport world. It is non-political, non-commercial and non-profit-making. Its membership spans the entire spectrum of professions and occupations that have an effect on, or are affected by, technological changes in the physical distribution of goods through world transport.

International Chamber of Commerce, 38 Cours Albert Ier, 75008, Paris, France

The International Chamber of Commerce operates from a headquarters in Paris, led by a Secretary General who is chosen by, and responsible to, the I.C.C. Council.

It is one of the most important bodies in international commerce, speaking with authority for businessmen of all types and seeking to promote international trade. It publishes a number of really authoritative documents, which every student should buy, such as *Incoterms 1953, Uniform Customs and Practice for Documentary Credits, Uniform Rules for the Collection of Commercial Paper*, etc. These publications are available from the I.C.C. National Committees in each particular country.

International Chamber of Shipping, 30–32 St. Mary Axe, London EC3A 8ET

The International Chamber of Shipping was formed in 1921 as the International Shipping Conference, and re-named in 1948. It is an association of national Chambers of Shipping from twenty-three countries, representing 50 per cent of the world's trading fleets. The Chamber deals with shipping policy in the broadest sense, seeking to promote the interests of its members in all matters of general policy. It co-operates with all technical, commercial and industrial interests or bodies on problems of concern to shipowners, and publishes handbooks on safety, operational methods, pollution control, etc.

International Civil Aviation Organisation (I.C.A.O.), 129 Kingsway, London WC2

The International Civil Aviation Organisation is an association of over a hundred sovereign states and a specialised agency of the United Nations. It was formed in 1944 after the Chicago Convention. Its assembly consists of the representatives of individual governments, and nowadays meets every three years. The Council of I.C.A.O. is elected by this assembly and has twenty-seven members. Persons with an active interest in airlines may not represent their governments.

The aims of the organisation are:

(a) To ensure safe and orderly growth of civil aviation throughout the world;
(b) To encourage the development of airports and navigation facilities for international civil aviation;
(c) To reduce wasteful competition;
(d) To ensure that all nations have a fair opportunity to operate international airlines;
(e) To avoid discrimination between contracting nations.

International Federation of Forwarding Agents Association (F.I.A.T.A.), 29 Brauerstrasse, P.O.B. CH-8026, Zurich, Switzerland

The International Federation of Forwarding Agents Association is an international body which represents the forwarding profession throughout the world. It has forty-six member organisations and more than 700 associates (including ports and airports) from 120 countries. It has official Consultative Status with the Economic and Social Council of the United Nations, and with many governmental and non-governmental bodies concerned with transportation on technical, legal, commercial and vocational training grounds.

F.I.A.T.A. has an Executive Committee which convenes a General Assembly every two years. There are twelve specialist committees able to deal with operational matters, seaborne transport, combined transport, road, rail, etc., and also with Customs matters, legal questions, documentation and the promotion of vocational training. Its Airfreight Institute tackles problems in air transport.

F.I.A.T.A. documents have achieved world-wide recognition, such as the forwarding agent's Certificate of Receipt, the forwarding agent's Certificate of Transport, the F.I.A.T.A. combined Transport Bill of Trading and the F.I.A.T.A. Warehouse Receipt.

International Road Transport Union (I.R.U.), Geneva, Switzerland

The International Road Transport Union has about sixty active members from over thirty countries. It is an international association of national federations for road transport, and also accepts Associate Members who are interested in its activities. It has consultative status in the United Nations and in the Council of Europe. Its main objective is to contribute to the development and the prosperity of national and international road transport. It seeks to do this by solving problems in the economic, social, legal and technical fields .

International Shipbrokers' and Agents' Protection and Indemnity Club Ltd., 15 St. Helen's Place, London EC3A 6DJ

This international association was founded in 1970 to assist those Shipbrokers and Agents throughout the world who do not qualify to be members of the Chartered Shipbrokers' Protection and Indemnity Association Ltd., but who nevertheless require similar services.

The services rendered to members are identical with those described in the section on the Chartered Shipbrokers' Protection and Indemnity Association (see above), and compensation can be in excess of U.S. $1 million.

International Union of Marine Insurance, Stadthausquai 5, 8001 Zurich, Switzerland

The International Union of Marine Insurance is a body composed of members of national associations of insurers, whose delegates meet together to discuss general problems facing marine insurers. Special committees are set up to deal with particularly difficult problems, and report back to open meetings which include both delegates and individual executives from marine insurance companies.

International Union of Railways (I.U.C.), 14–16 Rue Jean Rey, Paris XV, France

The International Union of Railways was set up in 1922 to co-ordinate international railway transport policies on any matters where mutual interests make it desirable. With headquarters in Paris, the I.U.C. has committees which deal with planning, commercial matters, railway operations, legal and financial problems, and study groups which review problems of management, control engineering, traffic trends, passenger services, etc. Its members include practically all the European railways, including British Rail, and railways in North America, African and Asia.

Lloyd's Register of Shipping, 71 Fenchurch Street, London EC3M 4BS

Lloyd's Register of Shipping began in 1760 as a committee to produce a Register of Shipping as a guide in the assessment of maritime risks. Classification by Lloyd's Register is accepted by owners, underwriters, charterers and national authorities as a guarantee of structural and mechanical efficiency. The Register employs 1,600 full-time engineers, naval architects, metallurgists and other professionals all over the world to provide a technical inspection and advisory service, primarily for ships but increasingly for engineering projects of many kinds, marine and non-marine.

National Dock Labour Board, 22–26 Albert Embankment, London SE1 7TE

The National Dock Labour Board is the statutory authority which administers the Dock Labour Scheme. The objects of the Scheme are to ensure greater regularity of employment for dock workers and to secure that an adequate number of dock workers is available for the efficient performance of dock work. Dock workers and port employers are represented on the National Board, which operates in the ports through a number of Local Boards. Among other functions the Board maintains a register of dock workers and employers, organises training and is responsible through its Local Boards for certain disciplinary procedure in the industry.

National Ports Council, Commonwealth House, 1–19 New Oxford Street, London WC1A 1DZ

The National Ports Council was established under the Harbours Act 1964 to secure the improvement and greater efficiency of the nation's harbours. It consists of a Chairman and not less than seven nor more than eleven other members, appointed by the Secretary of State for the Environment.

The Council's primary duties are to encourage and assist harbour authorities to perform their functions efficiently, and to advise the Secretary of State with regard to any necessary action to secure greater efficiency. In particular it advises the Secretary of State on all projects requiring more than £1 million, and on all loans he proposes to make to harbour authorities. The Council formulates plans for the development of the nation's ports, and its recommendations on estuarial groupings have been effected.

Its activities in the research, manpower development and educational fields have been most beneficial to the industry.

Road Haulage Association, Roadway House, 22 Upper Woburn Place, London WC1H 0ES

The Road Haulage Association is a trade association of road hauliers. Its 18,000 members carry 50 per cent of all the goods transported in the United Kingdom. It has a broadly based democratic network of 140 sub-areas serving every part of the country, reaching decisions and taking action on a wide variety of matters which arise in the day-to-day operations of road haulage. These sub-areas elect representatives to the fifteen area committees and thirteen functional groups with specialist interests. These are agricultural, bulk liquid, car transporters, caravan hauliers, express carriers, heavy haulage, international, livestock, long distance, meat and allied trades, milk carriers, tipping vehicles and waste disposal.

The Salvage Association, Lloyd's Building, London EC3M 7EU

The Salvage Association, formerly known as 'The Association for the Protection of Commercial Interests as respects Wrecked and Damaged Property', exists to seek out the truth about any maritime casualty and thus prevent fraud upon insurers. It does not operate ships, salvage plant or similar services. It acts for anyone who instructs it, charging fees on a time-and-trouble basis. Its expertise and experience enable it to discover the true facts about any casualty or loss of cargo. Over 20,000 cases are handled annually, by personal inspection either by an accredited Lloyd's agent or direct from London.

The Society of British Aerospace Companies Ltd., 29 King Street, St. James's, London SW1Y 6RD

The Society of British Aerospace Companies Ltd. is an association of about 300 firms in the aerospace industries, which encourages, promotes and protects the British Aerospace Industry and watches over the general interests of firms in the industry, but independently of any particular personal interests.

At the time of writing proposals for the nationalisation of the industry are being prepared—a policy which the association opposes. The association has in the past maintained very close liaison with the Government and the state-owned airline, and a close working relationship has been built up with the related Government departments. It remains to be seen how the Society will represent the industry in the new situation.

Society of Motor Manufacturers and Traders Ltd., Forbes House, Halkin Street, London SW1X 7DS

The Society of Motor Manufacturers and Traders Ltd. is the principal trade association for the British motor industry. It negotiates on behalf of the industry with the Government on all aspects of Government policy which may affect the industry. These include economic and fiscal aspects, matters to do with overseas trade and regulations about construction and safety.

GLOSSARY OF TRANSPORT TERMS

This section is designed to assist students with their background reading.

A.C.V. Air-cushion vehicles: vehicles which ride on a cushion of air. Though the principle has been applied to both land and sea vehicles, the best-known example is the marine hovercraft.

A.P.T. Advanced Passenger Train.

A.T.C. Air Traffic Control.

Ad valorem. According to value: a method of charging freight or customs duty on high-value goods.

Aligned documentation. A system of documentation based on standard designs for forms, so that all the completed documents required in connection with a particular consignment may be produced from one typing, or run off from one master copy, the object being to avoid the time-wasting process of copying information from one document to another, and to avoid the likelihood of omission or error inherent in such a process. Where it is desirable that some information, e.g. value, should not appear on all documents, this can be arranged by masking.

Autostrada. *See* Motorway.

BACAT. A system which links sea transport and inland water transport through 'barges on board catamarans'.

B.A.R.T. (Bay Area Rapid Transit)—the San Francisco computerised train service.

B.I.M.C.O. The Baltic and International Maritime Conference (*see* Appendix One).

B.O.B. Barge-on-board: another name for the LASH-type concept.

Break-bulk cargo. Another name for general or conventional cargo, i.e. non-unitised and non-bulk.

Bunkering. Replenishing a ship's fuel supplies.

C.I.M. (Convention Internationale de Merchandise)—the international agreement on the carriage of goods by rail.

C.I.T. The Chartered Institute of Transport.

C.I.V. (Convention Internationale de Voyageurs)—the international agreement on the carriage of passengers and their luggage by rail.

C.M.R. (Convention Merchandises per Route)—the international agreement on the carriage of goods by road, embodied in United Kingdom law by the Carriage of Goods by Road Act, 1965.

Cabotage. The practice of reserving to a nation the right to its own internal and coastal trade. Today the term is used to mean the right to pick up and set down goods (or passengers) within a country, and is the subject of road haulage agreements on a reciprocal basis.

Capacity ton-mile. The capacity of the vehicle multiplied by the number of miles travelled (*see* Load factor). A 10-ton capacity vehicle travelling 100 miles has travelled 1000 capacity ton-miles. This measurement is used as a unit of output to form the basis of a costing and rating system.

Carnet. A pad or set of international transport documents, as used in T.I.R. transport, to provide two copies for every frontier crossing.

Cash flow. The movement of money into and out of a business, as a result of revenue earned and expenditure incurred.

Cellular ships. The name given to container ships with holds fitted with vertical steel guides so that each container can be slotted in to a particular space, slot or 'cell' by the crane driver, without any assistance from shipboard labour.

Community transit. A system of transit documents for intra-Community use in the E.E.C. There are two procedures: those under 'movement certificates' and a full 'T form' transit procedure (*see* Chapter Nineteen).

Cost per freight ton-mile. A costing unit found by the formula.

$$\frac{\text{Cost of operating the vehicle}}{\text{Number of freight ton-miles carried}}$$

Cost per vehicle mile. *See* Pence per vehicle mile.

D.C.A. (differential cost analysis). A system of cost analysis which compares probable costs under alternative systems of distribution and hence seeks to find the best financial solution to a particular distribution problem.

D.C.F. (discounted cash flow). A method of evaluating capital expenditure by calculating the likely net cash flow to be earned by the new asset in years to come, and discounting it back to represent present-day receipts. If the earnings exceed the costs, when both are in present-day terms, it will be worth while proceeding with the investment.

Deadweight tonnage. The total load-carrying capacity of a ship measured in tons weight. The vessel's net registered tonnage is much less than deadweight tonnage as many cargoes stow at less than 100 cubic feet per ton (e.g. iron ore stows at about 20 cubic feet per ton). (*See* G.R.T. and N.R.T. for fullar explanation.)

Flowchart. A physical distribution chart showing how goods move from the point of production to the point of consumption. It pinpoints cost centres and enables the physical distribution manager to appraise them and compare present costs with those likely to be incurred by the use of alternative methods.

Freeway. *See* Motorway.

G.R.T. (gross registered tonnage). A term used in shipping to describe a vessel's active capacity. It is calculated by measuring the wholly enclosed spaces of the ship and dividing the total obtained by 100, i.e. every 100 cubic feet is regarded as 1 ton.

Groupage. A system of consolidation used to obtain the benefit of cheaper rates for full loads. A groupage agent (usually a freight forwarder) groups together small consignments from a number of exporters to make up a full container load or vehicle load, covering the single consignment with a House Bill of Lading or a similar document. At the destination (perhaps an I.C.D.) the consignment is broken down into its constituent parts for individual delivery.

H.M.C. (Her Majesty's Customs). The customs authority for the United Kingdom.

Hague rules. The body of rules laid down by the international convention on the carriage of goods by sea, and embodied into British law by the Carriage of Goods by Sea Act 1924 and re-enacted in 1971.

Headway. The timing between vehicles on the same track. Most frequently applied to railway operations.

I.A.T.A. International Air Transport Association (*see* Appendix One).

I.C.A.O. International Civil Aviation Organisation (*see* Appendix One).

I.C.D. (Inland Clearance Depot). Defined by H.M.C. as a place approved by them to which goods imported in containers may be removed for entry, examination and clearance and, equally, where goods intended for exportation may be made available for export control.

I.C.H.C.A. International Cargo Handling Coordination Association (*see* Appendix One).

I.M.C.O. Intergovernmental Maritime Consultative Organisation (*see* Appendix One).

I.S.O. International Standards Organisation: an international body devoted to the establishment of international standards. So far as transport is concerned, it has particular relevance in establishing internationally agreed standard sizes, e.g. for pallets and containers, and maximum permitted weights and standard design of fittings, e.g. the corner fittings of containers. These standards ensure complete compatibility with handling equipment, vehicles, etc., throughout the world.

Interface. The point in a transport system where passengers and goods are transferred between one mode of transport and another.

L.A.C.E.S. The London Airport Cargo Electronic Data Processing Scheme (*see* pages 56–7).

L.N.G. Liquefied natural gas.

L.P.G. Liquefied petroleum gas.

LASH. Lighters aboard ship—the first of the systems incorporating barge-carrying vessels.

Lead time. The time between the receipt of an order and its satisfaction by the supply of the goods, completion of the service, etc. The aim of the physical distribution industry is to satisfy demand with the least possible lead time.

Least time track. The method of 'pressure path' navigation which seeks to find optimum tracks for aircraft to take advantage of tailwinds or avoid head winds.

Lo-Lo Berth. Lift-on lift-off. A berth designed for the lift-on and lift-off of containers. Usually applied to a berth concerned with the short-sea routes.

Load factor. A ratio found by the formula

$$\frac{\text{Loaded ton-mile}}{\text{Capacity ton-mile}} \times 100$$

If the figures were (800/1000) × 100 the load factor would be 80 per cent. It is a measure of vehicle utilisation. It should be measured over a period and compared with a target load factor. Interpretation of the results may lead to the conclusion that the wrong type or size of vehicle is being used, or that the service is not being marketed properly, e.g. by failure to find suitable return loads. A low load factor may indicate that for most of the time the vehicle is being used in a partially loaded state, or that full-leg and empty-leg journeys are succeeding one another on most occasions.

Loaded ton-mile. The weight of the load actually carried the number of miles (*see* Load factor). A vehicle carrying 8 tons which travels 100 miles has travelled 800 loaded ton-miles. Used as a unit of output to form the basis of a costing and rating system.

Motorway. A divided highway, with very limited access, no conflicting traffic movements, no stopping (except in emergencies), restricted to certain classes of road users, and designed and constructed for high-speed travel. Alternative names used in other countries are: *Autobahn* (Germany), *autostrada* (Italy) and *freeway* or *turnpike* (U.S.A.).

N.C.R. No carbon required. A system of document-copying using coated papers which avoids the use of carbon paper, to give multiple copies of a single document or aligned documentation.

N.D.L.B. The National Dock Labour Board. This is the official body which maintains the registers of dock labour under the National Dock Labour Scheme. Not all ports are within the scheme at the time of writing, but if the proposals of the 1973 White Paper are implemented all dock workers will probably be brought within the scheme.

N.P.C. The National Ports Council (*see* Appendix One).

N.R.D.C. The National Research Development Corporation (*see* page 172).

N.R.T. Net registered tonnage of a ship. It consists of the gross registered tonnage (G.R.T.) less allowances for the space occupied by the engine room, crew accommodation and other non-earning parts of the ship. It is usually about 55–65 per cent. of the G.R.T. and is used as the basis for the calculation of port dues, canal dues, etc.

O.B.O. Oil-bulk-ore carrier.

Operating ratio. A unit of measurement used to test the viability of a service. It consists of the operating costs expressed as a percentage of receipts. The closer the figure is to 100, the less profitable is the service. If it exceeds 100 a loss will be incurred.

P.S.V. Public service vehicle, e.g. a bus or coach (*see* Road Traffic Act 1972 for legal definitions).

P.T.A. Passenger Transport Authority (*see* Transport Act 1968, Part II).

P.T.E. Passenger Transport Executive (*see* Transport Act 1968, Part II).

Payload. That part of the total load which earns freight or fares and hence contributes to the revenue of an undertaking.

Peak. The time of the day, week or year, when the demand for transport is greatest, and far exceeding the average. Satisfying this kind of demand requires an over-provision of transport facilities at other times and hence gives rise to the 'problem of the peak'.

Pence per passenger-mile. A costing unit found by the formula

$$\frac{\text{Cost of operating the vehicle in pence}}{\text{Number of passenger-miles}}$$

to give a standard cost per passenger-mile.

Pence per vehicle-mile. A costing unit found by the formula

$$\frac{\text{Cost of operating the vehicle in pence}}{\text{Number of vehicle-miles}}$$

to give a standard cost in pence per vehicle-mile.

Percentage satisfaction. The extent to which a firm can satisfy demand immediately from stock; 100 per cent satisfaction is the ideal in theory but in practice may be prohibitively expensive, tying up capital in slow-moving items.

Physical distribution. A term which has recently gained general currency to describe collectively a number of interrelated activities, such as freight transportation in all its forms, materials handling, storage, warehousing, packaging and unitisation.

Pratique. The health certificate issued to the master of a vessel if there is no infectious disease on board.

Prime mover. A type of engine giving motive power, which differs fundamentally from other classes of engines; e.g. a steam engine, diesel engine, etc. Sometimes used erroneously to describe the motive unit in an articulated lorry, to distinguish it from the trailer, or the combined motive unit and trailer.

Q.T.O.L. Quiet take off and landing. Also combined with S.T.O.L. to produce Q./S.T.O.L. A number of aircraft development groups have projects for Q./S.T.O.L. aircraft, and if developed they would cause far less noise offence than existing aircraft, apart from needing runways roughly one fifth the usual length. Development is likely to be hindered by the present financial climate.

R.O.C.E. Return on Capital Employed. Sometimes called R.O.C.I.—return on capital invested. The most fundamental ratio for determining the success of a business. The formula is

$$\frac{\text{Net profit}}{\text{Capital employed}} \times 100$$

Rapid transit. A system designed to deal with heavy surges of traffic, particularly in certain areas. The expression may be applied to either a road or rail service which has a high average speed, is capable of accepting heavy surges of traffic, and above all, operates on a completely grade-separated right of way (e.g. bus-only lanes).

Real-time. A computer system which controls a transport or other system by receiving data, processing them, and returning the conclusions almost simultaneously so that control can be exerted to affect the functioning of the system. Sometimes the computer is programmed to effect the necessary adjustments to the system.

Ro-Ro ship. A roll-on, roll-off vessel, with bow and/or stem doors through which vehicles are driven on or off, via adjustable ramps.

Ro-Ro terminal. A berth specially designed to facilitate the loading and unloading of roll-on, roll-off ships, being equipped with ramps and extensive marshalling areas for vehicles.

S.S.T. Supersonic Transport. Civil aircraft able to operate at a speed faster than the speed of sound. Concorde and the Russian Tupolev TU-144 are the first examples of this new generation of civil aircraft.

S.T.O.L. Short take-off and landing, a type of aircraft needing only short runways.

Seabee 'Sea barge'. A system where a 'swarm' of barges operates into inland waterways and small ports from a 'hive' mother ship (*see* page 91).

T Form procedure. The E.E.C. transit document procedure which will not only signal (indicate) to Customs Officers the status of goods in the Community, but which, provided their seals are unbroken, will enable them to cross frontiers without inspection.

T.I.F. (Transports Internationaux per Chemin de Fer). The international railway customs procedure similar to T.I.R. for road haulage.

T.I.R. (1) (Transports Internationaux per Route). The international road carnet system which enables goods in sealed approved vehicles or containers to cross frontiers without inspection by customs, so long as the seals are unbroken and the tilts, if employed, are undamaged.

T.I.R. (2). Commonly used as a form of shorthand to describe vehicles approved for T.I.R. operation, e.g. the company operates twelve T.I.R.s.

Tare. The unladen weight of a vehicle or container.

Tilt. A fabric cover over a framework secured to the platform of a lorry to form an easily removed, covered body. When used in connection with T.I.R. operations it must be capable of being laced and sealed with plastic-covered steel wire, and free from tears or repairs unless such repairs have been effected in accordance with the regulations.

Ton-miles. The weight carried multiplied by the length of the haul.

Total distribution cost. A concept which seeks to secure optimum efficiency in the distribution process by choosing that total system of storage handling and transport which moves goods from the point of production to the point of consumption with the least total expense, rather than dealing with each of the operations involved on an isolated basis.

Traffic Commissioners. The licensing authority for P.S.V.s and goods vehicles (*see* Road Traffic Act 1972).

Trim. The correct attitude of an aircraft when in flight, i.e. not nose-heavy or tail-heavy, but properly balanced. Also applied to vessels to describe their attitude to the water.

Turning radius. The distance between the centre of turn point of a forklift truck and the farthest point of the truck body. It is a measure of the skill of the designer in getting capacity and stability in as small a space as possible. The degree of success achieved will affect the space which must be provided for turning and manoeuvring, e.g. in warehouses and on stacking grounds.

Turnpike (1). Toll roads constructed by turnpike trusts in the United Kingdom between 1663 and 1895.

Turnpike (2). An alternative name for motorway used in the U.S.A.

Unit load concept. The concept which seeks to make one large load of many small loads by the use of pallets, containers, etc. The consolidation should take place as soon as possible in the journey from producer to consumer, the unit should be as large as can be handled by the vehicle and equipment connected with its journey, and should remain as a unit for the largest possible part of the journey before being deconsolidated.

V.L.C.C. Very large crude carrier: a designation usually reserved for vessels in excess of 200,000 tons deadweight tonnage.

V.T.O.L. Vertical take-off and landing: applied to aircraft capable of vertical ascent and descent. Sometimes called jump jets. The principle has been successfully applied to military aircraft, e.g. the 'Harrier', but as yet no successful commercial aircraft has been developed.

Warsaw Convention (1929). The original international agreement covering the carriage of goods by air, which has since been modified and amended by subsequent conventions and conferences but still forms the basis of the law of international carriage of goods by air.

INDEX

A.C.V., 262
A.D.R., 244
A.P.T., 101, 262
A.T.C., 262
Accounting,
  current purchasing power, 177
  historical cost, 176
  inflation, 176
Ad valorem, 262
Advanced passenger train (A.P.T.),
  101, 262
Affluence, effects of, 4
Air traffic control, 251
Air transport,
  advantages, 162
  control of, 248–51
  disadvantages, 162
  flying fish services, 160
  terminals and, 33–5, 52–7
Air Transport Licensing Board, 249
Air waybill, 215, 218–19
Airbrokers' Association, 253
Aircraft, 96–7
  Boeing 747, 96
  Concorde, 97
  freighters, 97
  motive power, and, 101–2
  unit of carriage as, 96–7
Airports,
  cargo facilities, 54–7
  community requirements, 34
  L.A.C.E.S., 56–7
  operational requirements, 33
  passenger facilities, 53–4
Aligned documentation, 203–6, 262
American Bureau of Shipping, 253
Ancillary equipment, materials hand-
  ling, 136-8
Anticipation inventories, 151
Articulated vehicles, 82
Artificial ways, 18
Automatic,
  battery chargers, 136
  warehousing, 140
  weighers, 138
Autostrada, 262

B.A.R.T., 262
B.I.M.C.O., 220-21, 253, 262
B.O.B., 262
Bacat Line, 91–3, 161
Balance sheet, 181
Baltic and International Maritime Con-
  ference, 253

Barge-carrying vessels,
  Bacat, 91–3
  barge units, 88, 90–92
  Lash, 88
  Seabees, 91
Berths,
  bulk wine, 75
  container, 70–71
  conventional, 68
  fruit, 74
  general, 68
  grain, 73
  heavy lift, 70
  meat, 74
  packaged timber, 71–3
  roll-on roll-off, 74
  side-loading, 74
  timber, 71–3
Bills of lading, 209
Boeing 747, 96
Break-bulk, 262
British,
  Association of Removers, 254
  Industrial Truck Association, 254
  Ports Association, 254
  Railways Board, 196
  Road Federation, 254
  Road Services, 163–5
  Ship Research Association, 254
  Shipping Council, 255
  Shipping Federation, 255
  Transport Docks Board, 254
  Waterways Board, 201
Budgets,
  capital, 182
  revenue, 183
Bulk transport, 143–50
  advantages of, 143–4
  clean product carriers and, 95
  company trains and, 146
  economies of scale and, 143
  freightliners and, 146–7
  grain carriers, 144
  L.N.G. carriers, 94
  L.P.G. carriers, 95
  methane carriers and, 94, 144
  Obo carriers and, 144
  pipelines, by, 148–50
  rail, by, 145–7
  road, by, 148
  sea, by, 144–5
  tankers, by, 144–5
  V.L.C.C.s, by, 92–4, 144–5
Bunkering, 65, 262

269